$65.99
619.85265TE(B)

369 0121168

KU-541-337

HEALTH AND HUMAN DEVELOPMENT

Health Improvement Library
Law House
Airdrie Road
Carluke. ML8 5EP
01698 377600

TREATMENT AND RECOVERY OF EATING DISORDERS

DATE DUE			
			PRINTED IN U.S.A.

HEALTH AND HUMAN DEVELOPMENT

JOAV MERRICK - SERIES EDITOR

NATIONAL INSTITUTE OF CHILD HEALTH
AND HUMAN DEVELOPMENT,
MINISTRY OF SOCIAL AFFAIRS, JERUSALEM

Adolescent Behavior Research:
International Perspectives
Joav Merrick and Hatim A. Omar (Editors)
2007. ISBN: 1-60021-649-8

Complementary Medicine Systems:
Comparison and Integration
Karl W. Kratky
2008. ISBN: 978-1-60456-475-4 (Hardcover)
2008. ISBN: 978-1-61122-433-7 (E-book)

Pain in Children and Youth
Patricia Schofield and Joav Merrick
(Editors)
2008. ISBN: 978-1-60456-951-3 (Hardcover)
2008. ISBN: 978-1-61470-496-6 (E-book)

Alcohol-Related Cognitive Disorders:
Research and Clinical Perspectives
Leo Sher, Isack Kandel and Joav Merrick
(Editors)
2009. ISBN: 978-1-60741-730-9 (Hardcover)
2009. ISBN: 978-1-60876-623-9 (E-book)

Challenges in Adolescent Health:
An Australian Perspective
David Bennett, Susan Towns,
Elizabeth Elliott
and Joav Merrick (Editors)
2009. ISBN: 978-1-60741-616-6 (Hardcover)
2009. ISBN: 978-1-61668-240-8 (E-book)

Children and Pain
Patricia Schofield and Joav Merrick
(Editors)
2009. ISBN: 978-1-60876-020-6 (Hardcover)
2009. ISBN: 978-1-61728-183-9 (E-book)

Living on the Edge: The Mythical,
Spiritual, and Philosophical
Roots of Social Marginality
Joseph Goodbread
2009. ISBN: 978-1-60741-162-8 (Hardcover)
2013. ISBN: 978-1-61122-986-8 (Softcover)
2011. ISBN: 978-1-61470-192-7 (E-book)

Obesity and Adolescence:
A Public Health Concern
Hatim A. Omar, Donald E. Greydanus,
Dilip R. Patel and Joav Merrick (Editors)
2009. ISBN: 978-1-60692-821-9 (Hardcover)
2009. ISBN: 978-1-61470-465-2 (E-book)

Poverty and Children:
A Public Health Concern
Alexis Lieberman and Joav Merrick (Editors)
2009. ISBN: 978-1-60741-140-6 (Hardcover)
2009. ISBN: 978-1-61470-601-4 (E-book)

Bone and Brain Metastases:
Advances in Research and Treatment
Arjun Sahgal, Edward Chow
and Joav Merrick (Editors)
2010. ISBN: 978-1-61668-365-8 (Hardcover)
2010. ISBN: 978-1-61728-085-6 (E-book)

Chance Action and Therapy:
The Playful Way of Changing
Uri Wernik
2010. ISBN: 978-1-60876-393-1 (Hardcover)
2011. ISBN: 978-1-61122-987-5 (Softcover)
2011. ISBN: 978-1-61209-874-6 (E-book)

**Advanced Cancer Pain
and Quality of Life**
Edward Chow and Joav Merrick (Editors)
2011. ISBN: 978-1-61668-207-1 (Hardcover)
2010. ISBN: 978-1-61668-400-6 (E-book)

**Advances in Environmental Health
Effects of Toxigenic Mold
and Mycotoxins**
Ebere Cyril Anyanwu
2011. ISBN: 978-1-60741-953-2

Alternative Medicine Yearbook 2009
Joav Merrick (Editor)
2011. ISBN: 978-1-61668-910-0 (Hardcover)
2011. ISBN: 978-1-62081-710-0 (E-book)

Behavioral Pediatrics, 3rd Edition
*Donald E. Greydanus, Dilip R. Patel,
Helen D. Pratt
and Joseph L. Calles, Jr. (Editors)*
2011. ISBN: 978-1-60692-702-1 (Hardcover)
2009. ISBN: 978-1-60876-630-7 (E-book)

**Child Health and Human Development
Yearbook 2009**
Joav Merrick (Editor)
2011. ISBN: 978-1-61668-912-4

Climate Change and Rural Child Health
*Erica Bell, Bastian M. Seidel
and Joav Merrick (Editors)*
2011. ISBN: 978-1-61122-640-9 (Hardcover)
2011. ISBN: 978-1-61209-014-6 (E-book)

**Clinical Aspects of Psychopharmacology
in Childhood and Adolescence**
*Donald E. Greydanus, Joseph L. Calles, Jr.,
Dilip P. Patel, Ahsan Nazeer
and Joav Merrick (Editors)*
2011. ISBN: 978-1-61122-135-0 (Hardcover)
2011. ISBN: 978-1-61122-715-4 (E-book)

**Drug Abuse in Hong Kong:
Development and Evaluation
of a Prevention Program**
*Daniel T.L. Shek, Rachel C.F. Sun
and Joav Merrick (Editors)*
2011. ISBN: 978-1-61324-491-3 (Hardcover)
2011. ISBN: 978-1-62257-232-8 (E-book)

**Environment, Mood Disorders
and Suicide**
*Teodor T. Postolache and Joav Merrick
(Editors)*
2011. ISBN: 978-1-61668-505-8 (Hardcover)
2011. ISBN: 978-1-62618-340-7 (E-book)

**Human Development: Biology
from a Holistic Point of View**
*Søren Ventegodt, Tyge Dahl Hermansen
and Joav Merrick*
2011. ISBN: 978-1-61470-441-6 (Hardcover)
2011. ISBN: 978-1-61470-541-3 (E-book)

**International Aspects
of Child Abuse and Neglect**
*Howard Dubowitz and Joav Merrick
(Editors)*
2011. ISBN: 978-1-60876-703-8 (Hardcover)
2010. ISBN: 978-1-61122-049-0 (Softcover)
2010. ISBN: 978-1-61122-403-0 (E-book)

Narratives and Meanings of Migration
Julia Mirsky
2011. ISBN: 978-1-61761-103-2 (Hardcover)
2010. ISBN: 978-1-61761-519-1 (E-book)

**Positive Youth Development:
Evaluation and Future
Directions in a Chinese Context**
*Daniel T.L. Shek, Hing Keung Ma
and Joav Merrick (Editors)*
2011. ISBN: 978-1-60876-830-1 (Hardcover)
2011. ISBN: 978-1-62100-175-1 (Softcover)
2010. ISBN: 978-1-61209-091-7 (E-book)

Positive Youth Development:
Implementation of a Youth Program
in a Chinese Context
*Daniel T.L Shek, Hing Keung Ma
and Joav Merrick (Editors)*
2011. ISBN: 978-1-61668-230-9 (Hardcover)

Principles of Holistic Psychiatry:
A Textbook on Holistic Medicine
for Mental Disorders
Soren Ventegodt and Joav Merrick
2011. ISBN: 978-1-61761-940-3 (Hardcover)
2011. ISBN: 978-1-61122-263-0 (E-book)

Public Health Yearbook 2009
Joav Merrick (Editor)
2011. ISBN: 978-1-61668-911-7 (Hardcover)
2011. ISBN: 978-1-62417-365-3 (E-book)

Rural Child Health:
International Aspects
Erica Bell and Joav Merrick (Editors)
2011. ISBN: 978-1-60876-357-3 (Hardcover)
2011. ISBN: 978-1-61324-005-2 (E-book)

Rural Medical Education:
Practical Strategies
*Erica Bell, Craig Zimitat and Joav Merrick
(Editors)*
2011. ISBN: 978-1-61122-649-2 (Hardcover)
2011. ISBN: 978-1-61209-476-2 (E-book)

Self-Management and the Health Care
Consumer
Peter William Harvey
2011. ISBN: 978-1-61761-796-6 (Hardcover)
2011. ISBN: 978-1-61122-214-2 (E-book)

Sexology from a Holistic Point of View
Soren Ventegodt and Joav Merrick
2011. ISBN: 978-1-61761-859-8 (Hardcover)
2011. ISBN: 978-1-61122-262-3 (E-book)

Social and Cultural Psychiatry
Experience from the Caribbean Region
*Hari D. Maharajh and Joav Merrick
(Editors)*
2011. ISBN: 978-1-61668-506-5 (Hardcover)
2010. ISBN: 978-1-61728-088-7 (E-book)

The Dance of Sleeping and Eating
among Adolescents:
Normal and Pathological Perspectives
Yael Latzer and Orna Tzischinsky (Editors)
2011. ISBN: 978-1-61209-710-7 (Hardcover)
2011. ISBN: 978-1-62417-366-0 (E-book)

Understanding Eating Disorders:
Integrating Culture,
Psychology and Biology
*Yael Latzer, Joav Merrick and Daniel Stein
(Editors)*
2011. ISBN: 978-1-61728-298-0 (Hardcover)
2011. ISBN: 978-1-61470-976-3 (Softcover)
2011. ISBN: 978-1-61942-054-0 (E-book)

Adolescence and Chronic Illness.
A Public Health Concern
*Hatim Omar, Donald E. Greydanus,
Dilip R. Patel
and Joav Merrick (Editors)*
2012. ISBN: 978-1-60876-628-4 (Hardcover)
2010. ISBN: 978-1-61761-482-8 (E-book)

AIDS and Tuberculosis: Public
Health Aspects
Daniel Chemtob and Joav Merrick (Editors)
2012. ISBN: 978-1-62081-382-9 (Softcover)
2012. ISBN: 978-1-62081-406-2 (E-book)

Alternative Medicine Yearbook 2010
Joav Merrick (Editor)
2012. ISBN: 978-1-62100-132-4 (Hardcover)
2011. ISBN: 978-1-62100-210-9 (E-book)

**Alternative Medicine Research
Yearbook 2011**
Joav Merrick (Editor)
2012. ISBN: 978-1-62081-476-5 (Hardcover)
2012. ISBN: 978-1-62081-477-2 (E-book)

**Applied Public Health: Examining
Multifaceted Social or Ecological
Problems and Child Maltreatment**
John R. Lutzker and Joav Merrick (Editors)
2012. ISBN: 978-1-62081-356-0 (Hardcover)
2012. ISBN: 978-1-62081-388-1 (E-book)

**Building Community Capacity:
Minority and Immigrant Populations**
*Rosemary M Caron and Joav Merrick
(Editors)*
2012. ISBN: 978-1-62081-022-4 (Hardcover)
2012. ISBN: 978-1-62081-032-3 (E-book)

**Building Community Capacity:
Skills and Principles**
*Rosemary M Caron and Joav Merrick
(Editors)*
2012. ISBN: 978-1-61209-331-4 (Hardcover)
2012. ISBN: 978-1-62257-238-0 (E-book)

**Child and Adolescent Health
Yearbook 2009**
Joav Merrick (Editor)
2012. ISBN: 978-1-61668-913-1 (Hardcover)
2012. ISBN: 978-1-62257-095-9 (E-book)

**Child and Adolescent Health
Yearbook 2010**
Joav Merrick (Editor)
2012. ISBN: 978-1-61209-788-6 (Hardcover)
2012. ISBN: 978-1-62417-046-1 (E-book)

**Child Health and Human Development
Yearbook 2010**
Joav Merrick (Editor)
2012. ISBN: 978-1-61209-789-3 (Hardcover)
2012. ISBN: 978-1-62081-721-6 (E-book)

Health Risk Communication
Marijke Lemal and Joav Merrick (Editors)
2013. ISBN: 978-1-62257-544-2 (Hardcover)
2012. ISBN: 978-1-62257-552-7 (E-book)

**Human Immunodeficiency Virus (HIV)
Research: Social Science Aspects**
Hugh Klein and Joav Merrick (Editors)
2012. ISBN: 978-1-62081-293-8 (Hardcover)
2012. ISBN: 978-1-62081-346-1 (E-book)

**Our Search for Meaning in Life:
Quality of Life Philosophy**
Søren Ventegodt and Joav Merrick
2012. ISBN: 978-1-61470-494-2 (Hardcover)
2011. ISBN: 978-1-61470-519-2 (E-book)

Public Health Yearbook 2010
Joav Merrick (Editor)
2012. ISBN: 978-1-61209-971-2 (Hardcover)
2012. ISBN: 978-1-62417-863-4 (E-book)

Public Health Yearbook 2011
Joav Merrick (Editor)
2012. ISBN: 978-1-62081-433-8 (Hardcover)
2012. ISBN: 978-1-62081-434-5 (E-book)

**Randomized Clinical Trials
and Placebo: Can You Trust
the Drugs are Working and Safe?**
Søren Ventegodt and Joav Merrick
2012. ISBN: 978-1-61470-067-8

**Textbook on Evidence-Based Holistic
Mind-Body Medicine: Basic Philosophy
and Ethics of Traditional Hippocratic
Medicine**
Søren Ventegodt and Joav Merrick
2012. ISBN: 978-1-62257-052-2 (Hardcover)
2013. ISBN: 978-1-62257-707-1 (E-book)

Textbook on Evidence-Based Holistic Mind-Body Medicine: Basic Principles of Healing in Traditional Hippocratic Medicine
Søren Ventegodt and Joav Merrick
2012. ISBN: 978-1-62257-094-2 (Hardcover)
2012. ISBN: 978-1-62257-172-7 (E-book)

Textbook on Evidence-Based Holistic Mind-Body Medicine: Healing the Mind in Traditional Hippocratic Medicine
Søren Ventegodt and Joav Merrick
2012. ISBN: 978-1-62257-112-3 (Hardcover)
2012. ISBN: 978-1-62257-175-8 (E-book)

Textbook on Evidence-Based Holistic Mind-Body Medicine: Holistic Practice of Traditional Hippocratic Medicine
Søren Ventegodt and Joav Merrick
2012. ISBN: 978-1-62257-105-5 (Hardcover)
2012. ISBN: 978-1-62257-174-1 (E-book)

Textbook on Evidence-Based Holistic Mind-Body Medicine: Research, Philosophy, Economy and Politics of Traditional Hippocratic Medicine
Søren Ventegodt and Joav Merrick
2012. ISBN: 978-1-62257-140-6 (Hardcover)
2012. ISBN: 978-1-62257-171-0 (E-book)

Textbook on Evidence-Based Holistic Mind-Body Medicine: Sexology and Traditional Hippocratic Medicine
Søren Ventegodt and Joav Merrick
2012. ISBN: 978-1-62257-130-7 (Hardcover)
2012. ISBN: 978-1-62257-176-5 (E-book)

The Astonishing Brain and Holistic Conciousness: Neuroscience and Vedanta Perspectives
Vinod D. Deshmukh
2012. ISBN: 978-1-61324-295-7

Translational Research for Primary Healthcare
Erica Bell, Gert. P. Westert and Joav Merrick (Editors)
2012. ISBN: 978-1-61324-647-4 (Hardcover)
2012. ISBN: 978-1-62417-409-4 (E-book)

Treatment and Recovery of Eating Disorders
Daniel Stein and Yael Latzer (Editors)
2012. ISBN: 978-1-61470-259-7

Adolescence and Sports
Dilip R. Patel, Donald E. Greydanus, Hatim Omar and Joav Merrick (Editors)
2013. ISBN: 978-1-60876-702-1 (Hardcover)
2010. ISBN: 978-1-61761-483-5 (E-book)

Alternative Medicine Research Yearbook 2012
Søren Ventegodt and Joav Merrick (Editors)
2013. ISBN: 978-1-62808-080-3

Building Community Capacity: Case Examples from Around the World
Rosemary M Caron and Joav Merrick (Editors)
2013. ISBN: 978-1-62417-175-8 (Hardcover)
2013. ISBN: 978-1-62417-176-5 (E-book)

Bullying: A Public Health Concern
Jorge C. Srabstein and Joav Merrick (Editors)
2013. ISBN: 978-1-62618-564-7 (Hardcover)
2013. ISBN: 978-1-62618-588-3 (E-book)

Conceptualizing Behavior in Health and Social Research: A Practical Guide to Data Analysis
Said Shahtahmasebi and Damon Berridge
2013. ISBN: 978-1-60876-383-2

**Health and Happiness
from Meaningful Work:
Research in Quality of Working Life**
Søren Ventegodt and Joav Merrick (Editors)
2013. ISBN: 978-1-60692-820-2 (Hardcover)
2013. ISBN: 978-1-61324-981-9 (E-book)

**Health Promotion: Community Singing as
a Vehicle to Promote Health**
*Jing Sun, Nicholas Buys and Joav Merrick
(Editors)*
2013. ISBN: 978-1-62618-908-9 (Softcover)

**Living on the Edge: The Mythical,
Spiritual, and Philosophical Roots
of Social Marginality**
Joseph Goodbread (Author)
2013. ISBN: 978-1-61122-986-8 (Softcover)

Managed Care in a Public Setting
Richard Evan Steele
2013. ISBN: 978-1-62417-970-9 (Softcover)
2013. ISBN: 978-1-62417-863-4 (E-book)

**Pediatric and Adolescent Sexuality and
Gynecology: Principles for the Primary
Care Clinician**
*Hatim A. Omar, Donald E. Greydanus,
Artemis K. Tsitsika, Dilip R. Patel
and Joav Merrick (Editors)*
2013. ISBN: 978-1-60876-735-9 (Softcover)

**Treatment and Recovery
of Eating Disorders**
Daniel Stein and Yael Latzer (Editors)
2013. ISBN: 978-1-61470-259-7 (Softcover)

Public Health Yearbook 2012
Joav Merrick (Editors)
2013. ISBN: 978-1-62808-078-0

TREATMENT AND RECOVERY OF EATING DISORDERS

DANIEL STEIN, M.D.
AND
YAEL LATZER, D.SC.
EDITORS

New York

Copyright © 2013 by Nova Science Publishers, Inc.

All rights reserved. No part of this book may be reproduced, stored in a retrieval system or transmitted in any form or by any means: electronic, electrostatic, magnetic, tape, mechanical photocopying, recording or otherwise without the written permission of the Publisher.

For permission to use material from this book please contact us:
Telephone 631-231-7269; Fax 631-231-8175
Web Site: http://www.novapublishers.com

NOTICE TO THE READER

The Publisher has taken reasonable care in the preparation of this book, but makes no expressed or implied warranty of any kind and assumes no responsibility for any errors or omissions. No liability is assumed for incidental or consequential damages in connection with or arising out of information contained in this book. The Publisher shall not be liable for any special, consequential, or exemplary damages resulting, in whole or in part, from the readers' use of, or reliance upon, this material. Any parts of this book based on government reports are so indicated and copyright is claimed for those parts to the extent applicable to compilations of such works.

Independent verification should be sought for any data, advice or recommendations contained in this book. In addition, no responsibility is assumed by the publisher for any injury and/or damage to persons or property arising from any methods, products, instructions, ideas or otherwise contained in this publication.

This publication is designed to provide accurate and authoritative information with regard to the subject matter covered herein. It is sold with the clear understanding that the Publisher is not engaged in rendering legal or any other professional services. If legal or any other expert assistance is required, the services of a competent person should be sought. FROM A DECLARATION OF PARTICIPANTS JOINTLY ADOPTED BY A COMMITTEE OF THE AMERICAN BAR ASSOCIATION AND A COMMITTEE OF PUBLISHERS.

Additional color graphics may be available in the e-book version of this book.

LIBRARY OF CONGRESS CATALOGING-IN-PUBLICATION DATA
Treatment and recovery of eating disorders / editors, Yael Latzer, Daniel Stein.
    p. ; cm. -- (Health and human development)
 Includes bibliographical references and index.
 ISBN 978-1-62808-248-7 (softcover)
 1. Eating disorders--Treatment. I. Latzer, Yael. II. Stein, Daniel, 1949- III. Series: Health and human development series.
 [DNLM: 1. Eating Disorders. WM 175]
 RC552.E18T739 2011
 616.85'26--dc23
                          2011022496

Published by Nova Science Publishers, Inc. † New York

CONTENTS

PREFACE

Eating disorders (EDs) and disordered eating behaviors are considered a major disease of the modern world, being among the most prevailing public health problems in female adolescents and young adults in recent decades, and reaching in many Western countries an epidemic proportion. They occur primarily in adolescent girls and young women, during a crucial developmental stage, and are linked to extensive morbidity and high mortality rates. EDs are complex, conflictual, misunderstood disturbances that often raise negative emotions such as bewilderment, mistrust and fear not only among lay people but also in treatment providers. These reactions are likely the result of failing to grasp why someone would not comply with the basic universal need of eating or put such an emphasis on weight and appearance that renders them more important than anything else in life. This book offers an up-to-date summary with respect to the putative treatment options in EDs.

Chapter 1 - Eating disorders (EDs) and disordered eating behaviors are considered a major disease of the modern world, being among the most prevailing public health problems in female adolescents and young adults in recent decades, and reaching in many Western countries an epidemic proportion (1). They occur primarily in adolescent girls and young women during a crucial developmental stage, and are linked to extensive morbidity and high mortality rates (1). EDs are complex, conflictual, misunderstood disturbances that often raise negative emotions such as bewilderment, mistrust and fear not only among lay people but also in treatment providers. These reactions are likely the result of failing to grasp why someone would not comply with the basic universal need of eating, or put such an emphasis on weight and appearance that renders them more important than anything else in life. As a result, individuals afflicted with EDs frequently feel misunderstood, unaccepted and isolated. This had led the authors to edit two books, written by renounced international and Israeli researchers, about ED-related problems. The authors' first book has focused primarily on aspects related to the history of EDs, diagnostic considerations, epidemiology, course and outcome, sociocultural influences, familial considerations, and prevention. For the current book they have conducted an extensive literature search to offer an up-to-date summary about putative treatment options and prognostic considerations in Eds.

Chapter 2 - Over 30 variables have been identified that may serve as risk factors for the development of eating disorders. Each factor is, in turn, multidimensional, making it highly unlikely that the interactions among these factors that are key to various stages in the genesis and maintenance of eating disorders can ever be adequately delineated or described. This level of complexity can lead to overspecialization and splintering within the field of eating disorders, as different disciplines focus on the investigation of separate risk factor areas with no shared framework within which to interpret, integrate, or apply new knowledge. A unifying framework is needed to maintain the integrity and cohesion of the increasingly complex etiological understanding of eating disorders. This chapter reviews the history of psychodynamic thought regarding the etiology of eating disorders. The contributions of psychodynamic theory to their current understanding of eating disorders are elucidated. Particular attention is paid to the pattern that emerges, over time, of psychodynamic theory as a flexible, integrative and self-correcting paradigm. Accordingly, a modern psychodynamic approach can provide an ideal organizing framework to unify and guide their efforts in the research, treatment, education, and prevention of eating disorders.

Chapter 3 - Objective: The purpose of this article is to provide an overview of the treatment literature on bulimia nervosa. The available published literature in this area was reviewed. Method: Following computer searches the psychotherapy and pharmacotherapy literature were reviewed in detail. Results: Psychotherapy remains the cornerstone of treatment for most patients with bulimia nervosa. The most intensively studied form has been cognitive behavioral therapy, although there are also data supporting the use of interpersonal psychotherapy, dialectic behavior therapy and family-based treatments for adolescents with bulimia nervosa. There is also a growing literature on the utility of self-help approaches. Two recently introduced therapies, which are currently being studied, include enhanced cognitive behavioral therapy and integrative cognitive-affective therapy. Relative to pharmacotherapy approaches, antidepressants remain the best studied form of drug therapy, focusing on the use of the serotonin reuptake inhibitors. Other medications which have been tried empirically include ondansetron and topiramate. Discussion: The treatment of bulimia nervosa has evolved to the point where both psychotherapy and pharmacotherapy approaches appear to be affective. Overall remission rates appear to be higher with empirically supported manual-based psychotherapy approaches, although many patients have benefited from drug therapy as well.

Chapter 4 - Psychopharmacological agents have been used since the early years of treatment of eating disorders because of the challenging nature of these disorders. There is nearly no new psychotropic agent which has not been studied in anorexia nervosa (AN) patients, usually with conflicting results. At this time it must be concluded that there are yet no first-line psychopharmacological agents that can be recommended in AN based on good clinical evidence. For bulimia nervosa (BN) and binge-eating disorder (BED), the evidence is better, having several promising data on the advantages of adding antidepressants and related agents to the psychotherapeutic work with these patient groups.

Chapter 5 - Successful weight loss is usually followed by weight regain. Numerous studies have attempted to clarify the basis for the difficulty in maintaining stable weight after successful weight loss, and have shown that reduced-obese subjects differ from never-obese individuals by an altered metabolism and different lifestyle and psychological adjustments to remain weight-stable. Understanding these differences and the features that characterize reduced-obese individuals who are more successful at maintaining weight loss may help devise strategies to combat this serious problem. In the present chapter, the authors review data on the metabolic, psychological and lifestyle characteristics of reduced-obese individuals. Successful weight maintenance requires restricted eating, strenuous regular exercise and frequent self-monitoring. These requirements for a *lifelong* commitment to significant lifestyle changes, possibly to oppose metabolic alterations that favor weight regain, and the psychological mind frame required to support this undertaking, may account for the low success rate of current treatment approaches.

Chapter 6 - High-quality care for patients with eating disorders is a challenge from the perspective of the affected individuals as well as from a health service point of view. This chapter will focus on the every day clinical practice of the dietitian's work with patients with eating disorders across the continuum of care. The dietitian assists patients in increasing information regarding self nurturance, effective vs. destructive behavior and thought patterns as well as developing consciousness-raising and self awareness regarding maladaptive defense patterns. The dietician creates an appropriate emotional climate for growth, helps patients develop open and trusting relationships with food and the body, as well as with others, helps patients engage in new alternatives for expressing feelings, positive self talk, self control and self nurturance using various tools, techniques and approaches. In addition, the nutritionist helps families return to effective communication patterns.

Chapter 7 - This chapter describes the rationale for conducting psychodynamic psychotherapy with eating disorders patients. Though there is strong endorsement for cognitive-behavioral approaches to treatment amongst eating disorder researchers, a review of the empirical literature suggests that 1) most eating disorder patients do not improve with cognitive behavioral approaches, 2) there is little empirical support for the theory of cognitive behavior therapy, 3) and most, if not almost all, clinicians use psychodynamic approaches in their work with eating disorder patients. An empirically based approach for combining cognitive behavioral and psychodynamic approaches is described as an alternative treatment for the eating disorders.

Chapter 8 - Specific and efficacious forms of cognitive behaviour therapy (CBT) have been developed for bulimia nervosa, anorexia nervosa and other eating disorders. Indeed the most recent refinement has been a 'transdiagnostic' CBT for all eating disorders. This chapter discusses the most well tested and manualised CBTs for eating disorders, their theoretical basis, evidence and principles of treatment. Specific issues for the overweight patient are also discussed and further reading recommended.

Chapter 9 - In eating disorders as in other psychopathologies, the twofold purpose of supervision is to provide learning for the supervisee and to optimize the service for the patient. This chapter addresses supervision in the treatment of eating disorders from two vantage points: case management and psychotherapy proper. With regard to case management, issues of hierarchy and leadership may influence the cohesiveness of the team and its therapeutic effectiveness and in this respect a structured eating disorders program has an advantage over an ad-hoc operation of private caregivers. With regard to psychotherapy, although cognizant and respectful of alternative and even more ubiquitous models of psychotherapy, the author has chosen to address the supervision of psychodynamic psychotherapy, congruent with her own orientation. The contemporary supervisory stance has parted from the previous purely didactic approach and recognizes the centrality of counter-transference. Unmotivated for change and difficult to treat, patients with eating disorders arouse in the therapist strong counter-transference reactions which reverberate in supervision: both therapists and supervisors are prone to experiencing frustration, anger, loss of value and confidence in their professional effectiveness. Traditional psychoanalytic devotion to the process, while delegating secondary attention to the symptoms is not realistic in eating disorders, notorious for their mortality risk. Artful navigation between activism and neutrality is one of the many challenges for both the therapist and the supervisor engaged in the endeavor.

Chapter 10 - The management of eating disorders goes beyond symptom management per se and indeed to the establishment of certain interpersonal conditions that are close to Winnicott's mother-infant holding environment. In this environment, there is an interactive play to facilitate cooperation and harmony between the medical and the psychological professional that stimulates different transference phenomena, creating a tension in the multidisciplinary team. Eating disorder patients feel duty-bound to induce strong feelings such as rage, hate, hopelessness, pity, sorrow, or love in those with whom they become involved, including their care-givers. The pseudo-family dynamics that may appear in the therapeutic milieu stimulate an intense emotional atmosphere recreating competition, parallel processes, and splitting dynamics that exert a great impact on the workplace atmosphere. The aim of this paper is to review the concept of countertransference in the context of treating eating disorders (ED). Additionally, the authors will discuss the team dynamics within this environment and their impact on treatment process and outcome. They shall discuss coping approaches to manage patterns of countertransference to facilitate effective treatment processes for the patient and the therapist.

Chapter 11 – The authors specialized in patient unit for the treatment of eating disorders has a long experience with involving families in the therapeutic process. Although the individual and family dynamics can vary a lot in the different cases, the authors make use of the therapeutic potential inherent to the common experiences of eating-disordered patients and their familes. Both for economic and psychological reasons they strongly advocate a group approach. In this paper, the authors report their multifamily intervention during inpatient treatment of eating-disordered adolescents. After discussing the rationale for this approach, they describe the goals and concrete methods of the multifamily groups. The authors conclude with a cost-benefit evaluation based on their own clinical practice.

Chapter 12 - Family-based treatment (FBT) is emerging as a treatment of choice for adolescent anorexia nervosa (AN) and bulimia nervosa (BN). This paper reviews the history of FBT, core clinical and theoretical elements, and key findings from the FBT for AN and BN treatment outcome literature. In addition, the authors address clinical questions and controversies regarding FBT for eating disorders, including whether FBT is clinically appropriate for all adolescents (e.g., older adolescents, patients with comorbid conditions), and whether it indicated for all types of families (e.g., critical, enmeshed, and non-intact families). Finally, they outline recently manualized, innovative applications of FBT for new populations currently under early investigation, such as FBT as a preventive/early intervention for AN, FBT for young adults with eating disorders, and FBT for pediatric overweight.

Chapter 13 - The majority of research data regarding recovery from anorexia nervosa (AN) relates to the therapists' perspective rather than to the patients' point of view. The few studies that documented the meaning and the supportive factors of recovery from the patients' perspective raised an important and significant understanding of the recovery process. The aim of the present study is to extend this scope of understanding from the patient's point of view, using qualitative methodology based on the phenomenological approach as a theoretical foundation. The key research questions were: How do women who recovered from AN experience the recovery process, and what meaning do they attach to this experience? The study was based on in-depth semi-structured interviews with 18 women who had recovered from AN about five years prior to the interview. The study findings show that the participants perceived recovery as resulting from a combination psychosocial and physical symptom changes (internal and external). They emphasized the gradual, stage-by-stage recovery process, starting with mental changes, moving through cognitive-behavioral, occupational, social and familial changes, and ending with physical changes and final relief from the symptoms. The study findings constitute the basis for a model that presents the whole range of discriminate factors for recovery from AN. The proposed model is unique, especially with regard to the definition of recovery from the patient's perspective. Clinical implications are discussed in light of the new findings presented, and recommendations for future research are suggested.

Chapter 14 - The aim of this chapter is to critically analyze the difficulties still inherent in studying recovery from anorexia nervosa (AN). A comprehensive literature review demonstrates that there are at least ten definitions of recovery from AN, differentiated according to several criteria: definition of normal weight; inclusion of only behavioral vs. both behavioral and psychological recovery; inclusion of comorbidity and overall psychosocial functioning in addition to eating-related recovery; and the minimal time required to define recovery. These discrepancies likely account for the wide variation in the range of patients defined as recovered from AN in different outcome studies (0-92%). A great variability also exists with respect to the factors predicting recovery. Another limitation to the research on factors that predict recovery in AN is that most outcome studies have used univariate analyses for this purpose, enabling the assessment of only separate independent predictors. By contrast, multivariate quantitative models allow for the measurement of the relative contribution of each variable for recovery, as well as for the assessment of the cumulative predictive power of all variables included. Unfortunately, only a few quantitative studies exist. Still, an overall worse prognosis has been found repeatedly to be associated with several factors: body image disturbances, compulsive exercising, comorbid anxiety disorders (particularly obsessive compulsive disorder), personality disorders and non-clinical personality traits, poor social skills, longer duration of illness prior to treatment, and shorter follow-up. In the second part of the chapter the authors aim to provide the reader with several potential options to standardize the definition of recovery and the design of outcome studies in AN.

Chapter 15 - This paper attempts to identify the unique way in which women who have recovered from bulimia nervosa (BN) describe their recovery process. This is a qualitative study, based on in-depth interviews with twelve women who have recovered from BN. Analysis of the interviews reveals that the women use metaphoric language to describe their recovery as a sharp transition transformation is described using three archetypal protagonists who embody three dimensions of change: the Self, the Bulimia, and the Environment. The recovery experience that emerges from the interviews is a complex and polarized one, encompassing a perception of achievement and victory over the disorder, coupled with a contradictory view of the Bulimia as chronic disorder. The findings of the research are discussed in reference to object relations theory and the use of the splitting mechanism.

Chapter 16 - This chapter addresses first issues in definition around the question of recovery in bulimia nervosa (BN), next the natural history, and third the outcome with treatment including predictors that may be modified to enhance remission and reduce relapse or later recurrence rates. Remission in BN is most often defined as the absence of binge eating and purging behaviours. In addition some studies have used reduction in psychopathology as an alternate indicator of recovery. These studies were based on a quantitative measure of eating disorder weight/shape (or other) concerns e.g. being less than one standard deviation above the community mean of the global Eating Disorder Examination score. There is a consensus that remission is most likely sustained after one year and relapse after that time may be termed recurrence. Naturalistic studies suggest that about half or more of those with BN may have a good outcome in the longer-term, but for the remainder the disorder is persistent. Treatment outcome studies indicate that for those who engage in specific interventions and evidence based treatments (particularly psychotherapies such as cognitive behaviour therapy for bulimia nervosa) developed since the 1980s the likelihood of recovery is significantly increased. Whilst there are mixed outcomes in studies of prognostic factors, consistent pre-treatment factors identified include a history of psychological advsersity, borderline personality structure, depression and obesity. Consistent post-treatment prognostic features are achieving abstinence and good psychosocial adjustment. Thus treatments should address improving psychological resiliency, coping and co-morbidities.

In: Treatment and Recovery of Eating Disorders
Editors: Daniel Stein and Yael Latzer

ISBN: 978-1-62808-248-7
© 2013 Nova Science Publishers, Inc.

Chapter 1

INTRODUCTION: TREATMENT STRATEGIES IN EATING DISORDERS: AN OVERVIEW

Daniel Stein, M.D.[1*] *and Yael Latzer, D.Sc.*[2]

[1]Director, Pediatric Psychosomatic Department, Edmond and Lily Safra Children's Hospital, Chaim Sheba Medical Center, Tel Hashomer, affiliated with the Sackler Faculty of Medicine, Tel Aviv University, Israel

[2]Faculty of Social Welfare and Health Sciences, Haifa University, Israel, Director, Institute for the Treatment and Study of Eating Disorders, Division of Psychiatry, Rambam, Health Care Campus, Haifa, Israel

INTRODUCTION

Eating disorders (EDs) and disordered eating behaviors are considered a major disease of the modern world, being among the most prevailing public health problems in female adolescents and young adults in recent decades, and reaching in many Western countries an epidemic proportion (1). They occur primarily in adolescent girls and young women during a crucial developmental stage, and are linked to extensive morbidity and high mortality rates (1). EDs are complex, conflictual, misunderstood disturbances that often raise negative emotions such as bewilderment, mistrust and fear not only among lay people but also in treatment providers. These reactions are likely the result of failing to grasp why someone would not comply with the basic universal need of eating, or put such an emphasis on weight and appearance that renders them more important than anything else in life. As a result, individuals afflicted with EDs frequently feel misunderstood, unaccepted and isolated. This had led us to edit two books, written by renounced international and Israeli researchers, about ED-related problems. Our first book has focused primarily on aspects related to the history of EDs, diagnostic considerations, epidemiology, course and outcome, sociocultural influences, familial considerations, and prevention. For the current book we have conducted an extensive

* E-mail address: danil49@netvision.net.il

literature search to offer an up-to-date summary about putative treatment options and prognostic considerations in EDs.

TREATMENT OF EATING DISORDERS

EDs are among the psychiatric disorders considered specifically difficult to treat, necessitating multi-professional interventions in patients with significant physiological and psychiatric morbidity that are often reluctant to receive treatment (2). Fore and foremost, any treatment of anorexia nervosa (AN), bulimia nervosa (BN), binge eating disorder (BED), or eating disorders not otherwise specified (ED-NOS) requires multi-modal interventions, with nutritional rehabilitation being a necessary, albeit insufficient, prerequisite for recovery (2).

Psychological Treatments

The study of psychodynamic psychotherapy as a possible treatment strategy for EDs is subject to considerable conceptual and methodological controversies and ambiguities, as this books aims to underline. At the start, each psychodynamic model relates to EDs - as is likely the case with respect to any psychopathology of putative psycho-developmental origin - according to its specific formulations and conceptualizations as derived from the treatment of already ill individuals. For example, classical psychoanalytic authors have hypothesized that fears during adolescence in relation to sexuality might lead the future to be AN patient to a regression from oedipal to pre-oedipal eating-related oral anxieties (3). The inherent problems with any such model are that hypotheses about predisposing psychological factors are derived from findings in patients who are severely ill not only psychologically but also physiologically when analyzed, and that these models cannot be subject to rigorous research. Furthermore, evidence-based studies assessing the effect of classical psychodynamic psychotherapies are scarce (4-7) and their findings are often subject to considerable ambiguity (8). Despite these limitations, the merit of psychodynamic viewpoints is that they may assist at least some ED patients (and their therapists) in understanding that their suffering has some personal relevant meaning; this, in turn, may offer an opportunity towards self-acceptance, and/or towards readiness for change (see Tobin, Banker, and Mitrani in this book).

Specific Psychological Treatment Modalities

Cognitive Behavioral Treatment (CBT)
The cognitive theory assumes that a complex multidirectional model may tie the development of an ED to specific maladaptive cognitions and behaviors. Accordingly, inborn dysfunctional core cognitions associated with lack of self-esteem may be associated in vulnerable individuals with an exaggerated inclination towards cognitive-related dichotomy, control, and perfectionism to correct such a pervasive sense of worthlessness. These cognitive distortions, may, in turn, lead to the development and perpetuation of complex interdependent interactions between extreme concern with weight and shape and the maintaining of relentless

strict dieting, likely culminating in diverse ED-related presentations. According to both classical (9), and modified transdiagnostic (10) cognitive formulations, these disturbances are more likely to appear and persist in the context of such premorbid personality attributes as rigidity, perfectionism, obsessionality, self-criticism, and intolerance to negative affects.

The application of the cognitive-behavioral model to the treatment of BN has been developed in the early 1980th by Fairburn (11), being implemented in several leading ED treatment centers in the UK and the USA several years later (12). It is noteworthy to note that two decades later, cognitive behavioral treatment (CBT), along with interpersonal therapy (IPT), are the only psychotherapeutic interventions currently validated, in randomized controlled trials (RCTs), to be effective in adult outpatients with BN and BED (13). Several RCTs have recently demonstrated the efficacy of CBT also in adolescent BN outpatients (14).

A full treatment manual has been published in the early 1990th (9), being subsequently successfully used in many independent RCTs (15). CBT is currently feasible within both an individual (9) and a group framework (16).

The classical CBT for BN and BED (9) is a structured intervention consisting of three interdependent stages. The behavioral stage applies systematic monitoring of eating and weight related preoccupations and behaviors in order to render these manifestations to become less automatic, to define the problematic behaviors and associated cognitions, and to set the ground for behavioral change. Cessation of dieting behavior is an important aspect of this first behavioral stage. The second cognitive stage is focused on identification and change of cognitive distortions related for the most part to weight and shape and their association with disturbances in self-esteem and self perception. The third and final stage is geared toward the consolidation of the changes achieved and to prevent relapse.

The classical CBT in BN and BED is a short term focal treatment (ranging between 16-24 weeks), emphasizing that important changes may continue in the months following the end of treatment (9). Longer modified versions exist in mores severe cases, or if the ED is accompanied by a personality disorder (particularly borderline personality disorder). A modified version lasting for around a year also exists for the treatment of obesity, showing seemingly promising results in maintaining reduction of weight at least in the short run (17).

CBT is considered the treatment of choice in BN and BED, being superior or a least as effective as any other psychotherapy, and superior to specific serotonin reuptake inhibitors (SSRIs) and tricyclic antidepressants (TCAs). The combination of CBT and SSRIs/TCAs has been found superior to each modality alone (18). Following treatment, around 40-50% of the patients cease both bingeing and purging, whereas at 1 to 6 years after treatment, around 50% of the patients have no bingeing/purging behaviors; although between 35-45% of the patients may still show evidence of an ED at follow up, it is usually less severe than at the beginning of treatment (19,20).

The lack of improvement with classical CBT in a significant minority of the patients has been associated with its focusing almost exclusively on "specific" core ED-related manifestations, likely not decreasing sufficiently other influential illness-maintaining processes (10). Additionally, a relatively high rate of drop out (between 15-35%) has been found with CBT, likely reflecting difficulties to carry out this procedure by both patients and treatment providers. This has led to the initiation of a modified transdiagnostic version of CBT-ED (10).

The transdiagnostic model is geared towards managing core aspects relevant to all ED types that have not been sufficiently addressed by the classical model, including clinical perfectionism, core low self-esteem, intolerance of negative affects, and interpersonal difficulties. This is done under the premise that these core "personality" traits likely interact with core ED-related manifestations to maintain the ED (21). This model has also the advantage that it can be tailored to the specific patient, regardless of the diagnostic subtype (22). The focus and therapeutic considerations in this strategy, described by the authors as an enhanced cognitive behavior therapy for EDs, would be, for example, different in a BN patient whose main concerns have to do with weight and body image in comparison to another BN patient with severe additional problems in the areas of perfectionism and mood intolerance (22). Indeed, a recent randomized controlled trial of transdiagnostic CBT in BN and ED-NOS patients with bingeing/purging disturbances (23) has found that whereas patients with mainly ED-related concerns improve better with a shorter "classical" CBT strategy, patients with additional disturbances in other core ED features react better to a modified "enhanced transdiagnostic" CBT version. Still, we are yet only at the early stages of the study of the modified transdiagnostic CBT. Future research is needed to examine whether this conceptual modification would be indeed found to overcome the serious limitations of classical CBT in the treatment of EDs.

In AN, there is still a lack of empirical evidence to favor any psychotherapeutic intervention over another (13), with the exception of the Multifactorial Interactional Family Therapy for adolescents with relatively short term AN (24). The improvement with any psychotherapeutic intervention – psychodynamic psychotherapy, CBT, or family therapy in adult AN patients is still only modest (25) .

The efficacy of CBT in AN patients is limited (5,26). This is the result of the resistance these patients often have with regard to change in general (27), and recovery in particular (27). Other factors interfering with CBT in AN include the need for weight gain and, if it is achieved, for its constant monitoring, and the little influence that CBT has on core AN features (10,27). CBT in AN is a long-term intervention, lasting for up to 24 months, and a considerable part of treatment is dedicated to acknowledging and deal with the patients' inherent fear of change, and increase their motivation toward change (27,28). The aim of treatment is to gradually make AN patients aware that their thoughts do not have to be entirely focused on ED-related issues to improve and maintain a sense of well-being, eventually increasing the scope of non ED-related issues that may be of relevance (27). Although evidence based research is still scarce, CBT might be more relevant in AN for relapse prevention that for the management of malnourished patients. One randomized controlled trial has, thus, found that previously hospitalized AN patients show significantly less relapse with individual CBT in comparison to standardized nutritional counseling (29). Another controlled pilot study in AN patients (7) has shown similar increase in weight and improvement in nutritional status persisting at one year follow-up with cognitive analytical and educational behavioral strategies.

Self Psychology

The self-psychological paradigm considers that a pervasive disturbance in self-esteem is an important factor in the predisposition to an ED. In an attempt to enhance their vulnerable sense of self-worth, future to be ED patients may be inclined at the start toward fulfilling the needs of significant others in the service of discarding their own needs (related to as selflessness), while simultaneously withdrawing from any reliance on these others as putative self-objects (30,31). At a later phase in their life, when still feeling unworthy, unloved and misunderstood despite their endless efforts, these individuals would turn to rely on food (in BN), or on actively refraining from food (in AN), as a fulfilling replacing self-object (30,31). The ability and choice to refrain from food may become in AN patients an important vehicle in their attempts to enhance their sense of self-worth and self-acceptance (31).

The conceptualizations of self psychology seem particularly suitable for the treatment of AN and BN because of the great emphasis put in this model on the potential of the therapist and therapeutic relationships to intervene with the ED-patient's pervasive disturbance in self-esteem. This is likely associated with the therapeutic stance of self-psychology that underscores the importance of empathic understanding "from within", from an experience-near stance where the therapist is highly tuned to the patient, in contrast to experience-distant interpretations "from without" that are characteristic of other types of psychotherapy. Another important contribution of self psychology lies in its potential to render the ED patient toward creating, or resuming, adaptive human-related self-object relationships with the figure of the therapist, which, in turn may enable the renunciation of hitherto cherished food (or lack of food)-related self-object relationships (30,31). Although self-psychology treatment in EDs has not been subject to rigorous controlled research, several important case-reports have alluded to its' efficacy, and one well-designed study has found self-psychology to be as effective as CBT in the treatment of EDs (4).

Family-based treatment interventions

Traditional models have put a great emphasis on the putative influence of the family in the predisposition to an ED. Minuchin (32) in the mid 1970th, in his conceptualizations about psychosomatic families, of which AN has been viewed as a prototype, has emphasized that the constellation of several important familial characteristics might predispose to the development of an ED. Similarly, systematic family theorists, including Selvini-Palazzoli (33) and Boscolo (34), alluded to the role of the family to predispose to an ED if it becomes a rigidly organized interactional system in which the symptoms of illness become a powerful homeostatic mechanism resistant to change from the outside.

These and similar theories have been severely criticized in later years, as many families with the allegedly "psychosomatic" characteristics have no evidence of an ED, and many ED families do not share these characteristics. Furthermore, these hypotheses have been developed according to studies in acutely ill patients, not taking into consideration the considerable effect of a chronic illness on the family's well-being and overall functioning. Most importantly, such conceptualizations might have generated, even if inadvertently, severe blame from others, including mental health authorities, towards the family of an ED patient, likely inducing considerable guilt in the family itself. This is specifically important when bearing in mind that families may have an important role in promoting healthier attitudes and behaviors towards eating, weight and shape, likely assisting and empowering ED patients in their endeavors towards recovery. Furthermore, non-shared environmental influences, namely those experiences that are unique to one sibling and not shared by other siblings reared in the same family, but not shared environmental influences, have been found to account for a significant percentage of the variance in the development of both AN and BN (0.17-0.46), interacting with hereditary influences (35). Still, despite the critique of traditional structural and strategic family-based theories in EDs, they have had an important role in generating the theoretical basis and clinical principles of the current evidence-based Multifactorial Family Based Treatment (FBT) approach (24).

FBT is currently considered the only effective evidence-based family intervention in the treatment of EDs, specifically, but not only, in AN. It is a structured, focused, and time-limited intervention, including 20 sessions conducted for around 6 months, and divided into three interdependent treatment stages (24). In the first stage, treatment focuses almost exclusively on weight restoration. Parents are actively involved and are temporarily put in charge on their child's eating. This stage includes once weekly sessions. It lasts between 3-5 months, and the family defers working on family conflicts until eating-disordered behaviors are resolved. In the second stage (treatment session every 2-3 weeks), the adolescent gets gradually increased responsibility for eating, although still being assisted to some extent by the parents. In the third stage (once monthly sessions) that starts upon achieving and maintaining a required weight, treatment focuses on age appropriate developmental tasks and relevant family conflicts, as well as on maintenance and consolidation of change, and on relapse prevention. Siblings do not take an active part in the management of ED behaviors in FBT, being rather encouraged to support the ED patient in her endeavors to overcome her illness.

The FBT model has shown showing promising results in several RCTs conducted in younger adolescents (<18) with relatively short term (<3 years) AN (36-39). It has been found effective primarily in youngsters with a relatively mild disorder and intact family, treated in outpatient settings, for both eating-related symptomatology and overall functioning. A modified version in which parents are seen separately from their offspring has been found superior to the traditional conjoint format in highly critical families (high levels of expressed emotion) (40). Moreover, the effect of FBT in younger patients with short-term AN has been found superior to any individual therapy in 1 to 5 years follow-up studies (36-39). Recent studies have shown a similar effect also in younger children diagnosed with AN (41).

The traditional FBT model has not been found suitable for BN adolescents and for adults with any ED, in whom individual psychotherapy is likely the preferable intervention. Recently, Le Grange & Lock (42), have initiated an adapted version of FBT geared for adolescents diagnosed with AN bingeing/purging type and BN. Similar to the treatment in AN, this adapted model includes 20 sessions conducted in around 6 months and parents are actively involved in the treatment. Preliminary findings suggest that parents are able to effectively decrease bingeing/purging behaviors in their children in addition to reversing severe dieting (43). Two randomized controlled trials using FBT have been conducted hitherto in BN adolescents. Schmidt et al (14) have found no difference between FBT and individual CBT in BN adolescents in bingeing/purging abstinence rates (around 40% abstinence for both modalities) at six months follow-up. Le Grange and colleagues (44) have found that significantly more BN adolescents treated with FBT have been abstinent from bingeing/purging behaviors following treatment and at 6-month follow-up compared to patients receiving either individual supportive psychotherapy or IPT, whereas no differences have been reported in patients receiving either family therapy or CBT.

Medications

Specific Serotonin Reuptake Inhibitors (SSRIs) and Tricyclic Antidepressants (TCAs)

Both SSRIs and TCAs have been found effective in the treatment of BN and BED in well designed RCTs (45-47). These medications reduce binge eating (mean reduction 55%, compared to 25% reduction or less with placebo in BN, and 33% in BED). In overweight BED patients, these mediations may also reduce weight. SSRIs have been shown also to have a beneficial effect on eating–related attitudes, including restraint, pursuit of thinness, eating-related obsessionality, and food-preoccupation. Nevertheless, apparently only a minority of BN and BED patients are completely abstinent from bingeing (and also from purging in the case of BN) with SSRIs at both short-term and long-term follow-up. Increased dosage is usually associated with a more favorable anti-bingeing effect. Interestingly, the anti-bingeing effect of SSRIs is not related to their anti-depressive effect.

The rationale for the use of SSRIs in BN and BED is related to an increase in the availability of intrasynaptic serotonin (5HT), which has the potential to reduce bingeing (food consumption) and increase satiety. Additionally, BN and BED share many comorbidities potentially mediated by 5HT, including depressive disorders, anxiety disorders, obsessive compulsive disorder (OCD), substance use disorders, and impulse control disorders (48). Indeed, the use of SSRIs has been associated with a reduction in symptoms related to these comorbidities in both BN and BED (46,47). Although SSRIs are effective in long-term treatment of BN and BED patients, follow-up studies have shown that relapse may occur if the antidepressant is discontinued (46,47). Furthermore, tolerance may develop to the anti-bingeing effect of these medications (although no tolerance has been found to occur with respect to their anti-depressive, anti-anxiety, and anti-impulsive effects), potentially increasing the risk of relapse.

Although many medications have been tried in AN patients, there is yet no established medication with the potential to improve weight gain in AN (25). Moreover, SSRIs are ineffective in underweight malnourished AN patients, as the absorption of tryptophan, the precursor of 5HT, is reduced in this condition compared to other essential amino acids (49). Most trials demonstrate treatment efficacy only for comorbid disorders (depression, anxiety, OCD) and only upon some correction of weight. One study has found that SSRIs may maintain the weight gain achieved, as well as reduce the extent of comorbid depression, anxiety, and ED and non-ED obsessionality, in weight-restored AN patients in comparison with placebo (50). However, in another study, SSRIs have not been found superior to placebo in reducing the risk of relapse in AN patients following weight restoration (51).

Topiramate

Topiramate is a sulphamate derivative of fructose approved as an add-on therapy in seizure disorders in adults and children over the age of two. It is associated with a number of reversible neurological and cognitive adverse effects, mostly impairment in cognitive functions of visual attention, attention, psychomotor speed, speech, and verbal memory (52). Topiramate is currently not approved as an anorectic agent in the treatment of overweight adults and children. Nevertheless, to date, three RCTs (53-55) as well as several open studies and case reports have shown significant reduction in binge-eating and weight with topiramate in adult BED patients. These studies have, thus, shown significantly greater reduction in mean binges per day, mean bingeing days per week, as well as in BMI following 14 weeks of treatment with topiramate in comparison to placebo. Between 60- 80% of the patients treated with topiramate have been abstinent from bingeing at the end of treatment compared to 26-61% of placebo-treated patients. In a long term (42 weeks) open-label monotherapy extension (56) of one controlled 14-week study (53), 10 of the original 61 patients have completed all 56 weeks of treatment. These patients have continued to show significant reduction in bingeing and BMI, as well as in eating-related obsessionality, at the end of treatment. Topiramate has usually been well tolerated, adverse effects being mostly minimal, and no differences in dropout rates have been shown between control and research patients.

Topiramate has been recently found effective also in BN. In an RCT performed for 10 weeks in adult BN women (57,58), a significant improvement in either bingeing or purging behaviors, or in both, has been found with topiramate in comparison to placebo. BN patients treated with topiramate have shown, in addition, significantly greater reduction in pursuit of thinness, body dissatisfaction, preoccupation with food and dieting, and anxiety. Most importantly, in contrast to the findings in BED, no significant reduction in weight has been found with topiramate in normal weight BN patients, suggesting that in BN, the use of topiramate is likely not associated with the induction of dieting. Mean dosage of topiramate in both BED and BN has been in the range of 100-200 mg/day. Because of the risk of neurocognitive adverse effects, it is suggested to start topiramate treatment in BN or BED with a low dose (25 mg/day) with weekly dosage increments of 25 mg/day thereafter.

Several mechanisms may account for the weight reduction potential of topiramate. Topiramate may act as an appetite suppressant and/or satiety enhancer, via its antagonist activities at hypothalamic glutamate receptors (glutamate elicits intense eating), and/or its potential to down regulate neuropeptide Y receptors (neuropeptide Y significantly stimulates feeding behavior). Topiramate–induced weight loss is associated with loss of fat rather than of lean body mass, likely related to its potential to inhibit fat deposition by reduction of food intake and/or stimulation of energy expenditure. Furthermore, topiramate may be effective in reducing disinhibition, impulsivity, and the cognitive restraint associated with eating.

Olanzapine

No medication has been yet proved effective for weight gain in AN, urging the research of novel strategies. In this respect, the use of olanzapine, an atypical antipsychotic medication associated with increased appetite and considerable weight gain due to reduced serotonergic activity (59), has been investigated in chronic AN patients resistant to any other intervention. Three randomized controlled trials (60-62), as well as a few open studies and case reports have found increase in weight in some AN patients treated with 5-10 mg/day of olanzapine, accompanied by a reduction in depression, agitation, eating-related obsessionality, pre-meal anxiety, and difficulty in eating. Currently, olanzapine is recommended only for chronic adult AN patients and only if multiple other treatments have failed.

Other Medications

The peripheral-acting orlistat has been found effective in the management of obesity and overweight associated with BED in both adults and children and adolescents (63). Preliminary findings support the effectiveness of the 5-HT3 antagonist ondansetron in some patients with BN (64). Recently, venlafaxine (a selective serotonin-noradrenalin reuptake inhibitor) has been found effective in reducing bingeing and BMI in BED (65). The use of Sibutramine, previously considered a modestly effective weight reduction agent in obese adults is currently contraindicated because of the finding of a greater risk of adverse cardiovascular effects in obese adult patients with pre-existing cardiovascular disease in comparison to placebo (66; see also Karwautz et al in this book).

CONCLUSIONS AND ACKNOWLEDGMENTS

The aim of this chapter is to bring up-to-date data regarding the most efficacious treatment options in EDs. The research of treatment in EDs is extremely complex, as the implementation of randomized controlled trials in many psychological interventions is subject to both methodological and treatment-related ethical controversies. Nevertheless, some important conclusions can be drawn from our extensive literature search. EDs are multicausal multidetermined disorders, where multiple bio-psycho-social factors interact to increase the liability to develop an ED. Whereas EDs, particularly AN, have been traditionally related to socio-cultural, familial, and individual psychological causations, it is currently conceived that genetic predisposition is likely of utmost importance in the predisposition to an ED, although it is yet to understand what this predisposition really encompasses. Psychosocial determinants may be of relevance if they operate in the context of this genetic vulnerability. Despite the genetic-biological etiopathology, psychological interventions, primarily CBT in adult BN and BED patients and FBT in adolescents with AN, are still considered the most effective in the management of EDs, if carried out in the context of adequate nutritional rehabilitation. The efficacy of any individual psychotherapy in AN is still limited. Thus, in a recent RCT comparing the long term effect (mean follow-up years 6.7±1.2 years) of CBT, IPT, and supportive therapy, only around 50% of the patients have had an overall good outcome, whereas another 50% show a poor outcome (67). No differences in recovery rates have been shown in this study, which is an extension of a previous RCT (26), among the different psychotherapies. On a more general level, it is of note that differential treatment strategies may have different effects in different types of EDs. Age is another factor that has to be taken into consideration when directing toward the most effective treatment for the specific patient.

The present book summarizes the knowledge and expertise of renounced international and Israeli researchers with respect to the most important treatment strategies in EDs. It includes detailed chapters of different models and points of view about CBT, psychodynamic psychotherapy, family therapy, and pharmacotherapy. Specific chapters deal with countertranference issues and the complexity of supervision in the treatment of difficult ED patients, as well as with the way to provide adequate interventions for the carers. Two chapters deal with specific complexities in the management of obesity.

The last four chapters of this book deal with issues related to the outcome and prognosis of AN and BN. The concepts of remission, recovery and chronicity are particularly relevant, albeit complex when it comes to EDs. This reflects the relevance of the dichotomy between behavioral remission and cognitive recovery, the influence of the high relapse rates on the distinction between recovery and remission, and the finding that some patients may recover even after many years of chronic sustained illness (see Stein et al and Hay in this book). We have been very fortunate to present, in addition to the therapists point of view, also the perspective of the patients about their own recovery.

We are very grateful to the clinicians and researchers form all over the globe for their effort and contribution to this endeavor.

Daniel Stein
Yael Latzer

REFERENCES

[1] Hoek HW. Incidence, prevalence and mortality of anorexia nervosa and other eating disorders. Curr Opin Psychiatry 2006;19:389-94.

[2] Halmi KA. Eating disorders in females: genetics, pathophysiology, and treatment. J Pediatr Endocrinol Metab 2002;15 Suppl. 5:1379-86.

[3] Mushatt C. Anorexia nervosa: a psychoanalytic commentary. Int J Psychoanal Psychother 1982-1983;9:257-65.

[4] Bachar E, Latzer Y, Kreitler S, Berry E. Empirical comparison of two psychological therapies: self psychology and cognitive orientation in the treatment of anorexia and bulimia. J Psychother Pract Res 1999;8:115-28

[5] Dare C, Eisler I, Russell G. Treasure J, Dodge L. Psychological therapies for adults with anorexia nervosa: randomized control trial of out-patient treatments. Br J Psychiatry 2001;178:216-21

[6] Garner DM, Rockert W, Davis R, Garner MV, Olmstead MP, Eagle M. Comparison of cognitive-behavioral and supportive-expressive therapy for bulimia nervosa. Am J Psychiatry 1993;150:37-46.

[7] Treasure J, Todd G, Brolly M, Tiller J, Nehmed A, Denman F. A pilot study of a randomized trial of cognitive analytical therapy vs. educational behavioral therapy for adult anorexia nervosa. Behav Res Ther 1995;33:363-7.

[8] Thompson-Brenner H, Weingeroff J, Westen D. Empirical support for psychodynamic psychotherapy for eating disorders. In: Levy RA, Ablon JS. Handbook of evidence-based psychodynamic psychotherapy: Bridging the gap between science and practice. New York: Humana Press, 2009:67-92.

[9] Fairburn CG, Marcus MD, Wilson GT: Cognitive-behavioral therapy for binge eating and bulimia nervosa: A comprehensive treatment manual. In: Fairburn CG, Wilson TG, Binge eating: Nature, assessment and treatment. New York: Guilford Press, 1993:361-404.

[10] Fairburn CG, Cooper Z, Shafran R. Cognitive behavior therapy for eating disorders: a "transdiagnostic" theory and treatment. Behav Res Ther 2003;41:509-28.

[11] Fairburn CG, A cognitive behavioral approach to the treatment of bulimia. Psychol Med 1981;11:707-11.

[12] Fairburn CG, Kirk J, O'Connor M, Cooper PJ. A comparison of two psychological treatments for bulimia nervosa. Behav Res Ther 1986;24:629-43.

[13] Fassino S, Piero A, Levi M, Gramaglia C, Amianto F, Leombruni P, Abbate Daga G. Psychological treatment of eating disorders. A review of the literature. Panminerv Med 2004;46:189-198.

[14] Schmidt U, Lee S, Beecham J, Perkins S, Treasure J, Yi I, et al. A randomized controlled trial of family therapy and cognitive behavior therapy guided self-care for adolescents with bulimia nervosa and related disorders. A J Psychiatry 2007;164:591-598

[15] Agras WS, Walsh T, Fairburn CG, Wilson GT, Kramer HC. A multicenter comparison of cognitive-behavioral therapy and interpersonal psychotherapy for bulimia nervosa. Arch Gen Psychiatry 2000;57:459-66

[16] Nevonen L, Broberg AG. A comparison of sequenced individual and group psychotherapy for patients with bulimia nervosa. Int J Eat Disord 2006;39:117-27.

[17] Cooper Z, Fairburn CG, Hawker DM. Cognitive behavioral treatment of obesity: A clinician's guide. New York: The Guilford Press, 2003.

[18] Mitchell JE, Peterson CB, Myers T, Wonderlich S. Combining pharmacotherapy and psychotherapy in the treatment of patients with eating disorders. Psychiatr Clin North Am 2001;24:315-23

[19] Jones R, Peveler RC, Hope RA, O'Connor M. Psychotherapy and bulimia nervosa. Longer-term effects of interpersonal psychotherapy, behavior therapy, and cognitive behavior therapy. Arch Gen Psychiatry 1993;50:419-28

[20] Fairburn CG, Norman PA, Welch SL, O'Connor ME, Doll HA, Peveler RC. A prospective study of outcome in bulimia nervosa and the long-term effects of three psychological treatments. Arch Gen Psychiatry 1995;52:304-12.

[21] Waller G, Ohanian V, Meyer C, Osman S. Cognitive content among bulimic women: the role of core beliefs. Int J Eat Disord 2000;28:235-41.

[22] Fairburn CG, Cooper Z, Shafran R. Enhanced cognitive behavior therapy for eating disorders ("CBT-E"): An overview. In Fairburn CG. Cognitive behavior therapy and eating disorders. New York, NY: Guilford Press, 2008a:23-34.

[23] Fairburn CG, Cooper Z., Doll H, O'Connor M, Bohn K, Hawker, D, et al.. Transdiagnostic cognitive-behavioral therapy for patients with eating disorders: a two-site trial with 60-week follow-up. Am J Psychiatry 2009:166:311-9.

[24] Lock J, Le Grange D, Agras WS, Dare C. Treatment manual for anorexia nervosa: A family based approach. New York: The Guilford Press, 2001

[25] Practice Guidelines for the Treatment of Patients with Eating Disorders, 3rd ed. Washington, DC: American Psychiatric Association, 2006.

[26] McIntosh VW, Jordan J, Carter FA, Luty SE, McKenzie JM, Bulik CM, et al. Three psychotherapies for anorexia nervosa: a randomized controlled trial. Am J Psychiatry 2005;162:741-7

[27] Garner DM, Vitousek KM, Pike KM: Cognitive behavioral therapy for anorexia nervosa. In: Garner DM. Garfinkel PW: Handbook of clinical treatments in Eating Disorders. Guilford Press, 1997:94-144.

[28] Fairburn CG, Cooper Z, Shafran R, Bohn K, Hawker DM, Murphy R, et al. Underweight and undereating. In: Fairburn, CG. Cognitive behavior therapy and eating disorders. New York, NY: Guilford Press, 2008b:147-182.

[29] Pike KM, Walsh BT, Vitousek KM, Wilson GT, Bauer J. Cognitive behavioral therapy in the post-hospitalization treatment of anorexia nervosa. Am J Psychiatry 2001;160:2046-9

[30] Goodsitt A: Eating disorders: A self-psychological perspective. In Garner DM, Garfinkel PE. Handbook of treatment for eating disorders. New York: The Guilford Press, 1997:208-228.

[31] Bachar E. The Fear of occupying space. Jerusalem: Hebrew University Magnes Press, 2001 (in Hebrew).

[32] Minuchin S, Roseman BL, Baker L. Psychosomatic families: Anorexia nervosa in context. Cambridge MA: Harvard University Press, 1978

[33] Selvini Palazzoli M. Self starvation: From the intrapsychic to the transpersonal approach. London: Chaucer, 1974

[34] Boscolo L, Cecchin G, Hoffman L, Penn P. Milan Systemic Family Therapy. New York: Basic Books, 1987

[35] Klump KL, Wonderlich S, Lehoux P, Lilenfeld LR, Bulik CM. Does environment matter? A review of nonshared environment and eating disorders. Int J Eating Disord 2002;3:118-35.

[36] Russell GF, Szmukler GI, Dare C, Eisler I.. An evaluation of family therapy in anorexia nervosa and bulimia nervosa. Arch Gen Psychiatry 1987;44:1047-56

[37] Robin AL, Siegel PT, Moye AW, Koepke T, Gilroy M, Denis, AB, Sikand A. A controlled comparison of family versus individual therapy for adolescents with anorexia nervosa. J Am Acad Child Adolesc Psychiatry 1999;38:1482-89.

[38] Eisler I, Simic M, Russell GFM, Dare C. A randomized controlled treatment trial of two forms of family therapy in adolescent anorexia nervosa: A five-year follow up. J Child Psychol Psychiatry 2007;48:552-60.

[39] Lock J, Le Grange D, Agras WS, Moye A, Bryson SW, Jo B. Randomized clinical trial comparing family-based treatment with adolescent-focused individual therapy for adolescents with anorexia nervosa. Arch Gen Psychiatry 2010;67:1025-32..

[40] Eisler I, Dare C, Hodes M, Russell G, Dodge E, Le Grange D. Family therapy for adolescent anorexia nervosa: The results of a controlled comparison of two family interventions. J of Child Psychol Psychiatry 2000; 41:727-36.

[41] Lock J, Le Grange D, Fordsburg S, Hewell K. Is family therapy effective for children with anorexia nervosa? J Am Acad Child Adolesc Psychiatry 2006;45:1323-38.

[42] Le Grange D, Lock J. Treating bulimia in adolescents: A family-based approach. New York: The Guilford Press, 2007

[43] Lock J, Le Grange D. Family-based treatment of eating disorders. Int J Eat Disord 2005;37 Suppl:S64-7; discussion S87-9.

[44] Le Grange D, Crosby RD, Rathouz PJ, Leventhal BL. A randomized controlled comparison of family-based treatment and supportive psychotherapy for adolescent bulimia nervosa. Arch Gen Psychiatry 2007;64:1049-56.

[45] Pederson KJ, Roerig JL, Mitchell JE. Towards the pharmacotherapy of eating disorders. Exp Opin Pharmacother 2003;4:1659-78.

[46] Shapiro JR, Berkman ND, Brownley KA, Sedway JA, Lohr KN, Bulik CM. Bulimia nervosa treatment: A systematic review of randomized controlled trials. Int J Eat Disord 2007;40:321-36.

[47] Brownley KA, Berkman ND, Sedway JA, Lohr KN, Bulik CM. Binge eating disorder treatment: A systematic review of randomized controlled trials. Int J Eat Disord 2007;40:337-348.

[48] Kaye W, Strober M, Jimerson D. The neurobiology of eating disorders. In Charney DS, Nestler EJ. The neurobiology of mental illness. New York: Oxford Press, 2004, p. 1112-1128

[49] Ferguson CP, La Via MC, Crossan PJ, Kaye WH. Are serotonin selective reuptake inhibitors effective in underweight anorexia nervosa? Int J Eat Disord 1999;25:11-7

[50] Kaye WH, Nagata T, Weltzin TE, Hsu LK, Sokol MS, McConaha C, et al. Double-blind placebo-controlled administration of fluoxetine in restricting- and restricting-purging-type anorexia nervosa. Biol Psychiatry 2001;49:644-52.

[51] Walsh BT, Kaplan AS, Attia E, Olmsted M, Parides M, Carter JC, et al. Fluoxetine after weight restoration in anorexia nervosa: a randomized controlled trial. JAMA 2006;295:2605-12

[52] Langtry HD, Gillis JC, Davis R. Topiramate: A review of its pharmacodynamic and pharmacokinetic properties and clinical efficacy in the management of epilepsy. Drugs 1997;54:752-73.

[53] McElroy SL, Arnold LM, Shapira NA, Keck PE Jr., Rosenthal NR, Karim MR, et al. Topiramate in the treatment of binge eating disorder associated with obesity: a randomized placebo-controlled trial. Am J Psychiatry 2003;160:255-61.

[54] McElroy SL, Hudson JI, Capece JA, Beyers K, Fisher AC, Rosenthal NR; Topiramate Binge-Eating Disorder Research Group. Topiramate for the treatment of binge–eating disorder associated with obesity: a placebo-controlled study. Biol Psychiatry 2007;61:1039-48

[55] Claudino AM, de Oliveira IR, Appolinario JC, Cordás TA, Duchesne M, Sichieri R, et al. Double-blind, randomized, placebo-controlled trial of topiramate plus cognitive-behavior therapy in binge-eating disorder. J Clin Psychiatry 2007;68:1324-32.

[56] McElroy SL, Shapira NA, Arnold LM, Keck PE, Rosenthal NR, Wu SC, et al. Topiramate in the long-term treatment of binge-eating disorder associated with obesity. J Clin Psychiatry 2004;65:1463-9.

[57] Hoopes SP, Reimherr FW, Hedges DW, Rosenthal NR, Kamin M, Karim R, et al. Treatment of bulimia nervosa with topiramate in a randomized, double-blind, placebo-controlled trial, part 1: Improvement in binge and purge measures. J Clin Psychiatry 2003;64:1335-41.

[58] Hedges DW, Reimherr FW, Hoopes SP, Rosenthal NR, Kamin M, Karim R, et al. Treatment of bulimia nervosa with topiramate in a randomized, double-blind, placebo-controlled trial, part 2: Improvement in psychiatric measures. J Clin Psychiatry 2003;64:1449-54.

[59] Barbarich NC, McConaha CW, Gaskill J, La Via M, Frank GK, Achenbach S, et al. An open trial of olanzapine in anorexia nervosa. J Clin Psychiatry 2004;65:1480-2.

[60] Mondraty N, Birmingham CL, Touyz S, Sundakov V, Chapman L, Beumont P. Randomized controlled trial of olanzapine in the treatment of cognitions in anorexia nervosa. Australas Psychiatry 2005;13:72-5.

[61] Bissada H, Tasca GA, Barber AM, Bradwejn J. Olanzapine in the treatment of low body weight and obsessive thinking in women with anorexia nervosa: a randomized, double-Blind, placebo-controlled trial. Am J Psychiatry 2008;165:1281-8.

[62] Attia E, Kaplan AS, Walsh BT, Gershkovich M, Yilmaz Z, Musante D, et al. Olanzapine versus placebo for out-patients with anorexia nervosa. Psychol Med 2011; Mar 22:1-6 [Epub ahead of print].

[63] Maahs D, de Serna DG, Kolotkin RL, Ralston S, Sandate J, Qualls C, et al. Randomized, double-blind, placebo-controlled trial of orlistat for weight loss in adolescents. Endocrinol Pract 2006;12:18-28.

[64] Faris PL, Kim SW, Meller WH, Goodale RL, Oakman SA, Hofbauer RD, et al, Effect of decreasing afferent vagal activity with ondanseron on symptoms of bulimia nervosa: a randomized, double-blind trial. Lancet 2000;355:769-70.

[65] Malhotra S, King KH, Welge JA, Brusman-Lovins L, McElroy SL. Pharmacologic treatment of binge eating disorder. Int J Eat Disord 2003;34 Suppl:S74-88.

[66] James WP, Caterson ID, Coutinho W, Finer N, Van Gaal LF, Maggioni AP, et al; SCOUT Investigators. Effect of sibutramine on cardiovascular outcomes in overweight and obese subjects. N Engl J Med 2010;363:905-17.

[67] Carter FA, Jordan J, McIntosh VW, Luty SE, McKenzie JM, Frampton C, et al. The long-term effect of three psychotherapies for anorexia nervosa: A randomized controlled trial. Int J Eat Disord 2010; Nov 10 [Epub ahead of print]

In: Treatment and Recovery of Eating Disorders
Editors: Daniel Stein and Yael Latzer

ISBN: 978-1-62808-248-7
© 2013 Nova Science Publishers, Inc.

Chapter 2

EATING DISORDERS ETIOLOGY AND PSYCHODYNAMICS: TOWARD A UNIFYING FRAMEWORK FOR THE UNDERSTANDING AND TREATMENT OF EATING DISORDERS

Judith D. Banker [†]
Center for Eating Disorders, Executive Director, Ann Arbor, MI, US

ABSTRACT

Over 30 variables have been identified that may serve as risk factors for the development of eating disorders. Each factor is, in turn, multidimensional, making it highly unlikely that the interactions among these factors that are key to various stages in the genesis and maintenance of eating disorders can ever be adequately delineated or described. This level of complexity can lead to overspecialization and splintering within the field of eating disorders, as different disciplines focus on the investigation of separate risk factor areas with no shared framework within which to interpret, integrate, or apply new knowledge. A unifying framework is needed to maintain the integrity and cohesion of the increasingly complex etiological understanding of eating disorders. This chapter reviews the history of psychodynamic thought regarding the etiology of eating disorders. The contributions of psychodynamic theory to our current understanding of eating disorders are elucidated. Particular attention is paid to the pattern that emerges, over time, of psychodynamic theory as a flexible, integrative and self-correcting paradigm. Accordingly, a modern psychodynamic approach can provide an ideal organizing framework to unify and guide our efforts in the research, treatment, education, and prevention of eating disorders.

[†] E-mail address: banker@umich.edu

INTRODUCTION

So six blind men of Indostan
disputed loud and long,
Each in his own opinion
exceeding stiff and strong;
Though each was partly in the right,
they all were in the wrong!

Six Blind Men and the Elephant - John Godfrey Saxe

How do we make sense of illnesses as multifaceted, paradoxical, and grave as eating disorders? Under the umbrella of gene and environment interaction, the risk factor model for the development and maintenance of eating disorders grows ever more complex. Over 30 variables have been derived from a range of biological, psychological, sociocultural, familial, developmental, and trauma influences and identified as potential risk factors for the development and maintenance of an eating disorder (1). Moreover, each of these factors by itself is multidimensional, making it highly unlikely that the exact interactions and reactions among these putatively predictive risk factors can be identified or described.

The danger, in the face of multivariate constellations and interactions of risk factors, is that a trend toward compartmentalization will develop in the field of eating disorders. Rather than grapple with the complexity of these illnesses, our field will focus on those risk factors that lend themselves to empirical study or clinical observation, seeking certainty and clarity within a particular discipline or theoretical point of view. Like the blind men and the elephant, we will hold fast to our small bits of information, confident in our increasingly specialized and compartmentalized knowledge, while a more realistic, integrated understanding of eating disorders eludes us. A cohesive, unifying principle is needed to prevent oversimplification, tangents, and splintering among the multiple disciplines in our field. In other words, what we need is, an overarching flexible framework that promotes the accurate interpretation and integration of new knowledge gleaned from eating disorders research and practice.

In the present chapter, I propose that psychodynamics, an integrative approach to the understanding of human personality and character development and the symptoms of mental illness, provides an ideal overarching framework to guide our understanding of eating disorders. I will trace psychodynamic conceptualizations of eating disorders from the earliest formulations to contemporary thought, to elucidate the themes that have emerged over the years to contribute to our current understanding of the etiology of eating disorders. I will further demonstrate the flexible, self-correcting, integrative nature of this approach that renders it an ideal guiding principal for our treatment, research, prevention and education efforts.

With its inception in the late 19th century, with the work of Sigmund Freud, psychodynamic thought has evolved from a single theory regarding the human condition to a wide range of theoretical views. Although earlier psychodynamic formulations have focused almost exclusively on individual psycho-sexual development, current psychodynamic thought integrates sociocultural, neurobiological, familial, cognitive, and behavioral factors, offering a framework that can encapsulate the depth and range of eating disorder risk factors. Despite the expanding synthesis of knowledge bases, several basic tenets underlying psychodynamics remain constant (2-6):

1) The therapeutic relationship is a core mechanism of change in psychological treatment.
2) Unconscious feelings, thoughts and motivations play a significant role in an individual's day to day functioning.
3) An individual can experience conflicting or opposing tendencies and needs that affect their behavior/reactions in particular relationships and situations.
4) Early childhood experiences, including attachment and caretaking experiences, play a key role in personality development and in the quality and dynamics of interpersonal relationships.
5) Internal representations of the self, subjectivity, and meaning inform the way people interact with others and the psychological symptoms they manifest.
6) Learning to self-regulate powerful drives and feelings through defense, coping and adaptation is part of the process of personality development and maturation.

Psychodynamics, then, is historically grounded in developmental, intra-psychic, and interpersonal perspectives. Constrained by limited knowledge and a single theory paradigm, some of the earliest psychodynamic models will come across as archaic and, perhaps, even preposterous to modern sensibilities. Language that includes references to fears of oral impregnation or "wishes…to acquire a penis" (e.g., 7, p. 9) may strike some as anachronistic at best. Yet, given the mysteriousness of mental illnesses and the emergence of these pioneering efforts in the earliest stages of psychological scientific inquiry, errant interpretations are to be expected. In this respect, the aim of the present chapter is to trace the evolution of the psychodynamic understanding of eating disorders from the single theory paradigm of Freud to the theoretical pluralism of contemporary psychodynamics. More importantly, it is the process of thought leading to the development of these theories that is the focus of this chapter.

The evolution of psychodynamic thought reveals consistent themes that are core to our current understanding of the etiology and treatment of eating disorders. Working through these themes would promote a dynamic integrative transtheoretical way of thinking that can be used to unify and advance our research, treatment, education, and prevention efforts. The historical development of psychodynamic models for the etiology of eating disorders will be reviewed in this chapter, with emphasis placed on these recurrent themes. Drawing from these themes, I will propose the adoption of an integrative psychodynamic framework to guide our understanding with respect to the etiology and treatment of eating disorders.

EARLY PSYCHOLOGICAL MODELS

One of the earliest written clinical accounts of anorexia nervosa was provided by Richard Morton (1689), an English physician who described a condition he called "nervous consumption". Morton offered a detailed description of the physical wasting associated with the disease along with his perspectives regarding the underlying psychological mechanisms:

> "The immediate cause of this distemper I apprehend to be in the System of the Nerves proceeding from a Preternatural state of the Animal Spirits... The Causes which dispose the Patient to this Disease, I have for the most part observed to be violent Passions of the Mind...At first it flatters and deceives the Patient, for which reason it happens for the most part that the Physician is consulted too late." (8, p. 591)

Morton identifies the underlying depression and anxiety associated with eating disorders as well as the anosognosia that accompanies them. To address these factors, Morton recommends the following treatment:

> "Let the Patient endeavour to divert and make his Mind cheerful by Exercise, and the Conversation of his Friends. For this Disease does almost always proceed from Sadness, and anxious Cares. "

Morton further recommends early intervention, a *"delicious and varied diet"* and a combination of *"Stomack-medicines"* and remedies to *"comfort and strengthen the Nerves"*. (8, p. 591)

In the 19th century William Gull (9) in England and Ernest-Charles Lasègue (10) in France provided further clinical descriptions of anorexia nervosa along with their theories about the psychological underpinnings of the illness. Gull has posited a psychosomatic model in which a "morbid brain force" or "energy" transforms thoughts and feelings into physical symptoms, recommending a psychological treatment to address the "unsound mind". Gull has recognized, as psychodynamic therapists do today, that an eating disorder takes on a meaning and purpose for the patient, assuming the role of enacting or subsuming emotional expression into the language of symptoms. Lasègue, in the meantime, has grasped perhaps the most perplexing and enigmatic aspects of anorexia nervosa, the unrelenting resistance to therapeutic intervention and the stunning ineffectiveness of standard medical approaches:

> Woe to the physician who, misunderstanding the peril, treats as a fancy without object or duration an obstinacy which he hopes to vanquish by medicines, friendly advice, or by the still more defective resource of intimidation. (10, p. 146)

Thus, as early as the late 19th century, key components of our current understanding of eating disorders were already established: the relationship between eating disorders and co-morbid mood disorders, the relationship between emotions and behavioral symptoms, the presence, in anorexia nervosa, of unrelenting resistance to treatment and denial of the illness per se or of its severity, and the importance of applying a specialized, multidimensional treatment approach tailored to the unique qualities of these illnesses.

THE DAWN OF PSYCHOANALYSIS

Whereas contemporary psychodynamic formulations for the etiology of eating disorders are flexible and tailored to the constellation of factors involved in each case, early psychoanalytic theorists sought a uniform model of the psychological mechanisms underlying all instances of these illnesses. In the late 19[h] and early 20[h] century, Sigmund Freud traced the causes of eating disorders to unconscious forces and instinctual drives. In a letter to a colleague he writes:

> Your patient obviously treats eating and talking as sexual activities.
> Little work has been done on food fads, but very often they have the same root as in your second patient. In the course of time you will increasingly fall in with the inevitable trend to trace back more and more to sex, to genital and functional details. (11, p. 79)

Freud's drive-conflict model proposed that psychopathology arose from disturbances among three central components of the human psyche: the id, ego, and superego. Symptoms of mental illness were manifested when powerful psychosexual developmental drives were thwarted. According to Freud, human psychosexual development occurred along a continuum of five stages: oral, anal, phallic, latency and genital. The nature of psychiatric symptoms reflected the stage of development where disturbance occurred.

Building on the work of Freud, mid-20th century psychodynamic theories have focused on difficulties arising during the oral phase of psychosexual development, which encompasses the first 18-24 months of life, as central to the development of eating disorders. During the oral phase, the infant/toddler's drives and instincts are primarily focused on the mouth---nursing, teething, sucking, crying, regurgitating, or breathing. Thus, within this early psychoanalytic framework, binge eating, refusing to take in food, or regurgitating food, seemed to suggest an obvious link between disturbed eating and the oral phase of psychological development, with eating disorder symptoms serving as a defense against instinctual oral drives and fantasies (7, 12-14).

In 1940, Waller et al (14), proposed that an adolescent girl who feels threatened by her budding sexual maturity may regress to an earlier stage of development where fantasies of oral impregnation were thought to be common. The symptoms of refusing food or vomiting what was ingested were viewed as attempts to act out and resolve unconscious conflicts activated by this developmental dilemma. This theory gained traction in the psychoanalytic literature during the 1940s and 1950s, a time period predominated by the views of Freud and his followers.

Still, psychoanalytic thought continued to evolve, and as it did, the views of newer schools of thought were reflected in the changing perspectives on the etiology of eating disorders (15). The ego psychology school of thought highlighted the role of ego development as an organizing factor in psychological health. With this change in theory, the models for eating disorder etiology shifted from a focus on disturbances related to sexual maturation and infantile fantasies of oral impregnation, to the ego psychology view that eating disorders reflect a deeper, psychotic-like disturbance in ego formation resulting from disruptions in early mother-child bonding experiences (16, 17). Sexual maturation was thought to activate the patient's unrequited need for a secure infantile attachment experience. The simultaneous flourishing of the patient's super-ego, fueled by the intensity of the drive for an infantile, dependent attachment, in the presence of innate ego-weakness, might lead to deep frustration, anxiety, and despair over this doomed pursuit. The symptoms of self-starvation, bingeing, purging, weight gain and weight loss symbolized in this context the grave nature of the patient's interpersonal experiences, at once "embracing cannibalistic aggression and self-sacrifice, devouring greed and saintliness, sadism and masochism, murder and suicide." (17, p. 395). Not to be obscured by the colorful language of this theory is the emergence of another dimension of our current model of eating disorders, that is, the role of attachment in the development, and maintenance of eating disorder symptoms (18, 19).

During this period, a single etiological model for eating disorders still continued to be pursued. However, it is important to note that this pursuit was accompanied by an ongoing effort to integrate the obvious physiological, genetic, familial, and environmental components of these illnesses. In 1939, for example, Rahman and colleagues wrote:

> The complexity of the factors present in the development of this syndrome is shown by an analysis of the heredity, personality, physical make-up, and environmental situations in the individual cases. (20, p. 364)

In regard to treatment, their recommendations were not unlike our current practice guidelines:

> Our observations emphasize the need for considering the individual as a unit while evaluating the psychic and somatic components. Treatment should be directed toward the institution of a regulated but flexible regimen and the analysis of personality features and emotional conflicts. (ibid, p. 364)

Interestingly, the psychoanalytic theories of the etiology of eating disorders developed to this point, were not invariably a part of a broader agenda to proselytize for the use of psychodynamic treatment in these disorders. Although using talk therapy to stimulate insight and bring unconscious material to conscious awareness was viewed by many as the treatment of choice to resolve eating disorders, others clearly cautioned against the sole use of talk or insight therapy. As Meyer & Weinroth (17) so eloquently state:

> …an attempt to interpret the regressive withdrawal and reactive anorexia is as seemingly irrelevant as an explanation to a drowning man of the principle of Archimedes." (p. 397)

This separation of theoretical framework from treatment approach early on demonstrates the transtheoretical utility of a psychodynamic framework. A psychodynamic understanding of eating disorders can, accordingly, serve to identify and integrate the salient factors, as well as the significant interactions among them, that contribute to the development of the eating disorder; this, in turn would guide the choice and application of appropriate treatment options.

ADVENT OF INTERPERSONAL THEORY, OBJECT RELATIONS AND SELF-PSYCHOLOGY

Toward the second half of the 20th century psychoanalytic thought began to emphasize interpersonal over intra-psychic factors and the importance of relationships for human psychological development. Based on the observational studies of infants and mothers conducted by Winnicott, (21, 22), Bowlby (23, 2 4), and others, there was an increased focus on attachment and the process of separation-individuation in the psychological understanding of eating disorders. Within this changing view in psychodynamic theory and treatment, eating disorders were seen as expressions of disturbances in family dynamics and disruptions or conflicts in the separation-individuation process producing a profound internal state of emptiness, disorganization, and depression. Eating disorder symptoms were conceptualized, in this context, to compensate for or fill this internal void and to impose a sense of psychic order (25). The seeds of diversification in our understanding of the etiology of eating disorders began to be sown during this period. Sours (26, 27) described four types of anorexia nervosa categorized according to age of onset, defense mechanisms, and infantile fixations, whereas Lacey (28) divided bulimia into three subtypes based on prior eating, weight, and diet behaviors and patterns. Lacey further suggested that *"it is the action of certain life events on these underlying factors in an already dieting woman which precipitates the disorder"* *(*28, p. 485).

During the latter 20th century, the emergent self-psychology school of psychodynamic thought has also been concerned with the role of early childhood attachment disruptions in the psychodynamic understanding of eating disorders. According to self-psychology scholars, inadequate mirroring and empathic failure in the child's relationship with the mother may result in problems with self-regulation, self-concept, and self-esteem when the child reaches adolescence (25, 29-31). The physical and emotional changes of adolescence and the inevitable push for independence from the mother create emotional conflict for an adolescent who lacks a strong sense of self. Struggling with feelings of being misunderstood, misperceived or unloved such an adolescent may withdraw from significant others, relying, instead, on food, or on actively refraining from food, as a way to cope with the loss of self. (25). In their study of individuals with bulimia nervosa, Sugarman (32) and Sugarman and Kurash (33) pointed to disturbances in the separation-individuation process and theorized that bingeing symbolized a connection to the mother and to symbiotic feeding experiences.

Therapists today who treat people with eating disorders, often observe a strikingly consistent negative self-concept or even a lack of sense of self in their patients. As one of my patient's recently shared, "Underneath my fears there is nothing; I am nothing." Hilde Bruch's groundbreaking work in the 1970s and 1980s identified and described this loss or lack of the self in terms of serious disturbances in early life interpersonal/family relationships, in particular in those between mother and child. In Bruch's view, early deficits in the mother-child dyad may produce in the child a sense of fraudulence, mistrust or lack of awareness regarding authentic feelings and thoughts, and the projection of a "false self" created from the perceived expectations and needs of others. The severe developmental disturbances she repeatedly observed in eating disorders patients led Bruch to propose a multi-model etiological approach to these disorders:

"I have come to the conclusion...that it is essential to delineate differences in the clinical course and psychological manifestations of various forms of eating disorders. Without clear-cut distinctions, investigations are meaningless, and appropriate treatment impossible." (34, p. 188)

In her book "Eating Disorders: Obesity, Anorexia Nervosa and the Person Within", Bruch (35) suggests that eating disorders can be described as a spectrum of disorders, ranging from anorexia nervosa and cachexia to binge eating and obesity, a view consistent with current research. She further emphasizes that faulty cognitive mechanisms underlie the features of dietary restraint, the rules and regulations regarding food, weight and, at times, physical activity, so characteristic of eating disorders patients. Bruch emphasizes the impact of malnutrition on the psychological functioning of the patient, clarifying that *"much of what is called "anorectic" behavior is a manifestation of starvation"* and draws the distinction that *"no true picture of the psychological problems can be formulated, nor can psychotherapy be effective, until the worst malnutrition is corrected...'*(36, p. 1535).

It comes as no surprise that similar to some early psychoanalytic theorists, Bruch points to the ineffectiveness of traditional psychoanalysis in the treatment of anorexia nervosa, instead recommending a multi-modal treatment approach that addresses improved nutrition, family issues including the involvement of the family in treatment, and cognitive restructuring (36). She further underscores that complex interactions exist between refeeding and psychological well-being, emphasizing that in addition to nutritional correction treatment must address the inner image of the patient...

At the same time Marie Selvini Palazzoli (37) also focused on the mother-child interaction in her understanding of the etiology of eating disorders. Incorporating the oral phase of development and object-relations theory, Selvini Palazzoli poses that eating disorders represent conflict over the incorporation by the critical, controlling maternal object. That is, in the act of eating, the helpless self is being taken over by the damaging aspects of her relationship with her mother. By refusing food or purging food, interruption of puberty or the alteration in body shape/maturation ensues, thus preventing incorporation by the maternal objectfor over-identification with her. According to Selvini Palazzoli (37) and other authors of that period (38) dysfunctional family dynamics involving impaired boundaries and obstructions to the process of separation and individuation are key to the development of eating disorders (38).

It is important to pause at this point, to address the extent to which disturbances in the family, and in particular, in the mother-child relationship have played a central role in the psychodynamic etiological models of eating disorders discussed thus far. Although in the latter part of the 20th century, psychodynamic theory increasingly incorporates findings of laboratory studies in child development, the models discussed here are still largely based on clinical observations gleaned from single and multiple case studies, thus being subject to inadvertent contextual/cultural bias. In addition, whereas the observations of the family and mother-child dynamics noted in these cases might be accurate, it is not clear that they are either causal or unique to the families or to the mother-child relationships of people with eating disorders, to the exclusion of healthy individuals or individuals with other types of mental illness. Although these models are no longer adhered to in the eating disorder field (39), they did, and, in many cases continue to, marginalize and stigmatize families, especially mothers, unwittingly interjecting undeserved blame and divisiveness into an already acutely stressed family situation.

CONTEMPORARY PSYCHODYNAMIC THEORY

Psychodynamic thought has continued to evolve in the second part of the 20th century and into the 21st century, leaving by the wayside those aspects of our understanding of eating disorders that have not stood the test of time. "Fears of oral impregnation" have bitten the dust along with the use of traditional psychoanalysis as the main mode of treatment, alongside misunderstandings about the role of families, and mothers in particular, in the etiology and maintenance of eating disorders. Contemporary psychodynamic thought has moved in the direction of theoretical pluralism, building on a relational perspective ushered in through the development of ego psychology, object relations psychology, self-psychology, and interpersonal psychoanalysis.. The relational view is an integrative paradigm that seeks to synthesize a wide range of disciplines including neuroscience, cognitive psychology, experimental psychology, personality and social psychology, philosophy, linguistics, political science, social thought, theology, literature, history, and education (2).

Integrative psychodynamic models for the understanding of eating disorders have began to take hold in the late 20th and early 21st centuries. Tobin and Johnson (41) have proposed a comprehensive approach to assessment and treatment that combines behavioral and psychodynamic strategies. Dare and Crowther (42) and Zerbe (43, 44, 45) build on the work of Bruch, Selvini-Palazzoli, and others to propose a multi-modal integrative approach that considers the interaction of individual and family dynamics, socio-cultural context and values, and biological factors. Feminist and feminist relational models challenge the applicability of the role of separation-individuation and the goal of autonomy in the female psychological development, positing that females develop eating disorders as a response to the social position and cultural pressures that are not in alignment with female psychological development (46, 47). Thus, by the beginning of the 21st century, psychodynamic theory regarding the etiology and treatment of eating disorders has assumed a trans-theoretical, integrative pluralistic view that values and incorporates the full range of biopsychosocial risk factors.

CONCLUSION

The history of psychodynamic understandings of eating disorders reveals an iterative, scholarly and increasingly integrative process. This process began, in the earliest instances, with observations based on single case studies of rare examples of anorexia nervosa and has evolved in to diverse formulations that integrate the wide range of eating disorder risk factors. From the beginning of psychodynamic thought, as theories developed, they were soon challenged and adapted by new theorists in an ongoing process. Explanations and interpretations of eating disorders that did not fit with new understandings of human psychological growth and development were replaced or altered to fit in a seamless progression, demonstrating an inherent quality of psychodynamic theory to self-correct.

Further, although there certainly were and are zealots of psychodynamic thought dedicated to promoting psychoanalytic treatment as a primary treatment, dynamicists in the field of eating disorders have, in the main, recognized and espoused the need for a multi-modal integrated approach to the psychological treatment of people with eating disorders that combines cognitive, behavioral and psychodynamic approaches (43,48, 41).

In closing, 1918 Nobel prize-winning German physicist and author of *Philosophy of Physics* Max Planck (49) wrote:

> Modern physics has taught us that the nature of any system cannot be discovered by dividing it into its component parts and studying each part by itself, since such a method often implies the loss of important properties of the system. We must keep out attention fixed on the whole and on the inter-connection between the parts. ... The whole is never equal simply to the sum of its various parts. (p. 751)

Similarly, while addressing the myriad components of eating disorder treatment, research, prevention, and education, including our basic understanding of eating disorders etiology, it is necessary and essential that we maintain a unifying framework in our overall understanding of these disorders. Psychodynamic theory has demonstrated its capacity to "keep its eye" on the whole as it has evolved over the last two centuries in to an approach that synthesizes knowledge from within and outside the field of eating disorders. The integrative, trans-theoretical approach of modern psychodynamics provides a flexible, adaptive, unifying framework through which we can interpret and integrate our changing understandings and new knowledge while guiding the delivery of our clinical treatments, and the directions for future research, prevention and education efforts

REFERENCES

[1]   Jacobi C, Hayward C, de Zwaan M, Kraemer HC, Agras WS. Coming to terms with risk factors for eating disorders: Application of risk terminology and suggestions for a general taxonomy. Psychol Bull 2004;130:19-65.
[2]   Borden W. Contemporary psychodynamic theory and practice: Toward a critical pluralism. Chicago: Lyceum Books, Inc.; 2009.
[3]   Wachtel PL. Relational theory and the practice of psychotherapy. New York: Guilford Press; 2008.
[4]   Roth A, Fonagy P. What works for whom? A critical review of psychotherapy research. 2nd ed. New York: Guilford Press; 2005.
[5]   Norcross J C, editor. Psychotherapy relationships that work: Therapist contributions and responsiveness to patients. New York: Oxford University Press; 2002.
[6]   Westen D. The scientific legacy of Sigmund Freud: Toward a psychodynamically informed psychological science. Psycho Bull 1998;124:333-71.
[7]   Masserman JH. Psychodynamisms in anorexia nervosa and neurotic vomiting. Psychoanal Q 1941;10:211-42.
[8]   Bhanji S, Newton VB. Richard Morton's account of "nervous consumption". Int J Eat Disord 1985;4:589-95.
[9]   Gull WW. The address in medicine. In: Kaufman MR, Heinman M. Evolution of psychosomatic concepts. New York: International Universities Press; 1964. p. 104-7.
[10] Lasègue EC. De l'anorexie hystérique. Arch Gén Méd 1873;21:385-403.

[11] Freud S. Letter from Sigmund Freud to Karl Abraham, February 2, 1909, In: Falzeder E. The complete Correspondence of Sigmund Freud and Karl Abraham 1907-1925.   London: Karnac Books, 2002. p. 79-80.

[12] Thomä H. Anorexia Nervosa. New York: International Press, 1967.

[13] Lorand S. Anorexia nervosa; report of a case. Psychosom Med 1943,5:282.

[14] Waller JV, Kaufman MR, Deutsch. F. Anorexia nervosa: psychosomatic entity. Psychosom Med 1940; 2:3-16.

[15] Kernberg O. Foreward. In: Sours JA. Starving to death in a sea of objects. New York: Jason Aronson; 1980. p. ix-xi.

[16] Eissler KR. Some psychiatric aspects of anorexia nervosa. Psychoanal Rev 1943; 30:121-45.

[17] Meyer BC, Weinroth LA. Observations on psychological aspects of anorexia nervosa. Psychosom Med 1957; XIX: 389-98.

[18] Eggert J, Levendosky A, Klump K. Relationships among attachment style, personality characteristics, and disordered eating. Int J Eat Disord 2007;40:149-55.

[19] Ward A, Ramsay R, Treasure J. Attachment research in eating disorders. B J Med Psychol 2000;73:35-51.

[20] Rahman L, Richardson HB, Ripley HS. Anorexia nervosa with psychiatric observations, Psychosom Med 1939;1:335-65.

[21] Winnicott D. The maturational process and the facilitating environment. London: Hogarth Press, 1965.

[22] Winnicott D. Primitive emotional development. In: Collected

[23] papers: Through pediatrics to psychoanalysis. London: Hogarth Press, 1958. p. 145-56.

[24] Bowlby J. Attachment and loss, Vol. 1: Attachment. New York: Basic Books, 1969.

[25] Bowlby J. Critical phases in the development of social responses in   man and other animals, In: Tanner JM. Prospects of psychiatricresearch; Oxford: Blackwell Scientific Publications; 1953.p. 80-5.

[26] Goodsitt A. Eating disorders: A self-psychological perspective, In: Garner DM, Garfinkel PE. Handbook of treatment for eating disorders. 2nd ed.. New York: Guilford Press, 1997. p. 205-28.

[27] Sours J. Starving to death in a sea of objects, New York: Jason Aronson, 1980

[28] Lacey HJ, Coker S, Birtchnell SA. Bulimia: Factors associated with its etiology and maintenance. Int J Eat Disord 1986;5:475-87.

[29] Goodsitt A. Self-regulatory disturbances in eating disorders. Int J Eat Disord, 1983:2:51-60.

[30] Goodsitt A. Narcissistic disturbances in anorexia nervosa. In: Feinstein SC, Giovacchini P. Adolescent Psychiatry Vol. 5. New York: Jason Aronson; 1977. p. 304-12.

[31] Kohut H. The analysis of the self. New York: International University Press, 1971.

[32] Sugarman A. Bulimia: a displacement from psychological self to body self. In: Johnson CL,. Psychodynamic treatment of anorexia nervosa. New York: Guilford Press, 1991. p. 3-33.

[33] Sugarman A, Kurash C. The body as a transitional object in bulimia,. Int J Eat Disord 1982;1:57-67.

[34] Bruch H. Perceptual and conceptual disturbances in anorexia nervosa. Psychosom Med, 1962;24:187-94.

[35] Bruch H. Eating disorders: Obesity, anorexia nervosa and the person within. Basic Books: New York, 1973.

[36] Bruch H. Anorexia nervosa: Therapy and theory. Am J Psychiatry, 1982;139:1531-8.

[37] Selvini Palazzoli M. Self-starvation: from individual to family therapy in the treatment of anorexia nervosa. New York: Jason Aronson, 1978.

[38] Swift WJ, Stern S. The psychodynamic diversity of anorexia nervosa, Int J Eat Disord, 1982;2:17-35.

[39] Le Grange D, Lock J, Loeb K, Nicholls D. Academy for Eating Disorders position paper: The role of the family in eating disorders, Int J Eat Disord, 2010;43:1-5.

[40] Tobin DL, Johnson CL. The integration of psychodynamic and behavior therapy in the treatment of eating disorders: clinical issue versus theoretical mystique. In: Johnson CL. Psychodynamic treatment of eating disorders. New York: Guildford Press. 1991. p.374-97.

[41] Dare C, Crowther C. Psychodynamic models of eating disorders. In: Szmukler G, Dare C, Treasure J. Handbook of eating disorders: theory, treatment and research. Oxford, England: John Wiley & Son; 1995. p. 125-39.

[42] Zerbe K. Integrated treatment of eating disorders: beyond the body   betrayed.   W.W.   Norton, 2008.

[43] Zerbe K. Feminist psychodynamic psychotherapy of eating disorders: theoretic integration informing clinical practice, Psychiatr Clin North Am 1996;19:811-27.

[44] Zerbe K. The body betrayed: a deeper understanding of women, eating disorders, and treatment. American Psychiatric Press, Inc., 1993.

[45] Steiner-Adair C. The body politic: normal female adolescent development and the development of eating disorders, J Am Acad Psychoanal Dyn Psychiatry 1986:14:95-114.

[46] Orbach S. Fat is a feminist issue: the anti-diet guide to permanent weight loss. New York: Paddington Press, Ltd., 1978.

[47] Tobin DL, Banker JD, Weisberg L, Bowers W. I know what you did last summer (and it was not CBT): A factor analytic model of international psychotherapeutic practice in the eating disorders psychotherapeutic practice. Int J Eat Disord 2007;40:754-57.

[48] Wang Y. Software engineering foundations: a software science perspective. Auerbach, Taylor & Francis Group, 2008.

In: Treatment and Recovery of Eating Disorders   ISBN: 978-1-62808-248-7
Editors: Daniel Stein and Yael Latzer   © 2013 Nova Science Publishers, Inc.

Chapter 3

AN UPDATE ON TREATMENT STRATEGIES FOR BULIMIA NERVOSA

James E. Mitchell[‡], James Roerig and Kristine Steffen
Neuropsychiatric Research Institute Fargo, ND, US

ABSTRACT

Objective: The purpose of this article is to provide an overview of the treatment literature on bulimia nervosa. The available published literature in this area was reviewed.

Method: Following computer searches the psychotherapy and pharmacotherapy literature were reviewed in detail.

Results: Psychotherapy remains the cornerstone of treatment for most patients with bulimia nervosa. The most intensively studied form has been cognitive behavioral therapy, although there are also data supporting the use of interpersonal psychotherapy, dialectic behavior therapy and family-based treatments for adolescents with bulimia nervosa. There is also a growing literature on the utility of self-help approaches. Two recently introduced therapies, which are currently being studied, include enhanced cognitive behavioral therapy and integrative cognitive-affective therapy. Relative to pharmacotherapy approaches, antidepressants remain the best studied form of drug therapy, focusing on the use of the serotonin reuptake inhibitors. Other medications which have been tried empirically include ondansetron and topiramate.

Discussion: The treatment of bulimia nervosa has evolved to the point where both psychotherapy and pharmacotherapy approaches appear to be affective. Overall remission rates appear to be higher with empirically supported manual-based psychotherapy approaches, although many patients have benefited from drug therapy as well.

[‡] E-mail address: Jmitchell@nrifargo.com

INTRODUCTION

A substantial treatment literature has developed regarding individuals with bulimia nervosa (BN) over the last 30 years. These treatments clearly impact on the course of this disorder, although further treatment development is needed.

In deciding on the proper treatment approach the goal is to provide the patient with the support and structure necessary for her to start eating regularly balanced meals and to cease binge eating and engaging in compensatory behaviors. Usually this can be accomplished effectively in outpatient treatment settings, but for some patients a more intensive setting, such as a partial hospital program or an inpatient stay may be necessary, particularly for patients who have co-occurring severe psychopathology or for those who fail to respond to outpatient care. Suicidality is the most common reason for such an increased level of care.

PSYCHOTHERAPY

Psychotherapy remains the cornerstone of treatment for most patients with BN. Unfortunately, the forms of treatment which have been shown to be effective have not been widely disseminated to the practice community, and many patients who are seen for treatment with eating disorders receive treatments that are not empirically validated (1). In considering psychotherapy certain general principles apply. First, both group and individual approaches are applicable. Second, there is evidence that more intensive treatment early on, such as seeing patients multiple times during the first few weeks of treatment, are helpful in achieving treatment success, eventually resulting in higher rates of abstinence (2).

Relative to specific techniques a variety of approaches have been studied. The one most intensively studied has been cognitive behavioral therapy (CBT). There are also data supporting the use of interpersonal psychotherapy (IPT), dialectic behavior therapy (DBT), and family based treatments for adolescents with BN. Recently there has been interest in a new generation of CBT-oriented approaches including enhanced CBT (CBT-E) developed by Fairburn and colleagues and integrative cognitive-affective therapy (ICAT) developed by Wonderlich and colleagues (3-6).

COGNITIVE BEHAVIORAL THERAPY

This therapy has been used in a variety of controlled trials and appears to be more effective than most treatments (with the possible exception of IPT), or waiting list controls (3,7).

Probably the leading evidence-based treatment for those with BN is a specific form of CBT developed for these patients (8). This therapy posits that low self-esteem enhances extreme concerns about weight and shape, which results in strict dieting, which then leads to binge eating and self-induced vomiting as a compensatory technique. This therapy is basically designed for those in a normal weight range. It focuses on the need to reduce dietary restraint and to address concerns about shape and weight. Emphasis early on is placed on the use of food logs as a self-monitoring approach, which are reviewed with the therapist each session. Patients are also asked to engage in only weekly weighing.

In the first phase there is an emphasis on educating patients about medical complications, stressing the ineffectiveness of vomiting and laxatives as methods of weight control, and education about the biology of weight and shape. Also three forms of dieting are discussed: 1) avoiding eating for long periods of time; 2) avoiding certain types of food and, 3) restricting total amount of food eaten. In the first phase various behavioral techniques are used including the prescription of regular eating patterns, the use of alternative behaviors, stimulus control techniques and psychoeducation of laxatives and diuretics.

In the second phase of treatment emphasis is placed on cognitive restructuring, systematic problem solving and the reintroduction of "forbidden" foods as well as continued work to reduced body image disparagement. The third phase focuses on relapse prevention strategies.

This therapy is generally administered in a treatment "package" wherein patients are seen twice a week for the first four weeks and then once a week thereafter for a total of 20 visits. The empirical literature supporting the efficacy of this approach is substantial.

INTERPERSONAL THERAPY

Interpersonal therapy (IPT) was originally developed as a treatment for depression by Klerman and colleagues (9). In the late 1980's this approach was modified for patients with BN. Wilfley and colleagues (10,11) developed a group format for IPT and demonstrated that it was an effective treatment for patients with BED. It has also been shown to be an effective treatment for patients with BN (7).

The theoretical model for IPT posits that interpersonal functioning is a critical component of psychological adjustment. The interpersonal roles of particular interest for IPT therapists involve the family as well as friends, and fellow workers and those in the neighborhood and community.

IPT for those with BN is again time limited and attempts to link interpersonal relationships to eating disorder symptoms. Four social domains can be addressed in the treatment: 1) interpersonal deficits, 2) role transitions, 3) interpersonal role disputes, and 4) grief. Generally one or at most two of these areas become the focus for treatment. IPT is generally delivered in 15-20 sessions or 4-5 months and includes three phases. In the initial phase, problem areas are identified; in the subsequent phase therapist and patient work on the target problems and in the final phase gains are consolidated and patients are prepared to do future work on their own.

A critical part of IPT is the interpersonal inventory which involves a thorough examination of each individual's interpersonal history. This includes an examination of relationships, social functioning, expectations of relationships and other interpersonal issues. This then leads to the interpersonal formulation which includes the identification of the primary areas of focus. The therapist presents a written version of this formulation to the patient and this is frequently referred to later in therapy. The therapy includes the encouragement of affect. IPT places considerable importance on establishing a strong positive therapeutic relationship with the patient. The therapy is goal directed. There is an ongoing need to draw connections between eating difficulties and interpersonal events.

DIALECTICAL BEHAVIOR THERAPY

DBT is a specialized form of CBT. It was originally developed to treat women with extreme emotion dysregulation, such as those with borderline personality disorder (12,13). This is skill-based approach that integrates dialectical philosophy derived from Zen that includes mindfulness skills and behavioral principles. It has now been adopted for use with patients with eating disorder and therefore may be particularly useful for patients with eating disorders who have comorbid personality disorders, a not uncommon pattern (14).

Two small non-randomized trials treating individuals with borderline personality disorder and eating disorders utilized the standard DBT (15,16). However, a form of DBT has been adapted specifically for patients with eating disorders, developed at Stanford University (17). Subsequently there has been one randomized trial in BN (17). In this study a wait list control was used as a comparison group. The results indicated higher rates of abstinence from binge eating and purging at the end of 20 weeks of treatment in the active treatment group (28.6%) versus the weight list control (0%).

In general DBT focuses on several issues, including self-acceptance, dialectic strategies, stylistic strategies, core strategies and case management strategies. Dialectical strategies focus on dichotomous thinking and behaviors and emotions. These may include the use of stories and metaphors. Stylistic strategies attempt to balance acceptance and the need for change. The therapist must convey interpersonal warmth and concern. Core strategies are those designed to promote acceptance and behavioral change and includes such things as an examination of antecedents and consequences and behavioral chain analysis. Case management strategies include teaching a patient to more effectively interact with the environment. Specific adaptations for patients with BN include a focus on decreasing mindless eating and food preoccupation, and capitulating or giving up to ones emotions and then binge eating. The model includes both individual and group sessions and includes an emphasis on distress tolerance, emotion regulation skills and relapse prevention.

FAMILY-BASED TREATMENT FOR ADOLESCENTS
WITH BULIMIA NERVOSA

In contrast to the substantial literature on the treatment of adults with BN very little research has focused on the treatment of adolescents with BN. Only two randomized controlled trials have been published both using a family-based therapy for BN (18,19). In the first of these studies le Grange and colleagues assigned 80 patients with full or subsyndromal BN, ages 12-19, to family-based therapy for BN or to individual supportive psychotherapy. Both groups received 20 therapy sessions over 6 months. The family-based approach had a clinically and statistically significant advantage over the comparison group at the end of treatment and at six-month follow-up, with more patients abstinent from binge eating and purging (39% vs. 18%) at end-of-treatment. In the other randomized controlled trial family-based therapy was compared to cognitive behavioral guided self-help. Subjects were age 12-20. Significantly more people in the CBT guided self-help group were abstinent from binge eating at post-treatment although there were no differences at six-month follow-up.

The theoretical underpinnings of family-based treatment for BN are an adaptation of an approach originally developed for treatment for anorexia nervosa (AN). In this model parents understanding of and the need to help their child are mobilized to promote changes in eating and weight. Since adolescents with BN tend to deny the importance of their symptoms parents are recruited to help move the adolescent toward a healthier adjustment. The approach is symptom focused and includes a strong emphasis on encouraging the parents to not assume a role of guilt. The role of the therapist is to serve as a consultant and educator while leaving decisions up to the parents.

In the first phase of this treatment, emphasis is placed on reestablishing healthy eating patterns. The sessions begin with a brief meeting between the therapist and the patient before meeting with the rest of the family. In the family meeting the therapist directs the discussion so as to strengthen the parental alliance. The family is carefully educated about medical and psychiatric sequellae of BN. Measures are taken to make it clear that the adolescent and the disorder are two separate things. This early part of therapy includes a family meal. This allows the therapist to establish rules around eating. The second phase of treatment focuses on helping the adolescent establish healthy eating behavior on their own, and the third phase of treatment focuses on adolescent issues and termination.

SELF-HELP FOR BULIMIA NERVOSA

The literature in this area has recently been thoroughly reviewed (20-22). The meta-analytic analyses, although hindered by a relatively small number of studies and relatively small sample sizes, suggests that partial self-help or guided self-help approaches do have some utility in the treatment of those with BN, and the follow-up results suggest that gains tend to be maintained. However, there isn't as of yet any firm evidence favoring one approach over another. However, the study by Walsh et al. (23) found that guided self-help provided by nurses did not add to the effectiveness of anti-depressant treatment, and was associated with a high dropout rate. This suggests that specialist care is probably needed for these types of interventions. Much of the development in this area has been motivated by health economic reasons but also problems with the availability of treatment. Clearly more work needs to be done looking at such approaches.

ENHANCED COGNITIVE BEHAVIOR THERAPY
FOR BULIMIA NERVOSA

Fairburn and colleagues have modified the traditional CBT for treatment to a transdiagnostic model designed to treat people with a variety of types of eating pathology. The full transdiagnostic treatment has been described in detail (4,5,24). Enhanced CBT or CBT-E posits that eating disorders are essentially cognitive disorders and that the core psychopathology is usually overvaluation of shape and weight, while for a subgroup the core is to control eating. The approach acknowledges that much diagnostic crossover exists in patients with eating disorder; hence, the needs for a transdiagnostic approach. Early in treatment a formulation is made that is personalized and then revised throughout treatment.

CBT-E is done in two forms, a focused version and a broad version which includes examination of mood intolerance, clinical perfectionism, low care self-esteem and/or interpersonal difficulties.

Therapy is delivered in 20 sessions over 20 weeks with a review session 20 weeks later. It is conducted in four stages. In the first stage patients are seen two times a week for four weeks. Emphasis is placed on engaging the patient, formulating the processes that maintain the disorder, and instituting weekly weighing and regular eating. The second stage is transitional in which progress is reviewed, barriers to change are identified and the formulation may be modified. Stage three is the main body of treatment and includes 8 sessions. Stage 4 is designed to insure that the changes are being maintained.

INTEGRATIVE COGNITIVE-AFFECTIVE THERAPY FOR THE TREATMENT OF BULIMIA NERVOSA

This therapy grew out of the observation that CBT does not sufficiently help many patients with BN. It has been argued that CBT might be improved by maintaining a stronger focus on affective and interpersonal issues (25) and enhancement of treatment techniques by integrating concepts for constructivist theories (26) including narrative strategies (27) utilizing the therapeutic relationship more thoroughly (28) and placing greater emphasis on developmental issues (29). In this model, greater emphasis is placed on self-discrepancy, interpersonal patterns, self-directed styles of behavior and emotional experience. The therapy is delivered in 21 sessions. A clinician manual and a patient workbook have been developed and palm top computers provide part of the therapy.

In terms of clinical principles ICAT attempts to increase awareness of emotional responses, identify situations that frequently illicit prominent emotional responses and to modify action tendencies in the face of situation-emotion units. It is delivered in four phases. The first is characterized by motivation and education, the second by meal planning, the third by a self-directed examination of interpersonal problems and the fourth by relapse prevention and work on termination.

PHARMACOTHERAPY

Considering CBT as the treatment of choice, it is unfortunate that CBT availability may be limited in the community. In a study by Crow and colleagues, (1) in a population of 353 women who were seeking treatment for BN, 65.4% had received previous treatment and of these, 96.7% reported receiving psychotherapy; however, only 6.9% of those reporting having received psychotherapy reported that the therapy included basic elements of CBT. With this in mind pharmacotherapy has been investigated for over twenty years (30).

ANTIDEPRESSANTS

Research over the past twenty years indicates that most antidepressants have efficacy in the treatment of BN (31). Classes of agents that have shown efficacy include the tricyclic antidepressants (TCAs), monoamine oxidase inhibitors (MAOIs) and selective serotonin reuptake inhibitors (SSRIs). The core agents utilized currently are the SSRIs and one agent (fluoxetine) carries an FDA indication for treatment of BN. Although in most studies there has been a significant advantage for active drug over placebo, the exceptions appear to be moclobemide and fluvoxamine. Responses to antidepressant medication in BN are not dependent upon the existence of a pretreatment depression (32). In a study of BN patients the effect of fluoxetine 60 mg/day was found to not correlate with the baseline Hamilton Depression Rating Scale (HAM-D) score or comorbid depression diagnosis (33).

RESPONSE VERSUS REMISSION

Despite multiple studies showing greater efficacy than placebo (34-36) questions remain as to the extent of antidepressant treatment efficacy. Several trials have not been able to differentiate active drug from placebo on important outcome variables (37,38). Also, despite impressive reductions in the frequency of target symptoms, the percentage of subjects free of symptoms (abstinent) at the end of treatment is also disappointingly low.

The mean abstinence rate associated with pharmacotherapy has been reported to be 24 % (39). In one sequential treatment controlled trial (40) those who did not achieve a 75% reduction in binge eating frequency with desipramine over 8 weeks were switched to fluoxetine. Pharmacological treatment occurred in combination with CBT, supportive psychotherapy or alone. Overall, 74% of eligible patients required the switch to the second pharmacological treatment. Cessation of binge eating behavior was then found in 29% of the medication only subjects by the end of the second treatment period. Studies of the combination of pharmacotherapy and CBT reported average remission rates of 42 to 49% versus average rates of 23 to 36% with any single therapy (24). However, response rates to subsequent therapies for patients who fail initial treatment have been variable. In one study, non-responders to CBT or IPT were given fluoxetine or placebo. The active drug was superior to placebo in improving symptoms (41). In another study of patients in whom CBT had not resulted in remission, the rate of response to subsequent IPT was 16%, and the rate of response to pharmacotherapy (fluoxetine followed by desipramine if indicated) was only 10% (36).

Maintenance studies utilizing pharmacological agents have demonstrated efficacy over placebo (42,43). However these studies have been characterized by high drop-out rates, which make them difficult to interpret. The largest and most recent maintenance trial was reported by Romano and colleagues (44). Subjects were treated in a single blind acute treatment phase, with those meeting response criteria (a minimum of 50% reduction of baseline frequency of vomiting during one of the final 2 weeks of a single blind phase) being randomized to fluoxetine 60 mg/day or placebo. One hundred and fifty patients were randomized to active drug or placebo for a period of one year. However, only 17.7% of the 150 patients were abstinent at the time of randomization. Of the 150 patients who entered the double blind phase only 19 completed the trial. The total number of patients who relapsed did not differ between groups, although fluoxetine did prolong the time to relapse. Thus, the weight of the evidence suggests that single agent pharmacological treatment does not provide a robust maintenance therapy for BN and patients achieving response but not remission appear to benefit little from maintenance treatment.

There is a strong need to develop new and better pharmacological approaches for these patients. Unfortunately there are no studies to date on the use of medication combinations or augmentation of pharmacological treatments, strategies that have been used with success in several other pharmacotherapy areas including the treatment of depression and anxiety disorders.

The concept of treating to remission has been developed as a focus in the treatment of affective disorders. It has been demonstrated that achieving remission (Hamilton Depression Rating Scale score < 8) versus only response (Hamilton Depression scale reduction of 50 %) is associated with better functioning (45) and prognosis (46,47). Unfortunately, studies which provide data on the outcome of patients who achieve abstinence in BN are few. In general, abstinence persisting at one year of follow up is quite variable (48) and in light of this, no consistent predictors of outcome have been identified (24). Thus an exploration of techniques to enhance symptom reduction is needed. Sequencing medication after failure to respond to CBT has shown mixed evidence. Medication addition was found helpful in a pilot trial by Walsh and colleagues (41). However a subsequent trial by Mitchell, et al. (40) found that after failure of CBT those who were randomized to medication derived little benefit. Yet combinations of medicine are often prescribed in clinical practice without evidence regarding efficacy or tolerability (49).

ONDANSETRON

Non-antidepressants have also been demonstrated to have efficacy in the treatment of those with BN. The serotonin 3 receptor (5-HT3) antagonist, ondansetron, was found to be efficacious in a randomized, double-blind trial (50). This agent is an antiemetic active at the vagus nerve terminals peripherally and at the chemoreceptor trigger zone centrally (51). Ondansetron is used extensively in chemo- and radiation- therapy induced nausea and vomiting. It is suggested that BN patients have satiety defects caused by post-binge eating vagal stimulation. In a four week randomized, double blind trial patients receiving ondansetron 24 mg/day reduced binge-vomit frequency from 12.8 ± 5.0/week to 6.5 ± 3.9/week, an estimated reduction of 6.8 episodes/week (p < 0.0001) while the placebo group reduced their mean binge-vomit frequency from 13.4 ± 9.9 to 13.2 ± 11.6 episodes per week.

TOPIRAMATE

Topiramate, an anticonvulsant associated with weight loss, has been explored for BN treatment. Topiramate's multiple pharmacological actions include a reduction of voltage-gated sodium currents, activation of potassium currents, increased postsynaptic GABA-A receptor currents, a reduction in the activation of AMPA-kainate glutamate receptor subtypes, and weak inhibition of carbonic anhydrase (52). There have been two randomized controlled trials of topiramate for BN treatment published (53,54). In addition, a recent review article summarizes the efficacy and tolerability of topiramate in the treatment of BN and binge eating disorder (55). The controlled trials in BN (53, 54) were both ten-weeks in duration and demonstrated reductions in binge/purge frequency as well as body weight with topiramate relative to placebo. Hoopes and colleagues (53) demonstrated that at a median topiramate dose of 100 mg/day (range 25-400 mg/day), binge and/or purge days were significantly reduced (44.8%) relative to the reduction observed with placebo (10.7%). Body weight also differed significantly between groups; with a 1.8 kg mean weight loss in the topiramate group compared with a 0.2 kg increase in the placebo group. Similarly, Nickel and colleagues (54) found that binge/purge frequency decreased by 3.3 episodes per week with topiramate (titrated to 250 mg/day) relative to placebo. The topiramate group in this study experienced significantly more weight loss (4 kg) compared to the placebo group (0.3 kg). Treatment-emergent adverse effects in the study by Hoopes and colleagues were reported more frequently with topiramate versus placebo. Effects reported by at least 10% of patients, included the following: fatigue, influenza-like symptoms, paresthesia, hypoesthesia, nausea, constipation, difficulty with concentration or attention, and nervousness. Study attrition due to adverse events was low, however, including only one of 34 patients in the topiramate group who experienced nausea. The study by Nickel and colleagues (54) reported headache as the only adverse effect which occurred more frequently with topiramate than with placebo, but the dosage used was not stipulated.

MISCELLANEOUS MEDICATIONS

Other treatments that have been studied include the androgen-antagonist flutamide, spironolactone, d-fenfluramine (no longer marketed), lithium, phenytoin and naltrexone, but none have evidenced clear efficacy, and none are commonly clinically employed in the treatment of those with BN at this time (56,57).

FUTURE PHARMACOTHERAPY RESEARCH

The first phase of investigation of pharmacotherapy for the treatment of BN has been completed. A variety of drugs have demonstrated benefit over placebo. However, the outcome for BN patients at this time is not optimal. It is time to embark on the second phase of pharmacotherapy investigation with BN. A next step in this search is exploring the augmentation of primary pharmacotherapy with secondary agents. Investigations to explore the efficacy of selected secondary agents can determine if symptom reduction is achievable after partial efficacy has been seen with the primary agent. This type of research is vital to explore the "next level" of pharmacotherapy.

Summary

Both psychotherapy and pharmacotherapy approaches appear to be useful in the treatment of patients with bulimia nervosa. Established forms of psychotherapy include cognitive behavioral therapy, which has been the form most intensively studied, dialectical behavioral therapy, interpersonal therapy and, two recently introduced approaches, enhanced cognitive behavioral therapy and integrative cognitive-affective therapy. Pharmacotherapy approaches have relied primarily on the use of antidepressant drugs, particularly the serotonin reuptake inhibitors. The only FDA approved drug for the treatment of bulimia nervosa remains fluoxetine hydrochloride although a number of other agents are also effective. Ondansetron and topiramate have also been studied in placebo-controlled trials.

References

[1]   Crow S, Mussell MP, Peterson C, Knopke A, Mitchell J. Prior treatment received by patients with bulimia nervosa. Int J Eat Disord. 1999;25:39-44.

[2]   Mitchell JE, Pyle RL, Pomeroy C, Zollman M, Crosby R, Seim H, et al. Cognitive-behavioral group psychotherapy of bulimia nervosa: importance of logistical variables. Int J Eat Disord. 1993;1477:287.

[3]   Wilson GT, Grilo CM, Vitousek KM. Psychological treatment of eating disorders. Am Psychol. 2007;62:199-216.

[4]   Fairburn CG, Cooper Z & Shafran R. Cognitive behavior therapy for eating disorders: A "transdiagnostic" theory and treatment. Behav Res Ther. 2003a;41:509-28.

[5]   Fairburn CG. Cognitive Behavior Therapy and Eating Disorders. New York: Guilford Press; 2008.

[6]   Wonderlich SA, Engel SG, Peterson CB, Robinson MD, Crosby RD, Mitchell JE, et al. Examining the conceptual model of integrative cognitive-affective therapy for BN: Two assessment studies. Int J Eat Disord. 41:748-54.

[7]   Agras WS, Walsh BT, Fairburn CG, Wilson GT & Kraemer HC. A multicenter comparison of cognitive-behavioral therapy and interpersonal psychotherapy for bulimia nervosa. Arch Gen Psychiatry. 2000;157:1302-8.

[8]   Fairburn CG, Marcus MD & Wilson GT. Cognitive behavior therapy for binge eating and bulimia nervosa: a comprehensive treatment manual. In: C.G. Faiburn & G.T. Wilson (Eds.). Binge Eating: Nature, Assessment and Treatment. New York: Guilford Press. 1993c.

[9]   Klerman GL, Weissman MM, Rounsaville BJ & Chevron ES. Interpersonal Psychotherapy of Depressions. New York: Basic Books. 1984.

[10] Wilfley DE, Frank MA, Welch RR, Spurrell EB & Rounsaville BJ. Adapting interpersonal psychotherapy to a group format (IPT-G) for binge eating disorder: Toward a model for adapting empirically supported treatments. Psychother Res. 1998;8:379-81.

[11] Wilfley DE, Welch RR, Stein RI, Spurrell EB, Cohen LR, Saelens BE, et al. A randomized comparison of group cognitive-behavioral therapy and group interpersonal psychotherapy for the treatment of overweight individuals with binge eating disorder. Arch Gen Psychiatry. 2002;59:713-21.

[12] Linehan MM, Armstrong HE, Suzrez A, Allmon D, Heard HL. Cognitive-behavioral treatment of chronically parasuicidal borderline patients. Arch Gen Psychiatry. 1991;48:1060-4.

[13] Linehan MM, Comtois KA, Murray AM, Brown MZ, Gallop RJ, Heard HL, et al. Two-year randomized controlled trial and follow-up of dialectical behavior therapy vs. therapy by experts for suicidal behaviors and borderline personality disorder. Arch Gen Psychiatry. 2006;63:757-66.

[14] Sansone RA, Levitt JL, Sansone LA. The prevalence of personality disorders among those with eating disorders. Eat Disord. 2005;3:7-21.

[15] Chen EY, Matthews L, Allen C, Kuo J, Linehan MM. Dialectical behavioral therapy for client with binge-eating disorder or bulimia nervosa and borderline personality disorder. Int J Eat Disord. 2008;41:505-12.

[16] Palmer RL, Birchall H, Damani S, Gatward N, McGrain L, Parker L. A dialectical behavior therapy program for people with an eating disorder and borderline personality disorder—description and outcome. Int J Eat Disord. 2003;33:281-6.

[17] Safer DL, Telch CF & Agras W. Dialectical behavior therapy for bulimia nervosa. Am J Psychiatry. 2001b;158:632-4.

[18] le Grange D, Crosby R, Rathouz P, Leventhal B. A controlled comparison study of family-based treatment and supportive psychotherapy for adolescent bulimia nervosa. Arch Gen Psychiatry. 2007;4:1049-56.

[19] Schmidt U, Lee S, Beecham J, et al., A randomized controlled trial of family therapy and cognitive behavioral guided self-help for adolescents with bulimia nervosa and related conditions. Am J Psychiatry. 2007;164:591-8.

[20] Perkins SJ, Murphy R, Schmidt U, Williams C. Self-help and guided self-help for eating disorders. Cochrane Database Syst Rev. 2006.

[21] Stefano SC, Bacaltchuk J, Blay SL, Hay P. Self-help treatments for disorders of recurrent binge eating: A systematic review. Acta Psychiatrica Scandinavica. 2006;113:452-9.

[22] Sysko R & Walsh BT. A critical evaluation of the efficacy of self-help interventions for the treatment of bulimia nervosa and binge-eating disorder. Int J Eat Disord. 2008;41:97-112.

[23] Walsh BT, Fairburn CG, Mickley D, Sysko R, Parides MK. Treatment of bulimia nervosa in a primary care setting. Am J Psychiatry. 2004;161:556-61.

[24] Fairburn CG, Harrison PJ. Eating disorders. Lancet. 2003b;361, 407–16.

[25] Safran JD & Segal ZV. Interpersonal process in cognitive therapy. Northvale, NJ: Aronson. 1996.

[26] Neimeyer RA. An appraisal of constructivist psychotherapies. J Consult Clin Psychol. 1993;61:221-34.

[27] Meichenbaum D. . Changing conceptions of cognitive behavior modification: Retrospect and prospect. J Consult Clin Psychol. 1993;61:202-4.

[28] Weston D. Commentary: Implicit and emotional processes in cognitive-behavioral therapy. Clin Psychol: Sci Practice. 2000;7:386-390.

[29] Guidano VF. The self as mediator of cognitive change in psychotherapy. In L.M. Hartman & K.R. Blankstein (Eds.), Perception of self in emotional disorder and psychotherapy (pp. 305-330). New York, NY: Plenum Press. 1986.

[30] de Zwaan M, Roerig J. Pharmacological treatment of eating disorders. In: M Maj K Halmi, JJ Lopez-Ibor, N Satorius (Eds.) Eating Disorders. West Sussex, England: Wiley. 223-285. 2003.

[31] Bacaltchuk J., Hay P. Antidepressants versus placebo for people with bulimia nervosa (Cochrane Review). In The Cochrane Library, Update Software, Oxford. 2003.

[32] Kaye WH, Walsh BT. Psychopharmacology of Eating Disorders, in Neuropsychopharmacology: The Fifth Generation of Progress. Edited by Kenneth L. Davis, Dennis Charney, Joseph T. Coyle, and Charles Nemeroff. American College of Neuropsychopharmacology Lippincott Williams & Wilkins Philadelphia PA. 2002.

[33] Goldstein DJ, Wilson MG, Ascroft, al-Banna M. Effectiveness of fluoxetine therapy in bulimia nervosa regardless of comorbid depression. Int J Eat Disorder. 1999;25:19-27.

[34] Fluoxetine Bulimia Nervosa Collaborative Study Group. Fluoxetine in the treatment of bulimia nervosa. A multicenter, placebo-controlled, double-blind trial. Arch Gen Psychiatry. 1992;9:139-47.

[35] Bacaltchuk J, Hay P, Mari JJ. Antidepressants versus placebo for the treatment of bulimia nervosa: a systematic review. Aust N Z J Psychiatry. 2000;34:310-7.

[36] Mitchell JE, Halmi K, Wilson GT, Agras WS, Kraemer H, Crow S. A randomized secondary treatment study of women with bulimia nervosa who fail to respond to CBT. Int J Eat Disord. 2002;32:271-81.

[37] Mitchell JE, Groat R. A placebo-controlled double-blind trial of amitriptyline in bulimia. J Clin Psychopharmacol. 1984;4:186-93.

[38] Carruba MD, Cuzzolaro M, Riva L, Bosello O, Liberty S, Castra R, et al. Efficacy and tolerability of moclobemide in bulimia nervosa: A placebo-controlled trial. Int Clin Psychopharmacol. 2001;16:27-32.

[39] Mitchell JE, Peterson CB, Myers T, Wonderlich S. Combining pharmacotherapy and psychotherapy in the treatment of patients with eating disorders. Psychiatr Clin North Am. 2001;24:315-23.

[40] Walsh B, Wilson T, Loeb K, Devlin M, Pike K, Roose S, et al. Medication and psychotherapy in the treatment of bulimia nervosa. Am J Psychiatry. 1997;154, 523-31.

[41] Walsh BT, Agras WS, Devlin MJ, Fairburn CG, Wilson GT, Kahn C, et al. Fluoxetine for bulimia nervosa following poor response to psychotherapy. Am J Psychiatry. 2000;157:1332-4.

[42] Pyle RL, Mitchell JE, Eckert ED, Hatsukami D, Pomeroy C, Zimmerman R. Maintenance treatment and 6-month outcome for bulimia patients who respond to initial treatment. Am J Psychiatry. 1990;147:871-5.

[43] Fichter MM, Kruger R, Rief W, Holland R, Doehne J. Fluvoxamine in prevention of relapse in bulimia nervosa: effects on eating-specific psychopathology. J Clin Psychopharmacol. 1996;16:9-18.

[44] Romano SJ, Halmi KA, Sarkar NP, Koke SC, Lee JS. A placebo-controlled study of fluoxetine in continued treatment of bulimia nervosa after successful acute fluoxetine treatment. Am J Psychiatry. 2002;159:96-102.

[45] Scott J, Teasdale JD, Paykel ES, Johnson AL, Abbott R, Hayhurst H, et al. Effects of cognitive therapy on psychological symptoms and social function in residual depression. Br J Psychiatry. 2000;177:440-6.

[46] Paykel ES. Remission and residual symptomatology in major depression. Psychopathology, 1998;131:5-14.

[47] Judd LL, Akiskal HS, Maser JD, Zeller PJ, Endicott J, Coryell W, et al. Major depressive disorder: a prospective study of residual subthreshold depressive symptoms as predictor of rapid relapse. J Affect Disord. 1998;50:97-108.

[48] Mitchell JE, Agras WS, Wilson GT, Halmi K, Kraemer H, Crow S. A trial of a relapse prevention strategy in women with bulimia nervosa who respond to cognitive-behavior therapy. Int J Eat Disord. 2004;35:549-55.

[49] Roerig JL, de Zwaan M & Mitchell JE. An evidenced based review of the pharmacotherapy of anorexia nervosa, bulimia nervosa and binge-eating disorder. Econ Neuroscience. 2004;45:235-7.

[50] Faris PL, Kim SW, Meller WH, Goodale RL, Oakman SA, Hofbauer RD, et al. Effect of decreasing afferent vagal activity with ondansetron on symptoms of bulimia nervosa a randomized, double-blind trial. Lancet. 2000;355:792-7.

[51] Lexi-Comp, Inc. Ondansetron Monograph, 1978-2009.

[52] McNamara JO. Pharmacotherapy of the epilepsies, in Goodman and Gilman's the pharmacological basis of therapeutics, 11th Ed. McGraw-Hill Medical Publishing Division, Brunton LL, Lazo JS, Parker KL (Eds).

[53] Hoopes SP, Reimherr FW, Hedges DW, Rosenthal NR, Kamin M, Karim R, et al. Treatment of bulimia nervosa with topiramate in a randomized, double-blind, placebo-controlled trial, part 1: improvement in binge and purge measures. J Clin Psychiatry. 2003;64:1335-41.

[54] Nickel C, Tritt K, Muehlbacher M, Pedrosa F, Mitterlehner FO, Kaplan P, et al. Topiramate treatment in bulimia nervosa patients: a randomized, double-blind, placebo-controlled trial. Int J Eat Disord. 2006;38:295-300.

[55] Arbaizar B, Gomez-Acebo I, Llorca J. Efficacy of topiramate in bulimia nervosa and binge-eating disorder: a systematic review. Gen Hosp Psychitry. 2008;30:471-5.

[56] Steffen KJ, Roerig JL, Mitchell JE, Uppala S. Emerging drugs for eating disorder treatment. Expert Opin Emerg Drugs. 2006;11:315-36.

[57] Wietersheim J, Muler-Bock V, Rauh S, Danner B, Chrenko K, Buhler G. No effect of spironolactone on bulimia nervosa symptoms. J Clin Psychopharmacol. 2008;28(2):258-60.

In: Treatment and Recovery of Eating Disorders
Editors: Daniel Stein and Yael Latzer

ISBN: 978-1-62808-248-7
© 2013 Nova Science Publishers, Inc.

Chapter 4

PSYCHOPHARMACOLOGICAL TREATMENTS FOR EATING DISORDERS

Andreas Karwautz[§], Julia Huemer and Gudrun Wagner
Medical University of Vienna, Department of Child & Adolescent Psychiatry,
Eating Disorders Unit, Waehringer Guertel, Vienna, Austria

ABSTRACT

Psychopharmacological agents have been used since the early years of treatment of eating disorders because of the challenging nature of these disorders. There is nearly no new psychotropic agent which has not been studied in anorexia nervosa (AN) patients, usually with conflicting results. At this time it must be concluded that there are yet no first-line psychopharmacological agents that can be recommended in AN based on good clinical evidence. For bulimia nervosa (BN) and binge-eating disorder (BED), the evidence is better, having several promising data on the advantages of adding antidepressants and related agents to the psychotherapeutic work with these patient groups.

Keywords: treatment, eating disorders, pharmacotherapy

INTRODUCTION

Eating disorders are psychiatric disorders challenging science and treating teams since they appear with growing prevalence in the community and in treatment centers. Although psychotherapeutic interventions are most important, other options can be added. Psychopharmacological agents have been used since the early years of the treatment of eating disorders because of the challenging nature of these disorders. There is nearly no new psychotropic agent which has not been studied in anorexia nervosa (AN) patients, usually with conflicting results. At this time it must be concluded that there are yet no first-line

---

[§] E-mail address: andreas.karwautz@meduniwien.ac.at

psychopharmacological agents that can be recommended in AN based on good clinical evidence.

Eating disorders – in particular AN - cannot be cured using psychotropic substances. However, the treatment of comorbid symptoms shows a more favorable outcome. For bulimia nervosa (BN) and binge-eating disorder (BED), the evidence is more favorable, having several promising data on the advantages of adding antidepressants and related agents to the psychotherapeutic work with these patient groups.

There are currently established criteria of evidence, the National Institute of Clinical Excellence (NICE) criteria (1) aiming to assist clinicians with respect to the choice of psychopharmacological treatment in eating disorders. These are summarized in table 1.

Table 1. Lists the levels and the grades of evidence according to NICE guidelines (NICE 2004)

Level of evidence I: Evidence obtained from a single randomised controlled trial or a meta-analysis of randomised controlled trials.

Level of evidence IIa: Evidence obtained from at least one well-designed controlled study without randomisation.

Level of evidence II b: Evidence obtained from at least one other well-designed quasi-experimental study.

Level of evidence III: Evidence obtained from well-designed non-experimental

descriptive studies, such as comparative studies, correlation studies and case-control studies.

Level of evidence IV: Evidence obtained from expert opinions and/or clinical experiences of respected authorities

Grade of evidence A : At least one randomised controlled trial (RCT) as part of a body of literature of overall good quality and consistency addressing the specific recommendation (evidence level I) without extrapolation.

Grade B of evidence: Well conducted clinical studies but no randomised clinical trials on the topic of recommendation (evidence level II or III); or extrapolated from level I evidence.

Grade C of evidence: Expert committee reports or committee reports or opinions and/or clinical experiences of respected authorities (evidence level IV) or extrapolated from level I or II evidence. This grading indicates that directly applicable clinical studies of good quality are absent or not readily available.

Different scientific organizations, including the American Psychiatric Association, (APA) (2) in the USA, and the, NICE in the UK (1) have published guidelines for the psychopharmacologic treatment of eating disorders. In the present chapter, to add to the conclusions of those associations, we sought to summarize the findings of all randomized controlled trials (RCTs), focusing primarily on the most recent studies and those with the largest sample sizes and most rigorous methodology (3). We have additionally added the results of some open pilot studies using new agents or exploring interesting hypotheses which could be promising for conducting RCTs in the future. Tables 2-6 summarize the results of studies using antipsychotic agents (Table 2), selective serotonin releasing inhibitors (SSRIs; Table 3), antidepressants other than SSRIs (Table 4), anticonvulsants (Table 5), and other agents (Table 6) (references 4-50). The NICE psychopharmacological treatment recommendations for eating disorders (1) will be used as guidelines for overall conclusions.

Table 2. Antipsychotics

Substance	Reference number, first author and year of publication	Milligram/day (duration)	N (active drug/placebo)	Age, age range (years)	Diagnosis	Study type	Results/significance/adverse effects
Atpyical Antipsychotics							
Olanzapine							
	4 Bissada 2008	2,5 – 10 mg; 6 mg in completers (for 10 weeks)	14/14	24 (SD 7) vs 30 (12)	AN-R: 16 AN-BP: 18 (at starting point)	RCT	More rapid weight gain; greater decrease in obsessions; decrease in depression and anxiety in both groups.
	5 Attia 2008	2,5-10 mg	12/10	29	AN-R: 14 AN-BP: 8	RCT vs aripiprazole	Olanzapine more effective in increase of weight and reduction of psychopathology
	6 Malina 2003	2,5 – 10 mg (3-70 weeks)	18	22 (SD 7)	AN	Open uncontrolled retrospective study	Decrease in core eating related symptoms and in anxiety
	7 Powers 2002	10 mg	18	27 (SD 12)	AN-R: 6 AN-BP: 12	Open trial	Weight gain, reduction in depression and negative symptoms
	8 Barbarich 2004	2,5-6,25 mg (3-6 weeks)	17	20 (SD 5)	AN-R: 12 AN-BP: 5	Open trail	Increase in BMI, reduction of depression, anxiety
	9 Brambilla 2007	2,5 - 5 mg (3 months)	15 vs 15	24 (SD 5)	AN-R: 18 AN-BP: 12	RCT	Increase in BMI, reduction in core eating-related symptoms, obsessions, depression, and aggression
Quetiapine							
	10 Bosanac 2007	520 mg (8 weeks)	8	33	AN	Open study	Reduction in obsessions, and AN-related thinking
	11 Powers 2007	150-300 mg (10 weeks)	19	14-65	AN	Open study	Reduction in, obsessions, depression, and anxiety
Aripiprazole	5 Attia 2008	5-15 mg	10 vs 12	29	AN	RCT vs. Olanzapine	See above
Amisulpiride	12 Ruggiero 2001	50 mg	12 vs 10 vs 13	24 (SD 6)	AN-R	CT vs fluoxetine vs clomipramine	Increase in weight with amisulpiride; no differences in psychological symptoms
Sulpiride	13 Vandereycken 1984	300-400 mg	18	24 (SD 6-10)	AN	RCT	No additional effect of medication

Legend: AN – anorexia nervosa; AN-R – restricting AN; AN-B/P- bingeing purging AN; BN – bulimia nervosa; BE - binge eating ; BED – binge eating disorder; SD – standard deviation; CT – control trial; RCT – randomized controlled trial (vs. placebo, unless stated otherwise); BMI – body mass index

Table 3. Antidepressants: SSRIs

Substance	Reference number, first author and year of publication	Milligram/day (duration)	N (active drug/placebo)	Age, age range (years)	Diagnosis	Study type	Results/significance/adverse effects
Fluoxetine	5 Attia 1998	60 mg (36 days)	15 /16	26.2 (16-45)	AN (12 AN-R, 19 AN-BP)	RCT	No effect vs. placebo; plasma levels measured
	14 Kaye 2001	20-60mg (11 months)	16/19	23 (SD 9)	AN-R: recovered	RCT	Improved outcome and reduced relapse rate; Plasma levels measured
	15 Ricca 1999	40 mg	24		AN atypical	RCT vs venlafaxine	Similarly effective on weight change and depression
	16 Walsh 2008	Mostly 60 mg	49 vs 44	16-45	AN: recovered	RCT	No effect on relapse prevention; plasma levels measured
	17 Arnold 2002	20-80mg Final mean dose 71.3mg/d (6 weeks)	60 (30/30) Completers 36 (23/13)	18-60	BED	RCT	Greater reduction in BE, BMI, and illness severity; no difference in adverse events; higher drop-out with placebo
	18 Grilo 2005	60mg (16 weeks)	108 (27/27/26/28)	21-59	BED	RCT vs placebo vs CBT+fluoxetine, vs. CBT+placebo	Fluoxetine not superior to placebo; no difference between CBT + fluoxetine vs. placebo; Both CBT conditions superior to fluoxetine and placebo
	19 Goldstein 1995	60 mg (16 weeks)	398	17-63 (Fluoxetine); 17-61 (Placebo)	BN	RCT	Greater reduction in BE, vomiting, both behaviors, and drive for thinness
	20 Romano 2002	60 mg/d (52 weeks)	76/74	Fluoxetine: 30 (SD 7), Placebo: 30 (SD 9)	BN	RCT	Less increase in BE, vomiting, eating-related preoccupation and symptom severity. Relapse occurred less frequently with fluoxetine n the first 3 months.
	21 Leombruni 2006	20-60 mg (12 weeks)	18/19	27 (SD 6)	BN	Single-blind RCT (fluoxetine vs. citalopram)	Greater reduction in introjected anger with fluoxetine; greater reduction in depressive feelings with citalopram; no overlap in efficacy profiles.
Sertraline	22 Santanostaso 2001	50-100 mg	11/11	14-34	AN-R	CT	Reduction in core eating-related symptoms and depression
	23 Milano 2004	100 mg (12 weeks)	24	24-36	BN	RCT	Greater reduction in BE and purging

Substance	Reference number, first author and year of publication	Milligram/day (duration)	N (active drug/placebo)	Age, age range (years)	Diagnosis	Study type	Results/significance/adverse effects
	24 McElroy 2000	50-200 mg (mean end-dose 187mg) (6 weeks)	34 (18/16) Completers (13/13)	18-60	BED	RCT	Greater reduction in BE, BMI and illness severity
Fluvoxamine	25 Hudson 1998	50-300mg (mean end-dose 260 mg) (9 weeks)	85 (42/43) Completers 67 (29/38)	18-60	BED	RCT vs. placebo	Greater reduction in BE, weight loss, and illness severity; drop out because of adverse events greater in fluvoxamine group
	26 Fichter 1997	300 mg maximum (15 weeks)	72	Fluvoxamine: 25 (SD5) Placebo: 24 (SD5)	BN	RCT	Fluvoxamine associated with higher binge abstinence rate, reduced clinical severity, and lower relapse rate. Fluvoxamine superior in limiting increases in BN behavior, global ED symptoms, fear of losing control, obsessive-compulsive symptoms, and, global severity during 12 week post-discharge phase.
	27 Sundblad 2005	20-40 mg (12 weeks)	Androgen receptor antagonist flutamide (n = 9), citalopram (n = 15), flutamide plus citalopram (n = 10), or placebo (n = 12)	21-45 (mean 26)	BN	Placebo controlled pilot study	Reduction in BE significant in both groups treated with flutamide but not in the groups treated with citalopram only or placebo. Blockade of androgen receptors may reduce some of the symptoms of BN in women.
Escitalopram	28 Guerdjikova 2008	10-30 mg (mean 26.5mg) (12 weeks)	44 (21/23)	18-60	BED	RCT	Greater reduction in weight and severity of illness. Reduction of BE not definite due to lack of statistical power. Effect size moderate

Legend: AN – anorexia nervosa; AN-R – restricting AN; AN-B/P- bingeing purging AN; BN – bulimia nervosa; BE - binge eating ; BED – binge eating disorder; SD – standard deviation; CT – control trial; RCT – randomized controlled trial (vs. placebo, unless stated otherwise); BMI – body mass index; SSRIs – specific serotonin reuptake inhibitors

Table 4. Antidepressants other than SSRIs

Substance	Reference number, first author and year of publication	Milligram/day (duration)	N (active drug/placebo)	Age, age range (years)	Diagnosis	Study type	Results/significance/adverse effects
SNRIs							
Venlafaxine	15 Ricca 1999	75 mg (6 months)	24 (12/12)	19	Atypical AN	RCT vs Fluoxetine vs clomipramine	Venlafaxine superior to other medications. Added to CBT
Milnacipran	29 El-Giamal 2003	100 mg (8 weeks)	10	19-38	BN	Report of 16 cases	Reduction in BE, vomiting and depression
NARIs							
Reboxetin	30 Fassino 2004	4 mg (3 months)	28	adults	BN	Randomized, double blind trial	Reboxetine improves BN symptoms, psychopathological features and social functioning
	31 El-Giamal 2000	8 mg (12 weeks)	7	28, 19-53	BN	Case series	?
Atomoxetine	32 McElroy 2007	40-120 mg (mean 106mg) (10weeks)	40 (20/20)	18-65	BED	RCT	Reduction in BE, BMI, Severity of illness, obsessions, hunger; more dry mouth in atomoxetine group
NASSAs							
Mirtazapine	33 Hrdlika 2008	22 mg (4 weeks)	18 (9/9)	15	AN	CT vs. no drug (without depression)	Weight gain faster in first week, then similar to no drug condition.
Amitryptiline	34 Biederman 1985	115 (50-175) mg	11/14/18	17	AN	RCT vs placebo vs no drug	No positive effects
	35 Halmi 1986	160 mg	72	13-36	AN of both subtypes	CT vs cyproheptadinbe vs placebo	No difference between amitrytiline and placebo
Cyproheptatine	35 Halmi 1986	32 mg	72	13-36	AN of both subtypes	CT vs amitryptilie vs placebo	Fewer days to target weight, less depressed mood with cyproheptadine
Desipramine	36 Walsh 1991	300 mg (8 weeks)	80		BN	CT vs Placebo	Reduction in BE of 47%

Legend: AN – anorexia nervosa; AN-R – restricting AN; AN-B/P- bingeing purging AN; BN – bulimia nervosa; BE - binge eating ; BED – binge eating disorder; SD – standard deviation; CT – control trial; RCT – randomized controlled trial (vs. placebo, unless stated otherwise); BMI – body mass index; SSRIs – specific serotonin reuptake inhibitors; SNRIs – serotonin norepnephrine reuptake inhibitors; NARI – noradrenergic reuptake inhibitors; NASSA - Noradrenergic and specific serotonergic antidepressants

Table 5. Anticonvulsants

Substance	Reference number, first author and year of publication	Milligram/day (duration)	N (active drug/placebo)	Mean age, age range (years)	Diagnosis	Study type	Results/significance/adverse effects
Topiramate	37 Claudino 2007	200mg (21 weeks)	73 (37/36)	18-60	BED	RCT+CBT vs. Placebo+CBT	Weight loss (-6.8 kg. vs. -0.9 kg), no reduction in BE and depression; paresthesias and taste perversion more frequent with topiramate.: insomnia more frequent with placebo
	38 McElroy 2003	25-600 mg Median end dose 212mg (14 weeks)	61 (30/31) Completers 34(16/18)	18-60	BED	RCT	Decrease in BE, illness severity, BMI, obsessions; more paresthesias, taste perversions, and confusion with topiramate
	39 McElroy 2004	268±223 (42 weeks; continuation of McElroy 2003	10 completers (of 61 patients at the start of the study	(18-60)	BED	Open label	Continuing reduction in BE, weight and obsessionality
	40 McElroy 2007	25-400mg (median300mg) (16weeks)	394 (195/199)	18-65	BED	RCT	Decrease in BE, weight (-4.5 kg vs. 0.2 kg), impulsiveness, obsessions, cognitive restraint, disinhibition, hunger; no difference in depression, and anxiety: more paresthesias, upper respiratory tract infection, taste perversion, difficulty with memory and concentration with topiramate
	41 Hoopes 2003	25-400 mg/mean 100 mg (10 weeks)	35/34	29	BN	RCT	Decrease in BE and purging behaviors
	42 Hedges 2004	25-400 mg/mean 100 mg (10 weeks)	35/34	29	BN	RCT	Decrease in drive for thinness, body dissatisfaction, preoccupation with food, dieting
	43 Nickel 2005	25-250 titrated within 6 weeks (10 weeks)	30 both groups	21 (SD 3)	BN	RCT	Greater reduction in BE, purging, and weight; medication appears safe
Zonisamide	44 Mc Elroy 2006	100-600mg; mean end dose 436 mg (16 weeks)	60 (30/30) Completers (12/18)	18-62 yrs	BED	RCT	Greater reduction in BE, BMI, illness severity, obsessions, compulsions and disinhibition; medication not well tolerated

Legend: AN – anorexia nervosa; AN-R – restricting AN; AN-B/P- bingeing purging AN; BN – bulimia nervosa; BE - binge eating ; BED – binge eating disorder; SD – standard deviation; CT – control trial; RCT – randomized controlled trial (vs. placebo, unless stated otherwise); BMI – body mass index

Table 6. Other agents

Substance	Reference number, first author and year of publication	Milligram/day (duration)	N (active drug/placebo)	Age, age range (years)	Diagnosis	Study type	Results/significance/adverse effects
Ondansetron	45 Faris. 2000	24 mg daily (6 weeks)	29 (completers 14/12)	29 (SD 6)	BN	RCT	Decrease in BE and vomiting Reduction in afferent vagal hyperactivity as mode of action
Memantine	46 Brennan. 2008	5-20mg (18.3mg) (12 weeks)	16	18-65	BED	Open label trial	Reduction in BE, disinhibition, no effects on BMI, depression anxiety, restraint and hunger
Opiate-antagonists							
Naltrexone	47 Marrazzi 1995	200mg/day (6 weeks)	6	20-36	AN/BP	RCT	Naltrexone in this high dosage significantly reduced BE and purging
Appetite suppressants							
Sibutramine	48 Appolinario. 2003	15mg/day (12 weeks)	60 (30/30) Completers (23/25)	18-60	BED	RCT	Reduction in BE, higher BE abstinence reduction in BMI and depression; dry mouth and constipation
	49 Berkovitz 2006	10-15 mg/day (12 months)	368/130	12-16	Overweight (BMI>95%)	RCT	Reduction in weight, waist circumpherence, HDL-cholesterol, triglycerides, glucose, insulin levels and insulin resistance
	50 Wilfley et al. 2008	15mg/day (24 weeks)	304 (Completers 100/86)	18-65 (completers 76%/62%)	BED	RCT	Reduction in BE, BMI, restraint, disinhibition, hunger; no changes in quality of life; Higher incidence of headache, dry mouth, constipation, insomnia, dizziness. Effect size for BED moderate, for weight loss large

Legend: AN – anorexia nervosa; AN-R – restricting AN; AN-B/P- bingeing purging AN; BN – bulimia nervosa; BE - binge eating ; BED – binge eating disorder; SD – standard deviation; CT – control trial; RCT – randomized controlled trial (vs. placebo, unless stated otherwise); BMI – body mass index

SUMMARY OF TREATMENT RECOMMENDATIONS

Anorexia nervosa (AN)

There is a long lasting interest in putative psychopharmacological treatments for AN, although currently there is no evidence for any first-line medication for this disorder (51, 52, 53). Several prevailing points of concern have to be taken into account whenever considering the feasibility of psychopharmacotherapy in AN (54). That is, can psychopharmacotherapy hold promise in the all important issues of direct influence on body weight resulting in weight gain (55), as well as the management of motor hyperactivity, cognitive restriction (56), rumination, body-related delusional symptoms, obsessional thinking, and the patients' all encompassing anxiety (57). Psychopharmacotherapy in AN has been also investigated when seeking to approach states of low motivation and facilitate motivational processes, as well as in the attempts to reduce the likelihood of relapse following remission or recovery.

With respect to weight and cognitive-related concerns, atypical antipsychotics have been found successful in enhancing weight gain in the short term and in reducing disturbed eating disorders-related cognitions in some patients (see Table 2), but they cannot be used without monitoring of potentially severe medical adverse effects. The rational for the use of these medications in AN stems from their weight increasing effect in patients diagnosed with schizophrenia, potentially related to 5-HT2 receptor blockade (54). Still, there are only case reports and case series regarding most of the antipsychotics studied in AN (risperidone), whereas others have not been studied yet (clozapine, zotepine). Recently (after the publication of the NICE Guidelines), olanzapine has been used in three RCTs (see Table 2) showing some effect on weight gain rate and on the reduction of obsessionality, ruminative thinking depression, and aggression. Currently, olanzepine use in AN is limited to Grade C evidence (see Table 1), although Grade A evidence might be given in future NICE revisions (57).

SSRIs are usually ineffective in the treatment of low-weight AN patients (58, 59), including in the management of comorbid anxiety and depressive states (see table 3). This is due to the effect of the underweight malnourished condition on neurotransmission activity, reduced absorption of necessary precursors, and the metabolism of the given medication. For example, in malnourished patients there is evidence of increased intestinal absorption of neutral amino acids at the cost of reduced absorption of tryptophan, the precursor of serotonin, leading, in turn, to reduced availability of tryptophan in the brain and to decreased brain serotonin synthesis (55). In addition, the initially hypothesized effects of SSRIs on relapse prevention (14) have not been substantiated in subsequent studies (16). Currently, SSRI use in relapse prevention of AN is limited to Grade C evidence

Table 7 summarizes the NICE guidelines on psychopharmacotherapy in AN, cautioning that there is a very limited base for the use of medications in this disorder, and that medications should not be used as the sole or primary treatment.

Bulimia nervosa (BN)

In a recent review by Shapiro et al. (60), forty-seven studies of medication only, behavioral interventions only, and medication plus behavioral interventions have been identified in BN. In terms of pharmacotherapy, good evidence exists that the SSRI fluoxetine (in a dosage of 60 mg/day) (19, 20) diminishes core symptoms of binge eating and purging as well as associated psychological features of the eating disorder, e.g., obsessionality, anxiety and depression in the short term (Grade B evidence, see Table 1).

Table 7. NICE guideline on psychopharmacological treatments of AN

4.4.3 Pharmacological interventions for anorexia nervosa (page 67)

There is a very limited evidence base for the pharmacological treatment of anorexia nervosa. A range of drugs may be used in the treatment of comorbid conditions but caution should be exercised in their use given the physical vulnerability of many people with anorexia nervosa.

4.4.3.1 Medication should not be used as the sole or primary treatment for anorexia nervosa. (C)

4.4.3.2 Caution should be exercised in the use of medication for comorbid conditions such as depressive or obsessive-compulsive features as they may resolve with weight gain alone. (C)

4.4.3.3 When medication is used to treat people with anorexia nervosa, the side effects of drug treatment (in particular, cardiac side effects) should be carefully considered because of the compromised cardiovascular function of many people with anorexia nervosa. (C)

4.4.3.4 Health care professionals should be aware of the risk of drugs that prolong the QTc interval on the ECG; for example, antipsychotics, tricyclic antidepressants, macrolide antibiotics, and some antihistamines. In patients with anorexia nervosa at risk of cardiac complications, the prescription of drugs with side effects that may compromise cardiac function should be avoided. (C)

4.4.3.5 If the prescription of medication that may compromise cardiac functioning is essential, ECG monitoring should be undertaken. (C)

4.4.3.6 All patients with a diagnosis of anorexia nervosa should have an alert placed in their prescribing record concerning the risk of side effects. (C)

Single or serial RCTs have also provided preliminary evidence for a similar efficacy of other SSRIs in BN including fluvoxamine (26), sertraline (23), citalopram (21), and escitalpram (28) (see Table 3). SSRIs are considered to exert their effects by increasing intersynaptic serotonin (5-HT) levels or activating 5-HT receptors at critical brain sites (54).

A Mono Amino Oxidase -Inhibitor (MAOI, brofaromine) (61) has been found to be associated with decrease of vomiting in the treatment of BN, although diet should be closely monitored. This limits the use of any MAOI in BN patients in the clinical practice (60).

Other antidepressants with preliminary evidence in reducing BN and associated symptoms include trazodone, the tricyclic antidepressants desmethylimipramine (36), serotonin noradrenaline reuptake inhibitors [(SNRIs; milnacipran, (29), venlafaxine (15), and duloxetine (62)], and the noradrenergic reuptake inhibitor (NARI) reboxetin (30) (see Table 4).

Medications other than antidepressants may also prove efficacious in the management of BN. Thus, in one RCT (27), a significant reduction in binge eating has been shown in BN patients treated with the androgen receptor blocking agent flutamide and with the combination of flutamide and citalopram but not in patients treated with citalopram only or with placebo.

Similarly, the anticonvulsant agent topiramate has been recently found effective in reducing binge-eating, purging, or both behaviors in BN patients in several RCTs (see table 5). BN patients treated with topiramate have shown, in addition, significantly greater reduction in pursuit of thinness, body dissatisfaction, preoccupation with food and dieting, and anxiety in comparison to placebo (41-43). Still, topiramate is currently not FDA approved in the treatment of eating disorders because of its potential adverse cognitive and neurological effects.

Lastly, in a small RCT involving 26 patients, the anti-emetic anti-vagal agent ondansetron has been found to decrease binge-eating and vomiting in BN patients (45).

Several points should be addressed regarding the utility of psychopharmacotherapy in BN in clinical practice. The combination of psychotherapy (usually cognitive behavioral therapy) and antidepressants has been found superior to psychotherapy alone. Whereas such a tendency exists also when comparing the combination of CBT and antidepressants to antidepressants alone, it has not been proven statistically significant (63). The use of medications, whether given as the only treatment or combined with CBT has been found less acceptable to BN patients in comparison to the psychotherapy alone. Accordingly, currently there is only preliminary evidence with respect to the optimal combination of medication and psychotherapy in for BN.

In addition, although SSRIs have been shown to be effective in long-term treatment of BN, relapse may potentially occur if the antidepressant is discontinued (60). Moreover, tolerance may develop to the anti-bingeing effect of the antidepressant (in contrast to its anti-obsessive, anti anxiety, and anti-depressive effects) potentially increasing the risk of relapse.

Table 8 summarizes the NICE guidelines on psychopharmacotherapy in BN. Currently only antidepressants are FDA approved as an alternative or additional first step to psychotherapeutic interventions, with SSRIs, specifically fluoxetine, considered the drugs of first choice in adult patients (Grade B evidence, see Table 1).

Table 8. NICE Guideline about psychopharmacological treatments of BN

7.3.6 Clinical practice recommendations (page 134)

7.3.6.1 As an alternative or additional first step to using an evidence-based self-help programme, adults with bulimia nervosa may be offered a trial of an antidepressant drug. (B)

7.3.6.2 Patients should be informed that antidepressant drugs can reduce the frequency of binge eating and purging, but the long-term effects are unknown. Any beneficial effects will be rapidly apparent. (B)

7.3.6.3 Selective serotonin reuptake inhibitors (SSRIs) (specifically fluoxetine) are the drugs of first choice for the treatment of bulimia nervosa in terms of acceptability, tolerability and reduction of symptoms. (C)

7.3.6.4 For people with bulimia nervosa, the effective dose of fluoxetine is higher than for depression (60 mg daily). (C)

7.3.6.5 No drugs, other than antidepressants, are recommended for the treatment of bulimia nervosa. (B)

In terms of future research, trials should be conducted to investigate treatment response in male BN patients (who are under-represented in clinical trials), and in different age groups, primarily in children and adolescents. Such trials should also take into consideration the influence of ethnic background and other socio-cultural factors. Further research is required to establish the long-term efficacy of relatively short-term medication trials, the optimal duration of medication treatment, the optimal strategy for the maintenance of treatment gains, and drug augmentation strategies (60). Lastly, novel medications that reduce the urge to purge (e.g., antiemetics) or diminish the extent to which binge eating and purging are experienced as reinforcing (e.g., opiate antagonists), are needed (see Table 6).

Binge Eating Disorder (BED)

Five major aims have to be taken into account in the treatment of binge eating disorder (BED); reduction of binge eating episodes and of specific eating-relate psychopathology; weight loss and/or prevention of weight gain; reduction of comorbid psychopathology (i.e. depression, anxiety or obsessionality); and improvement of the overall physical and psychological well-being and health condition.

With these aims in mind, SSRIs have been found to reduce the frequency of binge eating in adult BED patients by more than 60%, and to significantly improve comorbid symptomatology (see Table 3). However, reduction in binge eating does not always lead to substantial weight loss (see Table 3), likely leading to considerable frustration among affected patients.

Of the psychotropic medications specifically developed for weight reduction, only sibutramine, a centrally-acting nonselective serotonin, norepinephrtine and dopamine reuptake inhibitor may be effective for weight reduction in BED. Its weight reduction properties are related to the reduction of appetite and increase of satiety. Several RCTs (48-50) have shown a superiority of the active drug to placebo in reducing weight, HDL-cholesterol, triglycerides, glucose, insulin levels and insulin resistance (see Table 6).. Most of the studies have followed their patients for 6-12 months, so that weight-reducing long-term effects of sibutramine are still inconclusive. The medication has modest effects on total body weight (typically an additional 2-10 kg weight reduction), with most of the weight loss occurring within the first 4-6 months of treatment. Regain of weight may occur if the medication is discontinued (64)..

Nevertheless, the use of sibutramine is associated with potentially serious adverse effects, including hypertension, tachycardia, palpitations, headache, dizziness, insomnia, anxiety, and depression. In January, 2010, the Committee for Medicinal Products for Human Use (CHMP) of the European Medicines Agency (EMA) has voted to recommend the suspension of marketing authorizations for all anti-obesity medicines containing sibutramine in the European Union (EU) (64). The CHMP's recommendations have been based on early results of the SCOUT (Sibutramine Cardiovascular OUTcome Trial) (65). The full results of the SCOUT have been published in September 2010. In this study, 10,744 overweight or obese subjects, 55 years of age or older, with preexisting cardiovascular disease, type 2 diabetes mellitus, or both have been enrolled, to assess the cardiovascular consequences of weight management with and without sibutramine in subjects at high risk for cardiovascular events. All subjects have received sibutramine in addition to participating in a weight-management program during a 6-week, single-blind, lead-in period, after which 9804 subjects have undergone random assignment in a double-blind fashion to sibutramine (4906 subjects) or placebo (4898 subjects). The mean duration of treatment has been 3.4 years. The mean weight loss during the lead-in period has been 2.6 kg; after randomization, the subjects in the sibutramine group have achieved and maintained further weight reduction (mean, 1.7 kg). The rates of nonfatal myocardial infarction and nonfatal stroke have been 4.1% and 2.6% in the sibutramine group and 3.2% and 1.9% in the placebo group, respectively (hazard ratio for nonfatal myocardial infarction, 1.28; 95% CI, 1.04 to 1.57; P=0.02; hazard ratio for nonfatal stroke, 1.36; 95% CI, 1.04 to 1.77; P=0.03). The rates of cardiovascular death and death from any cause have not increased. The authors conclude that subjects with preexisting cardiovascular conditions receiving long-term sibutramine treatment have an increased risk of nonfatal myocardial infarction and nonfatal stroke but not of cardiovascular death or death from any cause. Currently, sibutramone is not in use in EU countries and in many other countries as well, including the USA.

To date several RCTs (38, 40, see Table 5) and meta-analyses and systematic reviews (66-69) have shown that topiramate may be associated with significant binge-eating and weight reduction in BED patients. These effects may be the result of topiramate down regulation of neuropeptide Y and glutamate receptors, with both peptides representing potent stimulants of feeding behaviors. In addition, topiramate-induced weight loss is related to loss of fat rather than of lean body mass. As in the case of BN, topiramate is not FDA approved for the treatment of BED.

To summarize, the most recent meta-analysis of pharmacotherapy in BED (66) has identified 14 randomized RCTs that have tested pharmacotherapy as primary intervention for BED, and 8 RCTs testing pharmacotherapy relative to or in combination with psychotherapy. There is now evidence that active medications may lead more often to cessation of binge eating and weight loss compared with placebo. However, the amount of weight loss is minimal, and often not clinically significant (3% vs. 0%). The combination of medications with psychotherapy usually fails to improve outcome in comparison to each treatment alone. Trials for psychopharmacotherapy are usually brief (6-24 weeks), and long-term follow-up studies of pharmacotherapy in BED are still missing. The only study with long- term follow-up data refers to D-fenfluramine, a medication withdrawn from use due to severe adverse events, has shown high relapse rates after medication discontinuation. It has also been critically commented that 12 of the 14 RCTs reviewed by Reas & Grilo (66), have been funded by the drug manufacturer

Despite these limitations, the NICE guidelines of psychopharmacotherapy in BED (see Table 9) recommend that SSRIs may be used as an alternative or additional first step in the treatment of BED, although their long term effects are still unknown (Grade B evidence, see Table 1). Additionally, the use of pharmacotherapy in BED should be conservative, as many BED patients may respond to the placebo effect of the medications.

Table 9. NICE Guideline about psychopharmacological treatments of EDNOS

8.3.5 Clinical practice recommendations (page 163)

8.3.5.1 As an alternative or additional first step to using an evidence-based self-help programme, consideration should be given to offering a trial of a SSRI antidepressant drug to patients with binge eating disorder. (B)

8.3.5.2 Patients with binge eating disorders should be informed that SSRIs can reduce binge eating, but the long-term effects are unknown. Antidepressant drugs may be sufficient treatment for a limited subset of patients. (B)

Non-BED Eating disorders not otherwise specified (EDNOS)

There are currently no systematic studies on the psychopharmacological treatment of EDNOS. From the perspective of clinical practice, EDNOS patients are usually treated with strategies that are closest to the respective defined full-blown eating disorder.

CONCLUSION

The use of psychotropic medications in anorexia nervosa, bulimia nervosa and binge-eating disorder has some good reason routed in both neurobiological and psychopathological understanding of these disorders. However, evidence is still low for most substances. Medications may be added individually and considered in a multimodal treatment plan as part of the therapy for more severe cases with comorbid psychopathology and in addition to psychotherapeutic interventions which are still recommended the first-line treatments for eating disorders.

REFERENCES

[1] NICE Guidelines: Eating Disorders: Core interventions in the treatment and management of anorexia nervosa, bulimia nervosa and related eating disorders http://www.nice.org.uk/Guidance/CG9, January 2004

[2] APA-Guidelines: Practice Guideline for the treatment of patients with eating disorders, third edition, APA 2006 Work group on eating disorders
http://www.psychiatryonline.com/pracGuide/pracGuideTopic_12.aspx

[3] Riedl A, Becker J, Rauchfuss M. Klapp BF. Psychopharmacotherapy in eating disorders: a systematic analysis. Psychopharmacol Bull 2008;41:59-84.

[4] Bissada H, Tasca GA, Barber AM, Bradwejn J. Olanzapine in the treatment of low body weight and obsessive thinking in women with anorexia nervosa: a randomized, double-blind, placebo-controlled trial. Am J Psychiatry 2008;165:1281-8.

[5] Attia E. Eating Disorders Research Society (EDRS) Congress. Montreal, Canada, September 2008.

[6] Malina A, Gaskill J, McConaha C, Frank GK, LaVia M, Scholar L, Kaye WH. Olanzapine treatment of anorexia nervosa: a retrospective study. Int J Eat Disord 2003;33: 234-7.

[7] Powers PS, Santana CA, Bannon YS. Olanzapine in the treatment of anorexia nervosa: an open label trial. Int J Eat Disord 2002;32:146-54.

[8] Barbarich NC, McConaha CW, Gaskill J, La Via M, Frank GK, Achenbach S, Plotnicov KH, Kaye WH. An open trial of olanzapine in anorexia nervosa. J Clin Psychiatry 2004;65:1480-2.

[9] Brambilla F, Garcia CS, Fassino S, Daga GA, Favaro A, Santonastaso P, Ramaciotti C, Bondi E, Mellado C, Borriello R, Monteleone P. Olanzapine therapy in anorexia nervosa: psychobiological effects. Int Clin Psychopharmacol 2007;22:197-204.

[10] Bosanac P, Kurlender S, Norman T, Hallam K, Wesnes K, Manktelow T, Burrows G. An open-label study of quetiapine in anorexia nervosa. Hum Psychopharmacol 2007;22:223-30.

[11] Powers PS, Bannon Y, Eubanks R, McCormick T. Quetiapine in anorexia nervosa patients: an open label outpatient pilot study. Int J Eat Disord 2007;40: 21-6.

[12] Ruggiero GM, Laini V, Mauri MC, Ferrari VM, Clemente A, Lugo F, Mantero M, Redaelli G, Zappulli D, Cavagnini F. A single blind comparison of amisulpride, fluoxetine and clomipramine in the treatment of restricting anorectics. Prog Neuropsychopharmacol Biol Psychiatry 2001;25:1049-59.

[13] Vandereycken W. Neuroleptics in the short-term treatment of anorexia nervosa. A double-blind placebo-controlled study with sulpiride. Br J Psychiatry 1984;144:288-92.

[14] Kaye WH, Nagata T, Weltzin TE, Hsu LK, Sokol MS, McConaha C, Plotnicov KH, Weise J, Deep D. Double-blind placebo-controlled administration of fluoxetine in restricting- and restricting-purging-type anorexia nervosa. Biol Psychiatry 2001;49:644-52.

[15] Ricca V, Mannucci E, Paionni A, Di Bernardo M, Cellini M, Cabras PL, Rotella CM. Venlafaxine versus fluoxetine in the treatment of atypical anorectic outpatients: a preliminary study. Eat Weight Disord 1999;4:10-4.

[16] Walsh BT, Kaplan AS, Attia E, Olmsted M, Parides M, Carter JC, Pike KM, Devlin MJ, Woodside B, Roberto CA, Rockert W. Fluoxetine after weight restoration in anorexia nervosa: a randomized controlled trial. JAMA 2006;295:2605-12.

[17] Arnold LM, McElroy SL, Hudson JI, Welge JA; Bennett AJ; Keck PE Jr. A placebo-controlled, randomized trial of fluoxetine in the treatment of binge-eating disorder. J Clin Psychiatry 2002;63:1028-33.

[18] Grilo CM, Masheb RM, Wilson GT. Efficacy of cognitive behavioral therapy and fluoxetine for the treatment of binge eating disorder: a randomized double-blind placebo-controlled comparison. Biol Psychiatry 2005;57:301-9.

[19] Goldstein DJ, Wilson MG, Thompson VL, Potvin JH, Rampey AH Jr. Long-term fluoxetine treatment of bulimia nervosa. Fluoxetine Bulimia Nervosa Research Group. Br J Psychiatry 1995;166:660-6.

[20] Romano SJ, Halmi KA, Sarkar NP, Koke SC, Lee JS. A placebo-controlled study of fluoxetine in continued treatment of bulimia nervosa after successful acute fluoxetine treatment. Am J Psychiatry 2002;159:96-102.

[21] Leombruni P, Amianto F, Delsedime N, Gramaglia C, Abbate-Daga G, Fassino S. Citalopram versus fluoxetine for the treatment of patients with bulimia nervosa: a single-blind randomized controlled trial. Adv Ther 2006;23:481-94.

[22] Santonastaso P, Friederici S, Favaro A. Sertraline in the treatment of restricting anorexia nervosa: an open controlled trial. J Child Adolesc Psychopharmacol. 2001;11:143-50.

[23] Milano W, Petrella C, Sabatino C, Capasso A. Treatment of bulimia nervosa with sertraline: a randomized controlled trial. Adv Ther 2004;21:232-7.

[24] McElroy SL, Casuto LS, Nelson EB, Lake KL, Soutullo CA; Keck PE Jr, Hudson JI. Placebo-controlled trial of sertraline in the treatment of binge eating disorder. Am J Psychiatry 2000;157:1004-6.

[25] Hudson JI, McElroy SL, Raymond NC, Crow S, Keck PE Jr, Carter WP, Mitchell JE, Strakowski SM, Pope HG Jr, Coleman BS, Jonas JM. Fluvoxamine in the treatment of binge-eating disorder: a multicenter placbo-controlled, double-blind trial. Am J Psychiatry 1998;155:1756-62.

[26] Fichter MM, Leibl C, Kruger R, Rief W. Effects of fluvoxamine on depression, anxiety, and other areas of general psychopathology in bulimia nervosa. Pharmacopsychiatry. 1997;30:85–92.

[27] Sundblad C, Landén M, Eriksson T, Bergman L, Eriksson E. Effects of the androgen antagonist flutamide and the serotonin reuptake inhibitor citalopram in bulimia nervosa: a placebo-controlled pilot study. J Clin Psychopharmacol 2005;25:85-8.

[28] Guerdjikova AI, McElroy SL, Kotwal R, Welge JA, Nelson E, Lake K, D'Alessio D, Keck PE Jr, Hudson JI. High-dose escitalopram in the treatment of binge-eating disorder with obesity: a placebo-controlled monotherapy trial. Hum Psychopharmacol Clin Exp 2008; 23:1-11.

[29] El-Giamal N, deZwaan M, Bailer U, Strnad A, Schüssler P, Kasper S. Milnacipran in the treatment of bulimia nervosa: a report of 16 cases. Eur Neuropsychopharmacol 2003;13:73-9.

[30] Fassino S, Daga GA, Boggio S, Garzaro L, Pierò A. Use of reboxetine in bulimia nervosa: a pilot study. J Psychopharmacol 2004;18:423-8.

[31] El-Giamal N, deZwaan M, Bailer U, Lennkh C, Schüssler P, Kasper S. Reboxetine in the treatment of bulimia nervosa: a report of seven cases. Int Clin Psychopharmacol 2000;15:351-6.

[32] McElroy SL, Guerdjikova AI, Kotwal R, Welge JA, Nelson EB, Lake KA, Keck PE Jr, Hudson JI. Atomoxetine in the treatment of binge-eating disorder: a randomized placebo-controlled trial. J Clin Psychiatry 2007;68:390-8.

[33] Hrdlicka M, Beranova I, Zamencnikova R, Urbanek T. Mirtazapine in the treatment of adolescent anorexia nervosa. Eur Child Adolesc Psychiatr 2008;17:187-9.

[34] Biederman J, Herzog DB, Rivinus TM, Harper GP, Ferber RA, Rosenbaum JF, Harmatz JS, Tondorf R, Orsulak PJ, Schildkraut JJ. Amitriptyline in the treatment of anorexia nervosa: a double-blind, placebo-controlled study. J Clin Psychopharmacol 1985;5:10-6.

[35] Halmi KA, Eckert E, LaDu TJ, Cohen J. Anorexia nervosa. Treatment efficacy of cyproheptadine and amitriptyline. Arch Gen Psychiatry 1986;43:177-81.

[36] Walsh BT, Hadigan C, Devlin M, Gladis M, Roose S. Long-term outcome of antidepressant treatment for bulimia nervosa. Am J Psychiatry 1991;148:1206-12.

[37] Claudino AM, De Oliveira IR, Appolinario JC, Cordas TA, Duchesne M, Sichieri R, Bacaltchik J. Double-blind, randomized, placebo-controlled trial of topiramate plus cognitive-behavior therapy in binge-eating disorder. J Clin Psychiatry 2007;68:1324-32.

[38] McElroy SL, Arnold LM, Shapira NA; Keck PE Jr, Rosenthal NR, Karim MR, Kamin M, Hudson JI. Topiramate in the treatment of binge eating disorder associated with obesity: a randomized, placbo-controlled trial. Am J Psychiatry 2003;160:255-61.

[39] McElroy SL, Shapira NA, Arnold, L.M., et al, Topiramate in the long-term treatment of binge-eating disorder associated with obesity. J Clin Psychiatry 2004;65:1463-9.

[40] McElroy SL, Hudson JI, Capece JA, Beyers K, Fisher AC, Rosenthal NR for the topiramate binge eating disorder research group. Topiramate for the treatment of binge eating disorder associated with obesity: a placebo-controlled study. Biol Psychiatry 2007;61:1039-48.

[41] Hoopes SP, Reimherr FW, Hedges DW, Rosenthal NR, Kamin M, Karim R, Capece JA, Karvois D. Treatment of bulimia nervosa with topiramate in a randomized, double-blind, placebo-controlled trial, part 1: improvement in binge and purge measures. J Clin Psychiatry 2003;64:1335-41.

[42] Hedges DW, Reimherr FW, Hoopes SP, Rosenthal NR, Kamin M, Karim R, Capece JA. Treatment of bulimia nervosa with topiramate in a randomized, double-blind, placebo-controlled trial, part 2: improvement in psychiatric measures. J Clin Psychiatry 2003;64:1449-54.

[43] Nickel C, Tritt K, Muehlbacher M, Pedrosa Gil F, Mitterlehner FO, Kaplan P, Lahmann C, Leiberich PK, Krawczyk J, Kettler C, Rother WK, Loew TH, Nickel MK. Topiramate treatment in bulimia nervosa patients: a randomized, double-blind, placebo-controlled trial. Int J Eat Disord 2005;38:295-300.

[44] McElroy SL, Kotwal R, Guerdjikova AI, Welge JA, Nelson EB, Lake KA; D'Alessio DA, Keck PE Jr, Hudson JI. Zonisamide in the treatment of binge eating disorder with obesity: a randomized controlled trial. J Clin Psychiatry 2006; 67:1897-906.

[45] Faris PL, Kim SW, Meller WH, Goodale RL, Oakman SA, Hofbauer RD, Marshall AM, Daughters RS, Banerjee-Stevens D, Eckert ED, Hartman BK. Effect of decreasing afferent vagal activity with ondansetron on symptoms of bulimia nervosa: a randomised, double-blind trial. Lancet 2000;355:792-7.

[46] Brennan BP, Roberts JL, Fogarty KV, Reynolds KA, Jonas JM, Hudson JI. Memantine in the treatment of binge eating disorder: an open-label, prospective trial. Int J Eat Disord 2008;41:520-6.

[47] Marrazzi MA, Bacon JP, Kinzie J, Luby ED. Naltrexone use in the treatment of anorexia nervosa and bulimia nervosa. Int Clin Psychopharmacol 1995;10:163-72.

[48] Appolinario JC, Bacaltchcuk J. Sichieri R, Claudino AM, Godoy-Matos A, Morgan C, Zanella MT, Coutinho W. A randomized, double-blind, placebo-controlled study of sibutramine in the treatment of binge-eating disorders. Arch Gen Psychiatry 2003;60:1109-16.

[49] Berkowitz RI, Fujioka K, Daniels SR, Hoppin AG, Owen S, Perry AC, Sothern MS, Renz CL, Pirner MA, Walch JK, Jasinsky O, Hewkin AC, Blakesley VA. Effects of sibutramine treatment in obese adolescents: a randomized trial. An Intern Med 2006;145:81-90.

[50] Wifley DE, Crow SJ, Hudson JI, Mitchell JE, Berkowitz RI, Blakesley V, Walsh BT. Efficacy of sibutramine for the treatment of binge eating disorder: a randomized multicenter placebo-controlled double-blind study. Am J Psychiatry 2008;165:51-8.

[51] Claudino AM, Hay P, Lima MS, Bacaltchuk J, Schmidt U, Treasure J. Antidepressants for anorexia nervosa. Cochrane Database Syst Rev. 2006; Jan 25 (1):CD004365.

[52] Bulik CM, Berkman ND, Brownley KA, Sedway JA, Lohr KN. Anorexia nervosa treatment: a systematic review of randomized controlled trials. Int J Eat Disord 2007;40:310-20.

[53] Crow SJ, Mitchell JE, Roerig JD, Steffen K. What potential role is there for medication treatment in anorexia nervosa? Int J Eat Disord 2009;42:1-8.

[54] Leibowitz SF. The role of serotonin in eating disorders. Drugs 1990;39:895-903.

[55] Ferguson CP, La Via MC, Crossan PJ, Kaye WH. Are SSRI's effective in underweight anorexia nervosa? Int J Eating Disorders 1999;25:11-7.

[56] Mondraty N, Laird Birmingham C, Touyz S, Sundakov V, Chapman L, Beumont P. Randomized controlled trial of olanzapine in the treatment of cognitions in anorexia nervosa. Aust Psychiatry 2005;13:72-5.

[57] Mehler-Wex C, Romanos M, Kirchheiner J, Schulze UM. Atypical antipsychotics in severe anorexia nervosa in children and adolescents--review and case reports. Eur Eat Disord Rev. 2008;16:100-8

[58] Fassino S, Leombruni P, Daga G, Brustolin A, Migliaretti G, Cavallo F, Rovera G. Efficacy of citalopram in anorexia nervosa: a pilot study. Eur Neuropsychopharmacol 2002;12:453-9.

[59] Bosanac P, Norman T, Burrows G, Beumont P. Serontonergic and dopaminergic systems in anorexia nervosa: a role for atypical antipsychotics? Aust N Z J Psychiatry 2005;39:146-53.

[60] Shapiro JR, Berkman ND, Brownley KA, Sedway JA, Lohr KN, Bulik CM. Bulimia nervosa treatment: a systematic review of randomized controlled trials. Int J Eat Disord 2007;40:321-36.

[61] Kennedy S, Goldbloom D, Ralevski E, Davis C, D'Souza J, Lofchy J. Is there a role for selective monoamine oxidase inhibitor therapy in bulimia nervosa? A placebo-controlled trial of brofaromine. J Clin Psychopharmacol 1993;13:415–22.

[62] Hazen E, Fava M. Successful treatment with duloxetine in a case of treatment refractory bulimia nervosa: a case report. J Psychopharmacol 2006;20:723-4.

[63] Bacaltchuk J, Hay P, Trefiglio R. Antidepressants versus psychological treatments and their combination for bulimia nervosa. Cochrane Database Syst Rev. 2001;(4):CD003385.

[64] European Medicines Agency (EMA). Questions and answers on the suspension of medicines containing sibutramine. EMA/H/A-107-1256/808179/2009. January 2010

[65] James WP, Caterson ID, Coutinho W, Finer N, Van Gaal LF, Maggioni AP, Torp-Pedersen C, Sharma AM, Shepherd GM, Rode RA, Renz CL; SCOUT Investigators. Effect of sibutramine on cardiovascular outcomes in overweight and obese subjects. N Engl J Med 2010;363:905-17.

[66] Reas DL, Grilo CM. Review and Meta-analysis of pharmacotherapy for binge eating disorder. Obesity 2008;16:2024-38.

[67] Stefano SC, Bacaltchuk J, Blay SL, Appolinario JC. Antidepressants in short-term treatment of binge eating disorder: Systematic review and meta-analysis. Eat Behav 2008; 9:129-36.

[68] Arbaizar B, Gómez-Acebo I, Llorca J. Efficacy of topiramate in bulimia nervosa and binge-eating disorder: a systematic review. Gen Hosp Psychiatry 2008;30:471-5.

[69] Brownley KA, Berkman ND, Sedway JA, Lohr KN, Bulik CM. Binge eating disorder treatment: a systematic review of randomized controlled trials. Int J Eat Disord 2007;40:337-48.

In: Treatment and Recovery of Eating Disorders
Editors: Daniel Stein and Yael Latzer

ISBN: 978-1-62808-248-7
© 2013 Nova Science Publishers, Inc.

Chapter 5

THE REDUCED OBESE STATE: METABOLIC, PSYCHOLOGICAL AND LIFESTYLE FEATURES

Maya Margalit and Elliot M Berry[**]

Departments of Internal Medicine & Human Nutrition & Metabolism
Braun School of Public Health
Hebrew University Hadassah Faculty of Medicine, Jerusalem, Israel

ABSTRACT

Successful weight loss is usually followed by weight regain. Numerous studies have attempted to clarify the basis for the difficulty in maintaining stable weight after successful weight loss, and have shown that reduced-obese subjects differ from never-obese individuals by an altered metabolism and different lifestyle and psychological adjustments to remain weight-stable. Understanding these differences and the features that characterize reduced-obese individuals who are more successful at maintaining weight loss may help devise strategies to combat this serious problem. In the present report, we review data on the metabolic, psychological and lifestyle characteristics of reduced-obese individuals. Successful weight maintenance requires restricted eating, strenuous regular exercise and frequent self-monitoring. These requirements for a *lifelong* commitment to significant lifestyle changes, possibly to oppose metabolic alterations that favor weight regain, and the psychological mind frame required to support this undertaking, may account for the low success rate of current treatment approaches.

Keywords: metabolic, psychological, behavioral changes, reduced obese state

---

[**] E-mail address: elliotb@ekmd.huji.ac.il

INTRODUCTION

In 2009, the majority of adults in the United States and other developed nations are overweight or obese, and obesity is becoming a major health concern in many developing nations. Studies of dietary and behavioral treatments for obesity have shown very high rates of recidivism, with rapid regain of the weight lost. The success rate of weight loss strategies depends on the definition of success and on study settings. While previous studies have demonstrated almost universal treatment failures (1), more recent estimates of successful long term weight loss, *i.e.* maintenance of >10% reduction of body weight for more than one year, are in the range of 20% (2). Gradual weight regain is also the norm following bariatric surgery, although these patients are much more successful at maintaining > 10% weight loss for a prolonged duration (3).

Over the years, attempts have been made to clarify the basis of the difficulty in maintaining stable weight after successful weight loss. Much data on the characteristics of reduced-obese subjects has emerged from the National Weight Control Registry (NWCR), a large prospective investigation of long-term successful weight loss maintenance, that is currently tracking over 5,000 adults who have lost significant amounts of weight (>13.6 kg) and kept it off for long periods of time (> 1 year) (4). The average weight loss reported by NWCR participants is 30 kg, and the average duration of weight maintenance is 5.5 years. About half of registry participants were overweight as children, and most report a family history of obesity. Almost all NWCR subjects have experienced previous unsuccessful weight loss attempts (4, 5). Despite certain methodological issues that may limit the generalizability of registry data and concerns that the requirements for weight loss maintenance may not be the same at different time points after initial weight loss, the NWCR is one of the most comprehensive resources for the study of long-term reduced-obese subjects.

Based on NWCR and other data, it is apparent that reduced-obese subjects differ from never-obese individuals of similar body mass index (BMI) and body composition in several important respects, including altered metabolism and different psychological and lifestyle requirements to remain weight stable. In the present report, we review data on these characteristics of reduced-obese individuals. The requirement for a lifelong commitment to significant lifestyle changes, possibly to oppose metabolic alterations that favor weight regain, and the psychological mind frame required to support this undertaking, may account for the low success rate of current treatment approaches.

PHYSIOLOGICAL CHARACTERISTICS OF THE REDUCED-OBESE STATE

In both obese and lean individuals, weight loss appears to trigger physiological responses that are directed towards increased metabolic efficiency (lower weight-maintaining energy requirements) to prevent further weight loss. Such responses, which share some features with those observed in energy deficiency states [e.g.. starvation, anorexia nervosa (6)] are observed in both lean and obese individuals (7), functioning to maintain usual body weight. (**Table 1**).

Energy expenditure and fat metabolism: Numerous studies have evaluated the effect of weight loss on total daily energy expenditure (TEE) and its components - non-resting energy expenditure (NREE), resting energy expenditure (REE) and the thermic effect of food (TEF).

Reduced-obese subjects appear to be characterized by decreased TEE (~15%, 300-500 kcal/d), which is explained mainly by reduced NREE (20-30%) (7). A reduction in NREE was consistently evident at both early (8 weeks) and late (1 year) time points after initial weight loss (8). In a series of rigorous experiments, Rosenbaum et al. showed that there is a significant contribution to reduction in NREE and TEE in weight-reduced individuals of increased skeletal muscle work efficiency, that is present at low workloads (such as those characteristic of a sedentary lifestyle) and is overcome by more intensive physical activity (9) Altered muscle work efficiency has also been suggested by other studies (10, 11).

REE is determined primarily by the fat-free mass (FFM); as weight reduction results in loss of both fat mass and fat-free mass, REE decreases inevitably in individuals who lose weight, although the loss of FFM is attenuated if the individual exercises. Studies on reduced-obese subjects have examined whether REE is decreased to a greater degree than expected by loss of fat free mass (REE/metabolic mass< REE/FFM), a finding that would signify increased metabolic efficiency at rest. Data on this matter remain inconclusive; some studies have suggested that REE/FFM may indeed be reduced (~10%) in reduced-obese individuals in comparison to both obese and never-obese subjects (7, 12, 13), while others indicate that such a reduction is minimal at most (9, 14, 15). Reasons for this discrepancy may relate to heterogeneous study populations, varying techniques for determination of REE, absence of weight stability at the time of testing, lack of weight-matched controls, variations in diet composition and physical activity (8) and variations in fat free mass composition in post-obese individuals (16). The TEF is probably not altered in the post-obese state (7, 16).

Other studies have examined the effect of weight loss on fatty acid trapping and metabolic fuel oxidation. Faraj et al. (18) demonstrated enhanced trapping of dietary triglycerides in peripheral tissues in weight-stable post obese women after gastric bypass surgery compared to controls. These results are compatible with those of another study, in which the area under the curve (AUC) for triacylglycerol was lower in post-obese than in never-obese women (19), and with the finding that adenylate cyclase activity in adipocytes is reduced in formerly morbidly obese women, which may result in decreased lipolysis (20). Data regarding fat oxidation are not consistent; while NWCR (14) and other data (12, 21, 22) suggest that lipid oxidation may be decreased in reduced-obese individuals compared to never-obese weight-matched controls, other studies suggest no change or increased fat oxidation after weight loss (9, 18, 23).

Neuroendocrine function: The reduced-obese state is associated with alterations of endocrine and autonomic nervous system function that are reminiscent of those observed in chronic energy deficiency states (**Table 1**). The most consistent findings are relative leptin deficiency, reduced levels of bioactive thyroid hormones, decreased sympathetic nervous system (SNS) tone (7, 13, 24) and increased parasympathetic system tone (7, 25). Increased insulin sensitivity (19, 26), increased serum free cortisol levels and reduced serum cortisol binding globulin levels have also been documented (27).

In reduced-obese individuals, thyroid hormone profiles are characterized by decreased thyroxine (T4) and triiodothyronine (T3) levels, and increased reverse triiodothyronine (rT3) levels (13). Catecholamine release in response to insulin-induced hypoglycemia and urine norepinephrine levels are reduced (13, 28). In a study that examined the correlation between urine catecholamine excretion and energy expenditure in individuals who lost 10% of their body weight, 25-40% of the change in TEE was explained by changes in catecholamine action (13). In another study, administration of a high-carbohydrate-low- fat diet enhanced sympathetic nervous system activity, as reflected by 24 hour heart rate and plasma norepinephrine concentrations, and resulted in higher energy expenditure in post-obese individuals (29). These findings may have therapeutic implications, and indeed, adherence to a high-carbohydrate-low fat diet characterizes most successful NWCR participants.

Table 1. Comparison of physiological parameters between chronic energy deficient (CED) and reduced-obese states

	CED	Reduced Obese
REE	↓	↓
NREE	↓	↓
TEF	↓	↔
Lipid oxidation	↑	↑/↓
Serum insulin	↓	↓
Insulin resistance	↔/↑	↓
Keto bodies	↑↑	?
Lipolysis	↑	↓
Serum non-esterified fatty acids (NEFAs)	↑	↓
Serum leptin	↓	↓
Serum glucagon	↑	↔
Sympathetic activity	↓	↓
Parasympathetic activity	↑	↑
Muscle fiber composition	↓ type II fibers	Unchanged

In recent years, much data has become available on the contribution of relative or absolute leptin deficiency to the metabolic profile of reduced-obese individuals. The primary functional role of leptin appears to be defense of body fat, by increasing food seeking and decreasing energy expenditure when fat stores are insufficient (7). The threshold for leptin sufficiency is determined by anatomical and functional characteristics of the hypothalamus and other brain areas, which may be amenable to modification by such factors as chronic changes in somatic fat stores. Thus, similar circulating leptin levels in never-obese and reduced-obese individuals of similar BMI and body composition may be perceived as sufficient or deficient, respectively, depending on hypothalamic thresholds. In addition, several studies have suggested that there may be less fat mass-adjusted secretion of leptin from adipocytes (30) and lower plasma leptin levels in reduced-obese individuals (18, 26, 30).

While administration of leptin to establish normal plasma levels corrects perturbations in congenital leptin deficient individuals (31), in obese subjects, no effect on weight loss is seen unless leptin is administered in markedly supraphysiological doses (32). Fascinatingly, Rosenbaum et al. have shown that administration of low-dose leptin to reduced-obese subjects to restore plasma leptin levels to those that were present prior to weight reduction reverses the effect of weight loss on energy expenditure (TEE and NREE), skeletal muscle work efficiency, sympathetic nervous system tone and circulating levels of thyroxine and triiodothyronine (24). Thus, such a therapeutic strategy might "fool" the reduced-obese body into more normal metabolic behavior.

Skeletal muscle structure and function: Rosenbaum et al. have found that increased skeletal muscle work efficiency in reduced-obese subjects is accompanied by increased lipid oxidation, as reflected by a reduced respiratory quotient (9), and Kern et al. demonstrated increased capillarity and oxidative capacity of skeletal muscle after weight loss (33). Other studies (34, 35) have identified decreased skeletal muscle expression of uncoupling proteins, particularly uncoupling protein 3 (UCP3), that may contribute to increased mechanical efficiency in reduced-obese individuals.

BEHAVIORAL, PSYCHOLOGICAL AND LIFESTYLE ASPECTS OF LONG-TERM REDUCED-OBESE INDIVIDUALS

Much of what is known about the psychological, behavioral and lifestyle characteristics of reduced-obese individuals is based on data from the NWCR. It should be noted that although the NWCR is a nationwide project in which participants have been recruited from all-over the United States, the profile of NWCR participants is very different from that of the American population at large, with prominent over-representation of women (77%), Caucasians (95%) and highly-educated individuals (82% college educated). It is not known how representative this highly-skewed profile is of the true population of successful weight losers, or results from biases that were introduced by the recruitment process. This issue should be kept in mind when considering the generalizability of NWCR data. The average age of registry participants is 45 years and 67% are married. Methods for initial weight loss of registry participants were diverse- 41% lost weight on their own, 36.5% participated in a commercial weight loss program, 15.7% used liquid formula diets, 4.2% used medications and 1.3 underwent bariatric surgery (4, 5, 26).

BEHAVIOR AND LIFESTYLE

Successful NWCR participants are characterized by continued long-term implementation of weight-related behavioral strategies that are similar to those employed by individuals who are actively losing weight, including attention to diet and eating habits, regular physical activity and frequent weight monitoring.

Compared to controls, registry members were consistently found to consume lower calorie diets with a low fat content (average 1295 kcal/d, 24.3% from fat in women; 1723 kcal/d, 23.5% from fat in men) and to actively employ more behavioral strategies (e.g. limiting intake of certain foods, limiting quantities of food eaten, counting calories, counting fat grams or calculating percentage of calories from fat) to decrease food intake (26). Successful NWCR participants reported increased dieting consistency (similar dietary habits on weekdays and weekends as well as on holidays compared to other days of the year) (36) and decreased dietary variety (consumption of a smaller variety of foods from all food groups) (37). Intake of fast food was low (26). Subjects consumed an average of 4.9 meals per day (26), a practice that may moderate the anabolic effects of swings in insulin levels. The majority of participants reported eating breakfast daily (38), and most meals were eaten at home (26).

NWCR weight maintainers were characterized by regular engagement in physical activity (>90% of participants), and made efforts to increase both lifestyle activity and regular planned exercise (5). Data from the NWCR suggest that the optimal amount of physical activity to maintain weight loss is about 1 hour per day, or an energy expenditure of approximately 2500-3000 kcal/week (26). In another study, weight loss and maintenance were significantly better in those whose level of physical activity was > 2500 kcal/week (39). In addition to engagement in physical activity, registry participants reported less sedentary activities; in particular, time spent watching television was significantly decreased in these individuals compared to the US national average (40). **Table 2** summarizes the energy balance in successful reduced obese subjects. It may be seen that women "live" on a net balance of ~.900 Kcals / day and men on ~.1200 kcals / day. These data illustrate why the required energy price for successful weight maintenance may be too high for the majority of obese individuals.

Table 2. Energy intake and volitional energy expenditure in successful reduced-obese subjects (51)

	All	Women	Men
Intake (kcal/d)	**1381**	**1295**	**1723**
Fat (%)	**24**	**24**	**23**
Protein (%)	**19**	**19**	**18**
Carbohydrate (%)	**55**	**56**	**56**
Physical activity (kcal/d)	**403**	**381**	**498**
Intake-physical activity (kcal/d)	**978**	**914**	**1225**

Another important aspect of weight maintenance in the NWCR was frequent weight monitoring (41). The vast majority of registry participants weighed themselves daily or no less than once a week. Frequent weighing also characterized successful weight maintainers in another clinical trial (42).

Inadequate adherence to a low calorie-low fat diet, failure to employ behavioral strategies to limit food intake, lower dietary consistency, higher dietary variety, and skipping breakfast were all predictors of weight regain in reduced-obese subjects (5, 26). Weight regain was also more common in subjects who did not comply with current physical activity recommendations for weight loss and maintenance, and in those who weighed themselves less frequently (26). Other factors that were found to predict weight regain in registry participants included a higher initial weight, a larger initial weight loss (>30% of body weight), a greater history of weight cycling and a shorter duration of weight loss maintenance (<2y) (26, 43). The presence of a medical trigger for initial weight loss was protective (44). No consistent link was found between subjects' initial weight loss method and the success of weight maintenance (45).

Two subgroups of individuals in the registry merit specific mention. Over the last few years there has been a growing number of NWCR participants who consume a low carbohydrate diet, a trend that probably reflects the growing popularity of this dietary regimen (46). These participants, who still comprise only ~10% of the registry, are characterized not only by consumption of more calories from fat, including saturated fat, but also by consumption of more calories per day, less dietary restraint and less physical activity (47). The basis for the ability of these individuals to remain weight stable is unclear, and may be related to moderation of swings in insulin concentrations by a low-glycemic index diet. In addition, although the small percentage of these subjects in the registry may reflect time trends in the popularity of low carbohydrate diets, it is also possible that the percentage of low carbohydrate dieters who succeed to satisfy registry criteria is smaller than that of low-fat-low- calorie dieters , and that the ones who do succeed are metabolically unique.

Successful weight maintainers who underwent bariatric surgery also display a markedly different, less restrictive lifestyle profile than other registry participants. These individuals report significantly increased consumption of fat and less consumption of carbohydrates. In addition, they eat breakfast less frequently, and are significantly less physically active (33% vs. 62% expend > 2000 kcal per week in physical activity (4). Interestingly, weight regain over time was not more common in either of these subgroups compared to other registry participants (4,47), who were significantly more susceptible to the deleterious effects of lifestyle deviations.

PSYCHOLOGICAL ASPECTS

It has been suggested that the intense physiological pressures produced by successful maintenance of weight loss may be accompanied by significant behavioral and psychological pressures. Keys et al noted that a 25% weight loss in normal-weight men produced extreme negative psychological consequences and short periods of binge eating in one subgroup (48). Other data have also suggested that weight suppression is associated with increased irritability, depression, social introversion, and preoccupation with weight, food, and hunger (49). In addition, psychological perturbations may be the consequence of weight loss itself. As discussed previously, the reduced-obese state shares certain common physiological characteristics with chronic energy deficiency states, in which changes in mood and mental status such as lethargy and depression are characteristic. This highlights the connection between food and mood (50).

Over 90% of NWCR participants reported that weight loss led to improvement in their overall quality of life, level of energy, mobility, general mood and self confidence (51). 30.3% of subjects rated weight loss maintenance as easy, 37.3% as moderately easy and 32.4% as hard. On the other hand, 14% and 20% of subjects reported a worsening in time spent thinking about food and weight, respectively, which suggests that in a minority of subjects weight loss is a cause of psychological stress (50) akin to an eating disorder (52). To study the association between psychological symptoms and weight loss, Klem et al. examined measures of mood, distress, restraint, disinhibition, binging and purging in 784 NWCR participants (53). They found that weight maintainers' levels of distress and depression as well as binge eating and purging rates resembled those of community-based samples. Levels of restraint and disinhibition in weight-reduced subjects were markedly different from those of subjects with binge eating disorder (BED) and bulimia, who scored significantly higher on hunger and disinhibition items and significantly lower on items related to cognitive restraint. Compared to never-obese healthy controls, reduced-obese individuals scored higher on cognitive restraint but similarly on hunger and disinhibition; this pattern was identical to that of individuals who were recently treated for obesity. A small but statistically significant negative correlation was found between the duration of weight loss and global distress, depression and disinhibition, indicating that psychological symptoms may wane with time in successful weight losers. The authors suggested that increased cognitive restraint in reduced-obese individuals is adaptive rather than pathological, enabling active, sustained implementation of behavioral strategies for weight loss maintenance. Notably, a study that was designed to address the concern that frequent weighing, a behavior strategy that was shown to prevent weight regain in post-obese individuals may have untoward psychological effects, did not document such psychological changes (54). Improvement of psychological symptoms (particularly depression, anxiety and binge eating) with weight loss achieved by behavioral weight loss programs was also reported in a review published by the National Task Force on the Prevention and Treatment of Obesity (55).

In comparison to successful weight maintainers who initially lost weight by non-surgical means, higher levels of depression, stress and night eating and lower dietary restraint may characterize similarly successful weight maintainers who attained initial weight loss by bariatric surgery (mostly Roux-en-Y gastric bypass), despite the fact that these individuals tend to employ less stringent behavioral measures to prevent weight regain (4). In addition, although quality of life and psychosocial function generally improve after surgery, results are mixed, with some studies indicating no improvement or a reversion to baseline levels of psychosocial distress (56). The basis for these differences is not clear, and may be related to effects of the post-surgical state, higher rates of baseline psychopathology in patients who undergo bariatric surgery, less physical activity, a less selected sample of individuals who manage to attain weight loss (selection of psychologically healthier individuals may be inherent in the process of sustained weight loss in non-surgical patients) or a protective effect of the cognitive resources that are utilized to sustain stringent lifestyle measures. It is to be noted that candidates for bariatric surgery have morbid obesity and may not be representative of obese patients in general. Further data are required to clarify this issue.

Other studies have examined psychological predictors for weight regain. NWCR and other data suggest that increased levels of dietary disinhibition, binge eating and depressive symptoms and decreased dietary restraint at baseline or follow-up predict weight regain in successful weight losers (26, 53). Notably, internal disinhibition (disinhibition of eating in response to internal cues) rather than external disinhibition was associated with worse outcomes (57). Reporting a desire to lose (rather than maintain) weight at entry into the registry also predicted weight regain; interestingly, an attempt to control weight was also found to be a risk factor for weight regain in an analysis using the National Health and

Nutrition Examination Survey (NHANES) database (58). Depressive symptoms, hunger and disinhibition at baseline and follow-up and decreased dietary restraint were also significantly associated with weight regain in the STOP regain trial (59), and increased disinhibition at baseline and over time was a strong predictor of weight-regain post bariatric surgery (3). These findings stress the importance of both emotional regulation skills and control over eating in long term successful weight loss. A further point is that regular exercise itself has been shown to improve mood and may contribute to well-being and better adherence to the lifestyle changes required for weight maintenance (39).

SUMMARY

'A three-fold cord is not quickly broken'

(Ecclesiastes iv, 12).

Although weight loss maintenance does not appear to cause significant psychological morbidity, it remains a formidable task that involves constant reliance on behavioral strategies and emotional skills to support a new lifestyle based on three components - *restricted eating, strenuous physical activity and frequent self monitoring*. Success requires permanent behavior changes of the kind that is generally recommended in weight loss programs. While difficulty to adhere to these lifestyle measures is probably the main explanation for the high failure rate of weight loss maintenance, certain physiological features of the reduced-obese state, including a reduced NREE due to increased metabolic efficiency and alterations of endocrine and autonomic nervous system function, may oppose successful weight loss and maintenance. Indeed, weight maintenance in reduced-obese individuals may be analogous to a constant state of starvation in never-obese persons.

Many more individuals are successful at losing weight than at sustaining weight loss, implying an ability to adapt to the required lifestyle measures only for limited periods of time. It is important to educate weight losers about the requirement for *long-term* lifestyle changes, and to provide them with strategies to *reinforce* continued implementation of behaviors that were adaptive during their weight loss process. Long-term participation in weight maintenance programs may enable timely detection of risk factors for weight regain and lapses from lifestyle requirements and desired weight. The importance of early detection of weight regain is underscored by the fact that even subjects who regain as little as 1-2 kg one year after initial weight loss are unlikely to lose this excess weight (60). It remains to be seen if measures targeting the physiological features of the reduced-obese state (i.e. leptin) will have a clinically significant role in long-term weight maintenance. As many of these features are prominent in workloads characteristic of a sedentary life style, but can be overcome by more strenuous activity, the importance of regular physical activity cannot be overstressed.

While an effective solution to the problem of weight regain is not yet apparent, there are some encouraging signs. According to NWCR data, implementation of lifestyle measures becomes easier over time (61), and maintaining weight loss for 2-5 years decreases the risk of subsequent weight regain by > 50% (43). Although it cannot be ruled out that this finding reflects "survival of the fittest who lose weight", for whom weight loss maintenance was easier in the first place, it may also reflect habituation to lifestyle measures, leading to decreased requirements for attention or conscious effort to maintain weight. Data on individuals who lose weight by a low carbohydrate diet (46) or bariatric surgery is also encouraging (62), as these methods allow weight maintenance to a degree that is similar to other NWCR participants with less stringent lifestyle measures. While it remains to be seen if the growing number of patients who lose weight by these methods will prove to be better weight maintainers, an additional benefit of bariatric surgery is the achievement of a greater degree of initial weight loss, that enables the patient to continue benefiting from the health advantages of weight loss for a long time despite gradual weight regain.

Finally, in view of the relatively poor outcome of weight loss maintenance, it would seem appropriate to ask the unorthodox question whether attempts at weight loss should be encouraged or withheld until more effective weight maintenance strategies become available. Large epidemiological studies have suggested that weight cycling may be detrimental to physical and mental health, and may increase all-cause and coronary heart disease-specific mortality. Although a subsequent report published by the National Task Force on the Prevention and Treatment of Obesity (63) concluded that the evidence is not sufficiently compelling to override the potential benefits of weight loss in obese individuals, it was stressed that conclusive data regarding the long term health effects of weight cycling are not available, and that obese individuals who undertake weight loss efforts should be ready to commit to lifelong changes in their behavioral patterns, diet and physical activity.

The question becomes even more compelling in view of data regarding the protective role of physical activity in obese patients. It is well documented that physical activity can ameliorate much of the increased morbidity and mortality associated with obesity, although disagreement persists about the degree of protection conferred, with some studies suggesting elimination of this risk and others – lesser degrees of attenuation and improvement of some but not all risk factors (64, 65). It has been shown that the outcome for patients who are "fat and fit" is better than that of patients who are "fat and lazy" and the same as or better than that of patients who are "lean and lazy". The health benefits of exercise may reverse many of the metabolic (and probably psychological) consequences of obesity, even if weight loss is not achieved. Thus, efforts to increase cardio-respiratory fitness in obese patients are undoubtedly warranted, although, considering the inverse relationship between BMI and cardio-respiratory fitness in large epidemiological studies, it remains to be determined if this goal is significantly more attainable than achievement of sustained weight loss.

REFERENCES

[1] Wadden TA, Phelan S. Behavioral assessment of the obese patient. In: Wadden TA, Stunkard AJ. Handbook of obesity treatment. New York: Guilford Press, 2002:186-226.
[2] McGuire MT, Wing RR, Hill JO. The prevalence of weight loss maintenance among American adults. Int J Obes Relat Meab Disord 1999; 23:1314-9.
[3] Karlsson J, Taft C, Ryden A, Sjoström L, Sullivan M. Ten year trends in health-related quality of life after surgical and conventional treatment for severe obesity: the SOS intervention study. Int J Obes 2007;31:1248–61.
[4] Bond DS, Phelan S, Leahey TM, Hill JO, Wing RR. Weight-loss maintenance in successful weight losers: surgical vs non-surgical methods. Int J Obes 2009;33: 173-80.
[5] Wing RR, Phelan S. Long term weight loss maintenance. Am J Clin Nutr 2005;82 (suppl): S222-5.

[6] Berry EM, The reduced obese syndrome and eating disorders. In: Guy-Grand B. Progress in obesity research: 8. London: John Libbey & Co. 1999:777-80.

[7] Rosenbaum M, Leibel RL, Hirsch J. Obesity. N Eng J Med 1997;337:396-407.

[8] Rosenbaum M, Hirsch J, Gallagher DA, Leibel RL. Long-term persistence of adaptive thermogenesis in subjects who have maintained a reduced body weight. Am J Clin Nutr 2008;88:906-12.

[9] Rosenbaum M, Vanderborne K, Goldsmith Rochelle, Simoneau J, Heymsfield S, Joanisse DR, Hirsch J, Murphy E, Matthews D, Segal KR, Leibel RL. Effects of experimental weight perturbation on skeletal muscle wok efficiency in human subjects. Am J Physiol Regul Integr Comp Physiol 2003;285: R183-92.

[10] Foster GD, Eadden TA, Kendrick ZV, Letizia KA, Lander DP, Connill AM. The energy cost of walking before and after significant weight loss. Med Sci Sports Exerc 1995;27:888-94.

[11] Larson-Meyer DE, Newcomer BR, Hunter GR, McLean JE, Hetherington HP, Weinsier RL. Effect of weight reduction, obesity predisposition and aerobic fitness on skeletal muscle mitochondrial function. Am J Physiol Endocrinol Metab 2000;278:E153-61.

[12] Buemann B, Astrup A, Christensen NJ, Madsen J. Effect of moderate cold exposure on 24-h energy expenditure: Similar responses in postobese and nonobese women. Am J Physiol 1992;263:E1040-5.

[13] Rosenbaum M, Hirsch J, Murphy E, Leibel RL. Effects of changes in body weight on carbohydrate metabolism, catecholamine excretion, and thyroid function. Am J Clin Nutr 2000;71:1421–32.

[14] Wyatt HR, Grunwald GK, Seagle HM, Klem ML, McGuire MT, Wing RR, Hill JO. Resting energy expenditure in reduced-obese subjects in the National Weight Control Registry. Am J Clin Nutr 1999;69:1189–93.

[15] Carey DG, Pliego GJ, Raymond RL. Body composition and metabolic changes following bariatric surgery; effects on fat mass, lean mass and basal metabolic .rate: six months to one year follow-up. Obes Surg 2006;16:1602-8.

[16] Leone PA, Gallagher D, Wang J, Heymsfield SB. Relative overhydration of fat-free mass in postobese versus never-obese subjects. Ann N Y Acad Sci 2000; 904:514-9.

[17] de Peuter, R, Withers RT, Brinkman M, Tomas FM, Clark DG. 1992. No differences in rates of energy expenditure between post-obese women and their matched, lean controls. Int J Obes. Relat Metab Disord 1992;16:801–8.

[18] Faraj M, Jones P, Sniderman AD, Cianflone K. Enhanced dietary fat clearance in postobese women. J Lipid Res 2001;42:571-80.

[19] Raben A, Holst JJ, Madsen J, Astrup A. Diurnal metabolic profile after 14 days of an ad libitum high starch, high sucrose or high-fat diet in normal-weight never obese and postobese women. Am J Clin Nutr 2001; 73:177-89.

[20] Martin LF, Klim CM, Vannucci SJ, Dixon LB, Landis JR, LaNoue KF. Alterations in adipocyte adenylate cyclase activity in morbidly obese and formerly morbidly obese humans. Surgery 1990;108:228-34.

[21] Larson DE, Ferraro RT, Robertson DS, Ravussin E. Energy metabolism in weight stable postobese individuals. Am J Clin Nutr 1995;62:735-9.

[22] Benedetti G, Mingrone G, Marcoccia S, Benedetti M, Giancaterini A, Greco AV, Castagneto M, Gasbarrini G. Body composition and energy expenditure after weight loss following bariatric surgery, J Am Coll Nutr 2000;19:270-4.

[23] de Castro Cesar M, de Lima Montebelo MI, Rasera I, de Oliveira AV, Gomes Gonelli PR, Aparecida Cardoso G. Effects of Roux-en-Y gastric bypass on .resting energy expenditure in women. Obes Surg 2008;18:1376-80.

[24] Rosenbaum M, Soldsmith R, Bloomfield D, Magnano A, Weimer L, Heymsfield .S, Gallagher D, Mayer L, Murphy E, Leibel RL. Low-dose leptin reverses .skeletal muscle, autonomic and neuroendocrine adaptations to maintenance of .reduced weight. J Clin Invest 2005;115:3579-86.

[25] Rissanen, P., Franssila-Kallunki, A., and Rissanen, A. Cardiac parasympathetic .activity is increased by weight loss in healthy obese women. Obes Res 2000;9:637–43.

[26] Wing RR, Hill JO. Successful weight loss maintenance. Annu Rev Nutr 2001;21: 323-41.

[27] Manco M, Fernández-Real JM, Valera-Mora ME, Déchaud H, Nanni G, Tondolo V, Calvani M, Castagneto M, Pugeat M, Mingrone G. Massive weight loss decreases corticosteroid-binding globulin

levels and increases free cortisol in healthy obese patients: an adaptive phenomenon? Diabetes Care. 2007;30:1494-500.

[28] Jung R, Campbell R, James W, Callingham B. Altered hypothalamic and sympathetic response to hypoglycaemia in familial obesity. Lancet 1982;1:1043-6.

[29] Astrup A, Buemann B, Christensen NJ, Madsen J. 24-hour energy expenditure and sympathetic activity in postobese women consuming a high-carbohydrate diet. Am J Physiol 1992;262:E282-8.

[30] Löfgren P, Andersson I, Adolfsson B, Leijonhuvuud BM, Hertel K, Hoffstedt J, Arner P. Long-term prospective and controlled studies demonstrate adipose tissue hypercellularity and relative leptin deficiency in the postobese state. J Clin Endocrinol Metab 2005;90:6207-13.

[31] Farooqi IS, Jebb SA, Langmack G, Lawrence E, Cheetham CH, Prentice AM, Hughes IA, McCamish MA, O'Rahilly S. Effects of recombinant leptin therapy in a child with congenital leptin deficiency. N Eng J Med 1999;341:879-84.

[32] Heymsfield SB, Greenberg AS, Fujioka K, Dixon RM, Kushner R, Hunt T, Lubina JA, Patane J, Self B, Hunt P, McCamish M. Recombinant leptin for weight loss in obese and lean adults: a randomized, controlled, dose-escalation trial. JAMA 1999;282:1568-75.

[33] Kern PA, Simsolo RB, Fournier M. Effect of weight loss on muscle fiber type, fiber size, capillarity and succinate dehydrogenase activity in humans. J Clin Endocrinol Metab 1999;84: 4185-90.

[34] Vidal-Puig A, Rosenbaum M, Considine RC, Leiberl RL, Dohm GL, Lowell BB. Effects of obesity and stable weight reduction on UCP2 and UCP3 gene expression in humans. Obes Res 1999;7:133-40.

[35] Mingrone G, Rosa G, Greco AV, Manco M, Vega N, Hesselink MK, Castagneto M, Schrauwen P, Vidal H. Decreased uncoupling protein expression and intramyocytic triglyceride depletion in formerly obese subjects. Obes Res 2003; 11:632-40.

[36] Gorin AA, Phelan S, Wing RR, Hill JO. Promoting long-term weight control: does dieting consistency matter? Int J Obes 2004; 28:278–81.

[37] Raynor HA, Jeffrey RW, Phelan S, Hill JO, Wing RR. Amount of food group variety consumed in the diet and long-term weight loss maintenance. Obes Res 2005;13: 883-90.

[38] Wyatt HR, Grunwald GK, Mosca CL, Klem ML, Wing RR, Hill JO. Long term weight loss and breakfast in subjects in the National Weight Control Registry. Obes Res 2002;10:78-82.

[39] Tate DF, Jeffery RW, Sherwood NE, Wing RR. Long-term weight losses associated with prescription of higher physical activity goals. Are higher levels of physical activity protective against weight regain? Am J Clin Nutr 2007;85:954-9.

[40] Raynor DA, Phelan S, Hill JO, Wing RR. Television viewing and long-term weight maintenance: Results from the National Weight Control Registry. Obesity 2006;14:1816-24.

[41] Butryn ML, Phelan S, Hill JO, Wing RR. Consistent self-monitoring of weight: A key component of successful weight loss maintenance. Obesity 2007;15:3091-6.

[42] Wing RR, Tate DF, Gorin AA, Raynor HA, Fava JL. A self-regulation program .for maintenance of weight loss. N Eng J Med 2006;355:1563-71.

[43] McGuire MT, Wing RR, Klem ML, Lang W. What predicts weight regain in a group of successful weight losers? J Consult Clin Psychol 1999;67:177-85

[44] Gorin AA, Phelan S, Hill JO, Wing RR. Medical triggers are associated with better short- and long-term weight loss outcomes. Prev Med 2004;39:612-6.

[45] McGuire MT, Wing RR, Klem ML, Seagle HM, Hill JO. Long-term maintenance .of weight loss: do people who lose weight through various weight loss methods use different behaviors to maintain their weight ? Int J Obes Relat Metabol Disord 1998;22:572-7.

[46] Dubnov-Raz G, Berry EM. Dietary treatment of obesity. Endocrine Clinics of North America 2008;37:873-86.

[47] Phelan S, Wyatt H, Nassery S, DiBello J, Fava JL. Hill, JO, Wing RR. Three-year weight change in successful weight losers who lost weight on a low-carbohydrate diet. Obesity 2007;15:2470-7.

[48] Keys A, Brozek J, Henschel A, Mickelson, O, Taylor, HL. The biology of human starvation (Vol. 2). Minneapolis: University of Minnesota Press, 1950.

[49] Stunkard AJ, Rush J. Dieting and depression reexamined: A critical review of reports of untoward responses during weight reduction for obesity. Ann Intern Med 1974;81:526-33.

[50] Canetti L, Bachar E, Berry EM. Food and Emotion. Behav Processes 2002;60:157-64.

[51] Klem ML, Wing RR, McGuire MT, Seagle HM, Hill JO. A descriptive study of individuals successful at long-term maintenance of substantial weight. Am J Clin Nutr 1997;66:239-46.

[52] Bonne OB, Bashi R, Berry EM. Anorexia nervosa following gastroplasty in the male. Int J Eating Disorders 1996;19:105-8.

[53] Klem ML, Wing RR, McGuire MT, Seagle M, Hill JO. Psychological symptoms in individuals successful at long-term maintenance of weight loss. Health Psychology 1998;17:336-45.

[54] Wing RR, Tate DF, Gorin AA, Raynor HA, Fava JL, Machan J. "STOP Regain": Are there negative effects of daily weighing? J Consult Clin Psychol 2007;75: 652-6.

[55] National Taskforce for the Prevention and Treatment of Obesity. Dieting and the development of eating disorders in overweight and obese adults. Arch Int Med 2000;160:2581-9.

[56] Elder KA, Wolfe BM. Bariatric surgery: A review of procedures and outcomes. Gastroenterology 2007;132:2253-71.

[57] Niemeier HM, Phelan S, Fava JL, Wing RR. Internal disinhibition predicts weight regain following weight loss and weight loss maintenance. Obesity 2007;15: 2485-94.

[58] Weiss, EC, Galuska, DA, Khan, LK, Gillespie, C, Serdula MK. Weight regain in U.S. adults who experienced substantial weight loss, 1999–2002. Am J Prev Med 2007;33:34–40.

[59] Wing RR, Papandonatos G, Fava JL, Gorin AA, Phelan S, McCaffery J, Tate DF. Maintaining large weight losses: the role of behavioral and psychological factors. J Consult Clin Psychol. 2008;76:1015-21.

[60] Phelan S, Hill JO, Lang W, Dibello JR, and Wing, RR. Recovery from relapse among successful weight maintainers. Am J Clin Nutr 2003;78:1079–84.

[61] Klem ML, Wing RR, Lang W, McGuire MT, Hill JO. Does weight loss maintenance become easier over time? Obes Res 2000;8:438-44.

[62] Canetti L, Berry EM, Elizur Y. Psychosocial predictors of weight loss and psychological adjustment following bariatric surgery and a weight-loss program: the mediating role of emotional eating. Int J Eat Disord 2009;42:109-17

[63] National Task Force on the Prevention and Treatment of Obesity. Weight cycling. JAMA 1994;272:1196-202.

[64] Wing RR, Jakicic J, Neiberg R, Blair SN, Cooper L, Hill HO, Johnson KC, Lewis CE and the Look AHEAD research group. Fitness, fatness and cardiovascular risk factors in type 2 diabetes: Look AHEAD Study. Med Sci Sports Exerc 2007; 39:2107-16.

[65] Lee DC, Sui X, Blair SN. Does physical activity ameliorate the health hazards of obesity? Br J Sports Med 2009;43:49–51.

In: Treatment and Recovery of Eating Disorders
Editors: Daniel Stein and Yael Latzer

ISBN: 978-1-62808-248-7
© 2013 Nova Science Publishers, Inc.

Chapter 6

NURTURING RATHER THAN FEEDING: COMMUNITY-BASED NUTRITION COUNSELING FOR PATIENTS WITH EATING DISORDERS

Moria Golan[tt]

Shahaf, Community Services for the Management of Eating Disorders
Nutrition Sciences Department, Tel Hai Academic College
School of Nutritional Sciences, The Hebrew University of Jerusalem,
Israel

ABSTRACT

High-quality care for patients with eating disorders is a challenge from the perspective of the affected individuals as well as from a health service point of view. This chapter will focus on the every day clinical practice of the dietitian's work with patients with eating disorders across the continuum of care. The dietitian assists patients in increasing information regarding self nurturance, effective vs. destructive behavior and thought patterns as well as developing consciousness-raising and self awareness regarding maladaptive defense patterns. The dietician creates an appropriate emotional climate for growth, helps patients develop open and trusting relationships with food and the body, as well as with others, helps patients engage in new alternatives for expressing feelings, positive self talk, self control and self nurturance using various tools, techniques and approaches. In addition, the nutritionist helps families return to effective communication patterns.

Keywords: eating disorder, nutrition, treatment, registered dietician

---

[tt] E-mail address: moriag@netvision.net.il

INTRODUCTION

High-quality care for patients with eating disorders is a challenge from the perspective of the affected individuals as well as from a health service point of view. This chapter will focus on the every day clinical practice of the nutritionist's work with patients with eating disorders. There are several resources providing practice guidelines for nutrition counselling in eating disorders (1-3). They will be presented here in brief while the skills and the different approaches to be used when addressing these goals will be discussed in detail.

According to the American Dietetic Association (2), "the registered dietician (RD) addresses food related problems—as demonstrated in the patient's thought processes, behaviors and physical status. First, the dietitian assesses the individual's nutritional status, knowledge base, motivation and current eating and behavioral status. In addition, the dietitian assists in medical monitoring of electrolytes, vital signs, physical symptoms, weight, nutritional intake and eating behaviors. The registered dietitian develops the nutrition section of the treatment plan in collaboration with the team and the patient's goals for recovery. The treatment plan is then implemented, with the dietitian supporting the patient in accomplishing the goals set out in the treatment plan. The cornerstones of nutritional treatment are nutrition education, meal planning, establishment of regular eating patterns, and discouragement of dieting" (2). Ideally, the dietitian has continuous contact with the patient throughout the course of treatment or if this is not possible, refers the patient to another dietitian if the patient is transitioning from an inpatient to an outpatient setting (2).

GOALS OF TREATMENT

1) To achieve freedom from the tyranny of the eating disorder
   a. Enroll patients and enhance patient's motivations to cooperate in the restoration of healthy eating patterns and participate in treatment.
   b. Create a wide coalition against the disorder by enlisting family support and providing family counseling, focusing on the appropriate division of responsibility according to the stages in the recovery process.
   c. Assess and treat physical complications.
   d. Restore or maintain healthy weight (at which menses and normal ovulation occur in females, normal sexual drive and hormone levels in males, and normal physical and sexual growth and development in children and adolescents are restored).
   e. Eliminate binge and purge behaviors.

2) To promote healthy eating and activity patterns and improve body image
   a. Provide education regarding healthy nutrition and eating patterns
   b. Correct core dysfunctional thoughts, attitudes, and feelings related to food, eating, dieting, and body image and achieve normal perceptions of hunger and satiety.
   c. Improve body image and body checking

3) To prevent relapse

1. ACHIEVING FREEDOM FROM THE EATING DISORDER'S TYRANNY

A. Enroll patients and enhance patient's motivations to treatment

First steps in the collaborative journey:

From most patients' point of view, nutrition counselling and getting rid of the eating disorders is an unacceptably perilous journey into appetites, desire, and passions, from which they must retreat or risk calamity. Most patients enter treatment due to pressure from family or friends. Thus, a confrontational approach, in which the patient is pressured to accept expert advice and is compelled to change old habits, is recommended only in cases of an immediate threat to one's life. However, since patients tend to see their disorder as an accomplishment rather than as an affliction, such an approach elicits patients' resistance.

The first step for collaborative journey and engaging patients to actively take part in their own recovery can be performed using motivational interview (4) or narrative interview techniques (5,6). Both approaches prefer the interview framework in which the therapist explains and models a collaborative journey towards understanding, developing an obligated stance against the problem, and coping with the journey toward freedom. The therapist adopts a curious, nonjudgmental stance, shows genuine interest in the client's experience, models ability to tolerate confusion, and seeks clarification as needed.

A central notion in the narrative approach is based on Foucault's epigram (7): 'The person is not the problem, the problem is the problem', which can be made more sophisticated by subsequently noting that, once the problem and the person can be conceived of as separable, the problem is neither the person nor the problem, but the person's relationship with the problem. Foucault has suggested that individuals internalize oppressive ideas in cultural, political, and social contexts. Thus, in narrative therapy clinical problems are conceptualized as restraining narratives that are influenced by one's culture and society (6).

A second central notion in the narrative approach is the use of "externalizing conversations" to help clients develop hostility towards the problem. For a narrative therapist, a person does not have eating disorder, but rather the eating disorder has him. When people can linguistically start to be disentangled from the problem and can discover that they, actually, might be otherwise than how "anorexia would have them believe themselves to be" (for example, "worthless"), perhaps other versions of themselves could be foundational to efforts of resistance to, and refutation of, the newly-defined problem.

A third notion in the narrative approach is the realization that the patient who is experiencing the problem is the expert. The change process involves helping clients replace their "dominant stories" with more empowering stories about their lives (8).

The first meeting

This meeting is significant in conveying the "collaborative" nature of the intervention, in which the treatment team, the patient, and family members are working together for one common goal: to achieve freedom from the eating disorder's tyranny and gain freedom of choices in life. At the first meeting, the counselor might be curious about the impact of the problem on the various fields in a patient's life. A beginning of collaborative storing of the patient's entanglement in the disease web is performed (9).

Using motivational interviewing as well as mapping the influence of the eating disorder and externalizing the relationship with the problem, patients typically move from recognizing the problems as a friend to a stage in which they may be considered as a foe (10). Although the patient acknowledges the sense of self-worth and self-control that is attributed to the eating disorder, he/she may also acknowledge that the eating disorder impedes his/her growth and autonomy, increasing interdependence with family members, and interfering with the formation of normal peer relationships. After recognizing the eating disorder as a destructive visitor rather than as an indication of an inherent weakness or a friend, the patient's values and wishes are discussed to elicit motivation to change and express a wish to start the journey to freedom. Freedom is defined by the patient himself, and it may start with freedom from family's 'intrusive caring', may continue with achieving freedom in choice behaviors, freedom from the preoccupied mind and cognition, etc.

At the end of this session, the patient should feel understood, not blamed, respected and assured that steps taken will be negotiated carefully and collaboratively to avoid panic and isolation as long as the patients is committed to recovery.

He also should leave the room with hope that the eating disorder is curable. However, although it is crucial to empower the patient's hopes, the nutritionist should avoid oversimplifying the ease of solving problems, encourage expression and sharing of fears, validating the patient's ambivalence and other feelings about having to cope with the disease (11). The ability to facilitate a commitment toward change is the key challenge of the therapist in the beginning phase of change.

The therapeutic alliance

The therapeutic relationship is a key function in the successful treatment of eating disorders. In general, a patient should feel as though he or she is a valid, significant part of the therapeutic alliance and has a personal role in the recovery process, decreasing the patient's feeling of being threatened or "controlled" through the treatment process. Patients are expected to honestly and accurately disclose information to nutritionists about history, present symptoms, current behaviors, and lapses or relapses, despite the eating disorders' temptations and intimidations. A clear stance should be taken against the problem, emphasizing the main priority of the alliance: aiding the process of recovery towards those issues that have been identified as difficult for the patient (not necessarily clinical symptoms) and what the patient feels are the important goals of treatment. The patient is an active participant and is accountable for his or her actions in the quest for behavior change and improvement of quality of life. Impositions will be operated only in relation to safety issues. In these situations, staff should clearly communicate to patients their intentions to take care of them and not engage in control battles, nor punish patients with aversive techniques.

The degree to which the autonomy of the patient is supported is often the degree to which the patient perceives his or her locus of control within the treatment structure. Whenever possible, dietitians should foster lower environmental control over the patient's behavior and increase responsibility and accountability of the patient for his or her own recovery and well-being. The therapeutic alliance with respect to confidentiality, information provided to parents, and crisis interventions should be discussed in a direct and clear manner during the initial consultation. A healthcare provider does not need to obtain parental consent to provide confidential treatment to any youth, as long as the youth understands the benefits and consequences of the proposed treatment (12). Still, parents are assured that if there is deterioration, they will be notified. If the progress of recovery is slow, a decision may be made to increase the level of care. This decision should involve the patient, the family, and/or support persons, so that they are allowed to be accountable for their actions and facilitation of recovery.

B. Creating a wide coalition against the disorders

The nature of eating disorders dictates the necessity to create a wide and strong coalition against the disorder with collaborative work employed by the interdisciplinary team (13). When working in community-based services, the nutritionist must communicate effectively with outward health care givers. If the dietitian does not communicate effectively with other in or outward team members that co-treat the patient, a split among therapists with respect to beliefs or approaches may occur, and the strength of the wide coalition may be cracked. This may nurture the eating disorder and weaken the patient's battle. A cohesive team of health care providers, who may even span various organizations in the community, allows the youth and family to see that everyone is on the same side working against the eating disorder.

The dietitian is obliged to support treatment goals within the guidelines of the nutrition care process and remain faithful to the messages and communication style agreed on by the team (2). Family members are a primary resource in recovery if they are assisted in learning how to cope during the crisis, to deal with the effects of the eating disorder, and to practice supportive parenting approaches. To enroll parents into the coalition against the eating disorder, therapists express curiosity about those aspects with which the disease intimidated relationships within the family and how food, weight, and health are being abused by the eating disorder. The therapist then invites parents to be part of the coalition against the disorder, a coalition in which the patient is the protagonist, the multidisciplinary staff is the guiding map, and the family is an auxiliary ego. Parents present the third rib of the alliance, and thanks to their encouragement, the child's persistence in the difficult battle is maintained. Individuals and family members are invited to consider ways in which they can gather their strength together to resist the problems. The family's/parents' role is tailored to the stage of illness and to the patient's age, in accordance with the therapeutic alliance. Nutrition counseling is focused on nutrition education as well as dividing responsibility according to the stages in the recovery process. Deciding how the parents can best support their child is most important in the process of recovery.

Parents' role may differ according to the institute's approach
In some places, parents might be in charge of child eating and activity patterns, while in others, the family will act as auxiliary ego and mainly has a supporting role.

The Maudsley approach, for instance (14, 15), involves the family from the outset of treatment and relies heavily on parent involvement in the re-feeding of the child with an eating disorder. In this approach, parents take on the nurses' role and have a primary role in confronting pro-anorexic or bulimic behaviors. Parents are encouraged to separate the eating disorder from the child while performing this task, and blame the eating disorder rather than the child, therefore minimizing the escalation of expressed emotion. Concurrently the siblings are recruited to ease the patient's distress, as well, in the same way. Different strategies are used to coach parents in performing their roles (15, 16). Once safe eating and weight are achieved through parental intervention, responsibility for these issues is gradually handed back to the adolescent (17, 18).

The Maudsley approach consists of three clearly defined phases, usually during one year of treatment: 1. Weight restoration 2. Returning control over eating to the adolescent 3. Establishing healthy adolescent identity. This approach, however, is not for the faint-hearted; some careers are somewhat skeptical and reluctant to be involved in family work (19). Moreover, oftentimes parents and patients are trapped in the care-taking position or the ill person position, respectively. The success of this approach seems to depend on the successful motivation of parents to take on this task and see it through, while simultaneously supporting the processes of adolescent development as they re-emerge, which is well documented (20). When sufferers feel "invisible" in their families, this type of intense involvement may suddenly act as a psychological facilitator in improving the overall relationship. It may help to make the sufferer feel seen, cared about, and loved, but this approach does not fit all families. Such an approach has disadvantages for families in which high levels of hostility or criticism toward the AN adolescent are present. Engaging these families in treatment can be a challenge (21).

Based on a solution-oriented approach, Nardone et al. (22) presented a model to treat eating with a systemic orientation. The authors suggest that direct or indirect attempts by the family to make the patient eat paradoxically increase his/her tendency to deny food and end up complicating the problem instead of solving it. They suggest that the family start a "conspiracy of silence," i.e., stop intervening or even mentioning the problem. In giving this prescription, the authors emphasize the importance of avoiding criticism of past actions, or any implication that the family is somehow guilty. Instead, counsellors use injunctive language, give positive connotations, and above all, avoid negative formulations, praising the parents for having been so patient at helping the daughter, being there for her, working to avoid the situation. Although it may seem strange, parents are asked to start observing without intervening. They must absolutely avoid talking about the problem. When followed, this prescription, as the authors report, stops the usual solutions attempted by the family. This often leads to surprising improvement in the eating disorder symptoms because it interrupts a retroactive vicious circle between the family and the young woman, which had been nourishing the problem (22).

Other approaches suggest that eating issues and the eating disorder's front should be managed between the nutritionist and the patient, while parents should revisit their primary role – nurturing rather than feeding. Parents are invited to sidestep eating disorder talks and arguments,reflect the child's difficulties, and empower him to persist in his battle, framing the conversation within the context of the life course, emotional life, and core values (23). This approach promotes sustained autonomy around food with the notion that maintaining a sense of control is often a key dynamic in these patients.

If the child fails to achieve his objectives, he is proposed to ask his parents' help in confronting the ED. According to this approach, in order to help the child regain control of his eating and life, he should be the main agent of change. This relies on the assumption that patients with eating disorders possess a powerful potential for change, given that they receive the necessary nutrients from their environment, although they occasionally engage in self-destructive behaviors (24). Obeying authoritarian images results in improvement in nutritional status but does not promote internalization of self-nurturance and self-control. The clinicians' task is to evoke and strengthen the child's inner resourcefulness and take the lead in the therapeutic process (25-27).

The nutrition counseling focuses on the therapeutic alliance between the therapist and the patient against the illness, and parents are considered as an auxiliary ego unless the child is asking them for a more active role. Their role might range from serving the food and confronting pro-eating disorders thoughts and behaviors to a minor responsibility where parents only make sure the food is available and serve as meal companions who model for the child normal eating behaviors. Families need to be kept up-to-date on the process, progress, and plans during treatment. They need to be informed directly, not just through their child, in order to avoid misinterpretation and misunderstanding. Whenever the nutritionist meets the parents, it is useful to meet with both parents and help them work as a team. This also helps to prevent secrecy, which is especially important if parents are separated or divorced. The young person feels relieved and valued when separated parents can put aside their differences in order to help. Parents are instructed to set rational limits with respect to the house food and cooking, and although it may upset the youth, in the long run, this can actually lead to a sense of control over the power of the eating disorder.

Whatever the institute policy is with respect to parents' role, parents should create a "good enough" environment. Explain the ""non-blaming" philosophy in which "the problem is the problem and not the patient, nor the parents."

Since the child reenacts conflicts, memories, and unconscious experiences with his parents, staff are often required to address parents' deprivations and introjections during the process of recovery. Direct discussion about self-blame, feelings of shame, and incompetence might be helpful as well as empowering to parents, reframing the admission to the program as a way to take responsibility - a step that reflects the parents' ability to help the child take an appropriate stance against the illness. Therapists should also help parents overcome the illusion of having a fast "cure" and the failure to "fix" the child (28).

Dietitians should provide parents with concrete instruction to follow, such as a meal plan, as well as prescriptions regarding what they should do under various circumstances during conflict at home over food and eating. Parents are asked to act as appropriate role models at home, demonstrating healthy eating and activity patterns, eating balanced meals and snacks, and modeling self care and positive body image, while avoiding diet talks (29-30). The dietitians exhibit openness and transparency when dealing with both the patient and family. Questions are welcomed, and the patient and family are encouraged to ask about anything that concerns them.

C. Assess and treat physical complications

Assessment

A careful assessment of the patient's history, symptoms, behaviors, and mental status is the first step in making a diagnosis of an eating disorder (1). For patients aged 20 years and younger, an individually appropriate range for expected weight and goals for weight and height may be determined by considering measurements and clinical factors, including current weight, bone age estimated from DEXA, menstrual history (in adolescents with secondary amenorrhea), mid-parental heights, assessments of skeletal frame, and growth charts.

History of restrictive and binge eating and exercise patterns and their changes, purging, and other compensatory behaviors should be made, as well as listing core attitudes regarding weight, shape, and eating, and associated psychiatric conditions. Most units use structured forms and various validated assessment tools like the EDEQ, EAT-26, EDI-2, and others (1). Many dietitians use assessment tools as a way to map the problems' influences and revisit these tools with the patients after 6 and 12 months, discussing and collaboratively researching the journey from being tangled in the eating disorder's arms to freedom. A family history of eating disorders or other psychiatric disorders, including alcohol and other substance use disorders, a family history of obesity, family interactions in relation to the patient's disorder, and family attitudes toward eating, exercise, and appearance are all relevant to the assessment. It is important to identify family stressors whose amelioration may facilitate recovery. It is essential to involve health professionals who routinely work with the patient.

Dietitians routinely assess young patients' status in relation to growth pattern, blood pressure, and heart rate, as well as monitor laboratory analyses if it is their role in the absence of physician at the clinic. According to the position of the American Dietetic Association (2), "dietitians demonstrate competence at assessing the physiologic effects associated with malnutrition and assisting the medical team member with monitoring laboratory values, vital signs, and physical symptoms" (31). Table 1 is application of Thomas D, a summation of the factors that should be included in dietetic assessment of patients with eating disorders (31).

Table 1. Factors to include in a dietetic assessment of eating disorder patient

Weight and eating history	From birth to present day; identifying periods of dieting, normal behavior, and times when food intake has been stressful
Current eating habits	Type, pattern, and format of food eaten. Particular food rules and food avoidance
Daily activity patterns	Level of energy expenditure
Binging and purging behaviors	Assess frequency of binges, vomiting, or laxative abuse
Present weight, height, body mass, percentage weight loss	Accurate measurement is important. This may be threatening for the patient, but dietitian should be firm about its necessity.
Body composition	Bone density, anthropometry
Blood chemistry and hematology	Low potassium levels and/or high amylase levels may suggest vomiting or laxative abuse
Issues around growth, illness	Previous points on growth chart should be requested, menstruation pattern.
Nutrition knowledge	Food rules, calorie restrictions
Family weight and issues around food	Helps to assess individual normal weight and food rules within the family
Body image	Body image disparagement and dissatisfaction may be accompanied by body shape avoidance or "fixing" attempts.
Readiness for change	Is the patient talking to you because he/she wants to, or because he/she has been brought by others?

Physical complications

Physical complications are brought to the patient's attention and are incorporated as part of the motivational enhancement talks. To reverse the medical effects of food-related problems, the dietitian provides medical nutrition therapy. Most symptoms (hypotension, bradycardia, hypothermia, dry skin, hypercarotenemia, lanugo, acrocyanosis, and atrophy of the breasts) will be spontaneously reversed when body weight and menses are restored.

Cardiovascular complications

If the dietitian finds marked orthostatic hypotension with an increase in pulse of 20 BPM or a drop in standing blood pressure of 20 mmHg, bradycardia <40 bpm, tachycardia >110 BPM, or an inability to sustain core body temperature, patient must be advised to go through hospital check up to prevent onset of medical instability (1-3). High prevalence of hematologic abnormalities were reported in women with eating disorders (1). Dietitians routinely monitor vital signs and blood tests, refer to physician, or assist with appropriate dietary advice.

Electrolyte abnormalities

Electrolyte abnormalities such as hypokalemia, hyponatremia, and metabolic acidosis or alkalosis may accompany frequent vomiting or laxative use. Although the results may be normal despite frequent vomiting or laxative use, an elevated bicarbonate level combined with hypokalemia, which usually does not occur with caloric restriction alone, can be a useful clinical clue that the patient is surreptitiously vomiting or using diet pills.

Symptoms associated with self-induced vomiting such as swelling of the parotid and submandibular glands are also reversed when vomiting is stopped, however, abnormal dentition, perimolysis (loss of dentin on the lingual and colossal surfaces of the teeth), and abrasions on the dorsum of the hand (caused by scraping against the incisors during attempts at vomiting) may be remnant (32). Patients often complain of dizziness, fatigue, and decreased energy, and their serum biochemical parameters may be normal or may show a hypokalemic, hypochloremic metabolic alkalosis. These changes have been attributed to chronic intravascular volume contraction associated with secondary hyperaldosteronism as a compensatory response to the dehydration (1). Most patients with normal weight bulimia nervosa appear to be able to tolerate these changes more readily than patients struggling with anorexia nervosa purging type. The use of oral potassium supplements (K-Dur, 2 mmol/kg a day, divided in three equal doses) in the setting of normal renal function may replete the total body potassium stores and decreases the serum hypokalemia. Where the electrolyte disturbance is more severe, a short admission to a medical unit to correct the metabolic changes may be necessary (12). In the case of hypokalemic, hypochloremic metabolic alkalosis, Pinzon & Beimers (12) reported that the best intravenous solution is 0.9% sodium chloride, with a maintenance dose of potassium chloride to restore effective intravascular volume and serum osmolality. Hyponatremia can occur with excess water intake, with inappropriate regulation of anti-diuretic hormone or severely abusing laxatives. Fluid limitation should be considered with the medical team.

Gastrointestinal complaints

Intestinal dilatation from chronic severe constipation and diminished intestinal motility as a result of chronic laxative abuse or withdrawal may be associated with either anorexia nervosa or bulimia nervosa. Both are manageable when implementing a structured meal plan with balanced nutrients (32). Common side effects of laxative and vomiting withdrawal are constipation, fluid retention, feeling bloated, and temporary weight gain. Most people suffer from these symptoms for 1 to 3 weeks after withdrawal.

Pro-motility agents such as metoclopramide or natural products may be useful for bloating and abdominal pains that occur during refeeding and purging behaviors in some patients. Gastroesophageal reflux (GERD) is also often reported by those who vomit. GERD usually occurs because the lower esophageal sphincter (LES) opens at the wrong time or does not close properly. Thus, stomach acid moving backward from the stomach into the esophagus - gastroesophageal reflux. Long-lasting reflux of stomach acid damages the tissue lining the esophagus, causing inflammation and pain and sometimes even cancer (36). Lifestyle modifications thought to be effective include elevating the head of the bed, reducing fat intake, quitting smoking, and remaining upright for three hours after meals. The dietitian can help the patient identify those foods that worsen the GERD symptoms. Some of the foods reported by patients include citrus fruits, chocolate, drinks or foods with caffeine, fatty and fried foods, garlic and onions, mint flavorings, spicy foods, tomato-based foods, like spaghetti sauce, chili, and pizza. The physician might recommend medication such as antacids and antirefluxants (e.g., alginic acid), which are viable treatment options for milder forms of GERD. A combination of the two therapies may be more effective than antacids alone. Histamine H2-receptor antagonists (H2RAs) have been shown to decrease gastric acid and can be used as premedication by patients who are able to predict symptom occurrence.

Stunted growth

Stunted growth with decreased adult final height is one of the most common long-term complications in children and adolescents with anorexia nervosa. There are reports of "catch-up growth," particularly when target weight is based on the pre-morbid height percentile, but complete catch-up growth may not be achieved (33). In the case of bulimia nervosa, linear growth complications are much less of an issue. The dietitian often challenges the patient's wishes to catch up growth and expresses curiosity about his/her wishes to favor time and act against the eating disorder and the resulting stunted growth. Some patients are motivated through reflection on pubertal development using Tanner staging.

Amenorrhea

The loss of normal estrogen levels causes amenorrhea and contributes to the development of osteoporosis, a serious side-effect of anorexia nervosa (34).

Delayed puberty is one of the cardinal features of anorexia nervosa during adolescence. The progesterone challenge is a common method to evaluate an adolescent with primary amenorrhea. The dietitian should involve the physician or gynecologist to address amenorrhea after weight restoration is achieved.

Osteopenia and osteoporosis

To address osteopenia and osteoporosis, body weight restoration and return of menses are main goals. Calcium (1,500 mg/day) with vitamin D (400 IU/day) supplements have shown some effectiveness, as have selective estrogen receptor modulators in women (35). The literature offers no definitive answer to the question about the potential benefits of using estrogen supplementation via oral contraceptives for improving bone accretion or preventing the development of osteopenia or osteoporosis. Oral contraceptives are usually incorporated with older and chronic patients.

D. Restore or maintain healthy weight

During the last few years, there has been considerable debate about the ethics of involuntarily feeding patients with anorexia nervosa (37-39). There is general agreement that children and adolescents who are severely malnourished and in grave medical danger should be re-fed, involuntarily if necessary, but that every effort should be made to gain their cooperation as cognitive function improves (1-3). Nutritional rehabilitation is aimed at promoting metabolic recovery, restoring a healthy body weight and growth, and improving eating habits and psychological behavior.

Intake levels

Total intake levels range from 30-40 kcal/kg/day during the first days to 70-100 kcal/kg/day. Intake is progressively increased while monitoring vital signs (Table 2 and 3 from ref. 1).

Anorexia Nervosa
a. Nutritional Rehabilitation

Help the patient to resume eating and to gain weight.
- Establish a target weight and rates of weight gain: a healthy goal weight is the weight at which normal menstruation and ovulation are restored or, in premenarchal girls, the weight at which normal physical and sexual development resumes.
- Usually begin intake at 30–40 kcal/kg per day (approximately 1,000–1,600 kcal/day); intake may be increased to as high as 70–100 kcal/kg per day.
- Reserve nasogastric feeding for rare patients with extreme difficulty recognizing their illness, accepting the need for treatment, or tolerating guilt accompanying active eating even when done to sustain life.
- Help the patient limit physical activity and caloric expenditure according to food intake and fitness requirements.
- Monitor vital signs; food and fluid intake/output; electrolytes; signs of fluid overload (e.g., presence of edema, rapid weight gain, congestive heart failure); or other evidence of a serious refeeding syndrome.
- Address gastrointestinal symptoms, particularly constipation, bloating, and abdominal pain.
- Provide cardiac monitoring, especially at night, for children and adolescents who are severely malnourished.
- Add vitamin and mineral supplements; for example, phosphorus supplementation may be particularly useful to prevent serum hypophosphatemia.
- Create a milieu that incorporates emotional nurturance and a combination of reinforcers that link exercise, bed rest, and privileges to target weights, desired behaviors, and feedback concerning changes in weight and other observable parameters.

3. Bulimia Nervosa
a. Nutritional Rehabilitation

→ Optimal weights should be determined and restored for all patients, since deviance from optimal weight may contribute to sustaining bulimia symptoms.

→ Provide nutritional counseling to help the patient
- establish a pattern of eating regular, nonbinge meals,
- increase the variety of foods eaten,
- correct nutritional deficiencies,
- minimize food restriction, and
- encourage healthy but not excessive exercise patterns.

Dietitians can help patients choose their own meals and can provide a structured meal plan that ensures nutritional adequacy and that none of the major food groups are avoided.

Nasogastric feeding is reserved for hospitalized patients with extreme difficulty in recognizing their illness, accepting the need for treatment, or tolerating guilt accompanying active eating even when done to sustain life. In contrast to the in-patient setting, in a community-based setting, food is negotiable and its quality and quantities are tailored to patients' readiness. Although the target is to address the DRI recommendations, with respect to intake of dietary proteins, fats, and carbohydrates, 15–20% protein of the daily energy intake consisting of 30% fats and 50–55% carbohydrates, in view of the approach presented here, it is actually subjugated to the patient's willingness to take this advice. Thus, sometimes the initial focus is on maximizing the nutritional value of what is eaten, which can improve health and feelings of well-being, even before weight is gained. Legitimate food allergies and patients' religious and cultural practices should be considered and discussed to limit patient rationalizations for restricted eating. For weight maintenance, Kaye et al. (40) found that weight-restored patients with anorexia nervosa often require 200–400 calories more than sex, age, weight, and height-matched control subjects to maintain their weight. The energy wasting of malnourished anorexia nervosa patients results in higher than normal resting energy expenditure (41).

The physician in most units monitors the blood tests regularly (its frequency depends on the setting and patient's position), while the dietitian reintroduces food gradually, starting at only 300-400 calories above the patient's preadmission daily intake to reduce the risk of refeeding syndrome and to support adherence. Caloric increases ranging from 300 to 500 calories per week are given to achieve the expected weight gain of 0.5-1 kg.

Laboratory tests are ordered and reviewed for the first 3 to 4 weeks but become less important as the patient becomes used to eating.

Refeeding syndrome

Refeeding syndrome involves a host of fluid and electrolyte derangements and leads to a constellation of cardiac, neurologic, and hematologic complications, including sudden, unexpected death, that occur in the weeks after the initiation of nutritional rehabilitation (42). The common pathway to develop refeeding syndrome may be ascribed to hypophosphatemia, but may include fluxes in potassium, magnesium, and sodium, acting concurrently, synergistically, and deleteriously with the classic shift in phosphorus levels (43). Most of the serious consequences from refeeding are seen with severe hypophosphatemia (serum phosphorus less than 1.0 mg/dl) (43). Admission to hospital for monitoring and management of refeeding syndrome is recommended in such conditions. Nutrition management of patients at risk for refeeding syndrome involves close monitoring of their symptoms and electrolyte status, particularly their phosphate and magnesium levels (2). Orenstein et al. (45) have found that serum phosphorus tended to improve dramatically within 24 to 48 hours when 250 mg to 500 mg per dose were administered. However, with oral supplements, there is the potential for inconsistent gastrointestinal absorption and diarrhea. Therefore, for individuals with severe hypophosphatemia, it is recommended to use intravenous supplementation at a dose of 20 to 30 mg/kg/day, in divided doses, usually infused over 6 hours (45).

Vitamin and mineral supplement

Some approaches suggest inclusion of vitamin and mineral supplements. To avoid deficiencies due to imbalanced electrolytes (for instance, excessive zinc ingestion may cause copper deficiency resulting in a variety of neurological symptoms), a broad vitamin and mineral replacement is suggested. Others prefer to encourage patients not to rely on external supplementation, but rather on regular foods. However, when hypophosphatemia or extreme hypokalemia are observed, phosphorus or potassium supplementation may be particularly useful to prevent cardiac arrhythmias.

Weighing and weight gain

The degree and rate of weight gain is based on psychological as well as medical considerations. Although the aim of most nutritional rehabilitation programs is to maintain a weight gain of approximately 400–800 g/week (1, 46), frequently the rate of weight gain is much slower due to perception that "if you cannot fight them, join them." Davies and Jaffa (46) suggest that the rate of weight gain should be fast enough to avoid negative "institutionalization" effects of inpatient stay but not so fast as to cause overwhelming anxiety to the patient, nor to result in an unacceptable risk of developing refeeding syndrome. Usually in the outpatient setting, patients are weighed once per week, and after weight regaining and stabilization, this may be reduced to once in two weeks, and then to once per month. Patients with bulimia are normally weighed once per week or once in two weeks. Some have suggested to adopt a strategy of limited weighing or to weigh patients with their back to the scale, in order to minimize the psychological effect of weighing. Others argue that patients should acclimatize to the notion of their weight, thus weighing in a modest frequency is part of desensitization (30).

Patients who require much lower caloric intakes or are suspected of artificially increasing their weight by fluid loading should be weighed in the morning after they have voided and are wearing only underwear; their fluid intake should also be carefully monitored (1). Urine specimens obtained at the time of a patient's weigh-in may need to be assessed for specific gravity to help ascertain the extent to which the measured weight reflects excessive water intake.

Meal Plan

The dietitian explains to the patients that they will start off with small meals and gradually build up to larger meals. Patients are introduced to such de-sensitization practices to decrease fear of food groups, such as fats. When patients panic upon receiving an increased-calorie diet, clinicians may limit negotiating by pointing out the endless desire of the eating disorder to bargain and request special considerations. Patients are encouraged to review the meal support guidelines and expectations before making a commitment, and are reminded that they may call for support if they encounter difficulties while performing the tasks. Daily intake is divided into three meals and two or three snacks. In order to control both binge eating and purging behavior, a structured meal plan is advised. Attention is paid to scheduling and meal content, two factors that are critical to establishing control of urges to binge.

Liquid nutritional supplementation

Calorie dense nutritional supplements (such as Ensure and Scandishake) are used as meal replacements for those who find it easier to exercise eating and control and consume more energy with less volume of food.

Gradually, patients should be exposed to regular food to avoid liquid feeding "addictions."

After most of the weight has been regained, in order to extend food variety, the dietitian may offer the patients to start with a "surprise menu" – or gradual exposure to foods. In this strategy, the dietitian brings a new food to every session, and the patient has to eat it as part of his agreement to enter the "game." Whenever the patient is overwhelmed by the eating disorder's threatening, the therapist focuses on Socratic questioning using questions such as, "Do you consider your growth arrest a problem? How do you think it will impact your every day life?" Do you want to try and limit the influence of the eating disorder on your life?"

Although it is an anxiety-provoking "game," it gets easier over time, and patients find it very helpful. Concurrently, a restaurant outing with the dietitian may be implemented to extend patients' social options.

Artificial Nutrition

Severe malnutrition could require the use of artificial nutrition to rapidly correct dangerous clinical conditions and to reverse medical complications, however this area is beyond the scope of this chapter.

Meal support therapy

Therapeutic meal support has been recognized as one of the cornerstones of treatment in specialized eating disorder programs (47, 48). It is a form of emotional and physical support provided to a person struggling with an eating disorder before, during, and after meals and snacks in an effort to increase the struggling person's success with meal/snack completion. Effective meal support is not just sitting down and watching someone eat. It is an active process that needs to be implemented with compassion and care (49). The clinician eats appropriate meals or snacks (normal amounts of food, balanced meal) with the patient.

According to the different stages of independency, the clinician's role is changed. In the beginning, the clinician sets up the trays (opens all containers), and eats with the patients while carrying out anti-anorexic/bulimic conversation as well as distraction techniques throughout the meals, in order to help the patient manage the preoccupied fears endorsed by the ED. The clinician promotes limited time meals starting from 50 to 20 minutes, depending on the patient's status. Following meals, to counter psychological and physical discomfort, the clinician may suggest a very slow walk, a distracting game, movie or any other post-meal support. With those wishing to purge, clinicians might advice deep breathing and other relaxation techniques lasting at least one hour following meals and 30 minutes following snacks. Gradually, patients are given increased levels of responsibility. They are encouraged to choose their own foods and serve their own portions while acknowledging the potential misperception that emerges by starvation and cognitive alternation, which reinforces a difference between subjective and objective measures of intake. The dietitian provides expert guidance on changes in the prescribed meal plan in order to stabilize body weight and identify individualized "appropriate" portions while encouraging variety, spontaneity, and increased flexibility.

Physical activity

Physical activity should be adapted according to the food intake and energy expenditure of the patient, taking into account the patient's bone mineral density and cardiac function (1). For the severely underweight patient, exercise should be restricted and always carefully supervised and monitored. Once a safe weight is achieved, the focus of an exercise program should be on the patient's gaining physical fitness as opposed to expending calories (1). An exercise program should involve exercises that are not solitary, are enjoyable, and have endpoints that are not determined by time spent expending calories or changing weight and shape. Sports such as soccer, basketball, volleyball, or tennis are examples. Some people diagnosed with eating disorders utilize compulsive exercise as a compensatory behavior to prevent weight gain. To manage this problem, patients should have a prescription for the amount and a specific schedule of physical activity that is allowed based on factors such as history of exercise abuse, current weight level, and medical risk factors.

E. Eliminate binge eating and purging behaviors and laxative abuse

Those who engage in binge eating and purging behaviors, as well as in laxative abuse, often find themselves swollen from excessive water retention and delayed bowel motility. The nutritionist may offer the patient several strategies to withdraw from these destructive behaviors, inviting the patient to choose which track fits better rather than challenging the patient's conflict with control issues. The patient may choose to implement a gradual breaking away from purging or abusing laxatives or to stop at once. The dietitian provides companionship and support when encountering the maladaptive behaviors, suggesting various strategies to distract negative emotions and cope with stressful situations.

Developing a pattern of normal eating, with three meals and appropriate snacks per day, is crucial in breaking chaotic eating behaviors (2). This allows the individual to become reacquainted with internal hunger and satiety cues while also changing behaviors, in order to move away from restriction and the binge–purge cycle. Energy intake should initially be based on the maintenance of weight to help limit hunger because this can be a trigger for a binge. Purging behaviors do not completely inhibit use of calories from the binge; an average retention of 1,200 kcal occurs from binges of various sizes and contents, and laxatives are ineffective at minimizing energy absorption but do substantially increase water losses (50). To promote normal bowel function, a fiber-rich diet is recommended. Patients are advised not to restrict fluid intake to avoid dehydration and worsening of constipation, and those with normal ranged weight may benefit from addition of regular physical activity, which assists in regulating bowel function. Binge eating is often precipitated by triggers such as negative affect, with overeating being identified as a tension-releasing coping mechanism, used to deal with emotional distress (51). Individuals with binge eating often engage in various behaviors to attempt to control their weight. For some patients, giving up severe dietary restrictions and restraints appears to increase binge-eating behavior, which is often accompanied by compensatory purging.

Nutrition education and cognitive behavioral therapy

Nutrition education and cognitive behavioral therapy (CBT) are two core skills implemented with these behaviors. Nutrition education encompasses principles of normal eating, psychological and physiological effects of starvation, nutritional requirements, and metabolism. It also counters misconceptions about body weight regulation and consequences of purging behavior. Patients are taught that inducing diarrhea by laxatives does not significantly change the absorption of food in the body, since laxatives work near the end of the bowel, where they primarily affect absorption of water and electrolytes (like sodium and potassium). Thus, they work after most of the nutrients from the food have been absorbed into the body and what appears to be weight loss is actually dehydration or water deprivation. Moreover, when bulk agents, like Metamucil and Colace are used as directed (with large amounts of water), they don't have the same physical effects on the bowel as the stimulant and osmotic laxatives. However, when these bulk agents are misused, they have the same psychological consequences as regular laxatives.

Cognitive behavior techniques are implemented to help the patient identify maladaptive behaviors and the associated cognitions. The therapist's first task is to help patients see that their dieting attempts are a problem since they are a major cause of preoccupation with thoughts about food and eating, they are anxiety provoking, and they restrict the way in which patients can eat. Rigid dietary rules are coupled with the tendency to react in an extreme and negative fashion to the intermittent breaking of these rules.

Patients are encouraged to self-monitor their daily behavior and thinking patterns, mapping the antecedents of maladaptive behaviors. Learning and utilizing skills is an important component of CBT for eating disorders, and it is likely that effective skill use facilitates symptom reduction. Usually, with CBT for eating disorders, patients are taught skills (e.g., thought restructuring, stimulus control techniques) and are asked to practice these skills between sessions (52).

Food records are the most common instrument used to identify and address maladaptive behaviors and cognitions. Self-monitoring is a central feature of treatment for eating disorders. It is recognized as a vehicle of data collection regarding a patient's dietary intake as well as associations between food intake, distressing situations, thoughts, emotions, and body image experiences. Patients are encouraged to monitor in the moment versus allowing significant time between an experience and recording the details of the experience. Food records may be formed in various levels of complexity. Initially, they may include details about time, place, companionship, and content of food eaten, as well as information regarding binge/purge episodes. Further on, they may focus on monitoring hunger and satiety cues, emotional eating, and obsessive compulsive rites related to food and eating. They may focus on qualitative as well as quantitative information. It is important that the dietitian review self-monitoring with the patient so that the patient can see the value of adhering to this aspect of the program, not only for improvements in eating disorder symptoms, but also for their overall quality of life, through increased knowledge of themselves and how they perceive and experience the world (53).

The cyclic nature of bulimic symptoms is perpetuated by negative effects and core beliefs. Negative effects are considered to be an antecedent to binge bulimic behaviors, including binge eating (54). *Cognitive restructuring* confronts dysfunctional cognitive schemas, beliefs, and interpretations regarding dieting and nutrition, as well as the relationship between eating patterns and physical symptoms. Food records are collaboratively discussed with the patient, and problem solving strategies are suggested. Since binge eating disorder and bulimia nervosa share common psychological and behavioral characteristics, binge eating disorder treatment has been highly influenced by bulimia nervosa treatment literature that encompasses cognitive behavior therapy and interpersonal psychotherapy (2). Normalization of eating behaviors is a primary goal, rather than weight loss, at any cost.

Weight maintenance may be a pivotal accomplishment and should be recognized as such by both the nutritionists and the patient because this can be an indicator of fewer or decreased binge episodes. In addition, appropriate physical activity components and leisure activities may provide stress management and also assist with energy balance.

2. PROMOTE HEALTHY THINKING, EATING, AND ACTIVITY PATTERNS AND IMPROVE BODY IMAGE

A. Normalizing eating and activity patterns

With weight restoration, food choices increase, food hoarding decreases, and obsessions about food decrease in frequency and intensity, although they do not necessarily disappear. Gradual incorporation of "forbidden or feared foods" into the diet is an important goal in nutrition counseling to increase variety of food eaten and counter restricted behaviors that limit patients' possibilities. During this process, patients are overwhelmed with concerns about their bodies. They describe a fear of gaining weight and may often state that they would rather be dead than fat.

Desensitization

Desensitization is a well known process in behavioral therapy. At the beginning of the treatment process, patients are aided in creating a "feared or forbidden foods" list in which they rank feared foods according to intensity of fear surrounding the particular foods (55). Through the treatment process, patients are assisted in neutralization of such fear through the practice of mindfulness and exposure therapy using a graduated hierarchy of progressively more feared foods. Mindfulness is the guiding factor for exposure therapy in that it sets the stage for a calm, focused, de-escalated, and nonjudgmental cognitive set for the experience. Exposure to other anxiety-provoking activities such as eating in a restaurant or eating with friends is often conducted, first verbally and then by modeling and simulating grocery shopping or eating out in restaurants. These situations allow the patient to practice utilizing healthy coping skills, such as problem-solving and mindfulness (55). The dietitian at this stage provides less supervision and more collaboratively researches the world of desires, fantasies, and boundaries with the patient. Food records are used to observe patient's tendencies, avoidance, and disinhibition behaviors. Various problem-solving strategies are advised.

Nutrition education

Nutrition education is a core feature in dietitian's role when breaking through these habits. Patients feel understood and respected when dietitians provide knowledge about basic food groups, the food guide pyramid, healthy eating habits, nutrient content of foods, as well as physiological and psychological consequences of restriction and semi-starvation. The psychobiological basis of hunger and satiety and the relatedness of nutritional status and behaviors to impaired concentration, indecisiveness, mood fluctuations, and sleep disturbance are discussed. The dietitian helps the patients develop an understanding of what they need from a physiological standpoint and to learn how to apply it to their own bodies. The goal is to normalize food intake, to help the individuals achieve normal satiety signals, so they can fuel themselves adequately to support health and allow them to achieve their life goals. Although done before, the dietitian addresses continually the potential difference between subjective and objective measures of intake and collaboratively researches with the patients what is an "appropriate" portion for them.

The dietitian discusses with patients the impact of the "numbers dictators" and helps patients choose alternative strategies for self-regulation and control. Some prefer to stick to calorie counting, while others are swept away to an obsessive course and would thus rather use schemes of eating portions and food exchanges.

Mindful eating should be encouraged, and *emotional eating* should be countered and its pattern explored. Clinician teaches patients to identify specific emotional triggers to food restrictions or binging and purging, challenge their irrational beliefs relating to weight, body image, and self-esteem, and develop healthy alternative behaviors to compulsive eating. Clinician may educate patients about mood intolerance and help explore unique events in which the patients have addressed such states with different effective strategies rather than eating or dieting.

B. Treating dysfunctional thoughts related to food, shape and weight

Poor body image at the end of treatment predicts poor prognosis (56). Dietitians should help patients deal with their concerns about weight gain and body changes, given that these are particularly difficult adjustments for patients to make.

Body image therapy
Body image therapy encompasses a host of components designed to improve mindfulness with regard to the experience of the body, decrease over-concern with body size and shape, address over-estimation of body size, decrease fear of situations that are associated with body shape concerns, decrease body checking rituals, and develop compassion and acceptance for the body and self (54). Patients are encouraged to accept their body size and shape as well as appreciate themselves for who they are, versus what they look like.

Media literacy
Media literacy is one of the tools aimed to build skills to resist social persuasion and empower the subjects to adopt a critical evaluation of media content so that they can identify, analyze, challenge, and propose alternatives to cultural ideals presented in the mass media. The main goal is to counter rigid internalized societal ideals of size and appearance, body dissatisfaction, and dieting, which were reported to be a causal risk factor for maladaptive eating patterns (57).

Mirror exposure

Mirror exposure is another tool that may be incorporated by dietitians. Mirror exposure involves deliberate, planned, and systematic exposure to body image. The approach is nonjudgmental, holistic in focus, and mindful of present emotional experience. Complementary behavioral assignments aim to reduce avoidance and excessive checking (58).

The clinician may use narrative therapy, which studies the internalized oppressive ideas in cultural, political, and social context (7). Most counsellors find it very productive when they share with the patients their personal experience in balancing their eating habits. Mahatma Gandhi said, "You must be the change you wish to see in the world." Thus counsellors should be good role models, modeling positive body acceptance by eliminating negative self statements.

C. Managing body checking behaviors

Some dietitians incorporate strategies of abolishing body checking behaviors. Body checking is the practice of repeatedly checking aspects of one's body in a range of ways (59). These behaviors include examining specific body parts, using the fit of clothing or jewelry to judge shape or weight, frequent weighing, and studying oneself in the mirror repeatedly. Each episode might last from a few seconds to a number of minutes. Fairburn et al. hypothesized that body checking magnifies perceived imperfections, serving to maintain body size preoccupation and the fear of losing control (thus maintaining dietary restriction). Because patients pay attention to even small changes, slight (and normal) fluctuations in weight can trigger mood change (60).

Mountford et al. (61) suggested that for an intervention to be successful in eliminating unhealthy checking or avoidance, the individual's underlying cognitions must be explicitly observed and challenged, as it is likely that a few key beliefs will underlie a number of behaviors. The therapist may ask patients why it is so important for them not to have to check their bodies every ten minutes. What knowledge does it add and how does it impact your thinking and affect?

3. RELAPSE PREVENTION

Follow-up meetings are crucial even after symptoms abstinence in order to support further progress and prevent relapse. Adhesion to anti-eating disorder steps can fluctuate. The dietitian increases hope while predicting more setbacks and reframing the fluctuating pattern of the journey to recovery. Meetings are focused on unique outcomes in which the patients enforce self-nurturance and self-regulation, aiming to empower patient self-efficacy. After identifying unique outcomes, patients are helped to ascribe significant meaning to these instances through re-storying, a therapeutic process designed to help patients create a sense of empowerment, self–efficacy, and hope (62). Re-storying might for example involve the counselor asking the patients, "What does this say about you and your ability to resist to society's messages?" "How would you name the strategy you employed when these ideas were driven away?" Gradually, a preferable story about patients' identity and coping style is re-authored (9).

During the follow-up sessions, patients are educated on the principles of relapse prevention, that is, the distinction between lapses and relapses and the development of plans to manage high-risk situations (63). Also, patient are trained to "get back on track" as quickly as possible once a lapse has occurred. It is important that patients are prepared for vulnerability to relapses during high-risk times. Patients are aided in identifying personal triggers and high-risk situations that may promote relapse and are trained through mindfulness to utilize awareness to recognize, prior to the lapse, that they have a choice in which behaviors they will choose, given the situation. In addition, patterns of thinking and destructive behaviors that may trigger relapse are identified. Patients are coached on how to reframe lapses as "slips" versus a complete relapse (55).

When patients are experiencing the urge to lapse to maladaptive behaviors (restrictions, binging, or purging), they are invited to phone their dietitian prior to engaging in such behaviors.

Wisniewski & Ben Porat (64) suggested using telephone skill coaching with DBT framework. They describe a telephone-based, semi-structured procedure that involves ascertaining the problem, evaluating what the patient has already tried to solve the problem, and developing, getting commitment for, and minimizing problems with an action plan. Generally, the goal of telephone skill coaching is to empower the caller to make a decision regarding the current crisis and to take appropriate action. In standard DBT treatment, telephone coaching is used to assist clients in generalizing the skills they are learning in treatment to everyday situations (11). Eating disorder patients are likely to become dysregulated when exposed to food-related stimuli as well as to interpersonal interactions. In such conditions, they might find a short conversation with their dietitian helpful to avoid relapse. The therapist needs to refrain from providing therapy and/or offering interpretative remarks regarding current behavior during telephone skill-coaching, as this attention could possibly reinforce crisis behavior (64). Interpretations regarding the episode, therefore, should be left for the individual session.

Solution focused strategy
Solution focused also offers techniques to overcome relapses. When some symptoms are re-engaged, the therapist may use techniques to remind the patient how he felt without the tyranny of the eating disorder. The "as if" technique is a useful tool in these situations. It is aimed to induce a positive, solution-oriented self-deception, where the fantasy of having overcome the problem becomes a self-fulfilling prophecy. This maneuver has two effects: It introduces a positive suggestion that takes advantage of the "logic of belief," suggesting that the "miracle" can happen and more importantly, shifts the person's attention away from the present symptom to a future free of the disorder. This change of perspective, obtained through suggestion, is therapeutic in itself, because it opens new horizons and projects the person beyond the problem (65).

Summary

The dietitain is an essential component of the team treatment of patients with eating disorders during assessment and treatment across the continuum of care. The dietitian assists patients in increasing information regarding self-nurturance, effective vs. destructive behavior and thought patterns, as well as developing consciousness-raising and self-awareness regarding maladaptive defense patterns. The dietitian creates an appropriate emotional climate for growth, helps patients develop open and trusting relationships with food and the body as well as with others, and helps patients engage in new alternatives for expressing feelings, positive self-talk, self-control and self-nurturance using various tools, techniques, and approaches. In addition, the dietitian helps families return to effective communication patterns.

REFERENCES

[1] American Psychiatric Association Working Group on Eating Disorders. Practice guideline for the treatment of patients with eating disorders, 3rd Edition, 2006, available at APA web site at www.psych.org.

[2] Position of the American Dietetic Association. Nutrition Intervention in the treatment of anorexia nervosa, bulimia nervosa and other eating disorders. J. Am. Diet. Assoc. 2006; 106; 12:2073-2082.

[3] National Institute for Clinical Excellence. Eating disorders: Core interventions in the treatment and management of anorexia nervosa, bulimia nervosa and related eating disorders. Clinical Guideline. Available at: www.nice.org.uk.

[4] Miller, W.R. & Rollnick S. Motivational interviewing: Preparing people to change addictive behavior. New York: Guilford, 1991.

[5] Epston, D. Catching up with David Epston: A collection of narrative practice-based papers published between 1991-1996. Adelaide: Dulwich Centre Publications, 1998.

[6] White, M. & Epston, D. Narrative Means to Therapeutic Ends. San Francisco: W.W. Norton, 1990.

[7] Foucault, M. Power/Knowledge: Selected interviews and writings, 1972-1977 (C. Gordon, Trans.). New York: Pantheon Books.

[8] White, M. Reflections on narrative practice. Adelaid, South Australia: Dulwich Centre Publication, 2000.

[9] Maisel, R., Epston, D., & Borden, A. Biting the hand that starves you. Inspiring resistance to anorexia/bulimia. New York: Norton, 2004.

[10] Serpell, L., Treasure, J., Teasdale, J. et al. Anorexia nervosa: Friend or foe? Int. J. Eat. Disord. 1999; 25:177-186.

[11] Linehan, M. Cognitive-behavioral treatment of borderline personality disorder. New York: Guilford Press, 1993.

[12] Pinzon, J.L. & Beimers, M.A. Medical complications in children and adolescents affected by eating disorders. B.C. Medical J. 2005; 47(1): 28-34.

[13] Rome, E.S., Ammerman, S., Rosen, D.S., Keller, R.J., Lock, J., Mammel, K.A., O'Toole, J., Rees, J.M., Sanders, M.J., Sawyer, S.M., Schneider, M., Sigel, E., & Silber, T.J. Children and adolescents with eating disorders: The state of the art. Pediatrics 2003; 111:e98-e108.

[14] Eisler, I., Dare, C., Russell, G., Szmukler, G., Le Grange, D., & Dodge, E. A five-year follow-up of a controlled trial of family therapy in severe eating disorders. Arch. Gen. Psychiat. 1997; 54:1025-1030.

[15] Lock, J., Le Grange, D., Agras, W.S., & Dare, C. Treatment Manual for Anorexia Nervosa: A Family-Based Approach. New York: Guilford Press, 2001.

[16] Lock, J. & Le Grange, D. Help your teenager beat an eating disorder. New York: Guilford Press, 2004.

[17] Le Grange, D., Binford, R., & Loeb, K.L. Manualized family-based treatment for anorexia nervosa: A case series. J. Am. Acad. Child Adolesc. Psychiatry 2005; 44: 641-646.

[18] Lock, J., Agras, W.S., Bryson, S., & Kraemer, H. A comparison of short-and long-term family therapy for adolescent anorexia nervosa. J. Am. Acad. Child Adolesc. Psychiatry 2005; 44: 632-639.

[19] Whitney, J. & Eisler, I. Theoretical and empirical models around caring for someone with an eating disorder: The reorganization of family life and inter personal maintenance factors. J. Ment. Health 2005; 14: 575–586.

[20] Rhodes, P., Gosbee, M., Madden, S., & Brown, J. Communities of Concern in the Family-Based Treatment of Anorexia Nervosa: Towards a Consensus in the Maudsley Model. Europ. Eat. Disord. Rev. 2005; 13:392–398.

[21] Le Grange, D., Eisler, I., Dare, C. et al. Family criticism and self-starvation: A study of Expressed Emotion. J. Fam. Ther. 1992; 14:177–192.

[22] Nardone, G., Verbitz, T., & Milanese, R. (eds.). Prison of Food: Research and Treatment of Eating Disorders. Karnac Books Ltd., 2005.

[23] Treasure, J., Sepulveda, A.R., Whitaker, W., Todd, G., Lopez, C. & Whitney, J. Collaborative care between professionals and non-professionals in the management of eating disorders: A description of workshops focused on interpersonal maintaining factors. Eur. Eat. Disorders Rev. 2007; 15: 24–34.

[24] Vitousek, K.B., Watson, S., & Wilson, G.T. Enhancing motivation for change in treatment-resistant eating disorders. Clin. Psychol. Rev. 1998; 18:391-420.

[25] Gelller, J., Drab-Hudson, D., Whisenhunt, B., & Srikameswaran, S. Readiness to change dietary restriction predicts outcomes in the eating disorders. Eat. Disord.: J. Treat. and Prev. 2004; 12: 219-224.

[26] Geller, G., Williams, K.D., & Srikameswaran, S. Clinician stance in the treatment of chronic eating disorders. Eur. Eat. Disorders Rev. 2001; 9:365-373.

[27] Vansteenkiste, M., Soenens, B., & Vandereychen, W. Motivation to change in eating disorder patients: A conceptual clarification on the basis of self-determination theory. Int. J. Eat. Disord. 2005; 37:3:207-219.

[28] Graap, H., Bleich, S., Herbst, F., Trostmann, Y., Wancata, J., & Zwaan, M. The needs of carers of patients with anorexia nervosa and bulimia nervsa. Eur. Eat. Disorders Rev. 2008; 16:21-29.

[29] Vitousek, K.B., & Hollon, S.D. (1990). The investigation of schematic content and processing in eating disorders. Cognitive Therapy and Research, 14, 191-214.

[30] Cooper, Z., Fairburn, C.G., & Hawker, D.M. Cognitive-Behavioral Treatment of Obesity, A Clinician's Guide. Guilford Press, 2004.

[31] Thomas, D. The dietitian's role in the treatment of eating disorders. Nutrition   Bulletin 2000; 25, 55–60.

[32] Rome, E.S. & Ammerman, S. Medical complications of eating disorders: An update, J. of Adolesc. Health 2003; 33(6):418-426.

[33] Modan-Moses, D., Yaroslavsky, A., Novikov, I., Segev, S., Toledano, A., Miterany, E. & Stein, D. Stunting of growth as a major feature of anorexia nervosa in male adolescents. Pediatrics 2003; 111(2): 270-276.

[34] Golden, N.H. & Shenker, I.R. Amenorrhea in anorexia nervosa: Etiology and implications. Adolesc. Med. 1996; 3:503-517.

[35] Mehler, P.S. Osteoporosis in anorexia nervosa: Prevention and treatment. Int. J. Eat. Disord. 2003; 33:113-126.

[36] Katzman, D.K. & Leslie, K. Anorexia nervosa in children and adolescents: The unique medical complications. Prim. Care Psychiat. 1997; 3:125-134.

[37] Russell, G.F. Involuntary treatment in anorexia nervosa. Psychiatry Clin. North Am. 2001; 24:337–349 124.

[38] Goldner, E. Treatment refusal in anorexia nervosa. Int. J. Eat. Disord. 1989; 8:297–306.

[39] Strober, M. Managing the chronic, treatment-resistant patient with anorexia nervosa. Int. J. Eat. Disord. 2004; 36:245–255.

[40] Kaye, W.H., Weltzin, T.E., Hsu,L.K., Bulik, C.M. An open trial of fluoxetine in patients with anorexia nervosa. J. Clin. Psychiatry 1991; 52:464–471.

[41] Winter, T.A., O'Keefe, S.J., Callanan, M., & Marks, T. The effect of severe undernutrition and subsequent refeeding on whole-body metabolism and protein synthesis in human subjects. J. Parenter Enteral. Nutr. 2005; 29:221–228.

[42] Birmingham, C.L., Alothman, A.F., Goldner, E.M. Anorexia nervosa: Refeeding and hypophosphatemia. Int. J. Eat. Disord. 1996; 20:211.

[43] Kraft, M.D., Btaiche, I.F., & Sacks, G.S. Review of refeeding syndrome. Nutrition in Clinical Practice 2005, 20:625-633.

[44] Ornstein, R.M., Golden, N., Jacobson, M.S. & Shenker, I.R. J. Adolesc. Helath 2003; 32:83–88.

[45] Agarwal, R. & Knochel, J.P. Hypophosphatemia and hyperphosphatemia. In: Brenner, B.M. (ed.). Brenner & Rector's The Kidney, 6th edition. Philadelphia: W.B. Saunders, 2000:1071–107.

[46] Davies, S. & Jaffa, T. Patterns of weekly weight gain during inpatient treatment for adolescents with anorexia nervosa. Eur. Eat. Disorders Rev. 2005; 13, 273–277.

[47] DeSantis, A. Therapeutic mealtime support: A treatment strategy for Disordered eating. Pulse 2002; 21:4-5.

[48] Noorduin, C. & Vandereycken, W. Coping with stressful family meals, patients, parents and therapists around the table. Eating Disorder Review 2003; 14:1-3.

[49] Leichner, M., Standish, K., & Leichner, P. Strategies for supporting youth with eating disorders when intensive treatment is needed. B.C. Medical J. 2005; 47:22-28.

[50] Kaye, W.H., Weltzin, T.E., Hsu, L.K., McConahan, C.W., & Bolton, B. Amount of calories retained after binge eating and vomiting. Am. J. Psychiatry. 1993; 50:969-971.

[51] Fairburn, C.G., Doll, H.A., Welch, S.L., Hay, P.J., Davies, B.A., O'Connor, M.E. Risk factors for binge eating disorder: A community based case-control study. Arch. Gen. Psychiatry.1998; 55:425-432.

[52] Wilson, G.T., Fairburn, C., & Agras, W.S. Cognitive-behavioral therapy for anorexia nervosa. In: Garner, D. & Garfinkel, P. (Eds.), Handbook of treatment for eating disorders Wilson, Fairburn, & Agras, New York: Guilford Press 1997: 67-93.

[53] Stewart,. T.M. & Williamson, D.A. Multidisciplinary treatment of eating disorders–Part I structure and costs of treatment. Behav. Modif. 2004; 28:812-30.

[54] Stice, E. Risk and maintenance factors for eating pathology: A meta-analytic review. Psychol. Bull. 2002; 128:825-848.

[55] Stewart T.M. & Williamson, D.A. Multidisciplinary treatment of eating disorders–Part II structure and costs of treatment. Behav. Modif. 2004; 28:831-853.

[56] Garner, D.M. & Garfinkel, P.E., eds. Handbook of treatment for eating disorders. New York: Guilford Press; 1997.

[57] Levine, M.P., Piran, N., & Stoddard, C. Mission more probable: Media literacy, activism, and advocacy in the prevention of eating disorders. In: Piran, N., Levine, M., Steiner-Adair, C., eds. Preventing Eating Disorders: A Handbook of Interventions and Special Challenges. Philadelphia: Brunnel/Mazel; 1999.

[58] Delinsky, S.S. & Wilson, G.T. Mirror exposure for the treatment of body image disturbance. Int. J. Eat. Disord. 2006; 39:108–116.

[59] Fairburn, C.G., Cooper, Z., & Shafran, R. Cognitive behavior therapy for eating disorders: A "transdiagnostic" theory and treatment. Behav. Res. Ther. 2003; 41:509–528.

[60] Shafran, R., Fairburn, C.G., Robinson, P., & Lask, B. Body checking and its avoidance in eating disorders. Int. J. Eat. Disord. 2004; 35:93–101.

[61] Mountford, V., Haase, A., & Waller, G. Body checking in the eating disorders: Associations between cognitions and behaviors. Int. J. Eat. Disord. 2006; 39:708–715.

[62] Guterman, J.T. & Rudes, J. A narrative approach to strategic evlecticism. J. Men. Health Couns. 2005; 27: 1-12.

[63] Marlatt, G.A. & Gordon, J.R. Relapse prevention. New York: Plenum, 1985.

[64] Wisniewski, L. & Ben-Porath, D.D. Telephone skill-coaching with eating-disordered clients: Clinical guidelines using a DBT framework. Eur. Eat. Disorders Rev. 2005: 13:344–350.

[65] Nardone, G., Giannotti, E., & Rocchi, R. The evolution of family patterns and indirect therapy with adolescents. London: Karnac Books, 2007.

In: Treatment and Recovery of Eating Disorders
Editors: Daniel Stein and Yael Latzer

ISBN: 978-1-62808-248-7
© 2013 Nova Science Publishers, Inc.

Chapter 7

THE RATIONALE FOR PSYCHODYNAMIC PSYCHOTHERAPY IN EATING DISORDERS: AN EMPIRICALLY CONSTRUCTED APPROACH

David L. Tobin[‡‡]
Tufts University Medical School, Springfield, MA, US

ABSTRACT

This chapter describes the rationale for conducting psychodynamic psychotherapy with eating disorders patients. Though there is strong endorsement for cognitive-behavioral approaches to treatment amongst eating disorder researchers, a review of the empirical literature suggests that 1) most eating disorder patients do not improve with cognitive behavioral approaches, 2) there is little empirical support for the theory of cognitive behavior therapy, 3) and most, if not almost all, clinicians use psychodynamic approaches in their work with eating disorder patients. An empirically based approach for combining cognitive behavioral and psychodynamic approaches is described as an alternative treatment for the eating disorders.

Keywords: psychotherapy integration, eating disorders, empirically constructed treatment

INTRODUCTION

This chapter will describe the rationale for conducting psychodynamic psychotherapy with eating disorder patients; it is important to understand this because if you are a clinician working with eating disorder patients, then you are probably already using some psychodynamic approaches with your patients. The probability here is very high, so high in fact, that in psychology we would say that the likelihood of you not using psychodynamic

---

[‡‡] E-mail address: DVTO2@aol.com

strategies in your practice reaches the null hypothesis (1). It should be noted that there are numerous schools of thought within the psychodynamic and psychoanalytic community. For the purposes of this chapter, I will be referring to a rather broadly defined approach to psychodynamic practice that is not tied to any particular meta-psychological school, because there is little or no evidence for any of the meta-psychologies of psychoanalysis, such as drive theory, or object relations theory, no matter how useful one finds them in clinical practice. To be fair, the same can be said for the cognitive models of clinical psychology, and this is why it would be advantageous to abandon theoretically based models of psychotherapy in favor of a strictly empirical approach which articulates treatment principles and strategies rather than an unsubstantiated, theoretically based model (e.g., 2).

Consistent with the vast majority of clinicians in the eating disorder field (1), my own approach, which I have labeled coping strategies therapy (2), has been to combine cognitive behavioral approaches to treatment, particularly the behavioral interventions, with psychodynamic strategies (3-6). The first principle of this approach is that the briefer the treatment, i.e., the smaller the dosage, the more it will resemble a behavioral approach, with the bulk of treatment comprising psychoeducation, behavioral assessment of target symptoms, and as concise a behavioral intervention as possible for target symptoms. Conversely, the longer the treatment, i.e., the greater the dosage, the more it will resemble a psychodynamic approach, in which a more broadly defined array of problems, such as interpersonal difficulties and/or emotional regulation patterns, are also included in the treatment. By broadly defined, I mean patterns that may appear in multiple contexts, such as in the patient's current life experiences, their family and interpersonal history, and in the emerging relationship to the therapist. Dosage theory, as described by Howard and his colleagues (7), is an empirical foundation for this approach, and dosage has been shown to be a predictor of outcome in patients with eating disorders (8, 9).

Findings regarding the benefits of high dosage, psychodynamic approaches have been replicated with a wide variety of patients who have serious psychiatric problems. Leihsernring and Rabnung (10), in a critical meta-analysis of long-term psychodynamic psychotherapy (LTPP) found that for a wide variety of complicated and comorbid disorders, patients who received LTPP were better off that 96% of their comparison sample. Similar to dosage studies in eating disorders, these authors found strong correlations between the various measures of outcome, including target problems (r = .62), general psychiatric symptoms (.54) and personality variables (.43), with the number of sessions; more sessions predicted more improvement. Several of the papers in this chapter are also included in Leihsernring and Rabnung's review, which suffers from the same problem as this one – there are simply not enough comparisons of psychodynamic treatments performed with quality, rigorous research designs.

In my own approach, psychodynamic focus and technique may emerge at any point in the treatment, but are more likely to be the focus of treatment during the third and fourth doses, which follow the first two doses that are brief, psychoeducational (dose 1) and cognitive behavioral (dose 2) in nature (2). Dose three, conceptualized in terms of a relatively short-term psychodynamic intervention, lasts about 20 visits and dose four, a long-term open-ended psychodynamic approach, can range from 50, to 100, to hundreds of visits. Dose three can entail any number of brief dynamic approaches, including interpersonal psychotherapy (IPT;11), supportive-expressive psychotherapy (SET; 12), and time limited dynamic psychotherapy (TLDP; 13). A cognitive behavioral treatment (CBT) that focuses on interpersonal issues could also fit within this framework. The common thread between these approaches is the focus on interpersonal problems, which are not only in the patient's day to day life, but can also appear in their past history and in the relationship to their therapist. A distinguishing feature between psychodynamic approaches and cognitive behavioral approaches, however, is the highlighting of three in-session principles. First, there is an emphasis in psychodynamic approaches, but not in CBT, on the primacy of whatever the patient is most strongly feeling in the moment. Second, there is an appreciation for the defensive processes by which the patient avoids painful emotions. And third, there is an appreciation for the interactions between the patient and the therapist as both a source of information and a mechanism for alleviation of the patient's interpersonal difficulties.

This latter principle is more commonly referred to the analysis of the transference, a term which has a negative connotation for many behavioral and cognitive theorists. However, much of this negative bias is a reaction to the meta-psychology in psychoanalytic literature such as drive theory and object relations theory. If, on the other hand, one could focus simply on the therapeutic processes, and choose whatever theoretical language one wished to use, then it is possible that acceptable descriptive language for cognitive and behavioral clinicians could be found. For example, transference could become "stimulus generalization", and the unconscious could become "tacit reinforcement schedules". The advantage of considering transference is that one can conduct "in vivo" assessment of a patient's difficulties, and find alternative reinforcement models, vis a vis the therapist's responses, that might directly help them build new patterns of thoughts and behavior. Several approaches to behavior therapy have, in fact, incorporated these techniques (14, 15).

In that there is more limited empirical data for patients with anorexia nervosa and those fitting into the eating disorder not otherwise specified (ED NOS) category, including binge eating disorder, much of the comments about empirical findings in this paper will be focused on patients with bulimia nervosa. Most reviews of treatment for eating disorders strongly endorse CBT as the treatment of choice for bulimia nervosa (e.g., 16), and in the UK there are official guidelines strongly recommending CBT for these patients (17). There have been statements made at eating disorder meetings suggesting that clinicians who do not use CBT for bulimia nervosa patients may be guilty of malpractice. Here is the attitude of one cognitive-behavioral research practitioner: "Even the most hardened cognitive-behavioral loyalist would have to concede that not all patients get better, even with CBT" (18, p 120). Waller (18) is inclined to blame clinicians for failing to implement CBT properly, but at least one meta-analysis suggests that most patients do not recover with CBT (19). When one looks closely at the evidence for CBT with eating disorder patients, there are significant limitations, noted even by official guidelines. For example, NICE guidelines (17) state that there are no benefits to CBT over behavior therapy for binge eating and purging at post treatment, and that there is no advantage to CBT over interpersonal therapy at follow-up. The other aspect of this treatment approach that Waller overlooks is that one of the "CBT" models he uses, dialectical behavior therapy (DBT) (15), is actually a treatment that combines CBT with psychodynamic approaches. Yet, the endorsement given for CBT by Waller and other CBT proponents is at the highest level.

EVIDENCE FOR PSYCHODYNAMIC PSYCHOTHERAPY FROM RANDOMIZED CLINICAL TRIALS

When it comes to psychodynamic approaches for eating disorders, there are simply very few controlled studies. An early study by Garner (20) for bulimia nervosa found that CBT was more effective than Supportive-Expressive psychotherapy (13), a manualized version of psychodynamic treatment. However, pretreatment differences on one of the comorbidity measures, the Borderline Syndrome Index (BSI), were quite large, with the mean score in the Supportive Expressive group at the same level as a group defined by Johnson and his colleagues (9) as having borderline personality disorder. In Johnson's study, patients with high BSI scores treated with psychotherapy integrating cognitive-behavioral treatment of bulimic symptoms with psychodynamic psychotherapy had significantly poorer outcomes than patients whose BSI scores were much lower, similar to the scores of patients in Garner's CBT group. Comorbidity, particularly of personality disorders, can impede the effectiveness of CBT (21) and plays an important role in justifying the use of psychodynamic approaches with eating disorder patients.

Only one other study of psychodynamic approaches has been completed to date with bulimia nervosa patients, a study by Bachar and his colleagues (22) comparing self psychology with nutritional counseling and a cognitive based treatment, though the trial also included anorexia nervosa patients. The study compared a self-psychology approach with CBT and a control group. Psychodynamic treatment was more effective than the control group, but not to CBT. The study is limited in the sense that self-psychology is somewhat constrained by the meta-psychology of one theorist, Heinz Kohut (23), and while important, misses a wide array of other psychodynamic approaches.

Despite there being relatively few studies for patients with anorexia nervosa with respect to treatment in general, there are, ironically, three studies using psychodynamic approaches with these patients: a study by Treasure and her colleagues using an approach they term "cognitive-analytic therapy (CAT)" (24), a study by Dare (25) using CAT and "focal psychoanalytic therapy", and the above mentioned study by Bachar. The psychodynamic treatments performed well in all three studies. Psychodynamic treatments had an equivalent, yet positive, outcome when compared to educational behavior therapy in Treasure's study, an equivalent outcome to family therapy in Dare's study with both treatments being superior to controls, and a positive outcome in Bachar's study, achieving superior outcome to the control group and equivalent outcomes to a cognitive treatment. Thus, from an empirical perspective, the biggest limitation of psychodynamic approaches for anorexia nervosa is the limited number of studies.

Thompson-Brenner and her colleagues (26) have recently reviewed the literature in this area and make a number of important points regarding 1) the inadequacy of research on psychodynamic therapy and 2) the limitations of empirically supported treatments, including CBT. As to the limitations of empirical support for CBT, they note that meta-analysis suggests that a only a minority, about 40%, of bulimia nervosa patients who enter treatment either complete treatment or achieve recovery (19). Second, they suggest that early trials of CBT have been inclined to exclude patients with significant comorbidity, particularly personality disorders. This second point has been disputed by cognitive behavioral researchers (16), but it is with comorbid conditions such as personality disorders that the need of for longer, more comprehensive treatments, including the kind of interventions provided by psychodynamic approaches, has emerged. For example, as noted earlier, Johnson and his colleagues (9) have found that bulimia nervosa patients scoring high on the Borderline Syndrome Index (BSI) are much less likely to recover at the end of one year of specialty clinic treatment than patients who have low scores. The other important finding of this study is that patients who have had high BSI scores and have still recovered, have had relatively high dosages of treatment, an average 100 sessions, and about twice that of high score patients who have not recovered. As noted previously, the higher the dosage, the greater the amount of psychodynamic strategies are likely to be included in the treatment. Succinctly put, most eating disorder patients, about 60%, do not recover with empirically supported treatments, and clinicians need to do something with their patients after behavioral or cognitive behavioral approaches fail to work. The longer they work with their patients, the more likely they will be using psychodynamic approaches.

EVIDENCE FROM CLINICAL PRACTICE

Several studies documented that clinicians who treat eating disorders generally do not use empirically supported treatments (EST) (1, 27-31). Early studies documented that EST's were not used, but gave little indication of what therapists did use. Two more recent studies looked at what clinicians did with their eating disorder patients with some detail. Thompson-Brenner and Westin (31) found that clinicians treating eating disorder patients in the community, who identified themselves as either psychodynamic or cognitive behavioral, used both psychodynamic and cognitive behavioral approaches. Similar to the findings on dosage, CBT clinicians were most likely to employ psychodynamic approaches when their patients had comorbid personality disorders.

A study by Tobin and his colleagues (1) found that of clinicians who attend eating disorder meetings, 99% were using psychodynamic interventions with their eating disorder patients, regardless of how they described their theoretical orientation. Furthermore, only 13% of therapists reported that they used a single theoretical approach with their patients. Ninety-nine percent of respondents indicated that they "examine what happens between me and my patient as a possible example of the patient's problem behaviors", representing one aspect of the analysis of the transference. Moreover, 100% of respondents reported that they "focus on the patient's feelings in the here and now, and 99% reported that they "ask about a patient's family life in the past", all core psychodynamic intervention strategies. Similar results were obtained for core CBT interventions, including psychoeducation, making behavioral suggestions, and teaching coping skills, which 98% of clinicians reported using. Furthermore, 93% of respondents reported using behavioral record keeping (e.g., food logs), a concrete indication of behavior therapy, and 91% reported that they "think that sometimes a patient finds a way to get me to feel what they feel, which is important to understand in the treatment". This last intervention involves the analysis of the countertransference, a psychodynamic strategy requiring a relatively high level of skill, training and experience. Thus, we must struggle with the discrepancy between the strong endorsement by researchers for cognitive behavioral approaches and their limited effectiveness, the relatively few studies of psychodynamic approaches, and the overwhelming vast majority of clinicians who use psychodynamic approaches with their eating disorder patients, typically in combination with cognitive behavioral approaches.

COMBINATION TREATMENTS

Treatments that combine psychodyanamic and behavioral approaches have probably been used since the first time clinicians began addressing eating disorders, and they have been written about for many years (2, 4-6, 32). Although it has been suggested by some researchers that combining CBT with other approaches risks reducing the effectiveness of CBT (16, 18), there is basically no evidence to support this concern. Furthermore, there are a number of treatments for patients with severe psychiatric difficulties, such as borderline personality disorder, that formally combine approaches from CBT and psychodynamic treatments. For example, Linehan's (15) DBT combines CBT techniques, psychodynamic strategies such as the analysis of transference and counteransference, and Zen Buddhism. For those unfamiliar with Linehan's incorporation of psychodynamic principles, note her description that: "the emphasis in DBT on therapy interfering behaviors is more similar to psychodynamic emphasis on 'transference' behaviors than it is to any aspect of standard cognitive behavioral therapies" (15, p. 29). Another integrative approach for difficult patients is schema therapy by Young and his colleagues (33), which combines cognitive behavioral approaches with "emotion focused" techniques. Young notes two important components of his treatment: (1) dosage of treatment; Young claims the success of therapy is strongly related to its duration and intensity (two sessions a week for 3 years), and (2) the importance of the therapeutic relationship. He claims that the relationship aspect of his treatment involves "limited parenting", and "is unlike any other approaches to treatment for borderline personality disorder". Young fully ackonowledges incorporating psychodynamic approaches into his work.

It is encouraging that these treatments are being developed and studied, and not surprising that they have such important overlapping components such as high dosage and a focus on the patient therapist relationship. However, it is somewhat discouraging to hear these developers claim to having "reinvented the wheel". It is even more frustrating to see that when developers or advocates of these treatments do a study, their approach always has superior effects to other treatments (34-36), likely suggesting researcher bias. Such bias and gamesmanship limits advancement in the field.

Nevertheless, similar to Linehan and Young, my own view is that the limited effectiveness of CBT can be enhanced by combining it with psychodynamic approaches, and that the biggest obstacle in demonstrating the success of such a combined approach is researcher bias. There is a vicious cycle here. Research costs a lot of time and money, and good researchers do not appear inclined to risk their careers to document something that their colleagues are not likely to fund. Thus, we face a long cycle of having researchers criticizing clinicians for practicing something that has little empirical support, when clinicians are in no position to conduct such research, and researchers are either unmotivated, or perhaps similar to clinicians, unable to do so.

Here is an illustration of the type of model I am suggesting (2); there are a number of core principles to this approach, referred to as coping strategies therapy (CST, 2). The first is that it should be based on empirical support and not on unsubstantiated theoretical models. Therapeutic processes should be empirically defined and studied, and unconstrained by any theoretical approach, leaving the possibility for a wide array of intervention strategies that might otherwise seem incompatible. For my model, I have combined dosage theory (7), the trans-theoretical model (37), and coping theory (1). These approaches help to define how much, what kind, and for whom we might apply different strategies. From dosage theory we predict that some patients may require only the briefest of interventions, while others may require years of treatment. This idea is reinforced by the trans-theoretical model, which predicts what patients are ready for active behavioral interventions and which patients might need longer treatments, in which therapeutic work is focused on the therapeutic alliance and on enhancing the patients' motivation for change. Lastly, coping theory provides an empirical model of change strategies that might nicely match the types of treatments typically used with both eating disorder and general psychiatric populations.

I will briefly describe the doses in the CST. Dose 1 involves 1 to 2 sessions of primarily psychoeducational strategies in which the patient is diagnosed, the problem is described, and a pathway of change is suggested to the patient. A relatively small percentage of patients are expected to recover with Dose 1. Dose 2 involves approximately 8 sessions of primarily cognitive behavioral intervention targeted for patients who ready to begin behavioral work. The treatment may utilize CBT interventions that focus on one or more types of symptoms, such as bulimia and depression, but is less likely to work with symptoms that reflect personality disturbance or other severe comorbid conditions (e.g., dissociative disorders). Dose 2 lasts about 8 visits. Dose 3 offers the patient the cognitive behavioral interventions of dose 2, but also includes a broader psychosocial focus that may involve interpersonal problems, somewhat focal emotion regulation difficulties, and trauma related illness (e.g., PTSD) that are uncomplicated by ongoing environmental reinforcement. In short, dose 3 combines CBT with short-term psychodynamic psychotherapy approaches, and there are a number of manualized examples to draw upon (e.g., 1-13). However, unlike the current zeitgeist, I view these manuals as research tools and teaching models, not rigid prescriptions. Dose 3 lasts about 20 visits.

The longest dose, dose 4, can range from 50 to 100's of visits. It should be noted that manualized treatments which address severe psychopathology such as personality disorders are typically 100 visits over the course of a year, or more (33,35,36). Patients who need dose 4 typically have very complicated comorbidity in addition to their eating symptoms, such as affective and/or anxiety symptoms. They may have trauma related histories that result in severe PTSD and dissociative disorders, and the incidence of personality disorders is overrepresented in this group. These patients may also have family and environmental issues which help to maintain their illness. One of the difficulties in dose 4 is that there can be so many problems that it can be difficult to know what to focus on, so a hierarchy of concerns is rank-ordered, starting with physical safety, emotional safety and threats to the treatment, followed by reducing symptom maintaining behaviors, developing interpersonal skills, and developing the self, and only lastly, addressing eating related difficulties. It may seem strange to treat the eating disorder last, but if one could treat it first, you would not need dose 4. This does not say that the therapist would not offer the patient the same behavioral suggestions a dose 1 or 2 patient would get; it just would not be very successful implementing those suggestions until other issues were addressed. Of course, sometimes the hierarchy gets turned on its head, such as when the eating symptoms constitute a physical threat to safety, and must be immediately addressed.

The sequence of interventions in CST goes something like this. The patients are assessed and feedback is given about their symptoms. Their readiness to take behavioral steps towards recovery is assessed, with their collaboration, and appropriate goals are suggested. If they seem willing and able, bulimia nervosa patients would be instructed at that stage to stabilize their meal pattern and keep food logs. As has been documented in the literature, a significant number of patients are able to make rapid progress with these suggestions and some early psychoeducational work, showing recovery in the first few visits. Rapid recovery has been shown to be one of the best predictors of positive outcome (38). If there is depression, I would suggest the patients to increase their activity, particularly social activity, and would similarly address other symptoms with specific behavioral suggestions (2). Behavioral analysis may be very useful in helping design suggestions.

It is when these straightforward behavioral interventions do not work that it is advantageous to move on to more psychodynamic aspects of treatment. When the logs and suggestions are reviewed and the behavioral work seems at a stand still, I tend to switch to a more dynamic approach of letting the patient guide the material to be examined and focusing on what is most affectively displayed. Sometimes it is the absence of affect, or concern, or even discussion, which is most prominent, and then this resistance must be examined. In manualized brief psychodynamic approaches such as interpersonal psychotherapy (IPT; 1), supportive-expressive psychotherapy (SET; 12), time limited dynamic psychotherapy (STPP; 13), and core conflictual relationship theme therapy (CCRT; 14), a method is used to identify a circumscribed dynamic focus, often interpersonal in nature. If the patient can respond more effectively to behavioral suggestion after a time limited approach to dynamic issues, then one can conclude with dose 3.

It is when everything seems to go wrong in treatment that we must apply dose 4 interventions. Patients who require dose 4 have severe and often multiple symptoms, family problems, personality disorders, and/or extensive trauma histories. They are not good with food logs, they miss sessions, or they threaten to kill themselves or act out in a variety of self-destructive ways. All these must be addressed before productive behavioral work on eating related issues can be implemented. Assessment is complex in these cases. If patients are suicidal, then one may need to insure their safety by hospitalization. Eating disorders patients requiring dose 4 often have very dysfunctional interpersonal relationships and traumatic histories. They expect that the therapist will similarly disappoint or hurt them, and this must be directly addressed when it emerges in the treatment, the analysis of the transference. It is here that a high dosage is necessary, as these patients have very little ability to hold onto the positive aspects of their involvement with the therapist, while having a very strong tendency to project their negative interpersonal experiences onto the therapist, causing them to expect disappointment and even abuse. Sometimes patients are able to influence the therapist to react negatively, and it becomes crucial for the therapist and patient to be able to examine this; this is the analysis of the countertrasnference. This type of work requires an intensive experience over a long enough period of time where the patients can not only observe and experience the therapist as wanting to help, but also as being capable of understanding and managing their tendency to recreate in treatment their negative interpersonal patterns.

It should be noted that I offer these patients the same behavioral suggestions for their eating-related symptoms, depression, or PTSD, that I offer patients in dose's 2 and 3, but I don't have the same expectation that they will comply as readily or as easily as patients who have less complicated or severe problems. For many of dose 4 patients, it is critical that they achieve a stable and benign sense of connection to the therapist before they can abandon their self-destructive behaviors and maladaptive coping strategies.

CONCLUSION

To summarize, while there are many studies of CBT for patients with eating disorders, particularly bulimia nervosa, the outcomes from these studies suggest that the majority of patients will not recover at the end of treatment. Yet, despite its limited effectiveness, researchers continue to strongly endorse that clinicians should adhere to CBT in their work with eating disorder patients. By contrast, it appears that the vast majority of clinicians practice with a combination of treatments that almost always includes aspects of both cognitive behavioral and psychodynamic therapy. It is unclear if the gap between research and practice will ever be closed in our field. From my own perspective, the ultimate irony in this situation is that while a treatment such as CBT can be described as empirically supported, the model from which it is derived cannot, as there is little or no basic science which supports our clinical models of "cognition". As I have already admitted, the same is true for psychodynamic theories. The pathway to resolution here is to abandon these unsupported theories, which cannot be adequately tied to basic research, in favor of developing a "science of psychotherapy", with the hope that it can eventually be tied to our basic research models in biology and psychology.

REFERENCES

[1] Tobin, DL, Banker JB, Weisberg L, Bowers W. I know what you did last summer (and It was Not CBT): A factor analytic model of international psychotherapeutic practice in the eating disorders psychotherapeutic practice. Int J Eat Disord 2007; 40:754–7.

[2] Tobin, DL. Coping Strategies Therapy for bulimia nervosa. Washington DC, American Psychological Association, 2000.

[3] Johnson C, Connors M, Tobin DL. Symptom management of bulimia. J Consul Clin Psychol 1987;55:668-76.

[4] Tobin DL, Johnson CL. The integration of psychodynamic and behavior therapy: Clinical issues vs. theoretical mystique. In: Johnson CL. Psychodynamic treatment for anorexia nervosa and bulimia. New York: Guilford, 1991:347-97

[5] Tobin DL. Psychodynamic psychotherapy and binge eating. In Fairburn CG, Wilson GT, eds. Binge eating: Nature, assessment, and treatment. New York: Guilford, 1993:287-313.

[6] Tobin, DL. Integrative Psychotherapy for bulimia nervosa with comorbid personality disorders. J Psychother Integr 1995;5:245-63.

[7] Howard KL, Kopt SM, Krause MS, Olinsky, DE. The dose effect relationship in psychotherapy. Am Psychol, 1986;41:159-64.

[8] Herzog T, Hartmann A, Sandholz Z, Stammer, H. Prognostic factors in out-patient psychotherapy of bulimia. Psychother Psychosom 1991;54:48-55.

[9] Johnson C, Tobin DL, Dennis A. Differences in treatment outcome between borderline and nonborderline bulimics at one year follow-up. Int J Eat Disord 1990;9:617-28.

[10] Leichsenring F, Rabnung S. Effectiveness of long term psychodynamic psychotherapy: A meta-analysis. JAMA 2008;300:1551-65.

[11] Klerman GL, Weissman MM, Rounsaville BJ, Chevron ES. Interpersonal psychotherapy for depression. New York: Basic Books, 1984.

[12] Strupp HH, Binder JL. Psychotherapy in a new key: A guide to time limited psychotherapy. New York: Basic Books, 1984.

[13] Luborsky L. Principles of psychoanalytic psychotherapy: A manual for supportive-expressive treatment. New York: Basic Books, 1984.

[14] Kohlenberg RJ, Tsai M. Functional analytic psychotherapy: Creating intense and curative therapeutic relationships. New York: Plenum Press, 1991.

[15] Linehan, MM. Dialectical-behavioral treatment of borderline personality disorder. New York: Guilford, 1993.

[16] Wilson GT. Psychological treatment of eating disorders. Annu Rev Clin Psychol 2005;1:439-65.

[17] NICE Guidelines: Eating Disorders: Core interventions in the treatment and management of anorexia nervosa, bulimia nervosa and related eating disorders http://www.nice.org.uk/Guidance/CG9, January 2004

[18] Waller G. Evidence-based treatment and therapist drift. Behav Res Ther 2009; 47:119–27.

[19] Thompson-Brenner H, Glass S, Westen D. A multidimensional meta-analysis of psychotherapy for bulimia nervosa. Clin Psychol: Sci Pract 2003;10:269-87.

[20] Garner DM, Rockert W, Davis R, Garner MV, Olmstead MP, Eagle M. Comparison of cognitive-behavioral and supportive-expressive therapy for bulimia nervosa. Am J Psychiatry 1993;150:37-46.

[21] Rossiter EM, Agras WS, Telch CF, Schneider JA. Cluster B personality disorder characteristics predict treatment outcome with bulimia nervosa. In J Eat Disorders 1993;13:349-57.

[22] Bachar E, Latzer Y, Kreitler S Berry EM. Empirical comparison of two psychological therapies, self psychology and cognitive orientation, in the treatment of anorexia and bulimia. J Psychother Pract Res 1999;8:115-28.

[23] Kohut H. The analysis of the self. New York: Basic Books, 1971.

[24] Treasure J, Todd G, Brolly M, Tiller J, Nehmed A, Denman F. A pilot study of a randomized trial of cognitive analytical therapy vs. educational behavioral therapy for adult anorexia nervosa. Behav Res Ther 1995;33:363-7.

[25] Dare C, Eisler I, Russell G, Treasure J, Dodge L. Psychological therapies for adults with anorexia nervosa: a randomized controlled trial of out-patient treatments. Br J Psychiatry 2001;178:216-21.

[26] Thompson-Brenner H, Weingeroff J, Westen D. Empirical support for psychodynamic psychotherapy for eating disorders. In: Levy RA, Ablon JS. Handbook of evidence-based psychodynamic psychotherapy: Bridging the gap between science and practice. New York: Humana Press, 2009:67-92.

[27] Arnow BA. Why are empirically supported treatments for bulimia nervosa underutilized and what can we do about it? J Clin Psychol 1999;55:769–79.

[28] Crow S, Mussell MP, Peterson C, Knopke A, Mitchell J. Prior treatment received by patients with bulimia nervosa. Int J Eat Disord1999;25:239–44.

[29] Haas HL, Clopton, JR. Comparing clinical and research treatments for eating disorders. Int J Eat Disord 2003;33:413–20.

[30] Mussell MP, Crosby RD, Crow SJ, Knopke AJ, Peterson CB, Wonderlich SA, Mitchell JE. Utilization of empirically supported psychotherapy treatments for individuals with eating disorders: A survey of psychologists. Int J Eat Disord 2000;27:230–7.

[31] Thompson-Brenner H, Westen D. A naturalistic study of psychotherapy for bulimia nervosa. Part 2: Comorbidity and therapeutic outcome. J Ner Ment Dis 2005;193:573–594.

[32] Lacey JH. An outpatient treatment program for bulimia nervosa. Int J Eat Disord 1983;2:209-14.

[33] Young, JE. Klosko, JS, Weishar, ME. Schema therapy: A practitioner's guide New York: Guilford, 2003.

[34] Giesen-Bloo J, van Dyck R, Spinhoven P, van Tilburg W, Dirksen C, van Asselt T, Kremers I, Nadort M, Arntz A. Outpatient psychotherapy for borderline personality disorder: A randomized trial of schema focused therapy versus transference focused therapy. Arch Gen Psychiatry 2006;63:649-58.

[**35**] Linehan M, Comtois A, Murray AM, Brown MZ, Gallop RJ, Heard HL, Korslund KE, Tutek DA, Reynolds SK, Lindenboim N. Two-year randomized controlled trial and follow-up of dialectical behavioral therapy vs. therapy by experts for suicidal behaviors and borderline personality disorder. Arch Gen Psychiatry 2006;63:757-66.

[36] Clarkin JF, Levy KN, Lenzenweger MF, Kernberg OF. Evaluating three treatments for borderline personality disorder: A Multiwave Study. Am J Psychiatry 2007;164:922-8.

[37] Prochaska JO. Systems of psychotherapy: A transtheoretical analysis. Homewood, Il.: Dorsey Press, 1979.

[38] Agras WS, Crow SJ, Halmi KA, Mitchell JE, Wilson GT, Kraemer HC. Outcome predictors for the cognitive behavior treatment of bulimia nervosa: Data from a multi-site study. Am J Psychiatry 2000;157:1302-8.

In: Treatment and Recovery of Eating Disorders
Editors: Daniel Stein and Yael Latzer

ISBN: 978-1-62808-248-7
© 2013 Nova Science Publishers, Inc.

Chapter 8

Cognitive Behaviour Therapy for Bulimia Nervosa, Anorexia Nervosa and the New 'Transdiagnostic' Approach

Phillipa Hay[1][§§] and Stephen Touyz[2]

[1] Foundation Chair of Mental Health, School of Medicine, University of Western Sydney, NSW, and Adjunct Professor of Psychiatry, School of Medicine, James Cook University, Townsville, Australia

[2] Professor of Clinical Psychology and Honarary Professor in the Discipline of Psychiatry, University of Sydney and Director of the Beumont Centre for Eating Disorders, Baulkham Hills, Sydney, NSW, Australia

Abstract

Specific and efficacious forms of cognitive behaviour therapy (CBT) have been developed for bulimia nervosa, anorexia nervosa and other eating disorders. Indeed the most recent refinement has been a 'transdiagnostic' CBT for all eating disorders. This chapter discusses the most well tested and manualised CBTs for eating disorders, their theoretical basis, evidence and principles of treatment. Specific issues for the overweight patient are also discussed and further reading recommended.

Keywords: psycho-education, monitoring, behavioural experiments, schema therapy, relapse prevention

Introduction

Cognitive Behaviour Therapy (CBT) combines behavioural experiments with rational disputation of patients' beliefs. The former experiments act to help patients disconfirm their

---

[§§] E-mail address: p.hay@uws.edu.au

original assumptions and confirm alternative attitudes. Following the seminal work of Beck and others, Fairburn developed CBT for the newly described 'bulimia' and subsequent bulimia nervosa (BN) in the 1980s, the therapy later known as CBT-BN (1). At the same time Garner and Bemis (2) also developed a longer term (1-2 years) CBT for anorexia nervosa (AN). Both have undergone refinement but CBT-BN has two attributes which place it at the leading edge of psychological therapies in eating disorders (EDs), namely it has evolved into a 'transdiagnostic' ED therapy, and it has been tested comprehensively in randomised controlled trials (3). For this reason this chapter will first discuss CBT-BN and next CBT for AN.

CBT for Bulimia Nervosa (CBT-BN)

CBT for BN developed out of a theoretical understanding of the origin of disordered eating and weight and shape concern based on a cycle of binge-eating followed by extreme dieting and/or weight-control behaviours which exacerbate extreme weight concern and reinforce in its turn the ED behaviours. This cognitive model was first introduced by Fairburn three decades ago (1). It has since been refined, extended and adapted but the core dieting/binge-eating/extreme weight-control behaviours cycle remains (4). In clinical practice therapists may adapt this so that a personalised schema is presented that includes early life experiences and other factors such exposure to a 'dieting' environment (e.g. ballet dancing school) that may have pre-disposed or place the person at risk of an ED.

CBT-BN is also easily adapted to patients with an ED who may not have all DSM diagnostic criteria for BN (3) but have like features i.e. those with EDNOS or BED who suffer from behaviours such as binge-eating and/or vomiting, laxative misuse, extreme exercise for weight and shape reasons, and severe restrictive dieting or fasting, in association with weight and shape concerns that are characteristic of an ED. Although lacking 'evidence', CBT is also sometimes used for patients who suffer from one or more of these behaviours but have primarily another psychological problem such as borderline personality disorder.

Generally evidence of efficacy of CBT for BN is good and it is the leading treatment recommended by national guidelines such as the National Institute for Clinical Excellence Guidelines (5). It has been tested in many randomised controlled trials (RCTs) comparing CBT-BN as developed by Fairburn et al, and variations of such CBT to wait list control groups, other psychotherapies, and pharmacological therapies (6). A number of systematic reviews have been conducted with all consistently finding CBT to be well supported (7). In these reviews (5,8-9), CBT has been found to be superior to wait list control groups with abstinence rates of forty percent or more at the end of treatment, compared to much lower (as low as 10%) abstinence rates for wait list control groups. It has also been found superior to other psychotherapies, most notably interpersonal psychotherapy, in the short-term. However, at one year follow-up, trials have found reduced differences in outcomes between CBT-BN and interpersonal psychotherapy (10). CBT has also been found to be effective compared to pharmacotherapy, most notably anti-depressant therapies (11), and attrition rates are notably higher in anti-depressant control groups.

Classic CBT for BN as developed by Fairburn and colleagues (12) is conducted over a series of twenty sessions that initially may be twice-weekly, decreasing to weekly and then having one or two follow-up sessions over a period of around four months. It is presented in four stages, the first being psycho-education, the second monitoring of eating behaviours, the third introducing behavioural experiments to prevent ED behaviours and promote self-control, and the fourth comprising cognitive challenging of ED attitudes.

In the first education phase, the patient is provided with information about BN and related EDs and an introduction to a personalised CBT formulation in diagrammatic form with the diet-binge-purge cycle at its core. Examples of such formulations can be found at the following website: www.psych.ox.ac.uk/credo/cbt_and_eating disorders. Specific discussion addresses the role extreme dieting plays in leading to binge-eating which often includes results of research studies of starvation (e.g. the classic study of Keys (13) or more recent laboratory research). Such an understanding of the antecedents to binge-eating is usually very well-received and provides some mitigation of the person's associated distress and self-disgust. The capacity for insight into the way early life experiences or their social and interpersonal context may have contributed to the onset of an ED is also often helpful in therapy.

The second phase of therapy starts with the behavioural monitoring and recording of eating and weight control behaviours. Patients often find keeping this distressing and need to be reassured of its core role in therapy. Forms are standardised but can be adapted into journal format and can be downloaded from the former website (see above). Records are reviewed at each session. The next step is instituting a meal plan of regular eating e.g. three meals and two snacks per day combined with dietary education. It is essential to avoid long periods without eating as this exacerbates the diet-binge cycle. The mid-phase of therapy focuses on cognitive strategies such as Socratic questioning and challenging of beliefs and attitudes which reinforce ED behaviours, such as valuing oneself according to one's weight and shape and "all or nothing" dichotomous thinking. Problem-solving is also usually incorporated here comprising the five steps of defining the problem, generating a solution, listing advantages and disadvantages of each, choosing a solution and trying it out and reviewing it and, if unsuccessful, revisiting other solutions. A good supplementary book for patients at this stage is the CBT self-help manual by Waller and colleagues (14) which also is a useful guide through therapy for carers.

The final phases of CBT involve relapse prevention and review of 'lapses'. Here advice is given that lapses will always occur but the patient will not resume "baseline" levels of binge-eating and purging. Patients may compile a record of strategies that have successfully helped them, such as monitoring and distractions at times of vulnerability to binge-eating. The use of relaxation, slow breathing and other anxiety management and coping strategies can also be usefully introduced during these later points in therapy.

The goal of therapy is normalising eating patterns and reducing extreme weight and shape concerns by identifying disrupted core beliefs and developing new coping mechanisms dealing with the impaired automatic way of thinking. By the end of therapy, the goal of a regular pattern of eating of varied and normal-sized food portions should be achieved. Binge-eating and self-induced vomiting and other behaviours should be reduced or absent and food, eating and weight no longer central to the patients self-view and self-esteem.

CBT-Extended or the trans-diagnostic approach

Fairburn has developed an extended manualised therapy (CBT-E) for all forms of an ED. CBT-BN is extended to include modules that address pre-disposing and, importantly perpetuating or maintaining factors for the ED (3). CBT-E has an additional core module for management of mood intolerance and three optional modules attending to issues in interpersonal relationships, clinical perfectionism, and low self-esteem. A full account and comprehensive treatment manual is found in the text by Fairburn (4).

The efficacy of CBT-E has been tested in a 2-site 20-week treatment and 60 weeks closed follow-up RCT with 154 normal weight ED patients (38% with BN) where it was found to offer advantages for those with more complex additional psychopathologies who appeared to benefit from the additional modules. For those without such problems however there were no differences in outcomes (15). Results for the underweight patient have not yet been reported (see below).

In the additional mood intolerance module, it is recognised that there are several ways mood and eating may relate. For example, people with anorexia may eat less to gain a sense of control over external events, or to demonstrate distress, defiance or anger. Emotional overeating is often found in those who are overweight and binge eating with or without vomiting or compulsive exercise may occur to cope with negative moods or adverse events. Education about the relationship(s) between moods and eating is provided, and explored with the patient. Problem solving and alternate mood modulation strategies are introduced and practiced via behavioural experiments that are encouraged, monitored and reviewed.

Self-esteem is addressed through exploring and challenging the cognitive schemas that promote core beliefs e.g. selective attention to information that supports a negative view of self-worth. Encouraging new activities and friendships and working on interpersonal relationships is also helpful. The specific interpersonal module closely follows that developed by Fairburn and colleagues as a stand alone control therapy for CBT-BN (16). Clinical perfectionism and the need to attain this through the ED is explored in a formulation that mirrors that of the role of over-concern about weight and shape on promoting ED behaviours. Perfectionism in ED is regarded as 'clinical' when it is so extreme that patients can never be satisfied with an achievement and any error is intolerable. In therapy mistakes can be 'reframed' as *'inevitable'* because *'no-one can be perfect - to err is human'*, and mistakes are important and necessary to provide opportunity for new learning.

CBT for anorexia nervosa (CBT-AN)

The central goal of CBT in AN is the normalization of eating behaviour to ensure consistent weight gain and medical stability to achieve a healthy weight with specific focus on the interaction between the thoughts, emotions and behaviours that are the core psychopathology of AN. Garner, Vitousek, and Pike (1997 page 109(17)) postulated the following principles of CBT in AN:

(i)   *the acceptance of conscious experience rather than unconscious phenomena.*
(ii) *focus upon belief, assumptions, schematic processing and meaning systems as mediating variables for maladaptive behaviours and emotions.*

(iii) *the employment of questioning as a prominent therapeutic strategy.*
(iv) *active participation by the therapist in treatment*
(v) *the essential contribution of homework sessions including self-monitoring*

The seminal CBT of Garner and colleagues (17) has been manualised and developed further by Pike and colleagues (18). This manualised CBT-AN follows three clearly defined phases of treatment:

Phase I: Building trust and setting treatment parameters. Here the principal goals are to build a positive therapeutic alliance, exploring and identifying the key features of the ED, providing education about starvation symptoms and other related topics, giving a rationale and advice for restoring normal nutrition and body weight, and prescribing eating patterns and establishing a regular eating pattern. Dietary restriction is addressed and patients are advised to eat regular meals at regular times and gradually increase portion sizes. Psycho-education about starvation and effects of AN is also important at his stage. (An excellent source is found in Garner (19)). This phase emphasises the need for the patient to move into an 'action' stage of change and motivational enhancement therapeutic strategies such as decisional analyses are utilised to help achieve this. This is crucial as outcomes are poorer where there is poor motivation to change and the majority of patients with AN who come for therapy are at a pre-contemplative or contemplative stage of change.

Phase II: Changing beliefs related to food and weight, then broadening the scope of therapy. The goals here are to continue the emphasis on weight gain and normalising eating and to bring these about by reframing relapse, identifying dysfunctional thoughts, exploring negative schema and thinking patterns, developing cognitive restructuring skills, modifying self-concept, and (like CBT-E above) developing an interpersonal focus in therapy.

Phase III: Preventing relapse and preparing for termination. Here the therapist clarifies the changes the patient has made, and prepares the patient for residual problems that may be found once therapy has concluded.

It must be emphasised that CBT-AN is also most appropriately and safely delivered within a multi-disciplinary context. This is where a physician will provide advice and monitor medical status (20) and if possible a dietician will provide expert and individualised nutritional advice.

There is small but mixed evidence base for CBT-AN in AN. Channon and colleagues (21) in a non-blinded RCT compared CBT to behaviour therapy alone and to a control "eclectic" therapy in 24 of 34 outpatients. Outcomes for participants in all treatment groups did not differ but improvements were modest. Serfaty and colleagues (22) compared a form of CBT over 20 weekly sessions with dietary advice in 35 patients followed to 6 months and no patients in the dietary advice group completed therapy. Those in the CBT arm had improved in ED and depressive symptom severity, and body mass index (BMI), but the mean BMI was less than 18. McIntosh and colleagues (23) in a small 20-week three armed study found that a manualised CBT was associated with a greater number of people rated as significantly improved (1 or 2 on their global scale) than those in the interpersonal psychotherapy group but differences were not significant for other outcomes. However, CBT was not associated with better outcomes compared to those in the control specialist supportive clinical management therapy. Finally, Pike and colleagues (24) found in 33 patients that

CBT-AN had a better outcome and longer time to relapse when compared to nutritional counselling therapy following hospital care and weight gain restoration.

The transdiagnostic CBT (CBT-E) developed by Fairburn and colleagues (4) is extended from CBT-BN (see above) but incorporates a module on therapy in the underweight "underweight and under-eating". This has many features similar to the CBT-AN of Pike and colleagues (18) but the focus is more on behavioural change (and monitoring of behaviours that reinforce the ED psychopathology such as body checking) and motivational enhancement strategies (excepting a decisional analysis) are not emphasised. Both therapies have monitoring weight as essential. CBT-E is more prescriptive of calorie needs, use of energy dense drinks to help achieve this, and a goal to 'maintenance' BMI of 19-20 with a weight gain of approximately 500 grams per week for outpatients. CBT-E recommends involving caregivers so that they help support the patient with all matters regarding food and eating in both psychological and pragmatic ways e.g. cooking with the patient. Randomised trials of CBT-E have been conducted but are yet to be published.

CBT in overweight patients

CBT for overweight patients was first described by Cooper & Fairburn in 2000 (25), with a program that is focussed on reducing weight loss to 5-10% and preventing weight regain or maintaining weight loss at the end of program. The style resembles CBT-BN. The treatment structure includes 24 sessions over an 11 month period, on a one-to-one basis. The program is based on two phases and nine modules, allowing the treatment to be tailored to the individual. The first and second phases are similar to CBT-BN, with the third phase focussing on weight maintenance and prevention of weight gain. However, in a longer term follow-up (26) of a randomised controlled trial comparing the CBT to guided self-help results were disappointing. In this trial at 3-years there were no differences between groups and most weight lost was regained by participants.

Patients who are overweight or obese and have an ED, such as binge eating disorder will benefit as well from CBT-E (4) as described above. In addition they may also need a supported weight loss program, particularly those patients with weight related medical problems such as diabetes or high blood pressure. In many cases, even a small weight loss such as the loss of 5-10% body weight, could reduce the risk of developing diabetes and/or cardiovascular diseases (27, 28). Patients should be therefore encouraged to set modest weight loss goals. This is important as studies investigating weight regain following obesity treatment, have found that those people who regain weight were the ones who set unrealistic weight goals and did not reach these goals (29). Weight loss advice and treatment should also take care not to undermine CBT for the ED. Strategies employed to assist the patient achieve modest weight loss include; increasing physical activity that is not compulsive but enjoyable and preferably sociable (e.g. tennis versus solitary gym exercises), minor alterations to meal and snacks choices to ensure meal patterns and portion sizes are in line with dietary guidelines, education on how to read nutrition information panels on processed foods to enable clients to make informed decisions when choosing between two or more similar products, and strategies to modify 'unhealthy' patterns such as eating when stressed or habitually overeating when not hungry. A helpful book incorporating many of these and others such as 'mindful eating' is the text by Kausamn (30) "If not dieting then what". Core to this is the framework that physical health and a healthy diet are not realised by any absolute weight but may be found within a wide range of BMI.

Conclusions and discussion

Forms of CBT have been developed as a treatment for bulimia nervosa, anorexia nervosa, binge eating disorder and weight disorder. Classically CBT in eating disorders will have an initial psycho-education and motivational phase which is followed by normalisation of eating with behavioural experiments and strategies to address body image and other typical cognitive schema. Therapy closes with preparation for termination and relapse prevention techniques. CBT may often be supplemented with other approaches including emotion regulation skills training, strategies to improve self-esteem and reduce extreme perfectionism and interpersonal therapy. All these are features of the extended to a transdiagnostic CBT-E (4).

The evidence base is strongest for specific CBT-BN and its next generation CBT-E (1,4). Long-term (5-year) maintenance of change has also been reported for CBT-BN (31) and it is generally regarded as 'first-line' treatment for BN. Evidence is present but weaker for CBT-AN and CBT used in other eating disorders. CBT has been developed for obesity but long term maintenance of weight loss has not been found. Further research is needed to establish the efficacy compared to other psychotherapies of CBT-AN and CBT-E in underweight patients.

Suggested reading

Touyz S, Polivy J, Hay P. *Eating Disorders*. In the series: Psychological Therapies and Behavioural Medicine Evidence-based Practice, Hogrefe & Huber, 2006.

Fairburn CG. *Transdiagnostic cognitive behavior therapy for eating disorders*. New York: Guilford Press, 2010.

REFERENCES

[1] Fairburn CG. A cognitive behavioural approach to the treatment of bulimia. Psychol Med. 1981;11:707-711.

[2] Garner DM, Bemis KM, A cognitive-behavioral approach to anorexia nervosa. Cognit Ther Res, 1982;6:123-150.

[3] Fairburn CG, Cooper Z, Shafran R. Cognitive behavior therapy for eating disorders: A "transdiagnostic" theory and treatment. Beh Res Therapy, 2003;41:509–529.

[4] Fairburn CG. Transdiagnostic cognitive behavior therapy for eating disorders. New York: Guilford Press, 2010.

[5] National Institute for Clinical Excellence (NICE). Eating disorders: Core interventions in the treatment and management of anorexia nervosa, bulimia nervosa and related disorders. Clinical Guideline Number 9. London: NICE, 2004.

[6] Touyz S, Polivy J, Hay P. Eating Disorders. In the series: Psychological Therapies and Behavioural Medicine Evidence-based Practice, Hogrefe & Huber, 2006.

[7] Hay P. Eating disorders. In Best practices in behavioral management of disorders of infancy, childhood, and adolescence. Trafton, JA, Gordon W Eds. Los Altos, CA: The Institute for Brain Potential, 2008.

[8] Shapiro JR, Berkman ND, Brownley KA, Sedway JA, Lohr KN, Bulik CM. Bulimia nervosa treatment. A systematic review of randomised controlled trials. Int J Eat Disord, 2007;40:321-336.

[9] Hay P, Bacaltchuk J, Claudino A, Ben-Tovim D, Yong PY. Individual psychotherapy in the outpatient treatment of adults with anorexia nervosa (Cochrane Methodology Review). In: The Cochrane Library, Issue 4. Chichester, UK: John Wiley & Sons, Ltd., 2003.

[10] Agras WS, Walsh BT, Fairburn CG, Wilson GT, Kraemer HC. A Multicenter Comparison of Cognitive-Behavioral Therapy and Interpersonal Psychotherapy for Bulimia Nervosa. Arch Gen Psychiatry, 2000;57:459-466.

[11] Claudino A, Bacaltchuk J, Hay P. Pharmacotherapy for eating disorders. Chapter 10 in Interventions for Body Image and Eating Disorders; Evidence and Practice. Paxton S, Hay P Eds. IP Communications, Melbourne. 2009.

[12] Fairburn CG, Marcus MD, Wilson GT. Cognitive behavior therapy for binge eating and bulimia nervosa: A comprehensive treatment manual. In Binge Eating: Nature, Assessment, and Treatment. Fairburn CG, Wilson GT Eds. New York: The Guilford Press, 1993:361-404.

[13] Keys A, Brozek J, Henschel A, Mickelsen O, Taylor HL. The biology of human starvation (Vols. 1–2). Minneapolis, MN: University of Minnesota Press, 1950.

[14] Waller G, Mountford V, Lawson R, Gray E, Cordery H, Hinrichsen H. Beating Your Eating Disorder. A Cognitive-Behavioral Self-Help Guide for Adult Sufferers and their Carers Bambridge, Cambridge, 2010.

[15] Fairburn CG, Cooper Z, Doll HA, O'Connor ME, Bohn K, Hawker DM, Wales JA, Palmer RL Transdiagnostic cognitive-behavioral therapy for patients with eating disorders: a two-site trial with 60-week follow-up. Am J Psychiatry, 2009;166:311-319.

[16] Fairburn CG, Jones R, Peveler R, Carr SJ, Solomon RA, O'Connor, M. E, Burton J,Hope RA. Three psychological treatments for bulimia nervosa: A comparative trial. Arch Gen Psychiatry,1991;48:463–469.

[17] Garner DM, Vitousek KM, Pike KM. Cognitive-behavioral therapy for anorexia nervosa. In Handbook of Treatments for Eating Disorders. 2nd edition. Garner DM, Garfinkel, PE Eds. New York: The Guilford Press, 1997:94-144.

[18] Pike KM, Carter J, Olmsted M. Cognitive Behavioral Therapy manual for anorexia nervosa. In The Treatment of Eating Disorders A clinical handbook. Grilo C, Mitchell JE Eds. The Guilford Press, 2010:83-108.

[19] Garner PE. Psychoeducational principles in treatment. In Handbook of treatment for eating disorders (2nd ed.) Garner DM, Garfinkel PE. Eds. New York: The Guilford Press. 1997: 145-177.

[20] Birmingahm CL, Treasure J. Medical management of eating disorders. (2nd Ed.) Cambridge: Cambridge University Press, 2010.

[21] Channon S, de Silva P, Hemsley D, Perkins R. A contolled trial of cognitive-behavioural and behavioural treatment of anorexia nervosa. Beh Res Therapy, 1989;27:529-35.

[22] Serfaty MA, Turkington D, Heap M, Ledsham L, Jolley E. Cognitive therapy versus dietary counselling in the outpatient treatment of anorexia nervosa:. Eur Eat Disorders Rev, 1999;7:334-50.

[23] McIntosh VVW, Jordan J, Carter FA, Luty SE, McKenzie JM, Bulik CM, Frampton CM, Joyce PR. Three psychotherapies for anorexia nervosa: a randomized controlled trial. Am J Psychiatry, 2005;162:741-747.

[24] Pike KM, Walsh BT, Vitousek K, Wilson GT, Bauer J. Cognitive behavior therapy in the post-hospitalization treatment of anorexia nervosa. Am J Psychiatry, 2003;160:2046-2049.

[25] Cooper Z, Fairburn. A new cognitive behavioural approach to the treatment of obesity Behav ResTher, 2001;39:499-511.

[26] Cooper Z, Doll HA, Hawker DM, Byrne S, Bonner G, Elizabeth E, O'Connor ME, Fairburn CG. A new cognitive behavioural treatment for obesity: A randomized controlled trial with three-year follow-up. Behav ResTher, 2010;48:706-13.

[27] National Health and Medical Research Council (NHMRC). Dietary Guidelines for Australian Adults. Canberra: Commonwealth of Australia, 2003.

[28] Vidal J. Updated review on the benefits of weight loss. Int J Obes, 2002;26:S25–S28.

[29] Byrne S, Cooper Z, Fairburn C. Weight maintenance and relapse in obesity: a qualitative study. Int J Obes, 2003; 27: 955-962.

[30] Kausman R. If not dieting then what? Allen & Unwin Ltd., Melbourne, 2005.

[31] Fairburn CG, Norman PA, Welch SL, O'Connor ME, Doll HA, Peveler RC. A prospective study of outcome in bulimia nervosa and the long term effects of three psychological treatments. Arch Gen Psychiatry, 1995;52:304-12.

In: Treatment and Recovery of Eating Disorders
Editors: Daniel Stein and Yael Latzer

ISBN: 978-1-62808-248-7
© 2013 Nova Science Publishers, Inc.

Chapter 9

THE ART OF SUPERVISION IN THE TREATMENT OF EATING DISORDERS

Edith Mitrany[***]

Training and supervising psychoanalyst, Israel Psychoanalytical Society and International Psychoanalytic Association
Formerly Head of the Department of Child and Adolescent Psychosomatic Medicine and Department of Eating Disorders, Sheba Medical Center, Tel Hashomer, Israel

ABSTRACT

In eating disorders as in other psychopathologies, the twofold purpose of supervision is to provide learning for the supervisee and to optimize the service for the patient. This chapter addresses supervision in the treatment of eating disorders from two vantage points: case management and psychotherapy proper. With regard to case management, issues of hierarchy and leadership may influence the cohesiveness of the team and its therapeutic effectiveness and in this respect a structured eating disorders program has an advantage over an ad-hoc operation of private caregivers.

With regard to psychotherapy, although cognizant and respectful of alternative and even more ubiquitous models of psychotherapy, the author has chosen to address the supervision of psychodynamic psychotherapy, congruent with her own orientation. The contemporary supervisory stance has parted from the previous purely didactic approach and recognizes the centrality of counter-transference. Unmotivated for change and difficult to treat, patients with eating disorders arouse in the therapist strong counter-transference reactions which reverberate in supervision: both therapists and supervisors are prone to experiencing frustration, anger, loss of value and confidence in their professional effectiveness. Traditional psychoanalytic devotion to the process, while delegating secondary attention to the symptoms is not realistic in eating disorders, notorious for their mortality risk. Artful navigation between activism and neutrality is one of the many challenges for both the therapist and the supervisor engaged in the endeavor.

[***] E-mail address: edmitran@netvision.net.il

Keywords: eating disorders, psychoanalytic psychotherapy, psychodynamic psychotherapy, supervision, counter-transference

INTRODUCTION

The treatment of eating disorders is composed of a number of simultaneous multidisciplinary interventions, undertaken on a secondary or tertiary care level.

Eating disorders are potentially severe, life threatening mental and physiological conditions. Anorexia nervosa (AN) alone has a high mortality risk (1, 2) including suicide, which is a common cause of death among these patients (3).

The front line intervention is therefore geared toward physiological stabilization, restoration of weight, normalization of alimentation and of aberrant eating habits and removal (or at least reduction) of the obsession with food and weight. The current core multimodal treatment protocol includes medical, pharmacological and dietetic management, rehabilitation and psychotherapy. The latter might be individual, family, or group therapy, long term psychodynamic, or short term crisis intervention, psycho-educational, supportive, cognitive-behavior therapy (CBT), interpersonal (IP), expressive-art therapies, etc. Each of these psychotherapies has its own merits provided they all abide by the basic principles of team collaboration and ongoing medical supervision. Treating anorexia single handedly is not a conceivable option (4).

The Merriam-Webster Dictionary (5) defines supervision as an act of overseeing, "a critical watching and directing of activities or a course of action" According to the Roget's Thesaurus (6) supervision is a synonym to (partial list): overseeing, surveillance, to inspect, scrutinize, contemplate, examine, to have control over, to manage, to direct, to conduct.

SUPERVISION

The following text will address two aspects pertaining to the supervision of treatment: case management and its supervision on one hand, and psychotherapy supervision on the other hand, with special emphasis on the unique dilemmas confronting the therapist vis-à-vis a patient suffering from an eating disorder.

Team Work and Case Supervision

Less severe cases of eating disorders are usually treated in the community, in private or public care, while patients with more severe eating disorders are hospitalized. The optimal care is usually provided by specialized eating disorders programs. At all levels of intervention, professionals working as a team is preferable to a number of professionals working in parallel (7, 8, 9).

Eating disorders programs, in hospital or outpatient settings, are hierarchically structured and consist of a department head and representatives of the different disciplines present (medicine, nursing, nutrition, psychotherapy, education, etc.) organized in one or several teams each led by senior professionals who function as case managers and treatment supervisors.

Team work is not an improvised, ad hoc partnership of several professionals working in tandem in pursuit of a common task but rather a group activity with its own particular dynamics and interactions. According to Yank (10) if properly invested, it will operate efficiently.

"The crucial property of teamness"--the key set of intangible phenomena that allow a team to function synergistically as more than the sum of its parts, and with a sense of team identity... Leadership activities promote team cohesiveness and boundary maintenance"(p.250) ".

Butterill (11) calls attention to possible team dysfunction caused by

"...poorly defined accountability, a lack of leadership, communication breakdowns, and boundary violations. Suggested interventions are education of team members about organizational theory, open discussion of contentious issues, and reinforcement of boundaries...."(p.370)

Team leadership in institutional programs is a pre-assigned function, emerging from a hierarchic system. Heads of department or chief psychologists are appointed, not democratically elected. The department head designs the treatment plan and delegates authority to the team leaders to oversee its implementation and coordinate the therapeutic activities, to supervise the management of the cases, their progress and vicissitudes.

There is a clear distinction between case management/supervision versus therapy supervision, whereas the former is service oriented and its purpose is to survey the diagnostic process and the accuracy and execution of the ensuing dispositions, the latter is focused on the psychotherapy process per se.

In ad-hoc settings, as opposed to structured eating disorder programs, the situation is quite different. Patients with eating disorders (or parents of an afflicted minor) who approach a private individual mental health professional will hopefully be advised to also see a dietician. Even in the fortunate but infrequent case where several basic disciplines (medicine, nutrition, psychiatry, psychology, social work) are actively collaborating, still, without a clear treatment algorithm, experience with previous shared cases and commonly agreed upon leadership, this format is not yet an eating disorders team. Individual care givers might initiate either sporadic consultation or regular supervision with a "specialist" in his, her own field, but this is an individual resource, outside the team. The mutual updating of treatment progress among the peer care givers – if there is any - has definite merits but still remains a default substitute for cohesive team work, case management and supervision as they are practiced in accredited eating disorders programs.

The following clinical case reflects underlying issues of hierarchy in leadership and interpersonal conflicts of such a "non-team" caregivers.

Case vignette 1

Anna, 16 yrs of age, began psychotherapy and dietetic counseling following a severe weight loss diagnosed as AN-RestrictingType. At some point, a psychiatric intervention was requested by all parties involved (parents and therapists) on account of suicidal thoughts and obsessive-compulsive manifestations. All three therapists from different disciplines worked in private practice and had no previous collaboration. Their involvement in this case was parallel and not interactive. At one point, the psychiatrist heard from the patient's mother that the dietician suggested day hospitalization. Surprised by this unshared initiative, the psychiatrist contacted the dietician who denied having made the recommendation. It was suggested that the family is manipulative and deceptive. The psychiatrist, a senior psychoanalyst himself, monitored medication while meeting with the patient every six weeks and exchanging by phone occasional update impressions with the psychologist and dietician. This psychiatrist experienced a certain frustration at carrying the bulk of the clinical responsibility while in effect filling only a marginal role vis-à-vis both patient and colleagues. This latent annoyance turned into overt vexation when, a few months later, the patient reported that she will be seeing a substitute psychologist for a while, since her therapist is about to take maternity leave. The surprised psychiatrist expressed disagreement with this recommendation and the same evening approached the psychotherapist to complain about the lack of communication and collaboration. "How is it possible that you have not informed me and consulted with me?" The reaction was: "it is your fault! You should have been more active in initiating collaboration between us and least of all share your disagreement with the patient." The psychiatrist protested that it was the therapist who took one-sided initiatives, that a 3 month (the length of the maternity leave) substitute new therapist might not be such a good idea, versus the more logical alternative of increasing the frequency of the visits with him, a known figure to the patient and an experienced therapist in his own right. The psychologist insinuated that both patient and parents would not feel comfortable with the psychiatrist as an alternative therapist. It was not said whether this was therapist's own inference or a de-facto communication by the patient. After a while, the patient declared herself sufficiently recovered and in no further need of professional help.

This is an example of a dysfunctional team, or in effect, a non-team, but rather a number of otherwise esteemed professionals who instead of collaborating, worked in parallel, competing for autonomy and leadership, and thus inadvertently collided along the way. In a "Solomonic Judgment" in reverse, the patient flew into health, relinquished both "parents" and regretfully dropped out of therapy while still in great need of treatment.

Supervision of psychotherapy[†††]

Of the plethora of practiced models in psychotherapy, this paper will address psychotherapy and its respective supervision from a psychoanalytic perspective, the author's area of expertise.

As psychotherapy itself, supervision of psychotherapy is a vast issue, informed by a great number of publications, subject of numerous theoretical and technical currents and controversies. (7) Addressing it in full would be way beyond the scope of this chapter.

A few salient points with regard to psychotherapy supervision per se will be briefly summarized, prior to shifting the focus to supervision in the treatment of eating disorders.

[†††] psychoanalytic psychotherapy and psychodynamic psychotherapy are used interchangeably

In the pre-qualification stage, supervision of psychotherapy involves trainees from various disciplines: psychiatric residents, clinical psychologists, clinical social workers, psychoanalytic candidates, etc. As a requirement of professional training, the supervision process is in many ways a close application of the above-mentioned Webster definition: the supervisee undergoes a learning experience through orientation and constructive criticism, and the patient benefits from "critical watching", both processes enabled by the supervisor. The task of supervision is to facilitate and develop learning. The supervisor can be experienced as a reliable mentor, someone to identify with, but he also can be considered judging and controlling. (12)

The subjective experience of the supervisee during the training phase of his/her career varies according to a number of factors, all orbiting around the three dyads involved: therapist-patient, therapist- own therapist (assuming that the supervisee is still undergoing personal therapy), supervisor-therapist, and their respective matching personalities. Addressing the way supervisees evaluate their supervisors, Beinart (13) refers to the findings of D.R.Green (author of "Investigating the Core Skills of Clinical Supervision", unpublished D. Clin.Psych. dissertation, University of Leeds-1988):

"using a qualitative research methodology Green found that special knowledge, credibility and integrity were terms used by trainees to describe influential supervisors." (p.42)

Some congruence of theoretical orientation between supervisor and supervisee is necessary for a good working alliance of the supervisor-supervisee dyad, although one may argue that exposure to diversity in theoretical paradigms enhances the learning process of the trainees.

The spectrum of the supervisory stance in psychoanalytic psychotherapy may vary from a didactic approach, at one end, which altogether avoids dealing with counter-transference, to an equally extreme position advanced by Balint (14) at the other end sustaining that the ideal supervisor would be the supervisee's therapist himself. The great diversification in psychoanalytic theory and practice has generated over the years a multitude of supervisory models in-between the two above mentioned poles.

In the Post-qualification stage a less motivated trainee might discontinue the supervision once his/her formal training requirements have been fulfilled, even though the case progress might still benefit from additional guidance.

At the opposite end, a dedicated therapist, although already formally qualified and even with years of experience, will unequivocally request supervisory assistance from a senior or peer and profit from it. Solnit (15) claimed that supervision, like psychoanalysis, is interminable.

In many institutional programs, supervision of psychodynamic therapy is mandatory even for qualified therapists

Setting: Psychodynamic therapy in eating disorders is often a complex proposition which in many respects cannot fully abide by the golden rules of practice. Public inpatient care has been increasingly shortened by heath policies, and unless there is a consecutive spectrum of daycare and outpatient service available, in many such settings the stay is too brief to allow for more than crisis intervention. If available and feasible, psychotherapy will better be supervised, for the benefit of all parties involved. According to Eckstein, R., and Wallerstein (16)

"The supervisor is directly related to the student but has a quasi-indirect relationship to the patient. On one hand his responsibility is to teach psychotherapeutic skills to the student, but there is an additional responsibility in maintaining clinical standards and seeing that patients benefit from the service." (p.12)

One distinct characteristic of supervision of psychodynamic psychotherapy in an eating disorder program – assuming that this option is not definitively extinct- is the inability to maintain the mutual anonymity of the supervisor-patient dyad as practiced in private psychotherapy. In most eating disorder centers the psychotherapy supervisors perform additional functions (psychiatric care, group therapy, etc) and often are otherwise involved with their supervisee's patients. However, there are settings that adhere to a more canonic stance and "import" the psychotherapy supervisors. Those are not members of the staff, hold no organizational functions and usually meet the supervisees in their own offices, away from the clinic.

Team Interaction and Supervision: Eating disorders programs traditionally hold group teaching activities in the format of case presentations either at the evaluation level (the so called "intake meeting") or as a treatment review. In addition, there are study groups either at peer level or led by a senior professional, local or imported, for the purpose of either consultation or continuous case supervision. This group of people, the "staff", by the mere virtue of working together will develop its own dynamics whether they sit in a circle in the meeting room or by themselves in their respective offices. Issues, to mention a few, such as achievement ambitions, competition, envy, exhibitionism, shame, passivity, control but also idealization and love, will emerge in the discussion, and are not exclusively related to the material presented. Patients with eating disorders present common characteristics such as chronicity, repeated relapses, lack of compliance, self destructive behaviors including suicide attempts which in the long run wear out the care givers. It will be incumbent on the supervisor to determine the demarcation line between group supervision and group therapy, a perennial challenge in all forms of psychotherapy supervision. A not uncommon occurrence is counter-transferential (supervisor vis-à-vis the group) causing the supervisor too to feel inadequate or ineffective, short of providing rescue solutions and subject to controversies as illustrated in the following case.

Case Vignette 2

Sally, 42 years of age, suffered from chronic AN-Purging Type since age 15. At present she was in her second year of twice weekly psychotherapy with Dr M. Due to a severe relapse of the anorectic symptoms, Sally needed urgent hospitalization and the only available eating disorders facility for the adult population in this country was headed by Dr. M. During her hospital stay, Sally, like the rest of the patients, was treated by a multidisciplinary team. The psychotherapist assignment presented a dilemma: on one hand it seemed inappropriate for Sally to continue therapy with Dr. M. (whose policy, as head of the department, was to refrain from seeing patients in the ward on an individual basis) but, on the other hand it made little therapeutic sense to assign Sally to a new psychotherapist, for the short period of expected hospitalization.

After serious staff debates it was decided to make an exception in this case and allow Sally to continue her twice-a-week sessions with Dr. M. Unsurprisingly, this decision put Sally in a special position vis-à-vis other patients (envy, sibling rivalry on their side, a sense of entitlement, bullying and acting out, on hers). The "special position" transpired to some members of the staff, in particular individual therapists and nursing personnel, all under Dr. M's leadership. By virtue of projective identification with other patients, displacement of envy and rivalry with regard to her special relation with Dr. M. and splitting, Sally became the focus of intensive preoccupation and debate.

During the few months of her hospitalization Sally captured many staff meetings and group supervision during which Dr. M. found herself overtly or covertly attacked, and deep inside deploring almost everything: the imperative inpatient admission, this particular eating disorder service under her chairmanship being the sole available resource, not having had temporarily discontinued psychotherapy, or not having assigned Sally, while hospitalized, to another colleague. Dr M was conscious of confronting negative countertransference feelings not only toward Sally but also toward her own team, vis-à-vis whom she fulfilled a supervisory function.

As an epilogue to this dilemma it is of interest to note that after the discharge and upon renewing the psychotherapy with Dr. M. on a private basis, Sally although recovered from the set back in her nutritional status and eating behavior, became a very resistant patient who eventually entered a negative therapeutic reaction which led to an insoluble impasse and ultimately discontinuation of treatment. Sadly, Sally had a life long difficulty in retaining her "good objects". During the following years, Sally had several relapses which required hospitalization in the same eating disorder setting, although without dilemmas with regard to the identity of the therapist since Dr. M has in the mean time retired from the service.

Supervision of individual psychotherapy of patients with eating disorders

The overall effectiveness of the various forms of psychotherapy in eating disorders remains controversial, the dropout rate is high and randomized controlled trials are extremely rare (17). Compared with briefer and symptom-oriented modes of therapeutic intervention, long term psychoanalysis is currently a rather uncommon treatment recommendation for eating disorders. Its next-of-kin, psychoanalytic psychotherapy, less rigorous in practice although founded on the same principles of analytic listening and empathic, but neutral in its nondirective exploration remains a worthy option and can be greatly beneficial to many such patients (4).

Individual psychodynamic oriented psychotherapy and its parallel supervisory process are not essentially different in eating disorders as compared to other psychopathologies, but they do possess specificities worthy of investigation.

The paramount dilemma of a the psychotherapist-supervisor pair informed by a psychoanalytic orientation vis-à-vis a patient with an eating disorder is how to artfully navigate between therapeutic neutrality dictated by one's own theoretical frame of reference, and the activism imposed by the unique vital necessities of a biologically endangered patient. This compromise is facilitated by the axiomatic rule of never operating as a single handed caregiver, which means that in all eventualities, the medical and nutritive situation is being monitored by the collaborating team members. Although not forcefully totally abstaining from addressing the weight and eating issues, the therapist need not necessarily focus on these preoccupations.

Mitrany (4) stressed:

> "The more symptom-oriented the psychotherapy, the more reluctant the patient is to cooperate and become coerced into a project geared towards an unwanted quest for change. Precisely for that reason, non directive psychotherapy, addressed to subjective feelings and preoccupations rather than to symptoms per se, might be perceived by the patient, for whom one of the central conflicts lies in a precarious sense of autonomy, as less intrusive and threatening, and thus more acceptable." (p. 201)

Bechar (18) emphasizes the unique contribution of self-psychology to the treatment of eating disorders.

> "Three main issues exemplify the opportunities and dilemmas that this new development in psychoanalytic theory brings to the fore in the treatment of eating disorders:
>
> [1] Empathy with deeds and attitudes of the patient that the therapist finds difficult to empathize with;
>
> [2] Empathic understanding "from within" from an experience-near stance vs. experience-distant interpretation "from without";
>
> [3] Self, selfobject relations with food and as a result of progress in therapy, with human beings." (p 147)

In their comprehensive paper on "Supervising the therapy of patients with eating disorders" Hamburg and Herzog (7) address in detail characteristic features of this endeavor and the replication in the supervisor-supervisee couple of certain currents (splitting, boredom) present in the therapist-patient pair.

Among the themes reviewed one finds the exaggerated need for control as well as a basic fear of being intruded upon, which are characteristic of the anorectic/bulimic patient. A too strenuous effort on the part of the therapist to obtain early revelations of the patient's hidden secrets with respect to both eating behaviors (vomiting, use of laxatives) or past and present possibly shameful life events (stealing. sexual assault, infidelity etc.) could be intrusive and needs to be intercepted and interpreted by the supervisor. The reverse situation, in which the therapist totally ignores endangering patterns could reflect a form of collusion between patient and therapist vis-à-vis an authoritative object impersonated by the supervisor. This interaction illustrates the role responsiveness reaction as conceptualized by Sandler (19) and warrants an urgent intervention by the supervisor. As already mentioned above, characteristic to the work with these patients is compromising between therapeutic neutrality on one hand and proper attention to the symptom, on the other.

COUNTERTRANSFERENCE

Among the issues emerging in all supervisory processes, perhaps the most salient is counter-transference. This concept gained a new dimension half a century ago owing to Searles (20), Eckstein and Wallerstein (16) who introduced the notion of a parallel process, meaning the interwoven interaction between patient, analyst, and supervisor.

Regarded from different perspectives, transference and counter-transference gained more attention and controversy than any other subject within the psychoanalytic domain. Until less than three decades ago counter-transference in supervision was avoided rather than accepted and utilized. For most supervisors the supervisee's counter-transference seemed to be a Pandora's Box they feared to open, out of concern that they may, from their position of authority, inappropriately intrude into the personality and inner life of the supervisee and turn supervision into psychotherapy. Over time, the initial trend of seeing these phenomena as pathological processes and impediments to therapy radically changed to considering transference and counter-transference normal components of all conscious and unconscious interactions. Wiener (21) wrote:

> "… although we may be in agreement that transference dynamics are alive and well in supervision, more difficult to assess is whether they are fostering or hindering the task of supervision." (p.53)

Far from claiming that counter-transference should be the sole subject matter of supervision, authors like Hunt (22) nevertheless relegated considerable weight to counter-transference emotions,

> "Supervision which lets in the counter-transference is the most helpful kind because it goes to the core of the therapist-patient relationship." "(p.370)

As applied to eating disorders, countertransference has been widely addressed (8,23,24 etc.), focusing on the impact -on both therapy and supervision –by typical phenomena on such as the tedious maintenance of boundaries, over identification or the opposite, frustration and exasperation with the patient.

The long and weary treatment of patients with eating disorders, described as unmotivated, unable to gain insight and enter transference inevitably reflects on counter-transference. The most common identified responses on the part of the therapist range from frustration and even a sense of failure at one end to narcissistic rage at the other, both endangering, with emotional depletion. Quoting Chessick (25)

> "any therapist who works with eating disorders must have ample independent sources of emotional supply and empathy in his personal life and must be free of the temptation to turn to his patients for gratification, soothing, or narcissistic massage."

The following clinical example will illustrate how these themes reverberate in the parallel process:

Case Vignette 3

Ruth a mother of three, in her mid-thirties, applied for evaluation on account of a protracted eating disorder (since the age of sixteen) with bulimic and purging symptoms. The referral was prompted by an intensification of the symptoms as a result of which Ruth became severely underweight and hypokalemic. The evaluation led to hospitalization in an eating disorders program, where Ruth became stabilized and relatively free of abnormal eating behaviors.

After discharge, Ruth continued follow up with a dietician who specialized in eating disorders and began psychotherapy with a psychiatrist. With the bulk of eating problems apparently behind her, Ruth became cognizant of her many other problems, which, even if present before, were apparently masked by her eating disorder symptoms. She was anxious and insomniac, obsessive/compulsive about her chores, felt insecure, unworthy but at the same time demanding and armed with a strong sense of entitlement towards the surrounding objects. On the surface, Ruth seemed very compliant with the therapy, she wanted so badly to be well and praised, but somehow she failed this intent. The therapist who had developed a protective attitude toward the patient, as if she were a weak, somewhat handicapped child in need of special care, failed to decode her numerous subtle contradictory messages and when alerted by the supervisor, reacted defensively. He perceived the patient as desperate, avoidant, tormented by vague traumatic memories. His supervisor on his side, suspected that this patient had a false self and behind messages of helplessness she was manipulative and in quest for exercising control.

At some point Ruth admitted having abruptly discontinued the medication without the therapist's permission. The therapist's main concern at this point seemed to be about the risk of withdrawal symptoms rather than the significance of the rebellious act itself. Shortly after, the patient began taking short vacations which incurred missing therapy sessions. The therapist continued to seem oblivious to patient's resistance and downright acting out, and sounded (again) protective of his patient (or of himself) vis-à-vis the supervisor. Only some time later, when the patient made a very important independent decision with regard to her career (or rather lack of) which also involved a very close tutorship by a coach with therapeutic ambitions, the therapist had a sudden change of heart: he felt furious, betrayed by the patient who had "pledged" loyalty to a rival, and impulsively confronted the patient with an ultimatum: "either me or him!"

The supervisor made a counter-transference interpretation commenting that the rage was in fact directed toward him rather than toward the patient, by a therapist who felt ridiculed and humiliated due to his compassionate naivety, caught in between a manipulative and dissimulating patient and a critical, unempathic supervisor. While cognizant of a sadistic temptation to declare: "I told you so!" the supervisor was also quite inclined to discuss the situation and even assume responsibility for forcing the therapist into a defensive identification with the so called attacked patient. This enactment could be seen as a manifestation of a projective counter-identification (26): the supervisor envied and reduplicated the supervisee's ability for compassion, a capacity he apparently felt somewhat lacking in himself. In addition, due to a mechanism of splitting, the therapist and supervisor identified each with a different aspect of the patient's psyche: the therapist with the helplessness, the supervisor with the quest for control.

Indeed, one particular expression of countertransference is the mechanism of projective identification [Klein (27) Segal (28), Sandler (29), J, Ogden (30) and many others].

Waska (31) summarizes: " Projective identification is a dynamic mental mechanism that naturally engages the therapist's countertransference and attempts to make use of the therapist as a translator, toxic dump, or special reservoir for the unwanted, confusing, or threatened parts of the self " (p. 160)

Gabbard (32) compares projective identification with countertransference enactment (putting an experience into behavior).

Regarded from a contemporary intersubjective perspective, Berman (34) considers the supervision experience as a form of transitional space, within which contents of therapy and supervision overlap and create a fertile therapeutic triad,

> "A crossroads of a matrix of object relations of at least three persons each brings her or his psychic reality into the bargain, creating a joint intersubjective milieu."

The following supervisory experience will attempt to illustrate the way these psychic processes may impact the therapist post-factum, mediated by a supervisory experience.

Case Vignette 4

Rachel started psychoanalysis at age 19, prompted by symptoms of restrictive anorexia which developed a few months earlier, shortly after beginning her two-year military service. The commanders of the specialized elite army unit to which she was assigned, fully informed of her condition, encouraged the treatment and allowed her to leave the military base in order to attend three weekly analytic sessions. Apparently, owing to her performance, she was very much appreciated by her superiors.

Rachel was very committed not only as a soldier but as patient as well. She was punctual, verbal, associated freely, unraveled memories, fantasized and remembered her dreams. Sadly though, not only was there no improvement whatsoever in her anorexia, but gradually she developed depressive symptoms: a sense of emptiness, purposelessness and lack of worth. In the center of her preoccupation was her parents' marital crisis, prompted by her father's extra marital affair and her sense of having been betrayed by him even more than her mother.

The military service was limited to office hours and Rachel slept at the family home. One night, Rachel called the analyst at about two o'clock in the morning announcing that she had cut her wrists and was bleeding profusely. To the analyst's question whether the parents are at home, Rachel replied she believed they were asleep in their bedroom. The analyst wisely did not inquire why had Rachel called her on the phone rather than alert the parents down the hall, and instead prompted Rachel to immediately wake the parents up and rush to the emergency room.

The next day, for the first time in the year and a half since the beginning of treatment, the analyst received a phone call from Rachel's father, requesting a meeting. The analyst was anxious to first meet with Rachel following the suicide attempt, and also to hear from her how she would feel about the proposed meeting with her parents. The analyst had promised to call the father back. Given all options: to oppose a meeting with parents, to accept and participate, or not participate, Rachel opted for the last. During that session, the analyst did ask the question:" why did you call me first?" Rachel couldn't find an answer and the analyst interpreted the guilt and the incumbent self-punishment over an otherwise unconscious forbidden oedipal (or primal scene) wish to penetrate the parent's bedroom. The meeting with the parents proceeded smoothly, they expressed appropriate concern, were not intrusive but rather offended that Rachel chose to call a "stranger" for help, while they were available to her, next door.

Now we come to supervision. The case was brought to an international forum of group supervision held in Europe. The forum included eight participants - associate members of the International Psychoanalytic Association- led by a senior training analyst. Some participants were adamant about the analyst meeting the parents, thus "corrupting" the neutrality of the analytic process and turning it into an "ordinary" psychotherapy with parental guidance. They would have opted for a different solution, such as referring the parents to a colleague for consultation or possibly couple therapy. Other participants joined the senior supervisor in commenting on the symbolic significance of Rachel's "cutting herself free" from infantile ties and thus dismissing her parents from their protective parental role.

The analyst, although appreciative of the different approaches and contributions, remained quite unsettled with regard to her so called "transgression" (meeting the parents). She also felt that the patient's message of loneliness had been somehow de-emphasized. The analyst could not help a feeling of being outvoted and categorized in a rigid and dogmatic way. She left the supervision session feeling rather confused but upon further reflection, had a sudden insight into a late projective identification vis-à-vis the patient ("each of us was trying so hard and ultimately felt so utterly alone") and on second thought, considered herself redeemed by the supervisory encounter.

CONCLUSION

Both psychotherapy of eating disorders and its corresponding supervision face issues basically similar to any other therapy/supervision endeavor. Here too, the supervisor-supervisee dyad faithfully echoes the therapist –patient saga. However, there are some unique features inherent to eating disorders pathology that merit emphasis. The main challenges facing both the therapist and the supervisor pertain to the psychotherapist's ability to function as a member of a team; to focus on the therapy process rather than on symptoms but in a way that balances therapeutic neutrality with concern for the patient's vital medical needs; to cope with issues of power struggle and quest for control as they emerge in the parallel process. Both the therapist and the supervisor may experience frustration, anger and narcissistic hurt vis-à-vis a resistant patient, unmotivated to change, and they are prone to a lessening of their sense of professional worth and personal value. This could be perceived as role responsiveness to the patient's unconscious malevolence.

In eating disorders as elsewhere, supervision is both an art and a métier. It could become a unique and memorable experience for a supervisory couple matched for personalities, theoretical congruence and transference/counter-transference sagacity. But it can also take a less profitable course and lead to impasse. Quoting Schlesinger (35):

> "There is art and science in facilitating learning through supervision. How to describe supervision that facilitates learning? To paraphrase Hippocrates, in the first place, it is important to do no harm."

The supervisory experience can be equally jeopardized by a supervisor's overly rigorous adherence to technique, too passive stance (which hampers learning), or activism and intrusiveness (which impair the supervisee's autonomy and creativity).

Supervision of psychotherapy does not mean interfering with the treatment, or outdoing the supervisee in his task. It is about being "there" and "with", but not "instead" of the therapist. As Winnicott (29) wrote:

"Responsible persons must be available when children play; but this does not mean that the responsible person need enter into the children's playing"

REFERENCES

[1] Fichter M. Six-year course and outcome of anorexia nervosa. Int J Eat Disord 1999;26(4):359-385.

[2] Fichter MM, Quadflieg N, Hedlund S Twelve-year course and outcome predictors of anorexia nervosa, Int J Eat Disord 2006;39(2):87-100

[3] Berkman ND, Lohr KN, Bulik CM. Outcomes of eating disorders: a systematic review of the literature. Int J Eat Disord 2007;40(4):293-309

[4] Mitrany E. Is psychoanalytic psychotherapy still an option in anorexia nervosa? Int J Child Adolesc Health 2009;2(2):197-204

[5] Merriam-Webster's Collegiate Dictionary, 10th ed., Merriam-Webster Inc. Springfield, Mass 1993, p.1184

[6] Roget's Thesaurus abridged edition, editor Betty Kirkpatrick, Penguin Books, UK1987, p. 342

[7] Hamburg P., Herzog D. Supervising the therapy of patients with eating disorders. Am J Psychother, 1990;44, (3): 369-380

[8] Lawrence M., The Anorectic Mind, London: Karnac, The Tavistock Series, 2008

[9] Fichter M, Inpatient treatment of anorexia nervosa, in Eating Disoeders and Obesity, edited by Brownell K, Faiburn C, New York, Kondon The Guilford Press, p, 336-343

[10] Yank GR, Barber JW, Hargrove DS, Whitt PD, The mental health treatment team as a work group: team dynamics and the role of the leader , Psychiatry 1992 Aug;55(3):250-64

[11] Butterill D, O'Hanlon J, Book H. When the system is the problem, don't blame the patient: problems inherent in the interdisciplinary inpatient team. Can J Psychiatry 1992 37(3):168-72, p.168

[12] Szecsödy, I. Supervision–a complex tool for psychoanalytic training. Scandinavian Psychoanalytic Review 1994;17:119-129

[13] Beinart H Models Of Supervision And Supervisory Relationship In Supervision And Clinical Psychology, Fleming I Steen L Brunner-Routledge, Hove And New York, 2004; p. 42

[14] Balint M. On the psycho-analytic training system Int J Psychoanal 1948;29:16-73

[15] Solnit A J Learning from psychoanalytic supervision. Int J Psychoanal 1970;51:359-362 p.361

[16] Eckstein R., Wallerstein R. The Teaching and Learning of Psychotherapy New York: International Universities Press, 1958 p. 12

[17] Halmi K. Treatment of anorexia nervosa, In: Wonderlich S, Mitchell J, De Zwann M, Steiger H, eds. Annual Review of Eating Disorders, Part 2. Abington: Radcliffe, 2006:159-67.

[18] Bachar E. The contributions of self psychology to the treatment of anorexia and bulimia. Am J Psychother. 1998 ;52(2):147-65.

[19] Sandler J. Countertransference and role-responsiveness. Int Rev Psychoanal 1976;3:43-47

[20] Searles HF, The informational value of the supervisor's emotional experiences, Psychiatry 1955;18:135-146.

[21] Wiener J The analyst's countertransference when supervising: friend or foe? J Anal Psychol, 2007;52:51–69, p. 53

[22] Hunt W. The Use of the countertransference in psychotherapy supervision. J Am Acad Psychoanal 1981:9: 361-373, p. 370

[23] Williams G. Reflections on some dynamics of eating disorders: No-entry defences and foreign bodies. Int J Psychoanal 1997;78:927-942

[24] Birksted-Breen D. Working with an anorectic patient. Int J Psychoanal 1989;70: 30-40

[25] Chessick RD. Clinical notes toward the understanding and intensive psychotherapy of adult eating disorders. Ann Psychoanal 1984;12: 301-322 p. 318

[26] Grinberg L.Countertransference and projective counteridentification In   Countertransference Ed. L. Epstein and A. H. Feiner. New York: Jason Aronson, Inc. 1979

[27] Klein M. Notes on some schizoid mechanisms. In Envy and Gratitude and Other Works, 1946-1963. New York: Delacorte Press/Seymour Laurence, 1975, pp. 1-24

[28] Segal H. An introduction to the Work of Melanie Klein. New York: Basic Books., 1964; p.27, 29

[29] Sandler J. The concept of projective identification. In Projection, Identification, Projective Identification, ed. J. Sandler. Madison, CT: Int. Univ. Press,1987; pp. 13-26

[30] Ogden T H. On projective identification.Int. J. Psychoanal. 1979;60: 357-373

[31] Waska RT. Projective identification, countertransference, and the struggle for understanding over acting out , J Psychother Pract Res 1999; 8:155-161.

[32] Gabbard GO. Countertransference: The emerging common ground. Int J Psychoanal 1995;76: 475-485 p.481

[33] Berman E. Psychoanalytic supervision: The intersubjective development. Int J Psychoanal 2000;81: 273-290 p.276

[34] Schlesinger HJ. Supervision for fun and profit: Or how to tell If the fun is profitable. Psychoanalytic Inquiry 1995;15:190-210, p.191

[35] Winnicott D. Playing and Reality. London: Tavistock 1971 p.50

In: Treatment and Recovery of Eating Disorders
Editors: Daniel Stein and Yael Latzer

ISBN: 978-1-62808-248-7
© 2013 Nova Science Publishers, Inc.

Chapter 10

MANAGING EATING DISORDERS. COUNTERTRANSFERENCE AND OTHER DYNAMIC PROCESSES IN THE THERAPEUTIC MILIEU

Moria Golan,[1,2,3]‡‡‡ *Amit Yaroslavski*[4] *and Daniel Stein*[4,5]
[1] Shahaf, Community Services for Eating Disorders, Kibbutz Naan
[2] School of Nutritional Sciences, Faculty of Agriculture,
Food and Environmental Quality Sciences,
Hebrew University of Jerusalem, Rehovot
[3] Department of Nutrition, Tel Hai Academic College, The Upper Galille
[4] Pediatric Psychosomatic Department,
Edmond and Lily Safra Children's Hospital,
Chaim Sheba Medical Center, Tel Hashomer
[5]Sackler Faculty of Medicine, Tel Aviv University, Ramat-Gan, Israel

ABSTRACT

The management of eating disorders goes beyond symptom management per se and indeed to the establishment of certain interpersonal conditions that are close to Winnicott's mother-infant holding environment. In this environment, there is an interactive play to facilitate cooperation and harmony between the medical and the psychological professional that stimulates different transference phenomena, creating a tension in the multidisciplinary team. Eating disorder patients feel duty-bound to induce strong feelings such as rage, hate, hopelessness, pity, sorrow, or love in those with whom they become involved, including their care-givers. The pseudo-family dynamics that may appear in the therapeutic milieu stimulate an intense emotional atmosphere recreating competition, parallel processes, and splitting dynamics that exert a great impact on the workplace atmosphere. The aim of this paper is to review the concept of countertransference in the context of treating eating disorders (ED). Additionally, we will

‡‡‡ E-mail address: moriag@netvision.net.il

discuss the team dynamics within this environment and their impact on treatment process and outcome. We shall discuss coping approaches to manage patterns of countertransference to facilitate effective treatment processes for the patient and the therapist.

Keywords: eating disorders, dynamic processes, therapeutic milieu

INTRODUCTION

The management of eating disorders (ED) calls for a lift above the multidisciplinary model to an interdisciplinary status. In recent years, the amount of research on the issue of staff countertransference and how it affects those providing services for psychiatric patients has increased. It is now well recognized that management of staff countertransference is a necessary condition for the provision and maintenance of high-quality services and the reduction of staff turnover (1-3). However, the impact of countertransference in the context of treating eating disorders has received only limited attention in the literature.

The management of eating disorders requires a highly structured and systemized treatment program in order to reduce maladaptive eating and to promote the development of the intrapsychic and interpersonal changes considered necessary for recovery. Management of these disorders goes beyond symptom management per se. Rather, establishment of certain interpersonal conditions that are necessary in order to conduct an effective intervention and for the patient to engage meaningfully in treatment is not a form of compliance, but a true developmental process (4). Management in this sense is close in its meaning to Winnicott's mother-infant holding environment (5) or to Kohut's self-object functioning (6). In this role, the staff has the potential to provide such functions as mirroring, tension regulation, vitalization, and integration to the ED patients. Through the events experienced and relived in the therapeutic environment, the patient's primitive needs may be resolved by the therapist's wish and ability to foster the good-enough environmental mother and the holding state (7). The keeping of boundaries is possibly the most vital, and at the same time the most difficult aspect of the work, because it is under constant attack, conscious or unconscious. The staff is working constantly to set and maintain boundaries that are "good enough," accommodating individual needs but holding firm the structures essential to managing what can become life-threatening states of despair and destructiveness (8).

Thus, milieu therapy and teamwork are essential components in ED programs. The meaning of milieu is "surrounding" or "environment." The milieu has both structured and unstructured components, the latter including the diverse interactions that take place among patients, staff, and other figures, such as visitors to the facility. The ED milieu usually consists of a multidisciplinary team. Within this therapeutic environment, the individual is expected to learn methods of positive coping skills, relationship skills, and life skills (9).

The pseudo-family dynamics that may appear in the therapeutic milieu stimulate an intense emotional atmosphere. The large spectrum of negative feelings that are likely to be evoked when treating ED patients tends to exert considerable impact on staff performance, treatment process and outcome, and the psychological climate in the treatment facility (10-13).

Pathological interpersonal patterns in the milieu may be induced via several dynamics, e.g., competition, parallel processes, splitting mechanisms, or projected fantasies, thereby exerting a great impact on workplace atmosphere. Empirical studies indicate that it is the overall pathology of the patient or specified clusters of patient characteristics (14) rather than discrete psychiatric diagnostic categories that evoke identifiable countertransference reactions. In order to work through the intense pain and anger that often dominate the ED therapeutic milieu, healthcare professionals have to take into account the effects of the intense transference and countertransference relationships that tend to develop when treating EDs, especially if treatment is done in the context of a large team with power relationships.

The aim of this paper is to review the concept of countertransference in the context of treating EDs. Additionally, we will discuss the team dynamics within this environment and their impact on treatment process and outcome. We shall discuss coping approaches to manage patterns of countertransference needed in order to facilitate effective treatment process for the patient and the therapist.

THE CONCEPTS OF TRANSFERENCE AND COUNTERTRANSFERENCE

Transference is defined as the displacement of patterns of feelings, thoughts, and behaviors originally experienced in relation to significant figures during childhood, onto a person involved in a current interpersonal relationship. In other words, transference may represent a current ubiquitous, automatic, unconscious repetition of past object relationships (15,16).

Countertransference, in general, is categorized into two recognizable subgroups. Freud and later "classicists" refer to countertransference in its "narrow" aspect, namely, as the therapist's unconscious response to the patient's transference (17). On the other hand, "totalists" support the broad definition of countertransference, which considers all of the therapist's conscious and unconscious feelings and emotional reactions to the patient's transferential and realistic needs, as well as to their own, evoked in the therapist during the therapeutic interaction with the patient (18-20).

Most definitions acknowledge, to varying degrees, that therapists' reactions to clients may be adversely influenced by therapists' unresolved personal conflicts. Research has demonstrated, for instance, that when therapists' unresolved issues are provoked, they may display avoidance behavior, engage in reactive as opposed to reflective thinking, feel anxious, and be prone to distorted perceptions of clients. Clients, in turn, may develop weaker alliances with therapists and perceive them to be less empathic when therapists display countertransference behavior (21).

Kornitzer (3) emphasizes the basic assumption that we can understand transference and countertransference relationships not only in the dialogue between patient and therapists but also in the dialogue between the patient and the multidisciplinary team.

The middle of the last century brought Will Menninger's "Guide to the Order Sheet" (22), which favored carefully designed interactions with milieu staff over individual therapy. Contemporary views suggest that patients recreate internal object relations within the interpersonal relationships they develop on their unit (23), making it necessary for milieu staff to interpret transferences and countertransference reactions in order to effect change in the patient's inner and outer worlds.

COUNTERTRANSFERENCE REACTIONS WHEN
TREATING ED PATIENTS

Clinicians who treat patients with EDs may feel inadequacy, helplessness, love, anger, hate, rejection and/or feeling rejected, overwhelmed, swallowed-up, anxious, sad, depressed, stressed, frustrated, jealous, controlled, punitive, impotent, or omnipotent. Franko et al. (11) found that that across ED diagnoses, patients diagnosed with anorexia nervosa (AN) may evoke more intense negative feelings (e.g., anger, helplessness, and stress) in therapists who specialize in the treatment of EDs, than do patients diagnosed with bulimia nervosa (BN) (11). Still, BN patients may also evoke very strong negative countertransference feelings, and the therapist may act out her/his hostility through retaliatory behavior.

The emotional reactions of ED patients are often very powerful, due to temperament characteristics and elevated reactivity (24,25). Additionally, this heightened emotional responsivity of ED patients may be related to their propensity to feel, think, and behave according to patterns that have been adaptive in the past, but are currently highly dysfunctional. Accordingly, these patients are duty-bound to induce strong feelings such as rage, hate, hopelessness, pity, sorrow, or love in those with whom they become involved, including their care-givers (26).

Burket and Sherman investigated the attitudes of 90 therapists towards patients with an ED, and found that 31% of these therapists were inclined not to treat such patients (27). Many of these therapists were male, they tended to advocate individual therapy as the sole treatment method, feelings of empathy were less common among them, and many claimed that the prognosis of ED was unfavorable. Therapist frustration, treatment resistance, and comorbid conditions predicted greater negative attitude.

Treatment providers who work with high-risk patients are vulnerable to personal emotional distress, which lingers long after the resolution of critical clinical events that often occur in these patients (28). In this respect, Herzog, Hamburg, and Bortman suggested that ED patients evoke intense reactions because of their neediness, and the likely probability of medical complications and suicidal behavior (29).

Dynamics in ED and the encountered countertransference

In working with the ED patient, the therapist may find himself in the painful grip of countertransference feelings evoked by identification with the patient (concordant) or with someone from the patient's world, like his parents (complementary). In many ED sufferers, an adaptive containment was not reliably available in early stages of development (4). As a result, the infant has developed an impaired sense of her own physical and mental boundaries and has not been able to come to experience herself as a whole person separate from her mother (30); she remains bound to her mother, identified with her, and unable to develop an autonomous identity. A similar wish of the patient in later years to be merged with the therapist is relentlessly sought and equally feared. If it is projected onto the therapist, it may induce similar turmoil among the entire treating staff through parallel processes which will be discussed later in this manuscript.

The inability to meet the challenges of life may often lead to libidinal and ego regression in ED patients. This regression likely stems from experiencing the parents as unavailable, inconsistent, or neglectful, enforcing too great a degree of separation too soon, or maintaining a merger with the child beyond the time in which it was appropriate (31).

Regression in ED patients can be expressed in several forms and evoke intense countertransference feelings. Because of the extreme distrust of the interpersonal environment found in ED patients, they often tend to "test" their therapists to see if they are similar to or different from the parental figures (4). Feelings evoked among the treating staff because of this "transference test" occur most frequently in relation to four developmental issues: control and structure, autonomy and initiative, tolerance of aggression, and fostering of the "true self" (4). A significant overlap often exists among these developmental dimensions.

TESTING THE PROVISION OF EXTERNAL CONTROL AND REGULATION

Clinicians who work with ED patients are often trapped in power struggles due to the patients' need for rigid control to overcome their embedded sense of ineffectiveness or due to their "no entry" defense mechanisms (32). The battle with the therapists gives the patients a sense of power and excitement. The "high" that these patients get from the omnipotent control protects them from the painful awareness of their actual inadequacy and from their underlying paralyzing anxieties (33). Unrealistic self-expectations associated with such power struggles have been identified as the single most critical factor in the development of caretakers' burnout (34).

Meninger suggested that frustrations might stem from the basic motivation of all healthcare personnel to help ill people and to restore them to health (35). The staff can also have a countertransference reaction to the patients' refusal to allow them to control the illness. Underneath the wish of the therapist to help others and ameliorate suffering, there is an unconscious need to master disease and control the patients' life and death. These wishes may often be expressed in the form of rescue fantasies. The patient who does not readily respond to therapeutic interventions challenges the treatment staff's sense of competence and confidence.

Transference tests in the area of autonomy and initiative are mainly tests in which the staff members are provoked to curtail the patient's autonomy via over-control, usually because the patient has acted out or expressed her independence needs in a self-destructive way (4). Sometimes the therapist's wish to "rescue" the patient from her distress leaves her feeling weak and impotent, or the patient may feel the therapist as seductive, resulting in the gratification of an unconscious oedipal wish that is unhelpful to the patient (36).

If therapy can be conceptualized as a kind of feeding (4), the therapeutic food in the case of ED may be experienced by the patients as unsafe and poisonous, as an extension of the mother's failure to nurture her child. ED patients may unconsciously want the care and support of their therapists. Overtly, however, they deny and resist any hint of dependency or intimacy, and bitterly and resentfully reject the therapist (26,37-39). Moreover, the therapist's interpretation is often experienced by the AN patient as a forbidden intrusion into her inner world, namely as a recapitulation of an early trauma in which she was told what she thought and felt by a superior significant other (40).

The treating staff may feel rejected under the assumption that the unresponsiveness of the patient is a function of their failure to properly understand and treat the patient in some way. Additionally, the patient's feelings of ineffectiveness and self-disgust may be projected onto the therapists, adding to their burden and sense of rejection (40). Feelings of inadequacy, impotency, and being rejected (vomited) as a consequence of response to the patient resistance, as well as being hooked in projective identification dynamics, are frequently expressed in the management of ED. Davis (41) suggested that the ED patient challenges the therapists' sense of self-effectiveness as well as the time-honored traditions of clinical work.

TRANSFERENCE TESTS IN THE AREA OF
TOLERANCE OF AGGRESSION

Transference tests in the area of tolerance of aggression are mainly in response to the patient's propensity to express her autonomy in such a way as to provoke retaliation or abandonment (usually by being provocatively noncompliant, demanding, rejecting, or unpleasant). ED patients are frequently demanding and highly sensitive, thereby often inducing a sense of burnout in those responsible for their treatment. They unconsciously direct the therapist into feeling as the patient does through the process of projective identification, just as the infant projects unwanted parts of herself (e.g., aggressive feelings) onto the mother, for her to hold it through her capacity for "reverie." The infant may then re-introject these parts in a more manageable form (42). In this case, the therapist is likely to feel locked in a dynamic interrelationship where he/she feels inadequate, impotent, and vomited upon, as the patient "spews out" her jumbled feelings. Therapists may feel that nothing they supply feels sufficient or right to the patient. The therapists may feel rejected, angry, and helpless and not infrequently, they will react via counter-projective identification processes.

Moreover, when the patient plays out her original, historical role and responds to the therapist as if being in a past relationship (often with her mother), the therapist may identify with the "depleted mother," i.e., the neglectful parent. A resulting risk of this process is when the therapist allows the patient subtly to take care of him/her, just as the patient learned to take care of her mother (43). When roles are reversed, the patient identifies with her mother, and the therapist is made to feel as the patient originally felt, that is in some cases being over-controlled, and in others being a caretaker to the parents, misperceived, invalidated, or merged.

TRANSFERENCE TESTS ASSOCIATED WITH
NOT FOSTERING THE "TRUE SELF"

Transference tests associated with not fostering the "true self" are those in which the staff members are provoked to push the patient away, to assert her own needs and feelings too quickly, not considering the adaptive role of her self-denial in the family and within her own ego ideal (4).

According to self-psychology (7,44), ED patients feel and behave like selfless souls serving others' needs. They cannot imagine that other people would be willing to give up, even temporarily, their own interests and viewpoints to fulfill their needs. In Kohutian terms, ED patients do not believe others can serve as self-objects for them (6). As a result, they often find themselves giving up their well-being and denying even their most basic needs, including nourishment. Geller et al. (45) stress that ED patients tend to "silence their self," or inhibit self-expression, in order to secure interpersonal relationships. Clinicians may be trapped in a parallel process where they give up their needs and find themselves preoccupied with the patient's needs and demands, or vice versa, provoked to push the patient away, to assert their own needs when the patient is immature and may respond in a counterproductive-regressive way, which in turn leaves the therapists frustrated and sometimes guilty. Other dynamics that often evoke intense counterstransference include:

- Concrete thinking and orientation. Early difficulties in differentiating between self and object may leave ED patients in a stage of concrete thinking in which symbolic equations have not yet given way to true symbols. The lack of symbolic capacity may render patients unable to engage in concrete body-oriented action or stimulation to regain the need-meeting object (46). Skarderud (47) emphasizes that the acting out nature of symptoms is an expression of deficit in reflective function and the patient may be difficult to engage, because she or he is trapped in the concreteness of body symbolism. This may cause therapists to encounter lack of commitment and patience; or worse— aggression and rejection. This concrete way of functioning mentally may represent paucity or absence of verbal accompaniment, often contributing to frustrating and non-productive silences in the therapeutic situation. Filled with such frustrations, therapists may elicit potentially treatment-destructive interventions (48).
- Competition on thinness. Frankenberg (49) studied the AN patient who may view the female therapist as another competitor in the never-ending battle for thinness. This competitive stance interferes with the establishment of a therapeutic alliance. It can leave the therapist, especially one who is overly concerned with her own weight, paralyzed by her negative reactions to the patient and her inability to connect empathically with the patient's painful sense of fragility and ineffectiveness (50). Shisslak et al. (51) found that 28% of the therapists they studied felt greatly affected by their work with ED patients. They reported a heightened awareness of food and their physical condition. This led some therapists to positive change in eating habits and body image, and increased awareness of their physical condition and appearance, while other therapists showed less favorable changes.

COUNTERTRANSFERENCE ENCOUNTERED
BY THE THERAPEUTIC MILIEU

In contrast to multidisciplinary teams in which different specialists all work independently on the patient, in the interdisciplinary teams, which is frequently the environment in which EDs are managed, different therapists communicate with each other in the process of patient care but have well-defined roles according to their training. In the context of treating EDs, when the staff attempts to control the patient's symptoms, this may block regressive expression of aggressive discharge in forms such as splitting, projective identification, or turning the anger against the self, i.e., introjections of hostility (52). Several dynamics were discusses in relation to milieu therapy when treating EDs:

- Different professional concepts. In this environment, the different professionals parallel play and at the same time are supervised for their interactive play to facilitate true cooperation and harmony despite different professional concepts. The medical system, which is often perceived to have a paternalistic nature, has to take into consideration issues such as physical danger to the patient and time constraints. These elements counter necessary psychological processes such as the provision of autonomy and psychological space, which are fostered by the psychological system – creating a tension in the multidisciplinary team. The balance between being strong and consistent, but also compassionate, is one of the great challenges of treating patients with EDs.

- Under-management and over-management. Goodsitt (7) warns of the hazards of the two extremes of under-management and over-management. Under-management is often a result of over-reliance on introspection and joining to the patient's point of view, while over-management is induced by relying exclusively on the external reality, namely, the view point of the treatment environment. The presence of a third party, often a coordinator who is not part of the team, is required to alert the staff to the existence of any of these "collusions." A frequent response to the patient's acting-out or asserting herself in a self-destructive way is that the team is provoked to be either over-controlling or under-controlling, i.e., providing too little structure in collusion with the patient's denial, deception, or false self-presentation. Such processes may set in motion powerful transference reactions and distorted projections. In this case, it is therefore likely that the angry feelings of patients will be expressed as bitter complaints about the program and/or staff, causing intense countertransference feelings of frustration in the milieu.

- Issues of impotence, importance, and competition. Frequently, staff members are likely to feel locked in a dynamic interrelationship where they feel inadequate and impotent as well as rejected, angry, and helpless, as described before. Feelings of omnipotence vs. impotence related to unresolved countertransference issues as well as preoccupation with issues of self-efficacy, competency, and being significant to others, which are amplified in the context of treating EDs, may be evoked to reactions such competitiveness and acting-out behaviors. These reactions may be amplified in the case of interdependent relationships between the medical staff and those responsible for the emotional components of therapy. Moreover, "depleted" therapists may feel that the organization in which they work does not endow them with adequate resources in the form of work place, salary, or administrative assistance.

- Splitting. ED patients often create chaos on the ward by splitting their surroundings, and by manipulating the staff and parents into antagonistic positions that charge the ward's atmosphere. A culture of blame is one of the most familiar manifestations of the tendency to split "good" from "bad" that was alluded to above. Splitting originates in the infant's need to sort out its sensations and hold on to the good ones while getting rid of the unpleasant or frightening ones. In pathological conditions that necessitate the continuation of primitive defensive mechanisms, splitting protects the patient's ego from conflicts by means of dissociation or actively remaining apart from introjections and identifications of a strongly conflicted nature (53-55). Patients tend to idealize some figures only to consider them as "bad" later on; the staff member feels demeaned, humiliated, and attacked. These dynamics tend to occur more frequently when there is co-morbidity of a personality disorder in addition to the primary ED diagnosis (4). Because of the panic attached to the hated "badness" in the self, there is tremendous intensity in the projections, and it can be acutely upsetting for conscientious staff members to find themselves on the wrong side of a split, and difficult to withstand the pressure to collude in one way or another in order to be seen as nice again.

- Triangulation dynamics can also be observed in the treatment of EDs. The three-party system may reenact some aspect of the therapist's oedipal conflict, or it may reenact a preoedipal theme in the context of a countertransferential process. In the latter instance, therapist and patient may be engaged in blissful symbiosis, with the supervisor or the professional manager perceived as an intruding outsider (17). Thus, these triangulation dynamics may cause a negative psychological climate in the therapeutic staff.

- Dynamics of parallel processes may also increase the burden on milieu work. Grey and Fiscalini (56) regard the parallel process as a chain reaction that can occur in any interconnected series of interpersonal situations that have dynamic similarity. The process may involve a significant person in the patient's life, who affects the patient, who, in turn, affects the therapist, who, in turn, affects the staff or manager (57). Some of these reenactments are negative (e.g., demandingness, rebellion, anger, or control), tending to harm the psychological climate and cause different reactions within the therapeutic milieu or towards the directors. In this respect, parallel process dynamics are likely to impair the decision process and the treatment outcome. Hughes (33) suggested that the therapist's countertransference is a repetition of the family dynamics, but it is also a unique opportunity to understand the parallel processes enacted in the ward.

THE EFFECTS OF COUNTERTRANSFERENCE ON TREATMENT OUTCOME

Countertransference feelings/reactions to patients may be regarded as a double-edged sword for therapists. If not understood and properly worked through, they are likely to lead to undesired behaviors on the part of the therapist, which, not surprisingly, are often destructive repetitions of the patient's past. Hayes et al. (58) reported that countertransference, measured by the Countertransference Factors Inventory, was found to be inversely related to the impact of treatment in cases with poor to moderate treatment results, these being in line with the amount of countertransference reactions exhibited. Therapists who are better self-integrated (have less fragmented personalities and more stable boundaries) tend to have fewer countertransference reactions (58). On the other hand, countertransference was unrelated to treatment impact in successful cases. Hayes and Gelso (59) suggested that the more a therapist engages in an "ego-oriented" behavior, the less likely the client and therapist are to be able to agree on the goals and tasks of therapy and to feel a close emotional bond. This finding by itself may stir up many unresolved conflict issues in the therapist.

Intensive countertransference reactions may bring about a failure to achieve a reparative therapeutic relationship, in which patient and staff growth is achieved, in the context of connection to others. In order for that growth to happen, relationships should be such that closeness is not fusion, separation is not detachment, and engagement is not enmeshment (60).

THE MANAGEMENT OF CLINICIANS' AND MILIEU DYNAMICS

Strains in the alliance when treating ED patients are inevitable (61), and one of the most important therapeutic skills in dealing therapeutically with this type of negative process and repairing ruptures in the therapeutic alliance is the management of countertransference issues, since failures on the part of the therapist are usually caused by countertransference (13).

The first step in the management of negative dynamics is identifying them. If therapists become aware of the countertransference process, it can serve as a valuable source of insight into the illness and treatment relationship (59). The patient's confusion between her internal world and family dynamics is often acted out in the therapeutic relationship, and if therapists are aware of their countertransference feelings, they will get a first-hand experience of the frustration that the patient and her family are suffering. Unidentified countertransference reactions may cause therapists to become furious with their patients, express desperateness, or even abandon or subvert therapy (62). Shaw (63) suggests that if psychotherapy is an investigation into the intersubjective space between client and therapist, then as a profession we need to take our bodily reactions much more seriously than we have so far because the body is the very basis of human subjectivity, and the therapist's body should be used as a means to monitor the psychotherapeutic process.

The second step is to enable the patient and the therapist to break out of the cyclical pattern and forge a new kind of healthier relational pattern in life. For example, when identifying a "hooked" therapist into countertransference enactment– kicking the patient– thus playing the role of the rejecting adult figure that fails her, therapists should be assisted to identify and break out the maladaptive pattern (13).

In order to work through the intense emotions of depression, anxiety, and anger that are often evoked when treating ED patients, the staff must become aware of their own bias towards these states as being destructive or constructive. Treatment providers are further required to examine how comfortable they are participating in working through these intense feelings within the context of the milieu.

Our goal in treatment is to transform a recurring maladaptive pattern of handling anger in an important relationship and/or to develop a stronger sense of a coping self that we can bring to other relationships. Correct identification and handling of countertransference reactions by the therapists in this case may assist the patients in communicating their hitherto unexpressed wishes, and preclude such maladaptive processes. It is essential that the staff learn to translate their anger towards the patients into clear, non-accusatory statements that give meaning to their own reactions. Anger and hostility can, in this sense, be both communicative and defensive. They can be used by a group as a resistance to working through other feelings (9). For example, Sullivan (64) wrote of the power of angry feelings to defend against the anxiety associated with disappointment and deprivation occurring within the context of interpersonal relationships charged with unfulfilled expectancy. Winnicot discussed hate and love, which always coexist in countertransference relations. The understanding and tolerance of such ambivalent feelings toward patients is necessary to facilitate effective and empathic interventions (65). Although the literature offers therapists a variety of strategies for dealing with "difficult" clients or overcoming client resistance, it offers little help in dealing specifically with a dislike or aversion to a client.

Williams and Day (66) suggested that in cases where the self of the therapist issues are mild, simply recognizing and acknowledging them may free the therapist to look at the client in a different (and more favorable) way. The therapist will need to be vigilant, however, to monitor his or her interaction with the client to avoid further problems. Sometimes it is possible to find something to like about a client if one looks at the individual from another person's perspective. Therapists also need to be alert to the possibility that other people's negative feelings about the client may influence their own perceptions. This can especially be a problem if a therapist hears negative views about a client from his appreciated colleagues.

It would also be prudent to seek out supervision or consultation to make sure the self of the therapist issues have not clouded the therapist's objectivity with the client. If a client elicits a strong countertransference response, then the therapist should also consider pursuing his or her own personal therapy.

Other strategies to manage negative dynamics include approaching the patient as separate from the problem. The narrative approach suggests that the person is not the problem, but the problem is the problem (67). This approach allows for compassion for the individual, but does not minimize the destructiveness of behaviors. Moreover, looking at the client from a multi-generational context can often develop greater compassion and empathy for a client (66).

Team work and support is an important component in the management of team dynamics. It is the responsibility of the staff to function as a communicative, cooperative, and cohesive team. An important task in the treatment process is the coordination of the treatment and collaboration with all disciplines. The job of the team is to implement the treatment plan across all treatment modalities. Therefore, it is important to establish a consensus of opinion about the structure, process, and content of the treatment plan for each patient (68). The team needs support in its efforts to hold onto an ordinary wholeness that includes mistakes and painful feelings, as well as hope, and a receptive frame of mind that can treat even the most hateful projections as desperate unconscious attempts to communicate. The quality of team interaction should facilitate therapists' autonomy, sharing of tasks, and decision making but provides structure, time limits, and leadership (69). Given and Simmons (70) indicated personal qualities vital to interdisciplinary team function. These include the ability to accept differences and perspectives of others; function independently; negotiate roles with other team members; form new values, attitudes, and perceptions; tolerate constant review and challenge of ideas; take risks; possess personal identity and integrity; and accept team philosophy of care. Holmqvist and Fogelstam (71) have found that units characterized by "work" and "pairing" regarding the group dynamics had high scores for helpful and autonomous feelings, while unhelpful feelings were evoked in units characterized by "dependency" and "fight."

Low levels of team support arise for both organizational and personal reasons. Therapists with less experience in the field of EDs reported feeling more frustrated and angry compared with more experienced therapists (11). This may be related to the ability of more experienced therapists to have a longitudinal view of EDs rather than to react negatively to more immediate experiences with a hostile or oppositional patient (12). Reluctance to ask for team support may stem from workers' fears that requests for team work, or team work itself, may lead to colleagues viewing them as weak or incompetent. Workers may fantasize that such views will culminate in painful rejection or criticism.

Van Wagoner et al. (72) identified five factors that promote the effective handling of countertransference: self-insight, anxiety management, conceptual skills, empathy, and self-integration. On the other hand, Hayes and Gelso (59) suggested that only two factors have been identified empirically as facilitating countertransference management: self-insight and self-integration. While the concept of self-insight relates to awareness about one's areas of unresolved conflict, self-integration is considered to reflect the degree to which one's conflicts are resolved.

At an organizational level, high case loads and a model of professional practice that encourages workers to manage families single handedly contribute to feelings of isolation. Compared to therapists with smaller case loads, those who see more patients each week score higher on the countertransference assessment subscales "frustrated," "manipulated," and "helpless/hopeless" (11).

The team leader should empower the staff struggle to hold boundaries and to maintain hope in the face of destructiveness in its different forms, counter being hooked in familial dynamics, and facilitate team spirit in a way that crises can be lived through and the possibility of recovery can be cherished, despite the ever-present threat (8).

An appropriate supervisory process is crucial for the management of team dynamics. Hamburg et al. (73) described how countertransference issues in the long-term therapy of patients with EDs are often mirrored in the supervisory process (73). Such countertransference phenomena may include being secretive, intrusive, shaming, over-controlling, overindulgent, or over-identified. Supervisors should offer empathy and support for the difficult feelings the patients arouse, but also—in the manner of a work-discussion group—make theoretical links that seem relevant, so that the thoughts about the feelings can be used in other interactions and can become part of the shared culture of the organization (8).

CONCLUSION

Intense countertransference reactions are common in the therapeutic milieu of ED units. These reactions arise from multiple sources including the therapists' and patients' histories and personal attributes, and the activation of intrapsychic and interpersonal processes such as identification, rejection, competition, testing, projective identification, splitting, or parallel processes. Often the same trait that allows the individual to become an excellent therapist, namely, the ability to empathize, can also leave him/her vulnerable to personal emotional distress as the result of the activation of maladaptive counter projective-identification processes. Working with high risk clients, such as those ill with EDs, produces all the effects frequently associated with treatment providers' burnout, including the loss of drive and motivation, the appearance of mental, physical, and emotional exhaustion, professional isolation, and the drain of always being empathetic and having to be content with only ambiguous success (74).

The therapeutic milieu should act as a holding environment in which staff members can be encouraged to use countertransferential feelings as the channel for moving inward to uncover the underpinnings of their own feelings. That is, it should become an environment that provides highly reinforcing opportunities for new patterns of thinking, feeling, and acting, as well as for the expression and examination of old patterns and motivations. Therapists must work through feelings associated with their unmet needs and desires if they are to be free to engage in mutually gratifying relationships in the here-and-now therapeutic situation. They should strive to understand the origin of their unmet countertransference feelings in order to be able to activate them in the best interests of the patients, rather than satisfying these needs through the patients.

Intervention within the milieu must interrupt the vicious cycle of malevolent transformation wherein the perceived need for tenderness in relation to the patient automatically brings foresight of anxiety or pain on the therapist's side. Through the appropriate interpretation of attitudes and behaviors with their transferential and countertransferential underpinnings, milieu staff can create an environment that keeps negative phenomena in check, is empathetic and responsive to the underlying needs of both patients and treatment providers, and offers healthier alternatives for the expression of intense, yet valid, feeling states. This environment should exist for both patients and care providers, who will then be in a position to provide ever better care.

REFERENCES

[1] Rose J. Stress and residential staff: towards an integration of existing research. Mental Handicap Res 1995;8:220–36.

[2] Hatton C, Emerson E, Rivers M, Mason H, Mason L, Swarbrick R, Kiernan C, Reeves D, and Alborz A.. Factors associated with staff stress and work satisfaction in services for people with intellectual disability. J Intellect Disabil Res 1999;43:253–67.

[3] Kornitzer S. Multiple professional staff countertransference toward hospitalized borderline patient. Isr J Psychother 2006;21(1):61-9.

[4] Stern S. The dynamics of clinical management in the treatment of anorexia nervosa and bulimia: an organizing theory. Int J Eat Disord 1986;5: 233–54.

[5] Winnicott DW. The maturation process and the facilitating environment. New York: Int Univ Press, 1965.

[6] Kohut H. The restoration of the self. New York: Int Univ Press, 1977.

[7] Goodsitt A. EDs: A self psychological perspective. In: Garner DM, Garfinkel PE, eds. Handbook of treatment for eating disorders. New York: Guilford, 1997:2005-28.

[8] Land P. Thinking about feelings: working with the staff of an eating disorders unit. Psychoanal Psychother 2004;18(4):390–403.

[9] Whalley P. Team approach to working through transference and countertransference in a pediatric/psychiatric milieu. Issues Ment Health Nurs 1994;15:457–69.

[10] Stern S, Whitaker CA, Hagemann NJ, Anderson RB and Bargman G J Anorexia Nervosa: The hospital's role in family treatment. Fam Process 1981;20: 395–408.

[11] Franko DL, Rolfe S. Countertransference in the treatment of patients with eating disorders. J Psychiatr 1996;59:108–16.

[12] Kaplan AS, Garfinkel PE. Difficulties in treating patients with EDs: a review of patient and clinician variables. Can J Psychiatr 1999;44:665–70.

[13] Mangis WM Kicking the patient: immediacy in the consulting room. J Psychol Theol 2007;35(1):43-51.

[14] Colson DB, Allen JG, Hamburg P, Herzog D. Supervising the therapy of patients with ED. Am J Psychiatr 1990;44(3):369–80.

[15] Moore BE and Fine BD. Psychoanalytic terms and concepts. New Haven: Yale Univ Press, 1990.

[16] Ellis A. How to deal with your most difficult client -You. J Ratio Emot Cognit Behav Therapy 2003;21:203–13.

[17] Tosone C. Countertransference and clinical social work supervision. Clin Super 1997;16:17–32.

[18] Kernberg O. Countertransference. J Am Psychoanal Assoc 1965;13:38-56.

[19] Racker H. Transference and countertransference. New York: Int Univ Press, 1968.

[20] Abend SM.. Countertransference and psychoanalytic technique. Psychoanal Q 1989;58:374–95.

[21] Hayes JA, Yeh YJ and Eisenberg A. Good Grief and Not-So-Good Grief: Countertransference in Bereavement Therapy. J Clin Psychol 2007;63:345–55.

[22] Menninger WC. Psychoanalytic principle applied to the treatment of hospitalized patients. Bull Menninger Clinic 1936;35-43.

[23] Gabbard GO. A contemporary perspective on psychoanalytically informed hospital treatment. Hosp Community Psych 1988;39(12):1291-96.

[24] Fassino S, Abbate DG, Amianto F, Leombruni P, Boggio S, Rovera GG. Temperament and character profile of EDs: a controlled study with the temperament and Character Inventory. Int J Eat Disord 2002;32(4):412–25.

[25] Steiner H, Kwan W, Shaffer TG, Walker S, Miller S, Sagar A, Lock J. Risk and protective factors for juvenile EDs. Eur Child and Adoles Psy 2003;12, Suppl 1, I38–46.

[26] Vitousek KB, Watson S, Wilson GT. Enhancing motivation for change in treatment-resistant EDs. Clin Psychol Rev 1998;18:391-420.

[27] Burket RC, Sherman LL. Therapists' attitudes about treating patients with eating disorders. South Med J 1995;88(8):813–8.

[28] Kleespies PM, Dettmer EL. The stress of patient emergencies for the clinician: Incidence, impact, and means of coping. J Clin Psychol 2000; 56(10): 1353–69.

[29] Herzog DB, Hamburg P, Bortman A. W. Psychotherapy and eating disorders: An affirmative view. Int J Eat Disord 1987;6:545–50.

[30] Mahler MS. On human symbiosis and the vicissitudes of individuation. New York: Int Univ Press, 1968.

[31] Sours JA. Starving to death in a sea of objects. New York: Jason Aronson, 1980.

[32] Williams G. Reflections on some dynamics of eating disorders: 'No Entry' defences and foreign bodies. Int J Psychoanal 1997;78:927-41.

[33] Hughes P. The use of the countertransference in the therapy of patients with anorexia nervosa. Eur Eat Disord Rev 1997;5:258–69.

[34] Scully R. The work setting support group: A means of preventing burnout. In: Farber B, ed. Stress and burnout in the human service profession. New York: Pergamon; 1983:93.

[35] Menninger W. Dealing with staff reactions to perceived lack of progress by chronic mental patients. Hosp Community Psych 1984;35:805–8.

[36] Gonzalez RG. Bulimia and adolescence: individual psychoanalytic treatment. In: Scwartz HJ, ed. Bulimia: Psychoanalytic treatment and theory. Madison: Int Univ Press, 1988:55-72.

[37] Yarock SR. Understanding chronic bulimia: A four psychology approach. Am J Psychoanal 1993;53:3–17.

[38] Geller J. What a motivational approach is and what a motivational approach isn't: reflections and responses. Eur Eat Disord Rev 2002;10(3):155–60.

[39] Messer SB. A psychodynamic perspective on resistance in psychotherapy: Vive la résistance. J Clin Psychol 2002;58(2):157–63.

[40] Bruch H. Eating disorders: Obesity, anorexia nervosa and the person within. New York: Basic Books, 1973.

[41] Davis WN. Reflections on Boundaries in the psychotherapeutic relationship. In: Johnson CL, ed. Psychodynamic treatment of anorexia nervosa and bulimia. New York: Guilford, 1991:68-85.

[42] Bion W. Learning from experience. London: Karnac, 1962

[43] Wooley SC. Uses of countertransference in the treatment of EDs; A gender perspective. In: Johnson CL, ed. Psychodynamic treatment of anorexia nervosa and bulimia. New York: Guilford, 1991:273.

[44] Bachar E. The contributions of self psychology to the treatment of anorexia and bulimia. Am J Psychother 1998;52:147–67.

[45] Geller J, Cockell SJ, Goldner EM, Flett GL. Inhibited expression of negative emotions and interpersonal orientation in anorexia nervosa. Int J Eat Disord 2000;28:8–19.

[46] Kreuger D. Body self, psychological self and bulimia: Developmental and clinical consideration. In: Scwartz HJ, ed. Bulimia: Psychoanalytic treatment and theory. Madison: Int Univ Press, 1988:55-72.

[47] Skarderud F. Eating one's words, Part I: 'Concretised metaphors' & reflective function in anorexia nervosa—an interview study. Eur Eat Disord Rev 2007;15:163–74.

[48] Skarderud F. Eating one's words, Part II: The embodied mind and reflective   function in anorexia nervosa—theory. Eur Eat Disord Rev 2007;15:243–52

[49] Frankenberg FR. Female therapists in the management of anorexia nervosa. Int J Eat Disord 1984;3:25–33.

[50] Derenne JL. The therapist's voice. Eating Disord 2006;14:335–39,

[51] Shisslak CM, Gray N, Crago M. Health care professionals' reactions to working with ED patients. Int J Eat Disord 1989;8:689–94.

[52] Strober M, Humphrey LL. Familial contributions to the etiology and course of anorexia nervosa and bulimia nervosa. J Consult Clinic Psychol 1987;55:654–59.

[53] Freud S. The ego and the mechanisms of defense. New York: Int Univ Press, 1946 [Original work published 1936].

[54] Klein M. Notes on some schizoid mechanisms. In envy and gratitude and other works, 1946-1963. New York: Free Press, 1975 [Original work published 1946].

[55] Kernberg O. Severe personality disorders: psychotherapeutic strategies. New Haven: Yale Univ Press, 1984.

[56] Grey A, Fiscalini J. Parallel process as transference-countertransference interaction. Psychoanal Psychol 1987;131:141-4.

[57] Lombardo LT, Greer J, Estadt B, Cheston S. Empowerment behaviors in clinical training: an empirical study of parallel processes. Clinical Super 1997;16:33–47.

[58] Hayes JA, Gelso CJ. Clinical implications of research on countertransference. Psychother Prac 2001;57:1041–51.

[59] Hayes JA, Gelso CJ, Van Wagoner SL, Diemer RA. Managing countertransference: what the experts think. Psychol Rep 1991; 69:139–48.

[60] Steiner CA. New maps of development new models of therapy: the psychology of women and the treatment of Eds. In: Johnson CL, ed. Psychodynamic treatment of anorexia nervosa and bulimia. New York: Guilford, 1991:225-43.

[61] Serpell L, Treasure J, Teasdale J, Sullvian V. Anorexia nervosa: Friend or foe? Int J Eat Disord 1999;25:177–86.

[62] Brotman WB, Stern TA, Herzog DB. Emotional reactions of house officers to patients with anorexia nervosa, diabetes and obesity. Int J Eat Disord 1984;3:71–7.

[63] Shaw R. The embodied psychotherapist: an exploration of the therapists' somatic phenomena with in the therapeutic encounter. Psychother Res 2004; 14(3):271–88

[64] Sullivan HS. The interpersonal world of the infant. New York: WW Norton, 1953.

[65] Winnicott DW. Hate in countertransference. Int J Psychoanal 1949;30:69–75.

[66] Williams L, Day A. Strategies for dealing with clients we dislike. Am J Fam Ther 2007;35:83–92

[67] Freedman J, Combs G. Narrative therapy: The social construction of preferred realities. New York: Norton, 1996.

[68] Stewart TM, Williamson DA. Multidiciplinary treatment of eating disorders – structure and costs of treatment. Behav Modif 2004;28(6):812-30.

[69] Haig AJ, LeBreck DB. Measurement of change in rehabilitation team dynamics with the team assessment profile (TAP). Int J Rehabil Res 2000;5(2):71–83.

[70] Given B, Simmons S. The interdisciplinary health-care team: Fact or fiction? Nurs Forum 1977;16(2):165–84.

[71] Holmqvist R, Fogelstam H. Psychological climate and countertransference in psychiatric treatment homes. Acta Psychiatr Scand 1996;93:288–95.

[72] Van Wagoner SL, Gelso C J, Hayes JA, Diemer RA. Countertransference and the reputedly excellent therapist. Psychother 1991;28:411–21.

[73] Hamburg P, Herzog DB, Bortman AW, Stasior JK. The treatment resistant eating disordered patient. Psychiat Ann 1989;19:494-9.

[74] Fox R and Cooper M. The effects of suicide on the private practitioner: A professional and personal perspective. Clin Soc Work J 1998;26:143–57.

In: Treatment and Recovery of Eating Disorders   ISBN: 978-1-62808-248-7
Editors: Daniel Stein and Yael Latzer   © 2013 Nova Science Publishers, Inc.

Chapter 11

FAMILIES AROUND THE TABLE: EXPERIENCES WITH A MULTI-FAMILY APPROACH IN THE TREATMENT OF EATING-DISORDERED ADOLESCENTS

Lies Depestele and Walter Vandereycken[§§§]
Eating Disorders Unit, Alexian Brothers Psychiatric Hospital, Tienen, Belgium

Abstract

Our specialized inpatient unit for the treatment of eating disorders has a long experience with involving families in the therapeutic process. Although the individual and family dynamics can vary a lot in the different cases, we make use of the therapeutic potential inherent to the common experiences of eating-disordered patients and their familes. Both for economic and psychological reasons we strongly advocate a group approach. In this paper, we report our multifamily intervention during inpatient treatment of eating-disordered adolescents. After discussing the rationale for this approach, we describe the goals and concrete methods of the multifamily groups. We conclude with a cost-benefit evaluation based on our own clinical practice.

Keywords: Eating disorders, multifamily therapy, family dynamics

INTRODUCTION

Already in the first case decriptions of anorexia nervosa in the 19th century a crucial role was assigned to the family: separating the patient from her parents was considered necessary for the recovery process. This idea of "parentectomy" would dominate the clinical literature far into the 20th century (1). In the 1970s, several systemic theories would reconceptualize the eating disorder as a symptom of a dysfunctional family system. Family therapy became a

---

[§§§] E-mail address: walter.vandereycken@ppw.kuleuven.be

popular approach in the last quarter of the previous century, but lost its appeal probably also because of a lack of controlled studies on its efficacy. In the new era of evidence-based medicine, one major research project kept the family approach to eating disorders alive. A series of studies at the London Maudsley Hospital, Institute of Psychiatry, became the point of reference for the use of family therapy in eating-disordered patients (2).

The "Maudsley model" of family-based treatment emphasizes that an active involvement of the parents is crucial for success in treatment. The adolescent with anorexia nervosa is viewed as not capable of making rational decisions about food and weight as long as her self-starvation remains active. Therefore, parents are put in charge of refeeding their child while showing respect and regard for the youngster's point of view. They are encouraged to distinguish the eating disorder from their daughter as a person. According to the Maudsley approach, this "externalizing" attitude contributes to the cooperation between the family members against the eating disorder instead of fighting against each other (3-5). Nowadays therapists assume that an eating disorder can develop in very different family contexts and that a family organizes itself around the eating disorder (6). This mechanism through which the eating disorder strongly influences the family life occurs parallel with the individual pathological process. The eating disorder increasingly contaminates the individual life just like it does at the family level.

Despite the differences in the organization processes Eisler (6) describes the following six trends in families of eating-disordered adolescents:

- Central role of the symptom in the family life: In most families the eating disorder holds a prominent place, either as a strict taboo or as the only theme of conversation.
- Focus on the here-and-now: The whole family gets focused on the current meal in such a way that a "bad" mealtime experience determines the whole atmosphere.
- Restricted interplay (the "frozen" family): Family members become aware that their ways of acting are useless but they are too fearful to handle differently.
- Reinforced dysfunction: Being faced with a life-threatening disorder reinforces particular interaction patterns (e.g., intense mother-daughter relation) which are often considered in terms of pathology instead of adaptation to an abnormal situation.
- Difficulties in life cycle problems: Because of the strain arising from an eating disorder
- Normal family stages can be experienced as extremely heavy.
- Powerlessness: The more involved parents are in confronting the eating disorder the more they feel helpless and powerless.

As a result of these developments parents fall into extreme positions: They either show over-adaptation to the eating disorder (complying with all the demands) in order to diminish the fear of their daughter, or they seek refuge in neglect and denial as expressed in acts of humiliation or threats towards the ill daughter. Often this dynamic ends in a polarization between the parents. Mothers tend to over-adaptation while fathers easily get into a struggle with their daughter. Existing relational problems can reinforce this polarization, but at the other hand it can also elicit or increase problems in the marital relationship. This organization and adaptation process becomes the point of entrance for family therapy in which the therapist conceptualizes the problem as a "normal" interplay provoked by the "abnormal" situation of an eating disorder. If this bottom line can be recognized in many families of eating-disordered adolescents, all showing similar adaptation processes as described by Eisler (6), then the logic step would be: Why not treating several families at the same time?

MULTIFAMILY THERAPY

The multifamily model — bringing together several families in a treatment setting — has a history of several decades. Usually multifamily therapy (MFT) combines group therapeutic aspects and psycho-educational elements (7). Since the beginning of this century a certain revival occurred with special applications in the area of eating disorders. Two treatment centers are especially promoting MFT. In Dresden, Germany, a special day format has been developed. The multifamily treatment for anorexic teenagers and their families amounts to 20 days (8 hours a day) over a period of one year. In parallel with this group approach there is some individual therapy with the eating-disordered youngsters as well as separate family therapy sessions (8,9). In cooperation with the Dresden project and inspired by MFT for adults (10), a similar program for eating disorders started at the Maudsley Hospital in London (11). This multifamily program consists of four days from 9 am to 5 pm over a period of six months. Both the Dresden and Maudsley program are characterized by a rather strict structure and an intensive involvement of the families. In the meantime other variants of MFT in eating disorders have been reported in the literature (12-14).

A multifamily group has a lot of therapeutic effects (7,8,15). First the communication and social interaction between different families is stimulated in a non-stigmatizing atmosphere: the multifamily group functions as a context for practice and experiment. Meeting other families in different phases of coping with a similar problem (i.e., an eating disorder) allows the exchange of experiences and gives hope for change. In a supportive context of mutual understanding, criticism and feedback are more easily accepted from "fellows" than from outsiders. When the therapist continuously invites the participants to express their views and opinions, an individual learning process in all group members can be stimulated. Referring to the above mentioned principles of the "Maudsley model" in family therapy of eating-disordered adolescents, responsibility is being returned to the parents: They have to get involved with the eating disorder of their daughter [because the great majority of eating disorder patients are female, we will only refer to "girls" or "daughters"]. The group format offers special opportunities such as cross-over of experiences: Parents are involved with the daughter of another family. Some interactions then become "acted-out" in a much more salient way that not only they become clearly recognizable but also that typical interactional strategies cannot be hided. The multifamily context requires a continuous adaptation to new situations and as such it offers ever new opportunities for specific observations which an individual session never can create.

OUR OWN PRACTICE

Within a specialized inpatient unit for eating-disordered patients (from age 15 on) we first experimented with a psycho-educational and problem-solving family group (16). In recent years, this multifamily group shifted to a more exploring and interactional process, melting narrative and psycho-educational elements. Families are in an experiential way stimulated to reflect on their manners of interacting with each other and with the eating disorder. After exploring these patterns they are invited to experiment with new ways of interacting with each other.

Table 1. Basic assumptions as framework for MFT

- The interrupted or dysfunctional family interaction is considered as a consequence of the eating disorder rather than a cause.
- The eating disorder is viewed as an "illness" out of the patient's control but she has the responsibility to get her life again in her own hands.
- Parents are stimulated to be firm but supportive in order to give the main responsibilities of life back to their daughter.
- The eating disorder is often caught in separation issues, confronting the adolescent with the dynamic between leaving home and being dependent on her parents.

In our MFT we work with four to five families (parents and admitted daughter). Six sessions are spread over two months and are taking place on a evening from 6 to 9 pm. The sessions are conducted by a family therapist (i.e., the first author) and a co-therapist, usually someone of the nursing staff.

Session 1. Introduction and psycho-education

The first session is a warming-up meant to get acquainted with each other and a kind of appetizer for the way of working in a group context. Family members are asked to introduce each other. The therapist stimulates a positive atmosphere by asking questions like "What do you appreciate your daughter/mum/dad for? What is typical for your family?". Sometimes the therapist tries to create a connection within the family by circular questions: "How would you describe the relationship between your daughter and your husband?". This first exercise confronts the participants with a barrier: "What can I reveal here about our relationships and what not?"

Joanna introduces her father and she is asked to mention a few positive things about him. She tells about the interests and hobbies they are sharing, and that she likes his peaceful character. But she misses doing things together. Mother says there is a kind of barrier between her husband and daughter since several months. Both Joanna and her father express their wish to change something in their "blocked" relationship.

Next we have a group conversation about some psycho-educational issues introduced by a few general statements (e.g., therapy is not just talking but also doing things, an eating disorder is a luxury problem). Although participants are free to get more or less actively involved in this discussion, the format is meant to create an interactive sphere.

Joanna's father tells he used to conceive eating disorders as a luxury problem: girls who want to be skinny like a fashion model. In the meantime he has learned that an eating disorder expresses something about dissatisfaction with one's own life. Another girl adds that anorexia also has to do with wanting attention and care from parents, but also with being afraid of growing up.

Sessions 2 and 3. Focusing on symptoms and weekends

The next two sessions start with a joint bread meal. Some girls bring their prepared meal from the ward while others — when they are far enough in their treatment — can share the meal that is served on the evening for the families (i.e. free choice). Most of the time these joint meals are experienced by the participants as an important social moment. Some groups spontaneously organize these joint meals outside the hospital before the remaining sessions that do not include a meal together.

In the first session, usually existing problems during mealtimes and the importance of a relaxed atmosphere have been discussed. Now during the joint meal a father asks. "Isn't this too difficult for you girls?". Some girls confirm this while others emphasize this can be a helpful experience: "Alone with my parents this would be most distressing, but here I feel more relaxed".

Now participants are stimulated to get in touch with a part of another family member. Family members are asked to change roles; for example, mother plays father, father plays daughter and daughter plays mother. From this position they have a conversation about how everyone experienced the last weekend together. Through this role playing they are forced to recognize the other's feelings and opinions. Together with circular questions from the therapists (e.g., "How would your father react in that case?") this empathic exercise may turn an otherwise tense discussion into a more relaxed conversation with usually a lot of laughing. It can become an eye-opener in different ways: Some family members are surprised about how good the others know what they were thinking or feeling; others are shocked because the role playing reveals that family members seem to be strangers for each other.

> Playing Joanna the father tells about the last weekend but forgets to mention that she was really upset after a date with an old friend. He doesn't seem to realize the importance and Joanna is irritated. In the individual family conversation afterwards, Joanna and her parents discuss how this misunderstanding could have happened. It's clearly a communication problem: Joanna has to express her concerns more directly and father should become more attentive.

After the role playing in group there is a moment of reflection for each family separately. Now they have to search for a particular issue they should pay attention to in the near future. What they have learned in the group exercise should be translated now into concrete actions. Each family presents their chosen point of interest in the group and after feedback from the other partcipants they have to take this as homework that will be evaluated in the next session.

> Kim has the need to organize every weekend in a very "planned" manner, especially the mealtimes. Her mother finds this difficult to accept because the family feels imprisoned by Kim's rules. Other girls recognize the problem: They explain this as a need for security — unexpected events are frightening — but realize it should not hinder the usual family life. Is a compromise possible? The girls exchange suggestions as to how Kim can loosen her fixed planning, if the family also shows some understanding.

Sessions 4 and 5. Family structure and adolescent development

In these sessions, participants are stimulated to reflect on their own family functioning and on how they experience the functioning of the other families. Which aspects do they assess as positive and which aspects do they want to change? Terms like "boundaries", "authority", "autonomy", "self-care" and "responsibility" can be a good entrance to start a group discussion about family functioning. We prefer to use the "goldfish-bowl" conversation. For example, all the daughters gather in the middle of the room and discuss a certain issue. The parents are sitting in a circle around them but are not allowed to interrupt the discussion. Afterwards parents and daughters change places and now the parents can comment on the previous discussion between their daughters. A similar exercise could be done with the fathers or the mothers as a separate group. After every group discussion the individual families have a moment for their own reflections. Finally, they are invited to tell in the group what they have learned about their family characteristics.

The family sculpture is another exercise which facilitates a reflection on family functioning. The families have to make a portrait of another family in a non-verbal way: family A must portray family B by using family C as a statue. Family B has to observe the statue and express how they experienced this portrait and what they want to change in the future. Each time we are struck how quickly these families get to know each other after only four sessions. The family statues are often very revealing and confronting for the families in question. That's why we suggest the families to keep the image of this statue in their mind and to talk about it at home.

> Joanna and her father are being sculptured as follows: father is sitting at the feet of his daughter asking for forgiveness. This statue is very expressive but its image is rejected by Joanna and her father: "Our relationship is not like that!" They now get the opportunity to remodel the statue in a form that corresponds with their experience of the relationship with each. Joanna makes a new statue that expresses a narrower distance between her and her father. The group discussion afterwards is centered around questions like: "What would this image mean in real life? How would Joanna and her father notice that their relationship is becoming stronger?"

Session 6. The future and relapse prevention

The final session anticipates on the family life after discharge from the hospital. The therapist focuses on what every family has learned during the previous sessions about themselves and about new strategies to beat the eating disorder. Possible pitfalls and emergency scenarios are discussed in group. Relapse is explained as a normal part of the recovery process. Emphasis is put on what people can do when they are confronted with signs of relapse. Finally, everyone can express how they have experienced the multifamily group sessions.

EVALUATION

Although we are doing now a systematic evaluation of our approach, so far we can only give some general impressions. No doubt, the most salient reaction is the enthusiasm on the part of the participating parents. They mention a growing feeling of solidarity between the participating families. Most parents feel relieved because of the recognition of their own situation in other families. The daughters already know this experience from their own inpatient treatment program, while for parents often it's the first time they feel understood. In the girls' opinion, the multifamily group is very useful because their parents get more insight in their daughter's problems and the ongoing treatment process.

For both the therapists and participating families the group format offers many opportunities of "mirroring", i.e. mutual observation, support, and exchange of ideas. When the therapist leaves the position of the expert and promotes this mirroring, families are given the opportunity to feel more competent than is usually possible in individual family therapy. The group sessions also occur in a more informal and relaxed atmosphere than in individual sessions with their higher risk of tension and less support. In a multifamily group a participant will seldom feel abandoned. The modelling by others will encourage participants to experiment with new interactions. Finally, therapists feel more at ease and less at risk to get absorbed in certain family conflicts or coalitions.

But the multifamily group has also its limitations and pitfalls. First, there is the barrier of safety well-known in group therapy: Participants, especially parents, may fear the confrontation in a group. A certain tendency towards social desirability — presenting oneself as "normal, without problems" — has been ascribed mainly to families of anorexia nervosa patients (1). Nevertheless, only a minority of the parents in our selection have refused to participate. This might be explained by the fact that they already have a longer treatment history than in an average outpatient sample. Perhaps the threshold is also lowered through the regular psycho-educational group meetings we organize for all parents of girls admitted to our unit (a total of 35 beds). If in this meeting some parents talk about their positive experience with the multifamily group, it is the best propaganda you can imagine.

Another problem is dealing with broken and/or renewed families: Some divorced parents do not want to meet each other in a group treatment. We then try to arrange that either mother or father joins the group and that we have parallel individual sessions with the other parent and the hospitalized daughter. Families with too high a level of conflict and criticism ("negative expressed emotion") might use a group to continue their internal fights, looking for fellow parents to get support for their own viewpoint. Based on clinical experience and research (17) we prefer to avoid the use of conjoint meetings of families with high levels of parental criticism. In these cases, separate parental counseling is more appropriate and perhaps later, when the intrafamilial atmosphere has been improved, these families are ready to join a multifamily group.

CONCLUSION

There is a growing body of clinical experience and research that supports the importance of involving families in the treatment of adolescent-onset eating disorders. A multifamily group has the potential to combine three basic aspects: Psycho-education, support, and therapy. Compared to individual family sessions, multifamily therapy is not only more economic but also allows the therapist to use a wider variety of techniques. Though certainly not a panacea, it is an enriching experience by melting the best of family therapy with the best of group therapy.

REFERENCES

[1] Vandereycken W, Kog E, Vanderlinden J. The family approach to eating disorders. New York: PMA Publishing, 1989.

[2] Le Grange D. The Maudsley family-based treatment for adolescent anorexia nervosa. World Psychiatry 2005;4:142-6.

[3] Rhodes P, Gosbee M, Madden S, Brown J. Communities of concern in the family-based treatment of anorexia nervosa: towards a consensus in the Maudsley model. Eur Eat Disord Rev 2005;13:392-8.

[4] Krautter TH, Lock J. Treatment of adolescent anorexia nervosa using manualized family-based treatment. Clin Case Stud 2004;3:107-23.

[5] Wallis A, Rhodes P, Kohn M, Madden S. Five years of family-based treatment for anorexia nervosa: the Maudsley model at the Children's Hospital at Westmead. Int J Adolesc Med Health 2007;19:277-83.

[6] Eisler I. The empirical and theoretical base of family therapy and multiple family day therapy for adolescent anorexia nervosa. J Fam Ther 2005;27:104-31.

[7] Asen E. Multiple family therapy: an overview. J Fam Ther 2002;24:3-16.

[8] Scholz M, Asen E. Multiple family therapy with eating disordered adolescents: concepts and preliminary results. Eur Eat Disord Rev 2001;9:33-42.

[9] Scholz M, Rix M, Hegewald K, Gantchev K. Treatment manual for multifamily therapy with anorexia nervosa (translated, revised and adapted by E. Asen). Dresden/London: Institute of Psychiatry, 2003.

[10] Colahan M, Robinson P. Multi-family groups in the treatment of young adults with eating disorders. J Fam Ther 2002;24:17-30.

[11] Dare C, Eisler I. A multi-family group day treatment programme for adolescent eating disorders. Eur Eat Disord Rev 2000;8:4-18.

[12] Cook-Darzens S, Doyen C, Bruneaux F, Rupert F, Bouquet MJ, Bergametti F, Mouron MC. Thérapie multifamiliale de l'adolescent anorexique [Multifamily therapy of the anorexic adolescent]. Thérapie Familale 2005;26:223-45. [French]

[13] Honig P. A multi-family group programme as part of an in-patient service for adolescents with a diagnosis of anorexia nervosa. Clin Child Psychol Psychiatry 2005;10:465-75.

[14] Salbach H, Bohnekamp I, Lehmkuhl U, Pfeiffer E, Korte A. Familienorientierte Gruppentherapie zur Behandlung von Patientinnen mit Anorexia and Bulimia nervosa: eine Pilotstudie [Family-oriented group therapy in the treatment of patients with anorexia and bulimia nervosa: a pilot study]. Z Kinder Jugendpsychiatr 2006;34:267-74. [German]

[15] Lemmens G, Eisler I, Migerode L, Heireman M, Demyttenaere K. Family discussion group therapy for major depression: a brief systemic multi-family group intervention for hospitalized patients and their family member. J Fam Ther 2007;29:49-68.

[16] Noorduin C, Vandereycken W. Coping with stressful family meals: patients, parents and therapist around the table. Eat Disord Rev 2003 ;14(6): 1-3.

[17] Eisler I, Simic M, Russell GF, Dare C. A randomised controlled treatment trial of two forms of family therapy in adolescent anorexia nervosa: a five-year follow-up. J Child Psychol Psychiatry 2007;48:552-60.

In: Treatment and Recovery of Eating Disorders   ISBN: 978-1-62808-248-7
Editors: Daniel Stein and Yael Latzer   © 2013 Nova Science Publishers, Inc.

Chapter 12

FAMILY-BASED TREATMENT FOR ADOLESCENT EATING DISORDERS: CURRENT STATUS, NEW APPLICATIONS AND FUTURE DIRECTIONS

*Katharine L Loeb[1,2]**** and Daniel le Grange[3]*

[1] Department of Psychology, Fairleigh Dickinson University, Teaneck, NJ, US
[2] Department of Psychiatry, Mount Sinai School of Medicine, New York, NY and
[3] Department of Psychiatry, University of Chicago, Chicago, IL, US

ABSTRACT

Family-based treatment (FBT) is emerging as a treatment of choice for adolescent anorexia nervosa (AN) and bulimia nervosa (BN). This paper reviews the history of FBT, core clinical and theoretical elements, and key findings from the FBT for AN and BN treatment outcome literature. In addition, we address clinical questions and controversies regarding FBT for eating disorders, including whether FBT is clinically appropriate for all adolescents (e.g., older adolescents, patients with comorbid conditions), and whether it indicated for all types of families (e.g., critical, enmeshed, and non-intact families). Finally, we outline recently manualized, innovative applications of FBT for new populations currently under early investigation, such as FBT as a preventive/early intervention for AN, FBT for young adults with eating disorders, and FBT for pediatric overweight.

Keywords: family-based treatment, eating disorders, adolescents

INTRODUCTION

While there are several schools of family therapy, Family-Based Treatment (FBT) specifically refers to a treatment modality originally developed in the late 1970s and early

---

**** E-mail address: loeb@fdu.edu

1980s by a team of clinical researchers led by two family therapists, Christopher Dare and Ivan Eisler. This team was based at the Institute of Psychiatry and the Maudsley Hospital in London, England. Consequently, this treatment has come to be known as the "Maudsley Approach" or the "Maudsley Method" (1).

FBT is a novel therapy in that it is theoretically agnostic and emphasizes parents as a resource, and empowers families in their effort to bring about recovery in their adolescent with an eating disorder. However, the first effort to include families in the treatment of adolescents with anorexia nervosa (AN) was made by Minuchin and his colleagues at the Child Guidance Clinic in Philadelphia (2). While treatment was quite mixed, the primary intervention was family therapy and the authors reported successful outcome in about 86% of patients. Given this success rate, as well as the theoretical model of the "psychosomatic family" upon which much of their work was based, Minuchin's work ultimately exerted considerable influence on ensuing efforts by the Maudsley group to involve families in the treatment of adolescents with AN.

The underlying theoretical principles and clinical application of Minuchin's structural family therapy, along with other school's of thought such as Palazzoli's (3) work from the Milan Group and Haley's (4) strategic therapy, served as the foundation for the development of FBT. This, in turn, gave rise to a number of controlled FBT studies which were pioneered at the Maudsley Hospital in London. FBT, as employed in these studies, contained several aspects of Minuchin's approach, but differed in significant ways.

Most important of these was that the Maudsley team, unlike Minuchin, encouraged parents to persist in their efforts until normal body weight had been achieved. In FBT, general adolescent and family issues are deferred until the eating disorder behavior was under control.

FBT remained limited to England from the time of its development until the mid 1990s. In 1994, Daniel le Grange, a member of the Maudsley team introduced FBT to his colleagues in the United States, when he trained at Stanford University. Through the relationships he established at Stanford University, he teamed up with James Lock to collaborate on manualizing (5) and studying this approach in clinical research trials targeting adolescents with eating disorders.

Much of their work, both collaboratively and independently, has led to the successful dissemination of FBT to other specialist centers in the United States, Canada and Australia.

THE FOUNDATION APPROACH

Core clinical and theoretical elements

FBT for adolescent AN is the original application of this model and its protocol (5) represents the foundation approach. In addition, manualized adaptations exist for bulimia nervosa (BN) (6), for the prevention of AN in children and adolescents with clinically significant, prodromal presentations (7), for young adults with AN (8), and for pediatric overweight (9). These newer applications will be described in detail below. FBT for adolescent AN is a short-term treatment designed to mobilize parents in assisting their ill child reverse his/her state of starvation acutely and ultimately achieve remission from AN. Given the profound physical and psychosocial liabilities associated with AN, a primary goal of FBT is to facilitate a return to a normal developmental trajectory, consistent with chronological age. FBT challenges the practical factors maintaining the AN, such as allowing the ill adolescent to make his/her own food choices, and makes no assumptions about the cause of AN. The treatment does not presuppose a familial pathology and in fact works to reduce parental self-blame regarding etiology. Moreover, FBT externalizes the illness, thereby reducing blame toward the ill adolescent for the symptoms s/he is experiencing. This aids in correcting misperceptions often held by siblings, who may believe their sister/brother is orchestrating the AN for attention. Sibling relationships are further protected by assigning a supportive role in treatment to siblings, reserving all supervisory responsibilities exclusively for the parents (10).

In the first of three phases of treatment, parents fully take charge of their ill child's eating, assuming the functions typical of an inpatient staff. The therapist helps parents develop and refine their techniques in an in-session family meal, a goal of which is for parents to convince their child to consume at least one more bite than s/he was originally willing. It is important to emphasize that this parental stance is unique to Phase I of FBT; once a minimal level of weight restoration is achieved (i.e., the adolescent crosses back over the diagnostic weight threshold) and conflict around eating is significantly reduced, control over food consumption is transferred back to the adolescent in Phase II of treatment. Phase III of FBT focuses on termination and more general issues of adolescent development. In its manualized format (5), FBT encompasses 20 sessions, although recent research indicates that a shorter course is as efficacious and arguably more cost-effective (11).

As suggested above, FBT incorporates an amalgam of techniques from family systems therapy, structural family therapy, and eating disorders- specific interventions. Also, as the treatment does not align with a particular therapeutic approach, etiological theory of AN, or model regarding maintenance of illness, hypothesized mechanisms of action of FBT for AN include exposure to forbidden foods and feared weight ranges, restructuring of family authorities and coalitions, and hormonal re- regulation as a function of weight restoration. FBT for AN has not been directly compared to inpatient behavioral interventions; however, long-term data across clinical trials and naturalistic follow-up studies indicate that treatment effects are more durable and relapse rates are markedly lower in FBT (12-14). Since FBT does not directly target the psychological feature of AN, such as fear of weight gain and body image disturbance, it is unlikely that improvements in these domains account for the sustained good outcome several years after completing FBT (12-14). However, indirect effects in these symptoms via the mechanisms noted above (e.g., exposure to feared weights, hormonal correction following full and sustained weight restoration) cannot be ruled out. Another possibility is that since FBT for adolescent AN by definition targets younger patients with a more recent onset of illness than their adult counterparts, this population is more responsive to treatment and has a better prognosis. However, randomized controlled trials (RCTs) of FBT versus individual psychotherapy show that even within this restricted age range, FBT is superior (12,15-17). Finally, it is likely that by training parents to create a zero- tolerance environment for self-starvation in their home and teaching them to identify signs and symptoms of AN, they keep relapse at bay. In that respect, parents can prevent a kindling effect, with each relapse increasing the likelihood of a subsequent one and of a more chronic course of illness.

FBT FOR ADOLESCENT ANOREXIA NERVOSA

Key findings from the literature

The efficacy of FBT for adolescent AN has been tested in RCTs (11-19). The first RCT of FBT for AN included a population of adolescent and adult patients. The only significant finding from this study demonstrated that FBT was particularly efficacious for patients 18 and younger. That is, FBT delivered better results in absolute clinical outcome and relative to individual treatment, acutely (one-year post- hospitalization) (17) and at five-year follow-up (12). These seminal studies provided preliminary evidence of FBT's utility in preventing relapse and facilitating continued improvement following inpatient weight restoration.

Since then, FBT for adolescents with AN has been subjected to further study in several additional RCTs, open trials, and clinical case series. Taken together, this literature has demonstrated that FBT is effective for a full course of outpatient weight restoration thereby preventing hospitalization (11,18,19) and that such gains are maintained 4-5 years after treatment ends (12-14); a version of FBT in which parents are seen separately from their adolescent is superior to the traditional conjoint FBT format when families are critical of their adolescent (high levels of expressed emotion) (18,21); that FBT yields a better outcome than either supportive individual psychotherapy (17) or a more focused and manualized ego-oriented individual therapy (15,16); that an abbreviated, 10-session course of FBT is as efficacious as the manualized 20-session version (11); that FBT can be disseminated in that it is feasible and effective when administered by investigators other than its developers (22,23); and that it appears to be as effective for children as it is for adolescents (24).

FBT FOR ADOLESCENT BULIMIA NERVOSA

Rationale for adaptation

Family-Based Treatment for bulimia nervosa (FBT-BN) (6) has been adapted from FBT for AN and, like its predecessor, is designed for adolescents. Until the development of this manual, only a limited number of either case series or case studies have been conducted for adolescents with BN. Most of these studies involve the patient's parents in the treatment. Moreover, AN - binge/purge subtype (about 20% of the samples studied) is typically responsive to FBT in terms of weight gain and reductions in binge and purge episodes. This suggests that parents are able to effectively decrease bulimic behaviors in addition to reversing severe dieting (11,18). Whereas AN and BN are distinct syndromes, considerable overlap in symptomatology is common Therefore, the efficacy of FBT for adolescent AN might be extended to include adolescent BN.

As in FBT for AN, this treatment modality for adolescents with BN is an outpatient intervention typically conducted in 20 sessions over 6 months. In some instances a shorter course is sufficient while additional sessions may be necessary for others. FBTBN consists of three phases. In Phase I parents are encouraged to assist their teen to reestablish healthy eating patterns and avoid engaging in binge eating and purging episodes. This process is collaborative in nature, however, parental authority is mobilized should this be required to manage the health crisis that the eating disorder poses. The adolescent's autonomy in other domains such as friendships and school is almost always kept intact at a level consistent with the patient's stage of development. In Phase II manages the return of control over eating to the adolescent at the time that acute symptoms have abated and regular eating patterns are established. Phase III addresses termination and issues of family structure and normal adolescent development.

In keeping with FBT for AN, FBT-BN also views the parents as a resource for resolving the eating disorder, and corrects misperceptions of blame directed to either the parents and their adolescent. Siblings are protected from the job assigned to the parents and are encouraged to play a supportive role in treatment. FBT-BN does not delve into what caused BN, instead, this treatment focuses on what can be done to resolve this serious disorder.

Key findings from the literature

The first of only two RCTs for adolescents with BN compared family therapy (n=41) (a form of FBTBN) and cognitive-behavioral guided self-care (n=44) (CBT-GSC) (25). These authors found no statistical differences at six months follow-up between the two treatments on binge/purge abstinence rates (around 40% for both). Direct cost was lower for CBT-GSC compared to family therapy, however, there were no other differences in cost between these two treatments. In the second RCT, Le Grange and colleagues (26) assigned 41 patients to FBT-BN and 39 to supportive psychotherapy (SPT), and unlike the Schmidt et al. (25), significant differences between the treatments did emerge. Categorical outcomes at post-treatment demonstrated significantly more patients in FBT-BN (39%) were binge/purge abstinent compared to SPT (17.9%). Somewhat fewer patients were abstinent at 6-month follow-up, however, the difference was statistically in favor of FBT-BN (29.3% vs 10.3%). Secondary outcome assessment, based upon random regression analysis, revealed main effects in favor of FBT-BN on all measures of eating pathology. Therefore, FBT-BN showed a clinical and statistical advantage over IPT at post-treatment and at 6-month follow-up. Reduction in core bulimic symptoms was also more acute for patients in FBTBN as opposed to SPT. But still it is the same results, when comparing FBT-BN to CBT-GSC. That is, FBT-BN and CBT-GSC are significantly favored treatments in comparison to SPT.

CLINICAL QUESTIONS AND CONTROVERSIES

Does FBT work for all adolescents with AN or BN?

Is FBT clinically appropriate across the child- adolescent age spectrum? Eating disorders impose significant developmental constraints on adolescents in both physical and psychosocial domains, with AN rendering the most severe liabilities. As described above, FBT works to restore the adolescent to his/her chronologically expected developmental state. In addition, FBT views the illness as directly responsible for impairing the adolescent's decision-making capabilities with regard to sensible food consumption and shape/weight standards. In that respect, the adolescent — even the older adolescent - is seen as functioning at a developmentally regressed level in his/her ability to appropriately self-feed. FBT asks parents to compensate for this discrepancy between chronological age and illness-influenced developmental state by temporarily taking charge of their child's eating until the eating disorder minimally recedes. In AN, this initial phase of treatment is characterized by parents assuming full responsibility for their child's eating; in BN, where the adolescent is typically less impaired and more on a par with her peers in terms of adolescent development, the process in Phase I is more collaborative between parents and child.

Given the equalizing force of the eating disorder in yielding a similarly regressed state across chronological age, FBT does not modulate its early techniques as a function of adolescent stage of development. However, Phase II, in which control is transferred back to the adolescent, and Phase III, in which broader issues of adolescence are addressed, are exquisitely sensitive to the subtle and gross differences between early, middle, and late adolescence. Importantly, even in Phase I, the therapist instructs the family to defer to actual stage of adolescent development in domains external to the eating disorder. For example, while parents may fully supervise meals, they would not supervise their adolescent's social encounters in the same manner. If parents do not afford sufficient respect to adolescent development in these other areas — whether pre- morbidly, as a function of general concern for their ill child, or based on a misunderstanding of their mission in FBT — the therapist actively corrects this.

Does the research support the application of FBT across the full child-adolescent age spectrum? While not yet tested in an RCT, FBT for children has generated promising results in a clinical case series (24) Within adolescence, compared to younger adolescents with AN, the evidence for the efficacy of FBT for older adolescents is somewhat mixed. A case series of adolescents with AN (22) showed no difference in outcome for younger (9-14 years) versus older (15-18 years) patients. Recent FBT trials for adolescent AN (12 to 18 years) (11) or BN (12 to 19 years old) (26) found that age was not a moderator of treatment outcome. In contrast, younger age was a predictor of remission for AN in univariate (but not multivariate) analyses (20). However, it is difficult to disentangle age from other variables that might be a proxy for severity of illness, such duration of illness, number of previous hospitalizations, and BMI, all of which loaded with age on the principal component analysis in that study (20).

Is FBT clinically appropriate for adolescents with greater levels of specific and comorbid psychopathology? In the only predictor analysis of adolescents with AN receiving FBT, Lock and colleagues (20) found that co-morbid psychiatric disorder predicted dropout and lower remission rates, and that the probability of remission increased with a reduction in child behavioral symptoms. Moderator analyses from the original trial (11) found that patients with higher levels of eating disorder-specific obsessions and compulsions fared better in a full course of treatment compared to an abbreviated course, but that that other severity indices (e.g., duration of illness, purging status) did not moderate outcome. In the only predictor analysis for adolescents with BN receiving FBT or SPT, findings indicated that participants with less severe Eating Disorder Examination (EDE) (27) eating concerns at baseline were more likely to be binge and purge abstinent (remitted) at post-treatment and follow-up, regardless of the treatment that they received (28). Participants with lower depression scores and fewer binge/purge episodes at baseline were more likely to be partly remitted (no longer meeting study entry criteria) at post-treatment and follow-up, respectively. In terms of moderators, participants with less severe eating disorder psychopathology (EDE global score), receiving FBT-BN, were more likely to meet criteria for partial remission at follow-up. Lower eating concerns are the best predictor of remission for adolescents with BN and FBT-BN may be most effective in those cases with low levels of eating disorder psychopathology. It is noteworthy that some severity-related factors with prior support as predictive of outcome, such as duration of illness and diagnosis (17,29), turned out to be neither predictors nor moderators of outcome in the present study. (28).

Does FBT work for all families?

Critical Families. Expressed Emotion (EE) has been studied in the families of patients with eating disorders (21,30-35), and has become a useful way to tap into the quality of the 'emotional life' of families of children with eating disorders. For instance, Minuchin and his colleagues (2,36) suggested that families of children with AN have several characteristics in common, such as enmeshment, and lack of conflict resolution. EE allows us to reliably measure several aspects of functioning in families with an eating disorder offspring.

Studies have shown that patients with AN are more likely to drop out of treatment prematurely, or have a poor outcome should they remain in treatment, if their parents are overly critical toward them (high EE family) (21,33,34). This fmding has recently also been replicated for adolescents with BN (31). Family interaction has important treatment implications. For instance, a version of FBT for AN in which parents are seen separately from their adolescent has shown to be superior to FBT in its conjoint format when families present with high levels of EE (high in terms of criticism) (18,21). This line of inquiry is still in its infancy and more work is clearly required.

Enmeshed Families. A traditional theory of eating disorders in adolescence, particularly AN, is that the illness represents a maladaptive attempt at separation and control in the context of an enmeshed family (36). Correspondingly, a prescription for recovery is often to afford more autonomy to the adolescent, especially with regard to eating, so as to prevent an exacerbation of symptoms. At its extreme, this recommendation excludes parents from treatment entirely, and has been labeled a "parentectomy" (37). In turn, a criticism that has been raised against FBT is that it prescribes, rather than proscribes enmeshment by virtue of Phase I techniques. This concern is predicated on four assumptions: first, that family enmeshment is implicated in the etiology of adolescent eating disorders; second, that FBT does not respect adolescent autonomy; third, that enmeshed parents would resist the transfer of control back to the adolescent in Phase II; and fourth, that FBT should ultimately worsen symptoms, even if it suppresses them in the short term. Each assumption is contradicted by or lacks support in research fmdings.

First, there are no longitudinal data to indicate enmeshment plays an etiological role in eating disorders. Even if large cross-sectional studies were to find an increased prevalence of enmeshment in eating disorder families relative to psychiatric and normal controls, it would be difficult to know whether this reflected cause of illness or the effect of having a child with a severe disorder, particularly one associated with a high mortality rate. Second, as noted above, FBT affords significant respect to adolescent autonomy, by maintaining domain specificity of parental control in Phase I, requiring transfer of control over food in Phase II, and directly addressing adolescent development, including issues pertaining to separation and individuation, in Phase III. In this respect, FBT can theoretically correct the expressions of an enmeshed family dynamic (while not directly treating the underlying family pathology) and would not be contraindicated for such a family. Third, there is no evidence to suggest that parents resist the transition to Phase II, which would be indicative of an enmeshed family process; in fact, clinical observations suggest a greater risk is parents' abrupt or rapid abdication of supervisory responsibilities once weight is minimally restored. Finally, follow up studies of FBT for AN (12-14) demonstrate sustained and robust improvement, without evidence of an ultimate symptomatic backlash in response to Phase I techniques. In other words, it is the eating disorder, not FBT, which appears to pose an insult to adolescent development.

Non-Intact Families. Another concern that has been raised about FBT is whether it is appropriate for a variety of family structures (e.g., divorced, separated, single parent, grandparent-headed households, etc.) beyond the traditional intact family. The treatment manuals (5,6) have the latitude to accommodate atypical family configurations provided that at least one parent or guardian can be involved in treatment. Moderator analyses from the Lock et al (11) comparison of 6-month versus 12-month FBT for AN showed that non-intact family status fared better with a longer treatment duration. Predictor analyses (20) from this study did not fmd family status to predict dropout or remission. In the BN literature, FBT was equally effective for intact and non-intact families (28). Collectively, these findings support the use of FBT with both intact and non-intact families, with the latter benefiting from a full, 12-month (20- session) course of treatment, per the published manual (5).

NEW APPLICATIONS UNDER INVESTIGATION

FBT for young adults with AN

The absence of FBT studies for young adults (1825 years) with AN is surprising for at least two reasons; there are similarities in terms of how fmancially dependent older adolescents and young adults are upon their parents, and there are significant challenges to engage and maintain adults in treatment. Young adults like older adolescents are substantially fmancially dependent on their parents, with nearly two-thirds of young adults in their early 20s receiving economic support from their parents (38). US census data from 1970-2000 suggest that the percentage of young adults living without fmancial dependence on family has declined significantly (39). Thus, dependence upon family resources continues later into the 20's for more young adults today than it did even a decade or two ago. Thus, it is surprising that we have not systematically used family treatment with young adults especially given the notorious difficulty in engaging and maintaining adults with AN in treatment (29). Involving family or other individuals who are concerned about the patient in treatment together with the AN patient may be a powerful way to maintain the patient's engagement. This is seen clearly in dropout rates for adult AN with the largest study reporting a dropout rate of 46% (29) and FBT treatment with adolescent AN showing dropout rates of 10-20% (11,40).

While young adults may still be substantially dependent upon parents, they also face different challenges than adolescents. It must also be noted that despite similarities, young adulthood has certain developmental differences from adolescence. For instance, young adults are legally regarded as adults, are more likely to be independent, and are more intellectually and socially experienced and skilled than adolescents. For instance, young adults are more likely to have moved out from home than adolescents with about half of the 27 million 18 to 24 years olds in the USA are not living with their parents (55.7%) (41). Due to this relative independence from family, young adults may struggle with new living situations, participation in the work-force or further educational challenges. Capitalizing on this ongoing leverage that parents may still have over their ill young adult offspring, FBT for this patient population is more collaborative. In other words, it is more in keeping with the model for BN as opposed to adolescent AN.

FBT for subsyndromal anorexia nervosa in children and adolescents

Early identification and treatment of AN is considered to have a positive prognostic impact on the course of illness in AN (42,43), although duration of illness remains a potential confound in these analyses (44). Given that (a) children and adolescents often present atypically on a number of dimensions relative to strict DSM (45) diagnostic criteria (Workgroup for Classification of Eating Disorders in Children and Adolescents (WCEDCA)), (46), (b) clinically significant but technically subthreshold presentations of AN (SAN) can reflect a disorder in evolution rather than a stable state or transient phase (e.g., 47, 48, 49) and (c) once the diagnostic threshold is crossed, AN is notoriously refractory to treatment, it is reasonable to target SAN at the intersect of prevention and intervention for AN. FBT is an excellent candidate preventive intervention for SAN in light of its efficacy for AN (50). In addition, an open feasibility/dissemination trial of FBT for AN- spectrum presentations found that FBT arrested and reversed AN symptoms in an SAN subset (23). An RCT is currently underway at Mount Sinai School of Medicine comparing FBT-SAN (7) to individual supportive psychotherapy in this potentially prodromal population.

While much of the core FBT for AN protocol (5) applies to clinically significant SAN patients, several important modifications are noted. First, the foundation approach is modified to address a wider range of developmental stages. While AN typically onsets in mid-late adolescence, prodromal AN by defmition precedes this. Second, for SAN participants who have lost weight but do not yet meet the weight cutoff for AN, regulation of eating patterns and the incorporation of a full range of foods in the child or adolescent's diet may be as important goals as weight gain early in treatment. Third, the goals and language of the treatment re modified to incorporate the notion of risk of progression from SAN to AN, while at the same time emphasizing the clinical severity of the SAN in and of itself, and the need for reduction and resolution of presenting symptoms. While we cannot be certain that all such patients would eventually go on to develop AN (i.e., that they are truly prodromal), their symptoms are sufficiently clinically severe to warrant intervention. Fourth, the revisions for SAN stress the importance of regular family meals at home and the modeling of healthy, non-restrictive eating habits by parents.

FBT for pediatric overweight

Parent involvement is a crucial element in reducing pediatric overweight (PO) in light of parents' ability to control and modify the family's home environment to promote the child's healthy behaviors. Data from the PO literature highlight that the most efficacious PO interventions include parental involvement to some degree (51,52). However, a recent review of studies with differing degrees of parental involvement provides mixed evidence of a positive relationship between greater parental involvement and better weight loss outcomes (53). It is possible that the relationship between family involvement and successful weight loss, as well as the optimal level of parental involvement, may vary as a function of the child's age and psychosocial development. In particular, the literature has not adequately addressed the unique needs of adolescents and the ideal quality and quantity of parental involvement at this crucial stage of development. Treatment of adolescent overweight must adequately navigate the dual challenge of the adolescent's increasing need for independence in the context of sustained reliance on a parent-influenced home environment. To date, no PO treatment study has targeted overweight across the child-adolescent age spectrum, nor has attempted to modulate parental involvement from a transdevelopmental perspective. FBT is a logical foundation approach to begin to resolve these deficits in the literature.

Inherent in the FBT model is a mission to increase parental empowerment, competence, and efficacy in facilitating healthy behaviors and outcomes for children, and in unapologetically assuming appropriate parental influence. Beyond this, FBT provides a strong foundation for application to the significant problem of PO because of its attention to parental engagement strategies, its demonstrated efficacy in correcting maladaptive eating and related behaviors, its explicit agenda of blame reduction, its disease-based model, and its emphasis on promoting normal physical and psychosocial development for the child or adolescent. Loeb and colleagues (9) proposed an innovative adaptation of FBT to PO (FBT-PO) that maintains the underlying tenets of the original FBT protocol but modifies it for a non-psychiatric weight disorder, with application to either psychiatric or primary care settings. FBT-P0 is currently being piloted at two sites (Mount Sinai School of Medicine and the University of Chicago.) Importantly, FBT-P0 recognizes that PO is not a psychiatric disorder and that children/adolescents are not developmentally regressed as they are in severe eating disorders. Therefore, FBT-P0 modulates the quality and intensity of parental involvement as a function of developmental stage. It also recognizes specific challenges of socioeconomically diverse populations (e.g., built environment, reduction in school-based physical activity), the challenges of concordance of overweight across family members, and the need for parents to model attitudes and dietary/physical activity habits associated with healthy weight. Finally, FBT-P0 addresses the multi- systemic toxic environment (54) that contributes to PO, and focuses on parent-driven, family-level change.

CONCLUSION

In conclusion, FBT is emerging as a treatment of choice for adolescent anorexia nervosa and bulimia nervosa, with promising adaptations for prevention of eating disorders in high risk children and adolescents, for young adult eating disorders, and for pediatric overweight. While the intervention continues to raise questions and controversies, it is gaining public and scientific acceptance in light of its demonstrated efficacy to date. However, additional and larger clinical trials are necessary to fully test its scientific merit. An NIMH five year two-site RCT (the University of Chicago and Stanford University) commenced in April 2004. In this study, adolescents with AN were randomly allocated to either FBT or Ego-oriented Individual Therapy (EOIT). This is the first large-scale treatment trial for adolescents with AN and should, upon completion, go some way toward verifying the relative efficacy of FBT for this clinical population. Another NIMH-funded multi-site study (with Stanford University as the Coordinating Center and 6 clinical sites) is examining FBT relative to family systems therapy as well as the adjunctive role of medication. Other studies underway involving FBT principles include a parent training treatment development study at Duke University; a study investigating the role of FBT in inpatient care at the University of Sydney; and a study of multi-family group FBT at the Institute of Psychiatry, London. Beyond these, future inquiries should focus on dismantling and step-care studies, as well as comparisons between FBT and treatment as usual, including inpatient and day treatment models. Larger trials for AN and BN, especially designs with two active treatments with hypothesized mediators, would permit investigation of mechanisms of FBT. It is also important to examine the relative moderating effect of symptom severity in terms of cognitions for a treatment that focuses on such symptoms, e.g., CBT, in order to determine whether these moderating effects would be similar between two specific treatments. Finally, the newly manualized and piloted adaptations of FBT described above require formal testing, as well as raise intriguing possibilities about the adaptation of FBT to other psychiatric disorders in adolescence, such as substance abuse.

ACKNOWLEDGMENTS

This work was supported in part by a Career Development Award granted to the first author by the NIMH (K23-MH 074506-01) and a Research Project Grant Program awarded to the second author by the NIMH (R01-MH 70620). The authors thank Lauren Alfano, BA, Angela Celio Doyle, PhD, Tom Hildebrandt, PsyD, and James Lock, MD, PhD for their contributions to the manuscript.

REFERENCES

[1] Lock J, Le Grange D. Family based treatment of eating disorders. Int Journal of Eat Disord 2005;37:S64-7.
[2] Minuchin S, Baker L, Rosman BL, et al. A conceptual model of psychosomatic illness in children: Family organization and family therapy. Arch Gen Psychiatry 1975;32:1031-8.
[3] Palazolli MS. Self starvation: From the intrapsychic to the transpersonal. London: Chancer Press, 1974.
[4] Haley J. Problem solving therapy. San Francisco: Jossey-Bass, 1976.
[5] Lock J, Le Grange D, Agras W, Dare, C. Treatment manual for anorexia nervosa: A family-based approach. New York: Guilford, 2001.
[6] Le Grange D, Lock J. Treating bulimia in adolescents: A family-based approach. New York: Guilford, 2007.
[7] Loeb KL, Le Grange D, Lock J. Family-based treatment for the prevention of anorexia nervosa. Unpublished Manual. New York: Mount Sinai School Med, 2005.
[8] Le Grange D, Chen E. Family-based treatment for young adults with anorexia nervosa. Unpublished Manual. Chicago: Univ Chicago, 2007.
[9] Loeb KL, Celio Doyle A, Le Grange D, Bremer J, Hildebrandt T, Hirsch A. Family-based treatment for child and adolescent overweight: A transdevelopmental approach. Unpublished Manual. New York: Mount Sinai School Med, 2006.
[10] Dare C, Eisler I. Family therapy for anorexia nervosa. In: Garner DM, Garfmkel PE, eds. Handbook of treatment for eating disorders, 2nd ed. New York: Guilford, 1995.
[11] Lock J, Agras WS, Bryson S, Kraemer HC. A comparison of short-and long-term family therapy for adolescent anorexia nervosa. J Am Acad Child Adolesc Psychiatry 2005;44:632-9.
[12] Eisler I, Dare C, Russell GFM, Szmukler G, Le Grange D, Dodge E. Family and individual therapy in anorexia nervosa: A 5-year follow-up. Arch Gen Psychiatry 1997;54:1025-30.
[13] Eisler I, Simic M, Russell GFM, Dare C. A randomised controlled treatment trial of two forms of family therapy in adolescent anorexia nervosa: A five-year follow up. J Child Psychol Psychiatry 2007; 48:552-60.
[14] Lock J, Couturier J, Agras WS. Comparison of long-term outcomes in adolescents with anorexia nervosa treated with family therapy. J Am Acad Child Adolesc Psychiatry 2006;45:666-72.

[15] Robin AL, Siegel PT, Koepke T, Moye AW. Family therapy versus individual therapy for adolescent females with anorexia nervosa. J Dev Behav Pediatr 1994;15:111-6.

[16] Robin AL, Siegel PT, Moye AW, Koepke T, Gilroy M, Denis, AB, Sikand A. A controlled comparison of family versus individual therapy for adolescents with anorexia nervosa. J Am Acad Child Adolesc Psychiatry 1999;38:1482-9.

[17] Russell GF, Szmukler GI, Dare C, Eisler I. An evaluation of family therapy in anorexia nervosa and bulimia nervosa. Arch Gen Psychiatry 1987;44:1047-56.

[18] Eisler I, Dare C, Hodes M, Russell G, Dodge E, Le Grange D. Family therapy for adolescent anorexia nervosa: The results of a controlled comparison of two family interventions. J Child Psychol Psychiatry 2000;41:727-36.

[19] Le Grange D, Eisler I, Dare C, Russell GFM. Evaluation of family treatments in adolescent anorexia nervosa: a pilot study. Int Journal of Eat Disord 1992;12:347-57.

[20] Lock J, Couturier J, Bryson S, Agras WS. Predictors of dropout and remission in family therapy for adolescent anorexia nervosa in a randomized clinical trial. Int J Eat Disord 2006;39:639-47.

[21] Le Grange D, Eisler I, Dare C, Hodes M. Family criticism and self-starvation: A study of expressed emotion. J Fam Ther 1992; 14, 177-92.

[22] Le Grange D, Binford R, Loeb KL. Manualized family-based treatment for anorexia nervosa: a case series. J Am Acad Child Adolesc Psychiatry 2005;44:41-6.

[23] Loeb KL, Walsh BT, Lock J, Le Grange D, Jones J, Marcus S, Weaver J, Dobrow I. Open trial of family-based treatment for full and partial anorexia nervosa in adolescence: Evidence of successful dissemination. J Am Acad Child Adolesc Psychiatry 2007;46:792-800.

[24] Lock J, Le Grange D, Fordsburg S, Hewell K. Is family therapy effective for children with anorexia nervosa? J Am Acad Child Adolesc Psychiatry, 2006;45:1323-38.

[25] Schmidt U, Lee S, Perkins S, Treasure J, Yi I, et al. A randomized controlled trial of family therapy and cognitive-behavioral guided self-care for adolescents with bulimia nervosa and related disorders. Am J Psychiatry 2007;164:591-8.

[26] Le Grange D, Crosby RD, Rathouz PJ, Leventhal BL. A randomized controlled comparison of family-based   treatment and   supportive psychotherapy for adolescent bulimia nervosa. Arch Gen Psychiatry 2007;64:1049-56.

[27] Fairburn CG, Cooper Z. The eating disorder examination. In Fairburn CG, Wilson GT, eds. Binge eating: Nature assessment and treatment, 12 ed. New York: Guilford, 1993:317-60.

[28] Le Grange D, Crosby R, Lock J. Predictors and moderators of outcome in family-based treatment for adolescent bulimia nervosa. J Am Acad Child Adolesc Psychiatry, in press.

[29] Halmi KA, Agras WS, Crow S, Mitchell J, Wilson GT, Bryson SW, Kraemer HC, Predictors of treatment acceptance and completion in anorexia nervosa: implications for future study designs. Arch Gen Psychiatry 2005;62:776-81.

[30] Dare C, Le Grange D, Eisler I, Rutherford J. Redefming the psychosomatic family: Family process of 26 eating disorder families. Int J Eat Disord 1994;16:211-26.

[31] Hedlund S, Fichter MM, Quadflieg N, Brandl C. Expressed emotion, family environment, and parental bonding in bulimia nervosa: A 6-year investigation. Eat Weight Disord 2003;8:26-35.

[32] Szmukler GI, Berkowitz R, Eisler I, Leff J, Dare C. Expressed emotion in individual and family settings: A comparative study. Br J Psychiatry 1987;151:174-8.

[33] Szmukler GI, Eisler I, Russell GF, Dare C. Anorexia nervosa, parental "expressed emotion" and dropping out of treatment. Br J Psychiatry 1985;147:265-71.

[34] Uehara T, Kawashima Y, Goto M, Tasaki S, Someya T. Psychoeducation for the families of patients with eating disorders and changes in expressed emotion: A preliminary study. Compr Psychiatry 2001;42:132-8.

[35] Van Furth EF, van Strien DC, Martina LML, van Son MJM, Hendrickx JJP, van Engeland H. Expressed emotion and the prediction of outcome in adolescent eating disorders. Int J Eat Disord 1996;20:19-31.

[36] Minuchin S, Rosman BL, Baker L. Pyschosomatic Families. Cambridge, MA: Harvard Univ Press, 1978.

[37] Harper G. Varieties of parenting failure in anorexia nervosa: protection and parentectomy revisited. J Am Acad Child Adolesc Psychiatry 1983;22:134-9.

[38] Gutmann MP, Pullum-Pinon SM, Pullum TW. Three eras of young adults home leaving in twentieth-century America. J Soc History 2002;35:533-76.

[39] Yelowitz A. Young adults leaving the nest: The role of cost-of-living. Lexington, KY: Dept Economics, Univ kentucky, 2006.

[40] Le Grange D, Lock J. The dearth of psychological treatment studies for anorexia nervosa. Int J Eat Disord 2005;37: 79-91.

[41] Rumbaut RG. Young adults in the United States: A profile. Research Network Working Paper, 2004.

[42] Deter HC, Herzog W. Anorexia nervosa in a long-term perspective: Results of the Heidelberg-Mannheim study. Psychosom Med 1994;56:20-2.

[43] Ratnasuriya R, Eisler I, Szmukler GI. Anorexia nervosa: Outcome and prognostic factors after 20 years. Br J Psychiatry 1991;156:495-6.

[44] Schoemaker, C. Does early intervention improve the prognosis in anorexia nervosa? A systematic review of the treatment-outcome literature. Int J Eat Disord 1997;21 (1):1-15.

[45] American Psychiatric Association. Diagnostic and statistical manual of mental disorders, 4th ed. Washington, DC: APA, 2000.

[46] Workgroup for the Classification of Eating Disorders in Children and Adolescents (WCEDCA). Classification of child and adolescent eating disturbances. Int J Eat Disord 2007;40: S117-22.

[47] Ben Tovim DI, Walker K, Gilchrist P, Freeman R, Kalucy R, Esterman A. Outcome in patients with eating disorders: A 5-year study. Lancet 2001;357: 1254-7.

[48] Herzog DB, Hopkins JD, Bums CD. A follow-up study of 33 subdiagnostic eating disordered women. Int J Eat Disord 1993;14(3): 261-7.

[49] Patton GC, Johnson Sabine E, Wood K, Mann AH. Abnormal eating attitudes in London schoolgirls: A prospective epidemiological study: Outcome at twelve month follow-up. Psychol Med 1990;20(2): 383-94.

[50] Le Grange D, Loeb KL. Early identification and treatment of eating disorders: prodrome to syndrome, Early Intery Psychiatry 2007; 1:27-39.

[51] Jelalian E, Saelens B. Empirically supported treatments in pediatric psychology: Pediatric obesity. J Pediatr Psychol 1999;24(3):223-48.

[52] Golan M. Parents as agents of change in childhood obesity: From research to practice. Int J Pediatr Obes 2006;1(2):66-76.

[53] Kitzmann KM, Beech BM. Family-based interventions for pediatric obesity: Methodological and conceptual challenges from family psychology. J Fam Psychol 2006;20(2): 175-89.

[54] Wadden TA, Brownell KD, Foster GD. Obesity: responding to the global epidemic. J Consult Clin Psychol 2002;70(3):510-25.

In: Treatment and Recovery of Eating Disorders
Editors: Daniel Stein and Yael Latzer

ISBN: 978-1-62808-248-7
© 2013 Nova Science Publishers, Inc.

Chapter 13

RECOVERY FROM ANOREXIA NERVOSA: THE PATIENT'S PERSPECTIVE

Meirav Shahar[1]††††, Yael Latzer[2] and Eli Buchbinder[3]

[1] Doctoral Student at the School of Social Work,
University of Haifa, Israel
[2] DSc. Associate Professor, Faculty of Social Welfare and Health Sciences,
University of Haifa, Israel. Director, Eating Disorders Clinic, Psychiatric Division,
Rambam Medical Center, Haifa, Israel
[3] Ph.D., Social Worker and Senior Lecturer at the School of Social Work,
University of Haifa, Israel

ABSTRACT

The majority of research data regarding recovery from anorexia nervosa (AN) relates to the therapists' perspective rather than to the patients' point of view. The few studies that documented the meaning and the supportive factors of recovery from the patients' perspective raised an important and significant understanding of the recovery process. The aim of the present study is to extend this scope of understanding from the patient's point of view, using qualitative methodology based on the phenomenological approach as a theoretical foundation. The key research questions were: How do women who recovered from AN experience the recovery process, and what meaning do they attach to this experience? The study was based on in-depth semi-structured interviews with 18 women who had recovered from AN about five years prior to the interview. The study findings show that the participants perceived recovery as resulting from a combination psychosocial and physical symptom changes (internal and external). They emphasized the gradual, stage-by-stage recovery process, starting with mental changes, moving through cognitive-behavioral, occupational, social and familial changes, and ending with physical changes and final relief from the symptoms. The study findings constitute the basis for a model that presents the whole range of discriminate factors for recovery from

---

†††† E-mail address: mshahar@univ.haifa.ac.il

AN. The proposed model is unique, especially with regard to the definition of recovery from the patient's perspective. Clinical implications are discussed in light of the new findings presented, and recommendations for future research are suggested.

Keywords: anorexia nervosa, recovery, qualitative methodology, eating disorders

INTRODUCTION

Anorexia nervosa (AN) is one of the most prevalent eating disorders in the Western world and has reached epidemic proportions (1). The prevalence rate ranges from 0.5%-1% in the entire population of the Western world, mainly among female adolescents and young adults, as well as a high mortality rate (2). The reported recovery rates from AN vary according to the different definitions of recovery used (3-5). Studies in the 1980s related to recovery of weight in terms of body mass index (BMI) and recommencement of menses as measures of recovery (6,7). However, in light of the finding that approximately 50% of patients have a relapse during the three years following the first remission (8), it appears that physical rehabilitation alone is not sufficient to claim recovery.

Indeed, more recent studies show that physical condition does not indicate complete recovery and that cognitive components should also be considered in the definition of recovery. Such measures include the absence of a distorted body perception, an excessive preoccupation with body shape and weight, and food phobias (4, 8-11).

It is also necessary to include the intra- and inter-personal components that form the basis of the illness and to strive to find adaptive methods of coping in order to attain full recovery (12-14). Moreover, adaptation in the social, educational and professional arenas should be included in the definition of recovery (11,15,16). It may be that the more components included in the definition, the lower the reported recovery rates.

Most studies on AN have focused on the therapists' standpoint. The few studies that did focus on the patients' point of view have provided an important perspective for understanding the meaning of recovery from the illness. Four studies found that self-definition, self-acceptance, and self-esteem were highly significant components in the patient's perception of recovery (17-20), thus contributing to the understanding that the patient's self-perception is an important indicator of recovery. The small number of studies addressing recovery from the patient's perspective calls for the need to expand and deepen knowledge of the subject. Therefore, the aim of the present study is to extend the scope of understanding of the recovery from AN from the patient's standpoint, using qualitative methodology based on the phenomenological approach as a theoretical foundation for the research.

METHOD

The qualitative research method used in this study is derived from the phenomenological-hermeneutic perspective, which observes the human world as composed of multiple subjective realities. The researcher's aim in this approach is to describe and interpret the meaning of recovery from AN as perceived by those experiencing it, thus enabling an understanding of significant, subjective processes without attempting to support or refute hypotheses (21).

Sample

Qualitative research is based on a small sample size of those who experience the phenomenon intensively (22). The inclusion criterion was full recovery from AN over a period of five consecutive years, in accordance with DSM-IV measures (23), using *the Mini International Neuropsychiatric Interview* (MINI) (24) for diagnosing AN. Of the 20 women recruited, 18 agreed to participate in the study. Two women refused on the grounds of lack of time and fear of dealing with the content. All the participants signed an informed consent form after receiving a detailed explanation of the study objectives and procedure.

All of the eighteen participants were Jewish and Israeli-born. Nine were married, and nine were single. In regard to education, seven were high school graduates, six were college students, and five had university degrees. Their age ranged from 20-33 years (27.4± 3.7). Eveven participants had suffered from AN restrictive-type and seven from AN binge-purge type. At the time of the interview, four did not express any fear of weight gain, seven had a normal perception of their body shape, and sixteen had regular menses (2 had irregular menses). All eighteen participants were free from binge-eating episodes and were no longer inducing vomiting or fasting. Seventeen participants did not sense a loss of control over their eating and did not abuse laxatives and/or diuretics. The majority (thirteen participants) did not engage in excessive exercise, and over half (ten) were not preoccupied with body and weight.

Instruments

Data were collected using in-depth semi-structured interviews designed to achieve meaningful, open, and rich descriptions of the participants' experiences, as expressed in their own words (25). The semi-structured interview guide was based on literature review dealing with recovery from AN as well as from a clinicians' who specializes in treatment of eating disorders (ED). This prior knowledge engendered theoretical sensitivity in the research process (26). The interview guide includes areas that focus on the participants' perceptions of the process, stages, and dynamics of the illness and recovery, aspects of change, and the influence of relationships with significant others throughout the recovery process. The interview protocol was composed of key questions, such as: "What does recovery from AN mean to you?" The purpose of the questions was to raise topics that might encourage the participants to provide in-depth, detailed descriptions of many different aspects (27).

Procedure

The participants were recruited by the staff at the Eating Disorders Clinic of Rambam Medical Center in the north of Israel after receiving approval from the hospital's Helsinki Committee, under the auspices of the Ministry of Health. The interviews were conducted in the women's homes and lasted approximately three hours each. They were recorded and transcribed in full for the purpose of precise analysis. All of the participants' names were changed in order to ensure anonymity.

Data analysis

Data analysis was conducted in four stages. In the first stage, the interviews were reread repeatedly for in-depth understanding of the participants' perceptions, thoughts, and feelings, as expressed in the interviews (28). In the second stage, units of meaning were identified and sorted using two methods: identifying repeated statements about themselves and locating statements that had a broad meaning for the participants. For example, "self-acceptance" and "sense of control in life" were identified as significant in most participants' perceptions of their recovery. This stage ended when saturation was reached for the different recovery components. In the third stage, similar units of meaning were clustered. Using focusing, comparison, confrontation, and synthesis, the components that constituted the conceptual skeleton of the theme were consolidated (25). The following components were identified as recovery modules which cannot be achieved without completing the previous module in the fallowing order: mental, cognitive, behavioral, occupational, social, familial, and physical. In the fourth stage, connections were made between the sub-themes through focusing, comparison, and confrontation, with the aim of constructing a conceptual model (29). The analysis finished with the clustering of sub-themes into a complete narrative, describing the recovery process and components from the participants' perspective. This narrative included internal components (mental and cognitive), external components (social and familial), and physical (bodily) components of the recovery.

Trustworthiness

The researchers focused on attempting to expand and deepen the understanding of anorexia, while creating a coherent picture of the participants' subjective meaning of their recovery (30). Lincoln and Guba (31) noted that a qualitative study is trustworthy when the researchers succeed in demonstrating credibility in their description of varied realities, based on in-depth interviews, direct experience, ongoing intervention, and deeper exploration of the participants' perceptions. Credibility is also achieved based on grounding and using precise quotes alongside analysis, thus enabling the readers to evaluate whether and how the researchers' conceptual interpretations and constructions reflect the participants' subjective perspectives (32).

FINDINGS

The participants perceived their recovery from AN as composed of changes in different areas of life that together create a uniform narrative of change. This narrative can be referred to as "internal and external harmony" and represents the participants' change process while on the road to recovery. From the participants' descriptions, it appears that the change process is modular, whereby each change draws on the last until full recovery is achieved.

The first meaningful change occurred on the mental level and was expressed through the transition from a conflicted self, which drains vital energy, to the experience of self-acceptance and recognition of one's inner strength. Intra-personal change enabled a shift in the thinking patterns and negative beliefs that dominated their lives while afflicted with AN, thereby contributing to its preservation. This change in thinking patterns gradually led to changes in behavior, including the release of compulsive behaviors that controlled their world. The sense of energy that they experienced as a result of this release facilitated their gradual inclusion in normative life tasks and paved the way to creating social relationships and a change in family patterns. Changes in the attitude toward their bodies served as final evidence of recovery from the illness.

Mental Changes

The narratives revealed that the road to recovery from AN is a long and complex one, beginning with mental changes such as the transition from denial to an awareness of the underlying difficulties of the illness. Dana describes this transition as follows:

> "From my point of view, recovery occurred when I finished therapy. This was mainly mental. For me, the weight gain is almost meaningless because after three months of home hospitalization, I reached my target weight, but to say that I'd recovered? I wish I had recovered. It was totally physical and not related to anything else; the problems and layers were still embedded there. For me, recovery was the day on which I could say to my psychologist: 'Now I can go my own way because the answers are inside me.' That was when I understood how to help myself. I think that this was the point at which I could really say: 'I've recovered'" (014).

Dana made a distinction between physical and mental recovery, indicating that the physical recovery is only a stage in the process. Dana was helped through the process by psychotherapy, which provided her with more constructive and effective coping tools to replace her self-punishing behaviors. When she sensed that she was no longer controlled by the illness, she was able to regain her internal locus of control and understood that she was on the right path to recovery.

Shelley tells how deepening her insight led to a change in the recovery process:

> "I became aware of my personality, of who I am, and recognized my fears more openly. I worked on my social difficulties, on my lack of self-confidence, the fear of bringing myself forward, fear of others. Today, I can say that in relation to my body, when I feel fat, I understand that I'm actually dealing with another kind of difficulty. It means making changes on a deeper level, observing, exploring and taking the available possibilities and deciding what I'm going to do with them, and instead of killing myself, using them. This is actually what happened in the final recovery process." (017).

Shelley explains the importance of this insight in the process of change on the way to recovery, allowing her to cope for the first time with the underlying fears, character traits, and non-adaptive patterns of the illness. Moreover, she was able to identify alternative coping strategies at her disposal and to choose between them. She describes how all previous distress and difficulty was automatically transformed into anxiety about her body weight. When she finally realized that her perception about her body weight was a hindrance and served only to preserve the illness, she was able to move from a position of weakness to a position of strength with the help of therapy, and to adopt more effective coping strategies.

Tali viewed her newfound self-acceptance, self-love, and self-esteem as mental measures of recovery:

> "Learning to love and accept yourself just as you are is related to the cessation of the illness, as the moment you love yourself, you won't get stuck with that kind of disease. It's a matter of self-esteem; accepting yourself is the key issue here." (009)

Tali also describes her long life struggle with perfectionism, which led to feelings of inferiority, self-loathing, and self-criticism. As the self-loathing increased, the self-punishment followed and was finally manifested in the illness. At a certain stage, "excelling" even in weight loss became her central self-esteem criterion, thereby contributing to the preservation of the illness. Her recovery was made possible by relinquishing her aspirations to perfection, making way for the sense of both internal and external self-acceptance.

Cognitive-behavioral changes

Changing obsessive thoughts about food, weight, and body image and eradicating the related compulsive behaviors were additional factors that contributed to the participants' recovery. Adi and Michal describe this process as follows:

> "For someone who has recovered, food is not the central focus of her life, the thing that motivates her. For me, someone with anorexia is someone who thinks only about food, calories and weight, someone who is preoccupied with this. That's what I was like, and the sign that I have recovered is that I no longer think about it." (002)

> "The most important thing is that your weight doesn't rule your life. It isn't shocking, there's flexibility, no obsession with calories and less involvement with sport. There's sport and healthy eating, but this shouldn't rule your life. It's part of life, but not the main thing." (001)

The fear of weight gain was clearly a central factor in creating and maintaining the participants' illness. They completely surrendered themselves to this fear, which controlled their thoughts and led to a variety of compulsive behaviors, including incessant calorie-counting, intensive physical exercise, and constant preoccupation with external appearance. Weight loss became their central goal in life, demanding total, unconditional dedication and leaving no room for flexibility or spontaneity in their lives. In contrast to the period of the illness, their recovery was characterized by normative attitudes to food, weight, and body image. They no longer experienced the fear of weight gain as a "motivation" or "ruling force" in their lives, as they had in the past. By exploring the source of their fear and learning how to cope with it effectively, their obsession with food, weight, and body shape was reduced and they regained control of their lives.

Functional changes

Once the dysfunctional thinking and behavioral patterns were pushed aside, the participants were able to gradually return to normative life and become reintegrated into regular life frameworks. Rotem describes this transition as follows:

> "Up until the final 'down' phase, I was functioning to the point of exhaustion. When I recovered, I gradually returned to normal functioning. When I think about the acute period, I hardly functioned at all. I have no idea how I got through my matriculation exams or where I found the strength to go to school. Today, I do a hundred and one different things. I was in the army, I left home, got married, and gave birth. Life flows much more easily, with fewer limits." (015)

Rotem depicts the illness as a period of her life when she was depleted of energy and had difficulty functioning. Going through the motions without enthusiasm, life passed her by and did not engage her in the usual teenage experiences. At the same time, her internal world was in chaos. After overcoming the illness, Rotem succeeded in reintegrating into the mainstream of life and participating in normative developmental tasks for her age, namely, army service, marriage and childbirth. Her life changed from one extreme to the other and since recovery has been full with activity and experience that is rich in both quantity and quality.

Carmit shares her feelings that accompanied these changes:

> "On the functional level, I enjoy going to work, working out at the gym, and dancing salsa. When I'm at work, I'm focused, I can analyze, explore things in-depth. The intellectual side was always there, but during the hardest time, before hospitalization, it just wasn't how it should have been." (006)

The time since Carmit's recovery has been characterized by a sense of joy in life. Her activities are not merely mechanical and lacking in interest or reason, but rather are full of enjoyment and curiosity. Following recovery, she has discovered new activities and hobbies, such as dancing salsa. In the past, she related to her body in a punishing, destructive and alienating manner, whereas today she listens to its needs, strengthening, nurturing and reviving it. Carmit tells of how, during the illness, her "intellectual side" was damaged. This can be explained by two phenomena: one is malnutrition and the poor physical condition that harmed her cognitive faculties, while the other is the "internal noise" that reverberated within her, making it difficult to concentrate on external factors. In contrast, today she reports functioning well as a social worker as well as being emotionally available.

Social changes

Changes in relationships with others constituted a highly important component in the participants' perception of recovery. These changes began with the development of a positive attitude toward the self, which in turn led to the establishment of genuine, meaningful relationships within the peer group. Dana describes this change in self-perception in relation to others as follows:

> "I used to be a nice, friendly girl who did everything I was supposed to do. I was playing a role, or at least an ideal of the kind of person I thought I should be. My pre-illness relationships were not genuine. I used to tell a lot of lies, and this prevented me from developing true relationships. The more I accepted myself, the less need I had to tell untruths. I began to talk to people more, to be genuine, with the attitude of, 'that's the way I am, so accept me, and if you don't like it, that's also fine.'" (014)

Prior to the illness, the need to please others was central to Dana's interpersonal relationships. This led to distancing herself from her "true self" and adopting a façade that not only diminished her internal strengths and resources, but also damaged the authenticity of her relationships with her peers. The illness ultimately forced her to face this façade through her process of self-exploration, self-discovery, and self-acceptance. This change enabled her to gradually discard the "mask" that she had worn and to stay true to herself, without surrendering to the pressure to adapt her personality to the demands of society.

Likewise, Carmit describes significant social changes that marked her recovery period:

> "Beforehand, the social world was limited. Everything revolved around food, weight, and work. Then I started from the beginning, all sorts of initial steps to find my place, and when I saw that people wanted to be close to me, I opened up, and today I have lots of good friends. So from my point of view, the measure of success is in the social sense. As soon as you allow yourself to accept something, feedback, the fact that you have some kind of social system with the outside world. Today, I no longer bottle up all my problems and cope alone, but I am helped and help others within my own fixed boundaries. Also, developing an intimate relationship with a man, **having normative relationships**." (006)

Carmit describes a poor social life before the illness. She experienced the illness as closing in on her, preventing her from establishing significant relationships and leaving her isolated from society. It may be that focusing on external factors helped her to protect herself from the terrible sense of loneliness. In contrast, Carmit's current life is rich with relationships that enable her to fulfil her own needs, while maintaining the balance between responding to her personal needs and those of the environment. Moreover, previously she was afraid of her sexual and emotional maturity and fought against it by starving herself, but today she allows herself to enjoy her femininity and sexuality. Indeed, she believes that developing intimate relationships is a measure of recovery.

Familial changes

The family system was perceived as a major component of preserving the illness. This was manifested in blurred parent-child boundaries, conflict avoidance, overprotection, lack of direct communication, and inadequate sensitivity to others' needs and differences.

Dana describes how family therapy helped her to change familiar communication patterns and to cope effectively with conflicts and difficult feelings:

> "It opened up a communication channel with my parents. It made us talk more, listen more, and understand better. We're very different, my parents and I, but we learned to be tolerant of these differences. This is something that didn't exist before. In our house, a conversation would start with someone making a statement, which would develop into shouting and arguing within a minute, and then everyone would go off and do their own thing. And because I was always the one who externalized emotions, I was the one who let it out through the anorexia." (014)

It is not hard to see how AN can be maintained by constant conflict avoidance in the family. When family members avoid discussions involving conflicts, disagreements and differences of opinion in order to maintain the balance within the family system, any attempt to solve a conflict can leave them with a sense of frustration, tension, and anxiety. Dana tried to make her family see its distress and how her illness served as a "cry for help." Deterioration in her medical and emotional condition forced the family to change their communication patterns by creating an environment that was conducive to open and direct communication, expressing personal opinions, mutual listening, and coping with conflict.

Other family dynamics can also serve to preserve the illness. Carmit describes how she succeeded in escaping the destructive "triangle" that was defining her family:

> "When I was sick, I was the 'contact person' between Mom and Dad. They used me to send all kinds of messages to each other when they were having problems, and I would get drawn in. It used to be, 'tell him this,' and 'tell her that.' It doesn't happen today because I throw the ball back in their court with 'tell him yourself.'" (006)

Thus, the AN served as a symptom of the latent couple-related difficulties in the parents' intimate sub-system. When the parents had difficulty in directly resolving their conflicts, they "drew in" Carmit to serve as an emotional and communications mediator. Although this role may have served the parents in some way, it left Carmit trapped in a loyalty conflict and burdened with a responsibility that was inappropriate for her age. Forced to push aside her own developmental needs for the sake of preserving the family unity and her parents' couple functioning, she sought a release from the destructive triangle through her illness.

Chen also describes feeling trapped during her illness and the legitimization of autonomy and self-identity that she received from her family during the recovery period:

> "I used to be a spoiled child. I received excessive attention and was more attached to Mom than anyone else in the family, for good and for bad. Since then, our relationship has changed and Mom understood that I had to have six tattoos, travel to the Far East, and not get two degrees like my brothers and sister, that I needed to do things at my own pace." (018)

Chen's relationship with her mother prior to the illness was characterized by her mother's devoted care, pampering, and excessive attention, but at the same time by her over-protectiveness and restriction of autonomy. Chen responded to the demanding, inflexible family norms by using her body as an outlet in order to achieve a sense of control, autonomy, and self-expression. When the illness confronted the mother with Chen's distress and needs, it brought about a change that released Chen from the grip of the illness, allowing her to begin a journey of self-cohesion, independent decision-making, and separation from her mother.

Physical and symptom changes

The participants' narratives show that the rehabilitation of the body was the final step in their path to full recovery from the illness. While their physical symptoms were clearly exposed, their emotional distress was hidden and repressed. Coping with these factors enabled their release from the symptoms and the accompanying medical complications.

Or and Carmit vividly describe the damage caused by the disease:

"During the illness, my hair fell out, my skin was dry, I had white marks on my nails because of calcium deficiency. My teeth lost their enamel because I ate so little. My bones hurt, everything hurt. Today I have a regular menstrual cycle, my weight is normal, my hair is healthy, I have no symptoms." (013)

"I found it hard to fall asleep because I was hungry. I started having bone loss, and I had pains in my back and legs and painful joints. At that time, the therapist said that my BMI was terrible, and I was in danger of a heart attack or cardiac arrest. I had trembling of the knees, low blood sugar. Today I have much more energy, with strength to get up for work, to go from place to place, whereas I used to drag myself.." (006)

The participants describe a kind of betrayal of the body during the period of the illness, the body became a burden instead of a source of vitality. Their poor health caused by malnutrition led to serious medical complications, weakening of the immune system, and deterioration in general functioning. These complications were manifest in underweight, dryness of the skin, pallor, balding, rotting teeth, absence of menses, insomnia, muscle depletion, osteoporosis, heart problems, fatigue, loss of consciousness, and more. Just as abstention from eating during the illness led to physical deterioration, the return to eating during recovery led to a general improvement in the functioning of most bodily systems. Among other things, the participants experienced weight gain, the return of menstruation, and high energy levels. Today the body is their source of life, providing the basis from which to go out into the world and live a full and self-actualizing life.

DISCUSSION

The aim of this study was to describe and analyze the meaning of recovery from AN from the perspective of women who have recovered from the illness. The study findings show that recovery is due to many factors, including rehabilitation of the patient's mental, cognitive, behavioral, occupational, social, family, and physical condition. The findings also indicate that the process of change is modular, whereby each change draws on the last until full recovery is achieved.

These findings support those of other studies (12). According to the participants, the most significant component and turning point in the recovery process was their mental rehabilitation and insight into the illness, which allowed for direct coping with the problems and non-adaptive patterns that had contributed to its development. Additionaly, in line with previous research showing that the replacement of passive coping patterns with an active one is a criterion for recovery from AN (33). Another way in which mental rehabilitation was expressed by the participants was through self-acceptance and a significant improvement in their self-image and self-esteem. They described how the despair and pessimism characterizing the period of their illness had been replaced by self-fulfillment and satisfaction with life (19,34).

Cognitive changes included the reduction in compulsive thoughts about food and external appearance, the drive for thinness and the fear of weight gain. As a result, accompanying changes also occurred on the behavioral level, including a decrease in compulsive weight-related behavior, such as purging, binge-eating, intensive physical exercise, fasting, and abuse of laxatives and diuretics. These findings support those of previous studies showing that a reduction in the fear of weight gain and the preservation of normative eating patterns for over a year constitute significant discriminate measures of recovery (11,23). Similarly, the participants in the present study reported that their normative attitudes toward body, weight, and food afforded them the time, space, and energy to integrate and function well in various frameworks, such as school, army, and work, from which they had dropped out during the illness. Inclusion in these kinds of frameworks was found to be an additional discriminate measure of recovery in other studies as well (35).

The study participants noted that recovery was also made possible by an improvement in their social life. During the illness, they suffered from isolation, which was derived, among other things, from their preoccupation with food, weight, and body shape. This isolation and social withdrawal is described in the literature as one of the initial symptoms of AN. A study examining this subject found that 60% of people with AN had no close friends and that the majority avoided any social activity (36). In the recovery stage, however, it was found that approximately 87.5% were well-adapted socially (37) and enjoyed intimate relationships and intact sexual functioning (38).

The participants in the present study manifested their social reintegration in their creation of meaningful peer relationships, their inclusion in normative social activity, and their establishment of intimate relationships.

Rehabilitation of family functioning was found to be an additional important phase in recovery. The participants observed that changes in communication and interaction patterns led to forming clearer boundaries within the family, coping with conflicts in a direct and open manner, and allowing separationand autonomy. These results support previous findings that view family therapy and parent-focused therapy as central to recovery from AN (39-41).

The patient's perspective for recovery from anorexia nervosa: A proposed model

Physical
Intact BMI
Regular
menses
Absence of
medical
complications
Sound functioning
of bodily systems

Familial
Intact hierarchy, clear
boundaries between
sub-systems, Adaptive
communication patterns,
Separation and autonomy,
Supportive, and positive family
atmosphere

Social
Meaningful peer relationships
Inclusion in social activity
Establishment of intimate relationships

Functional
Inclusion in normative life frameworks,
such as army, studies, work

Behavioral
Absence of compulsive behavior related to food, weight
and body, such as purging, binge-eating, intensive physical
exercise, fasting, and abuse of laxatives and diuretics

Cognitive
Reduction in fear of weight gain, absence of obsessive thoughts about
food and physical appearance, decrease in drive for thinness, sound
perception of body weight and shape, flexible thinking patterns

Mental
Self-esteem, self-acceptance, internal locus of control, sense of cohesive
identity, adaptive strategies for coping with difficulties and problems,
and absence of psychiatric morbidity

Physical rehabilitation was the final step of the recovery process and was proof that the participants had reached its completion. It was manifested in sound physical functioning, the absence of medical complications, the recommencement of menstruation, and normal body weight. The literature places primary emphasis on physical recovery, whereas the findings of the present study indicate physical rehabilitation to be the final module of the recovery process. However, it is important to note that they relate to the final stage of the symptom relief. Thus, in line with the previous literature, the first stage of symptom relief is crucial for achieving the next steps of recovery, yet it will not be internal and full symptom relief without completing the other modules. Therefore, in many cases, achieving full relief of symptoms during hospitalization without continuous intensive psychotherapy and rehabilitation, leads to revolving door phenomenon. Meaning, recurrent relapse and re-hospitalizations over and over again. The participants maintained that the return to intact physical functioning completed the long recovery process. They perceived their physical rehabilitation as a final step in the recovery process, though they emphasized the importance of focusing at the same time on the other areas and not measuring recovery according to this factor alone (42).

In conclusion, the study findings propose a recovery model that supports the recovery measures presented in the literature, but with different emphases on the order and importance of each stage, as perceived from the participants' perspective. They perceive the first stage of recovery as beginning with cracks that indicate denial, opening up an internal, emotional exploration of the processes and difficulties that form the basis of the illness. The next stages include rehabilitation on the cognitive, behavioral, occupational, social, and family levels, and the entire process is completed with physical rehabilitation. Each module cannot be achieved without completing the previous module. From the participants' perspective, in spite of the importance of the physiological recovery, it will not endure without accompaniment by the prior rehabilitation processes.

STUDY LIMITATIONS

The study has several methodological limitations. First, it is hard to generalize from the study results due to the small sample size. The second limitation stems from the research tool. The interview is a type of intervention that may influence the interviewees; therefore, the participants' personal exposure to the interviewer may have influenced the interview's development and content. The third limitation is related to the credibility of the analysis. Qualitative research, by its nature, is based on the researcher as a significant research tool, as being responsible for gathering and analyzing the data. The women were interviewed by one interviewer only, which may have limited the observation point and perception of meanings that emerged from the interview content. The researcher can never be totally free of pre-conceived attitudes, perceptions, and thoughts in relation to the study objectives. This reality can influence both the data analysis process and the study results.

Due to these limitations, and in order to explore additional layers in the recovery process, as well as the different experiences and meanings attached to them by the participants, further research in this area is needed. In addition, the variables can also be examined using quantitative tools in order to validate and generalize the findings. Finally, the present study focused only on the meaning of recovery from AN. Thus, additional studies should be conducted on the meaning of recovery from bulimia and binge-eating disorders in order to determine whether the meaning of recovery, as described in this study, is unique to AN or is characteristic of recovery from other eating disorders as well.

REFERENCES

[1]   Currin L, Schmidt U, Treasure J, Jick H. Time trends in eating disorders incidence. Br J Psychiatry 2005;186:132-5.

[2]   Latzer Y, Gur E, Stein D. Eating disorders: update, controversies, and the Israeli perspective. Isr J Psychiatry 2005;42:141-5.

[3]   Costin C, Johnson CL. Been there, done that: clinicians' use of personal recovery in the treatment of eating disorders. Eat Disord 2002; 10: 293-303.

[4]   Jarman M, Walsh S. Evaluating recovery from anorexia nervosa and bulimia nervosa: integrating lessons learned from research and clinical practice. Clin Psychol Rev 1999;19:773-88.

[5]   Woodside B. Treatment of anorexia nervosa: more questions than answers. Int J of Eat Disord 2005;37: 41-2.

[6]   Crisp AH, Hsu LKG, Harding B, Hartshorn J. Clinical features of anorexia nervosa: a study of a consecutive series of 102 female patients. J Psychosom Res 1980;24:179-91.

[7]   Falk JR, Halmi KA. Amenorrhea in anorexia nervosa: examination of the critical weight hypothesis. Biol Psychiatry 1982;17:799-806.

[8]   Norring CE, Sohlberg SS. Outcome, recovery, relapse and mortality across six years in patients with clinical eating disorders. Acta Psychiatr Scand 1993; 87:437-44.

[9]   Eckert ED, Halmi KA, Marchi P, Grove W, Crosby R. Ten - year follow - up of anorexia nervosa: clinical course and outcome. Psychol Med 1995; 25:143-56.

[10] Finfgeld DL. Anorexia nervosa: analysis of long - term outcomes and clinical implications. Arch Psychiatr Nurs 2002;16:176-86.

[11] Pike KM. Long term course of anorexia nervosa: Response, relapse, remission and recovery. Clin Psychol Rev 1998;18:447-75.

[12] Couturier J, Lock J. What is recovery in adolescent anorexia nervosa? Int J of Eat Disord 2006; 39: 550-5.

[13] Federici A, Kaplan AS. The patient's account of relapse and recovery in anorexia nervosa: a qualitative study. Eur Eat Disord Rev 2008;16:1-10.

[14] Fennig S, Fennig S, Roe D. Physical recovery in anorexia nervosa: Is this the sole purpose of a child and adolescent medical psychiatric unit? Gen Hosp Psychiatry 2002;24:87-92.

[15] Steinhausen HC, Glanville K. A long – term follow up of adolescent anorexia. Acta Psychiatr Scand 1983;68:1-10.

[16] Steinhausen HC, Glanville K. Follow-up studies of anorexia nervosa: A review of research findings. Psychol Med 1983;13:239-49.

[17] Granek L. "You're a whole lot of person" – understanding the journey through anorexia to recovery: a qualitative study. Humanist Psychol 2007;35:363-85.

[18] Lamoureux MMH, Bottorff JL. Becoming the real me: Recovering from anorexia nervosa. Health Care Women Int 2005; 26: 170-88.

[19] Tozzi F, Sullivan PF, Fear JL, Mckenzie J, Bulik CM. Causes and recovery in anorexia nervosa: the patients perspective. Int J of Eat Disord 2003;33:143-54.

[20] Weaver K, Wuest J, Ciliska D. Understanding women's journey of recovering from anorexia nervosa. Qual Health Res 2005;15:188-206.

[21] McLeod J. Qualitative research in counselling and psychotherapy. London: Sage, 2001.

[22] Patton MQ. Qualitative methods in social work research: Challenges rewards. Thousand Oaks, CA: Sage, 2002.

[23] American Psychiatric Association. Diagnostic and statistical manual of mental disorders (4th edition). Washington DC: Author, 2000.

[24] Sheehan DV, Lecrubier Y, Sheehan KH, Amorim P, Janavs J, Weiller E, Hergueta T, Baker R, Dunbar GC. The Mini International Neuropsychiatric Interview (M.I.N.I): the development and validation of a structured diagnostic psychiatric interview for DSM-IV and ICD-10. J Clin Psychiatry 1998;59:34-57.

[25] Rubin HJ, Rubin IS. Qualitative interviewing. Thousand Oaks, CA: Sage, 1995.

[26] Strauss A, Corbin J. Basics of qualitative research: Grounded theory procedures and techniques. Newbury Park: Saga, 1990.

[27] Sparadley JP. The ethnographic interview. New York: Holt, Rinehart & Winston, 1979.

[28] Kvale S. InterViews: An introduction to qualitative research interviewing. Thousand Oaks, CA: Sage, 1996.

[29] Shkedi A. Multiple case narrative. Amsterdam/Philadelphia: John Benjamins, 2005.

[30] Lieblich A, Tuval-Mashiach R, Zilber T. Narrative research: Reading, analysis, and interpretation. Thousand Oaks, CA: Sage, 1998.

[31] LincolnYS, Guba EG. Naturalistic inquiry. Beverly Hills, CA: Sage, 1985.

[32] Maxwell JA. Qualitative research design: An interactive approach. Thousand Oaks, CA: Sage, 1996.

[33] Bloks H, Van - Furth EF, Callewaert I, Hoke HW. Coping strategies and recovery in patients with a severe eating disorder. Eat Disord 2004;12:157-69.

[34] Bachar E, Latzer Y, Canetti L, Gur, E, Berry, EM, Bonne O. Rejection of life in anorexic and bulimic patients. Int J of Eat Disord 2002;31: 43-8.

[35] Zipfel S, Lowe B, Reas DL, Deter HC, Herzog W. Long- term prognosis in anorexia nervosa: lessons from a 21- year follow up- study. Lancet 2000;355:721-2.

[36] Deter HC, Herzog, W. Anorexia nervosa in a long- term perspective: results of the Heidelberg- Mannheim study. Psychosom Med 1994;56:20-7.

[37] Strober M, Freeman R, Morrell W. The long -term course of severe anorexia nervosa in adolescents: Survival analysis of recovery, relapse, and outcome predictors over 10-15 years in prospective study. Int J of Eat Disord 1997;22:339-60.

[38] Newton M. Exploring the experiences of romantic relationships and intimacy for women with anorexia nervosa. Sci Eng 2005;65:62-85.

[39] Latzer Y, Gaber LB. Pathological conflict avoidance in anorexia nervosa: family perspectives. Contemp Fam Ther1998;20:539-51.

[40] Latzer Y, Hochdorf Z, Bachar E, Canetti L. Attachment style and family functioning as discriminating factors in eating disorders. Contemporary Family Therapy 2002;24:581-99.

[41] Lock J, le Grange D. Family treatment of eating disorders. In: Powers PS, Yager J. Clinical manual of eating disorders. Washington, DC: American Psychiatric Publishing, 2007: 149-70.

[42] Goodsitt A. Eating disorders of self-psychological perspective. In: Garner DM, Garfinkel PE. Handbook of psychotherapy for eating disorders (2nd ed.). New York: Guilford, 1997: 205-228.

In: Treatment and Recovery of Eating Disorders ISBN: 978-1-62808-248-7
Editors: Daniel Stein and Yael Latzer © 2013 Nova Science Publishers, Inc.

Chapter 14

RECOVERY FROM ANOREXIA NERVOSA

Michal Yackobovitch-Gavan[1,2]‡‡‡‡, Rachel Bachner-Melman[3] and Daniel Stein[4]

[1] School of Nutritional Sciences, Faculty of Agricultural, Food, and Environmental
Quality Sciences, Rehovot, The Hebrew University, Jerusalem, Israel
[2] Institute for Endocrinology and Diabetes, National Center of Childhood Diabetes,
Schneider Children's Medical Center of Israel, affiliated with the Sackler Faculty of
Medicine, Tel Aviv University, Tel Aviv, Israel
[3] Eating Disorders Unit, Adult Psychiatric Department, Hadassah University Medical
Center, Ein Kerem, Jerusalem, Israel; Rothberg International School, Hebrew University
of Jerusalem, Jerusalem, Israel
[4] Pediatric Psychosomatic Department, Edmond and Lily Safra Children's Hospital,
Chaim Sheba Medical Center, Tel Hashomer; affiliated with the Sackler Faculty of
Medicine, Tel Aviv University, Tel Aviv, Israel

ABSTRACT

The aim of this chapter is to critically analyze the difficulties still inherent in studying
recovery from anorexia nervosa (AN). A comprehensive literature review demonstrates
that there are at least ten definitions of recovery from AN, differentiated according to
several criteria: definition of normal weight; inclusion of only behavioral vs. both
behavioral and psychological recovery; inclusion of comorbidity and overall
psychosocial functioning in addition to eating-related recovery; and the minimal time
required to define recovery. These discrepancies likely account for the wide variation in
the range of patients defined as recovered from AN in different outcome studies (0-92%).
A great variability also exists with respect to the factors predicting recovery. Another
limitation to the research on factors that predict recovery in AN is that most outcome
studies have used univariate analyses for this purpose, enabling the assessment of only
separate independent predictors. By contrast, multivariate quantitative models allow for
the measurement of the relative contribution of each variable for recovery, as well as for

---
‡‡‡‡ E-mail address: michalyg2000@gmail.com

the assessment of the cumulative predictive power of all variables included. Unfortunately, only a few quantitative studies exist. Still, an overall worse prognosis has been found repeatedly to be associated with several factors: body image disturbances, compulsive exercising, comorbid anxiety disorders (particularly obsessive compulsive disorder), personality disorders and non-clinical personality traits, poor social skills, longer duration of illness prior to treatment, and shorter follow-up. In the second part of the chapter we aim to provide the reader with several potential options to standardize the definition of recovery and the design of outcome studies in AN.

Keywords: anorexia nervosa, recovery, eating disorders

INTRODUCTION

Anorexia nervosa (AN) is a chronic disorder with an often unfavorable course, imposing a considerable burden on inflicted individuals, their families and society at large (1,2). Treatment providers need a good understanding of what is meant by remission and recovery from AN, so that sound decisions can be made with respect to the planning of appropriate intervention strategies for this eating disorder (ED), and the optimal time range for their provision. For example, for patients who are not fully remitted, treatment may be increased or changed, whereas treatment can be discontinued if recovery is reached (3). Regrettably, the study of the exact criteria required is hampered by problems such as the prolonged course of AN until recovery is reached and the high relapse rate of the disorder within a relatively brief time period (4,5), as well as because of difficulties in defining and agreeing on standard criteria for recovery (2,5,6). Currently, definitions vary widely with respect to the required criteria and the duration required for recovery, creating difficulties in comparing the course and outcome of AN across different studies.

The aim of the present chapter is to provide a critical description of the different definitions for recovery from AN, emphasizing theoretical, clinical, and research-related conclusions associated with each definition. We further aim to provide a better understanding of the meaning of the distinction between remission and recovery. This distinction is of greater relevance in AN in comparison to other psychiatric disorders because of the high mortality, morbidity, and relapse rate associated with this disorder (5,7,8). Lastly, we relate to the critical issue of the relevant biopsychosocial dimensions influencing the course and outcome of AN and the complex interactions occurring among these dimensions in the all-important process of recovery. Recommendations for future research are also provided.

DEFINITIONS OF OUTCOME IN ANOREXIA NERVOSA

Definitions of response to treatment, remission, and recovery in AN vary widely in the research literature, and reflect considerable confusion between these terms. Definitions differ both with respect to the criteria required and the duration of time needed to define them. According to Couturier & Lock (6):

Response to treatment – A significant clinical change or a significant change in a specific index (e.g. a score on an assessment scale) following a period of treatment, as compared to the baseline period. Time duration is not part of this definition.

Remission – The patient has been symptom-free at least for a brief period of time.

Recovery – A symptom-free condition maintained for a prolonged period of time.

Both remission and recovery are not related to the effect of treatment and may occur spontaneously, in line with the natural course of the illness. Still, the duration required to define both varies significantly, ranging from eight weeks to one year or more (5,6,9).

We now present the different definitions of remission and recovery reported in the AN literature. Probably the oldest and most commonly used scale for assessing the outcome of AN is the Morgan-Russell Scale (10). This scale defines three possible outcomes: good, intermediate, and poor, based on criteria of weight and menstruation. A "good" outcome is defined as weight not less than 85% of normal weight range according to age, gender, and height, combined with the presence of normal and regular menstruation. An "intermediate" outcome is defined as weight not less than 85% of the normal range, but menstruation is unstable, and/or irregular. A "poor" outcome is defined as weight lower than 85% of the normal weight range and the absence or near absence of menstruation. This instrument is limited in that an individual may be defined as fully recovered based on normal weight and menstruation, while still displaying pathological attitudes and behaviors regarding eating and body weight. The minimal duration required to define any outcome with the Morgan-Russell Scale is 8 weeks.

As an alternative, Strober and associates (5) have defined "good recovery" as a good outcome according to the Morgan-Russell Scale, whereas "full recovery" is defined as absence of all symptoms, both behavioral and preoccupational/attitudinal required for the diagnosis of AN. Accordingly, "full recovery" requires normal body weight, menstruation and eating related behaviors, and the absence of preoccupations and maladaptive attitudes concerning weight and shape. The other possible outcomes (partial recovery and poor recovery) are defined according to the Morgan-Russell criteria. The minimal duration required to define a respective outcome according to Strober et al (5) is similar to that of the Morgan-Russell Scale, namely 8 weeks.

Steinhausen and Glanville (11) modified the semi-structured interview of Stuzenberger et al (12) to develop a scale that would define recovery from AN not only qualitatively (i.e., present or absent), but also from a quantitative (i.e., extent of recovery) perspective (11,13,14). Furthermore, this scale defines recovery with respect to both ED symptomatology and sexual and psychological functioning. Each of its 11 factors is scored on a scale of four points, reflecting severity and frequency (absent, minimal, moderate, or severe). These ratings lead to three scores: 1. An ED score, based on five factors – restricting behaviors, bingeing, vomiting, use of laxatives, and amenorrhea; 2. A psychosocial score based on six factors – lack of interest in sex, abstinence from sexual activity, unsatisfying interpersonal relationships, dependence on one's family, unsatisfying social life, and a deficient professional career; 3. A general score based on all eleven factors, which encompasses both the ED and the psychosocial functioning score.

Herzog et al (15) have developed another scale assessing recovery from AN, the Psychiatric Status Rating Scale (PSR). Scores range from 1 to 6, with 1 representing full recovery ["usual self" with no evidence of AN and with normal body weight (defined as

100% of ideal body weight) and menstruation], and 6 representing active, severe AN ("definite criteria, severe" – a diagnosis of full-blown AN and severe overall dysfunction, such as a need for hospitalization). The PSR allows for several options in the definition of each stage of recovery, and it also takes measures of AN-related attitudes and behaviors into consideration. For example, "full/good recovery" are defined as eight consecutive weeks with a PSR score of 1 or 2, respectively, whereas "partial recovery" can be defined as eight consecutive weeks with PSR score of 3 or 4, or less than eight consecutive weeks with PSR score of 1 or 2 (15).

Eckert et al (16) has developed another scale consisting of seventeen items, based on the criteria of the Morgan-Russell Scale and on Garfinkel et al's (17) Global Clinical Score. Scoring is based on a general rating of clinical outcomes as well as on sixteen items encompassing current weight and height, and pathology in seven areas: AN like behaviors and/or attitudes, menstruation, sexual attitudes and behaviors, social adjustment, educational and/or occupational adjustment, and psychological adjustment. Scores are based on the past six months. Each item is rated on a four-point scale, from "absent" to "extreme." Data from this scale classify each case into one of four recovery categories: recovered, good outcome, intermediate outcome, and poor outcome.

Kaye and his group (18) defined recovery from AN as a condition requiring normal weight (defined as weight of 90% of average body weight) and menstruation (defined as 10-12 menstrual cycles in 12 months), as well as complete abstinence from bingeing, purging and restrictive eating behaviors for at least 12 months prior to assessment. This group was the first to define normal menstruation in term of number of cycles required, and among the first to require a prolonged 12-month duration criterion.

Casper (19) uses criteria similar to those of most other studies, but also adds a requirement for a substantial improvement in eating-related preoccupations and in attitudes related to food, physical appearance, and weight. Accordingly, Casper defines a "good recovery outcome" or "physiological recovery" as body weight within 85% or more of average body weight along with regular menstruation. "Psychological recovery" is established based on results of a rating scale, the Eating Attitudes Test-26 (EAT-26) (20), with "full recovery" defined as physiological recovery together with a score within no more that two standard deviations from the normal EAT-26 score. Like Kaye and his group, Casper also requires a period of no less than 12 months to define recovery.

Kordy et al's (21) criteria require weight of more than 88% of ideal body weight [body mass index (BMI)>19 kg/m^2], and a score within the normal range on a standardized clinical interview assessing eating-related behaviors and attitudes [the Eating Disorder Examination (EDE) (22)] for a period of no less than 3 months, to define remission. A similar lack of symptoms for at least 12 months defines recovery.

Pike (23,24) sets stringent criteria for remission and recovery. For both, normal weight (BMI=20 kg/m^2, or more than 90% of recommended weight), normal menstruation status and normal eating behaviors have to be achieved. In addition, recovery is attained only when the overall functioning and risk of recurrence of the symptoms is comparable to that of a control group of healthy women. To achieve this condition, Pike requires the presence of normal eating related behaviors and attitudes, defined as not more than 1 standard deviation of a normal comparison group on the EDE, and lack of AN-related acute health problems. Pike does not require a specific time duration to define recovery, but mentions that the requirement of Morgan & Russell (10) and Strober et al (5) for 8 weeks may be a reasonable starting point for defining the stage of recovery.

Lastly, Von Holle and associates (9) define recovery from AN as three consecutive years without ED symptoms (including low weight, no or disturbed menstruation, and the presence of restricting, binging, or compensatory behaviors). In explanation of their choice of the three-year time frame, these authors emphasize their intention to maximize the probability that recovery would be diagnosed in those who are truly recovered rather than in cases of temporary remission, given that most relapses occur during the first year after the completion of treatment (4,5)

Table 1 summarizes many of the problems associated with the criteria required for remission and recovery from AN..

Table 1. Summary of criteria for recovery from anorexia nervosa

	Weight (% of normal weight)	Behavioral recovery only	Behavioral & psychological recovery	Overall (non-ED) Functioning	Duration
Morgan Russell (10)	85%	+	-	-	8 weeks
Strober (5)	85%	+	-	-	8 weeks
Steinhausen (11,14)	BMI≥17.5	+	-	+	No defined time period
Herzog (15)	100%	-	+	-	8 weeks
Eckert (16)	85%	+	+	+	6 months
Kaye (18)	90%	+	-	-	12 months
Casper (19)	85%	-	+	-	12 months
Kordy (21)	88%	-	+	-	12 months
Pike (23,24)	90%	-	+	-	No defined time period
Von Holle (9)	No defined weight range	+	-	-	36 months

Firstly, is the lack of ED-related symptoms and behaviors (i.e., normal weight, and/or normal menstruation and/or cessation of restricting/bingeing/purging behaviors) sufficient for the definition of recovery, as suggested by some researchers (e.g., 9,10,18), or should full remission be described only in the absence of eating/weight-related preoccupations and body image disturbances, as suggested by others (e.g., 5,15,16,19,21,23)? The inclusion of eating-related behaviors only suggests a "narrow" definition of recovery, whereas the addition of eating-related preoccupations and attitudes suggests a "broad" definition (6). This differentiation not only influences the proportion of individuals who recover from a studied sample, but also the time required to reach recovery. Not surprisingly, behavioral recovery appears to occur more often and at a shorter duration than psychological recovery (2,5,6.21). Secondly, should recovery be limited only to the ED per se (see 5,9,10,19), or should a reduction in psychiatric comorbidity (e.g., depression, anxiety or non-ED obsessionality) and/or an improvement in overall psychosocial functioning and general health be also included in the definition of recovery (see 11,14,16,23)? A third difficulty is related to discrepancies in the definition of normal weight [e.g., either 85% (5,10,16,19), 88% (21), 90% (18,23) or 100% (15) of required weight, presented in terms of ideal (21) or average (18) body weight range, and BMI (14)]. Similar problems exist in the definition of normal menstruation, often leading to poor inter-rater reliability (25). Varying definitions of "normal weight" and "normal menstruation" may also affect the time frame (ranging from 8 weeks to 3 years) required for recovery.

From a different perspective, recovery rates in AN may also reflect in part the assessment tool used, i.e., higher rates in the case of rating scales, and lower rates if clinical interviews are used (26). Moreover, with the exception of Kordy et al (21) and Pike (23), none of the criteria proposed differentiate remission from recovery, except for the criterion of time, despite the likelihood of earlier remission representing a good predictor of later recovery (3). Lastly, most of the studies so far relate to adult female populations. Studying males likely requires a whole different set of criteria, which have still not been studied in depth. Similarly, the definition of recovery in adolescents is likely even more ambiguous than in adults, because recovered adolescents may have still not reached their final adult height (and in turn, their ideal weight), or not have had their first menstrual period. In this respect, the issue of menstruation represents a major problem in the study of recovery in AN, because periods are often irregular even in recovered patients, and many adolescent and young adult females nowadays use contraceptives.

RECOVERY RATES IN ANOREXIA NERVOSA

AN is a chronic disorder, with recovery occurring mostly after 4-10 years from the onset of the illness (2,9), although it may happen even after 15 years of illness (9). The large variability in the definition of recovery and in the duration required for recovery, alongside variations in patient parameters (e.g., age, age at the onset of illness, the country in which the study takes place, or inclusion of outpatients vs. inpatients), and in study characteristics [e.g., selective attrition, duration of the follow-up period, the time period at the start of the study (representing a cohort effect) or the type of treatment provided], likely account for the large variability in remission/recovery estimates in AN.

Indeed, two comprehensive reviews, those of Herzog et al (27) and Steinhausen (2), summarizing the results of 33 and 119 outcome studies, respectively, have found recovery rates ranging from 17-77%, (27) and 0% to 92% (2). More recent studies have also shown a similar variability of outcome (4,9,21). These considerable discrepancies preclude meaningful comparisons among different studies. Still, on average, full recovery occurs in less than 50% of the patients, with 30% showing some improvement, and 15-25% remaining chronically ill (2,23).

Recently, Couturier and Lock (3,6) assessed the rate of remission and recovery from AN according to different sets of relevant criteria. In their first study (3), remission was defined along the criteria sets proposed by Morgan-Russell, Pike, Kordy et al, and the definition of AN according to the DSM-IV-TR, 2000 (28), taking into consideration different thresholds for normal weight and the absence/presence of psychological disturbances (i.e., attitudinal eating-related preoccupations on the EDE). Remission was assessed 12 months after the start of treatment. A wide range of remission rate was found, the lowest being 3% (full criteria according to Pike) and the highest 96% (if weight within 85% of ideal body weight was the only criterion required for remission). The authors suggested that combining the definition of normal weight (85% of ideal body weight) and normal eating-related behavioral and psychological condition (EDE scores within 1-2 standard deviations of normal) appeared to reduce the variability in remission rates to the greatest extent.

In the second study, Couturier and Lock (6) defined recovery using various thresholds for normal weight (85-95%) and for normal eating-related behaviors and attitudes (EDE scores within 1 or 2 standard deviations from normal). Recovery was assessed 2-6 years after the start of treatment. A wide range of recovery rates was found, the lowest being 57.1% (scores for all EDE scales within 1 standard deviation of normal), and the highest 94.4% (if weight within 85% of ideal body weight was the only criterion required for remission). Of interest, all definitions of recovery showed a similar temporal trend, with no substantive changes occurring after 12 months. Accordingly, if remission was present for no less than 12 months, it was also maintained at long term follow-up. In addition, weight recovery occurred around one year earlier than behavioral and psychological recovery (an average of 12 vs. 24 months, respectively). Likely, it was necessary to achieve normal weight to alter eating-related behaviors and attitudes (29). The variability in recovery rates was the least when combining normal weight (defined as 85% of ideal body weight) and normal easting-related behavioral and psychological condition (EDE scores within 1 standard deviation of normal). All former patients fulfilling these criteria were functioning well at follow-up both from an occupational and a social perspective. Attainment of normal weight and normal scores on the restraint subscale of the EDE (but not on other EDE subscales or the total EDE score) at 12 months was highly correlated with normal scores in these two parameters at long-term follow-up. Theses findings led Couturier and Lock (3,6) to conclude that weight restoration and low EDE restraint scores might be excellent predictors of long-term recovery.

PREDICTORS OF ANOREXIA NERVOSA OUTCOME

Studies assessing predictors of recovery from AN have mostly used longitudinal follow-up designs, or, less often, retrospective chart reviews. The earliest predictive factors are related to the time of onset of the illness, usually assessed with retrospective descriptions of patient and family during the index follow-up assessment, or according to medical charts. Other predictors of recovery can be assessed prospectively from different relevant points during the course of the illness, e.g., the return of the menstrual cycle (physical point of reference), when leaving home for college (psychosocial point of reference) or upon discharge from inpatient treatment (treatment-related point of reference).

Although a wide range of predictive factors have been found in different studies, reflecting the wide variability in the definition of recovery, the design of the outcome study, and the length of the follow-up period, several parameters seem repeatedly to have a greater power to predict outcome than others. The following summary of data is based on the reviews of Herzog et al, (27) Pike (23), and Steinhausen (2), as well as on more recent data:

1. **ED-related variables**–An overall worse prognosis is associated in particular with the presence of elevated drive for thinness, disturbances in body image (23) and vegetarianism (30) at any point during the course of the illness, the emergence of bingeing/purging behaviors in patients originally diagnosed with restrictive type AN (2,23), the likelihood of eating less varied food and/or food with lower caloric density (31), and the presence of more compulsive exercising following discharge from inpatient treatment (5). Conversely, the lack of these variables may predict an overall more favorable outcome. Of interest, severity of dieting behavior and extent of emaciation during the course of AN have been usually found not to exert a significant influence on outcome (2,23).

2. **Comorbidity** –
   Anxiety disorders – The likelihood of elevated rates of anxiety disorders, primarily non-ED obsessive compulsive disorder (OCD) and social phobia, both before the onset of AN (32) and during the course of the illness (33-35), suggests that elevated anxiety may have a role both in the predisposition to AN and in increasing the risk for non-recovery (36). Accordingly, patients not recovering from AN have been found to have a significantly greater incidence of anxiety disorders preceding the emergence of the ED compared to recovered patients (37). Similarly, a history of non-ED OCD in AN patients has been significantly correlated with a longer duration of the illness (35).
   Personality disorders – Long-term outcome studies in AN have found that the presence of concomitant personality disorders, primarily obsessive compulsive personality, during the course of the illness may be a marker for an overall worse prognosis of the ED (2,27,38,39). By contrast, hysterical personality has been linked to an overall more favorable outcome (2).
   Non-clinical personality traits - Elevated levels of personality attributes such as harm avoidance, rigidity, inhibition, perfectionism and obsessionality, have been associated with an overall worse prognosis of AN in several long-term outcome studies (2,33,40), as well as in studies comparing recovered AN to non-ED control patients (41).

3. **Other demographic, psychosocial, and treatment-related factors** – The association between age at onset of the AN and prognosis is inconclusive, with younger age being linked to a better outcome in most (2,9,23), although not all (27) studies. Similarly, there is no evidence that the time period in which the study has been carried out (i.e. older vs. recent studies) has an influence on the outcome of AN (2). By contrast, longer duration of follow-up has been associated almost invariably with a better prognosis (2,9), whereas longer duration of illness until receiving treatment (2,23,27) and longer duration of treatment (13,14,43) have been associated with a less unfavorable outcome. With respect to psychosocial effects, the presence of disturbed parent-child relationships (2,27) and poor social skills (5,42) has been linked to an unfavorable outcome, particularly in adolescent AN.

4. **Quantitative Models for the Prediction of Outcome in Anorexia Nervosa**

Another limitation in the investigation of predictors of recovery in AN is that most outcome studies use univariate analyses for this purpose, enabling the assessment of only separate independent predictors. By contrast, multivariate quantitative models allow for the measurement of the relative contribution of each variable for recovery, or, alternatively, to what extent each factor affects outcome independently. These analyses further enable the assessment of the cumulative predictive power of all variables included, and whether risk accumulates as the number of predictive variables increases (23). Unfortunately, only a few quantitative studies exist (5,13,43-47).

In the first of these studies, Strober et al (5) followed 95 women 10-15 years after being hospitalized during adolescence because of AN. The use of stepwise logistical regressions detected two variables predicting a chronic course of AN: compulsive exercising at discharge from the index hospitalization and a history of problematic social relationships prior to the onset of AN. The use of a regression equation explained 13.2% of the variance for a chronic course of AN.

The group of Herzog et al (47) in Germany followed 66 patients for an average of 12 years from hospitalization because of AN. The results of a stepwise multiple regression indicated three laboratory measurements performed at admission to this hospitalization that predicted a chronic course of AN: high levels of creatinine, low levels of albumin, and low fasting glucose levels.

Other long-term follow-up studies of this group (45,46) tracked 84 patients over the course of 21 years on average from the first hospitalization due to AN. The use of ordered logistical regression analyses identified five variables as significant predictors of non-recovery: longer duration of illness prior to the index hospitalization, lower BMI and lower weight gain during this hospitalization, diagnosis of bingeing/purging type AN, and greater severity of psychological and social problems.

The group of Herzog et al (44) in the USA examined the course and outcome of AN over an average follow-up period of 7.5 years in 136 patients. The use of a Cox statistical model for follow-up studies indicated two variables predicting longer duration to full recovery: longer duration of illness and lower body weight.

Steinhausen et al (13) followed 242 adolescents treated for AN at five inpatient centers in Europe for an average period of 6.4 years after the start of treatment. The use of multiple regression analyses identified three significant predictors of poor outcome: longer duration of outpatient treatment following the index hospitalization, postponement of, or early dropout from treatment, and the presence of a comorbid psychiatric disorder at follow-up. All three variables were directly correlated with an overall worse recovery outcome. The use of a regression equation explained 26% of the variance for a chronic course of AN.

Lastly, Fichter et al (43) followed 103 AN patients for a period of 12 years from their admission to inpatient treatment. The use of logistic regression analyses detected four variables predicting an overall worse prognosis: sexual problems, impulsivity, and longer duration of AN and of the index inpatient treatment. The use of a regression equation explained 45% of the variance for a chronic course of AN.

THE FINDINGS OF ISRAELI OUTCOME STUDIES

The authors of this chapter have recently carried out the first two long-term outcome studies of Israeli AN patients. Yackobovitch-Gavan et al (48) assessed 36 remitted AN inpatients, 24 non-remitted AN inpatients and 31 non-ED controls. Remission was defined according to Strober's (5) criteria, but we extended the required duration of remission to 12 months. Mean duration from index hospitalization to the follow-up assessment was 8.9 years. Only variables differentiating among the groups in separate analyses were included in the forward stepwise logistic regressions used in this study to create quantitative models for remission. By comparing past and follow-up parameters in remitted and non-remitted AN patients, the authors sought to identify factors predicting and contributing to remission, respectively. A similar comparison between remitted and control participants aimed to define factors potentially predisposing to the development of AN [see Srinivasagam et al (18) for the explanation of this paradigm].

Five past variables predicted non-remission from AN: more hospitalizations and greater duration of ambulatory treatment following the index hospitalization, a history of vegetarianism, greater inclination to display anxiety, and sexual abuse during childhood. The use of a regression equation correctly predicted non-remission in 87.0% of the cases (sensitivity) and remission in 94.4% of the cases (specificity). It further explained 91.5% of the variance for non remission, considerably higher than the respective values in previous studies (13.2-45%). The explained variance (R^2) of this equation was high: $R^2=0.724$. The accuracy of the diagnostic test of this model, depending on its ability to correctly separate remitted from non-remitted AN patients, was excellent [the area under the receiver operating characteristic curve (ROC) (49) equaled 0.938].

Three follow-up variables contributed to non-remission from AN: vegetarianism, higher total follow-up Eating Disorders Inventory-2 (EDI-2) (50) score, and lower BMI .The use of a regression equation correctly identified non-remission in 65.2% of the cases (sensitivity), and remission in 88.9% of the cases (specificity), correctly explaining 79.7% of the variance for non-remission. The explained variance of this equation was high: $R^2=0.621$, and the accuracy of the diagnostic test of this model was excellent (the area under the ROC curve equaled 0.907).

The use of univariate analyses showed that that remitted patients had elevated anxiety and eating-related obsessionality compared to the controls, suggesting that these variables may predispose to AN. In this respect, the results of this study highlight the specific role of anxiety in increasing the risk for both the predisposition to AN and for non-remission.

Another Israeli study by Bachner-Melman and associates (51) explored the implications of adopting different definitions of recovery. Two hundred and twenty-five women with a lifetime diagnosis of AN were interviewed, diagnosed, and assessed for level of recovery. When broad criteria for recovery were adopted (BMI of at least 19, regular menstruation for at least three months, and no bingeing or purging behaviors for at least eight consecutive weeks), 74 women (33%) were defined as recovered. When a more stringent definition was used (adding lack of body image distortion and fear of fatness to the aforementioned criteria), only 32 women (14%) were classified as recovered. The 32 women fulfilling the more stringent criteria were referred to as "behaviorally and cognitively recovered", whereas the 42 women who had recovered according to the broad but not the stringent criteria were referred to as "behaviorally recovered".

A battery of self-rating scales measuring current ED symptomatology (disordered eating, body dissatisfaction, and drive for thinness) and core ED-related personality characteristics (endorsement of the thin ideal concern for appropriateness, drive for success, fear of failure, harm avoidance, obsessionality, perfectionism, and self-esteem) was completed by the two groups recovered from AN and by 253 non-ED control women. On all scales, the scores of the behaviorally recovered women were significantly more pathological and in the direction expected from ill AN patients, in comparison to women who were also cognitively recovered; the latter, in turn, were indistinguishable from the control women on all measures.

Similar to the findings of Couturier & Lock (3,6), these results highlight the need for a standardization of the definition of recovery. These findings also underscore that full return to normal functioning, both behavioral and cognitive, albeit infrequent, is possible even in a chronic debilitating illness such as AN. Thirdly, this study replicates earlier studies (18,19,40,48,52), in showing an elevation of personality attributes characteristics of AN (in the present study elevated perfectionism, obsessionality, harm avoidance and fear of failure, and lower self-esteem and drive for success) in behaviorally recovered patients in comparison to non-ED controls. Whereas some of the traits differentiating between the two samples might reflect the consequences of prior illness, the assumed absence of confounding nutritional influences in recovered patients raises the possibility of assessing in this case potential vulnerability factors that predispose certain individuals to the development of AN (18). On the other hand, the lack of difference between cognitively recovered AN women and never-ill controls, raises the possibility that these personality traits may actually be associated with the condition of the illness (i.e., appearing in behaviorally but not cognitively recovered patients).

DISCUSSION, CONCLUSIONS, AND DIRECTION FOR FUTURE RESEARCH

The present chapter presents the multitude of problems associated with the study of recovery from AN. Based on the findings described; we highlight several points for further discussion.

1. Criteria for recovery: in the ongoing disagreement between favoring "narrow" and "broad" criteria for recovery, Couturier and Lock (6) favor the second option, as their definition of recovery requires normal weight range (likely associated with an overall stable physical condition) and lack of pathological eating-related behaviors and attitudes. We agree with most of the researchers excluding the condition of comorbid disorders from the definition of recovery, as many studies have shown elevated comorbidity to be present even in a high percentage of recovered AN patients (2,48). Still, since comorbidity may affect the functioning of AN patients above and beyond the influence of the ED per se, we suggest adding an evaluation of psychosocial functioning to Couturier and Lock's (6) criteria, so that recovery would reflect, at least to some extent, the patient's overall condition.

2. Behavioral vs. psychological recovery: The study by Bachner-Melman et al (51) supports previous studies (5,19) in emphasizing the differences between behavioral and psychological recovery, and that in order to lead a normal productive life, it is not enough for the recovered AN patient to be in an overall stable physical condition and to eat well. The persistence of eating and weight-related obsessionality and of pathological attitudes toward the body may considerably interfere with occupational, social, and sexual functioning despite the presence of physical and behavioral recovery (14,23). Moreover, studies focusing on the patients" own perspectives have shown that factors such as personality strength, self-confidence, identification and expression of emotions, and feeling understood (53), as well as feeling a connection within oneself and others and that life has a meaning (54), are important ingredients of recovery. It is our opinion, therefore,

that outcome studies should relate to both definitions of recovery and to the similarities and differences in the factors predicting them.

3. Methodological considerations: In our opinion, outcome studies in AN should combine prospective longitudinal designs assessing the patient's condition at different time points during the course of the illness, with follow-up comparisons of recovered, non-recovered, and non-ED participants, analyzing the results with quantitative statistical models. Such combined designs would enable the assessment of factors potentially predisposing to AN, vs. factors determining the course and outcome of the disorder.

4. Recovery in male AN patients: Understandably, most outcome studies in AN have related only to female patients, with only a few studies including additional small samples of male patients. This precludes the formulation of adequate recovery criteria in this population at the present time. It is most likely that gender differences beyond the issue of menstruation would be found in the process of recovery from AN.

5. Recovery vs. remission: Only the two studies of Couturier and Lock (3,6) have attempted to differentiate directly between remission and recovery from AN. According to these authors, the only difference between the two constructs is shorter vs. longer duration, respectively. The rationale for this paradigm is plausible, allowing for the investigation of a putative association between short-term remission and long-term recovery, and for the comparison of factors predicting the two conditions. Nevertheless, in our opinion, duration is not the only factor that should differentiate between recovery and remission. Remission may differ from recovery not only on clinical but also on theoretical grounds. For example, we believe that psychological (or cognitive) recovery should be part of the definition of long-term recovery, but not of short-term, potentially temporary, remission. If that is the case, future research should determine the factors increasing or decreasing the likelihood of progressing from remission to recovery. In keeping with the more broad differentiation between remission and recovery, Pike (23) suggests that although similar clinical criteria are required for both conditions, recovery can, nevertheless, be attained only when the overall functioning and risk of recurrence of the ED symptoms is comparable to that of never-ill women

6. The interrelationships between recovery and relapse: The ambiguity in the definition of recovery likely leads also to considerable problems in the characterization of relapse. In particular, should relapse be established only if a full AN syndrome recurs, or is the mere reappearance of interfering symptoms sufficient? Secondly, what is the minimum duration of a symptom-free condition required to define symptomatic reappearance as a relapse, rather than a part of an index episode?

In conclusion, the study of recovery from AN and of the factors increasing or decreasing its likelihood of is of vital importance. Although many outcome studies do exist, the multitudes of problems in defining recovery, and the great variations among the studies, still preclude a uniform definition of the construct. In light of these findings, the standardization of the definition for recovery from AN and of the design of future outcome studies is of vital importance to improve our ability to compare the results of different studies, to draw sound conclusions, and to plan appropriate treatment interventions.

REFERENCES

[1] Hoek HW. Incidence, prevalence and mortality of anorexia nervosa and other eating disorders. Curr Opin Psychiatry 2006;19:389-94.

[2] Steinhausen HC. The outcome of anorexia nervosa in the 20th century. Am J Psychiatry 2002;159:1284-93.

[3] Couturier J, Lock J. What is remission in adolescent anorexia nervosa? A review of various conceptualizations and quantitative analysis. Int J Eat Disord 2006;39:175-83.

[4] Carter JC, Blackmore E, Sutandar-Pinnock K, Woodside DB. Relapse in anorexia nervosa: A survival analysis. Psychol Med 2004;34:671-9.

[5] Strober M, Freeman R, Morrell W. The long term course of severe anorexia nervosa in adolescents: Survival analysis of recovery, relapse, and outcome predictors over 10-15 years in prospective study. Int J Eat Disord 1997;22:339-60.

[6] Couturier J, Lock J. What is recovery in adolescent anorexia nervosa? Int J Eat Disord 2006;39:550-5.

[7] Kaye W, Strober M, Jimerson D. The neurobiology of eating disorders. In: Charney DS, Nestler EJ, eds. The neurobiology of mental illness. New York: Oxford Press, 2004:pp. 1112-28.

[8] Neumarker ICI. Mortality and sudden death in anorexia nervosa. Int J Eat Disord 1997;21:205-12.

[9] Von Holle A, Poyastro Pinheiro A, Thornton LM, Klump KL, Berrettini WH, Brandt H, et al. Temporal patterns of recovery across eating disorder subtypes. Aust N Z J Psychiatry 2008;42:108-17.

[10] Morgan HG, Russell GFM. Value of family background and clinical features as predictors of long term outcome in anorexia nervosa: Four- year follow- up study of 41 patients. Psychol Med 1975;5:355-71.

[11] Steinhausen HC, Glanville K. Follow up studies of anorexia nervosa a review of research findings. Psychol Med 1983;3:239-49.

[12] Sturzenberger S, Cantwell PD, Burroughs J, Salkin B, Green JK. A follow-up study of adolescent psychiatric inpatients with anorexia nervosa. J Am Acad Child Psychiatry 1977;16:703-15.

[13] Steinhausen HC, Boyadjieva S, Griogoroiu- Serbanescu M, Neumarker KJ. The outcome of adolescent eating disorders: Findings from an international collaborative study. Eur Child Adolesc Psychiatry 2003;12(Suppl. 1):91-8.

[14] Steinhausen HC, Seidel R, Winkler-Metzke C. Evaluation of treatment and intermediate and long term outcome of adolescent eating disorders. Psychol Med 2000;30:1089-98.

[15] Herzog DB, Sacks NR, Keller MB, Lavori PW, Ranson KB, Gray HM. Patterns and predictors of recovery in anorexia nervosa and bulimia nervosa. J Am Acad Child Adolesc Psychiatry 1993;32:835-42.

[16] Eckert ED, Halmi KA, Marchi P, Grove W, Crosby R. Ten-year follow-up of anorexia nervosa: clinical course and outcome. Psychol Med 1995;25:143-56.

[17] Garfinkel PE, Moldofsky H, Garner DM. Prognosis in anorexia nervosa as influenced by clinical features, treatment and self-perception. Can Med Assoc J 1977;117,1041-5.

[18] Srinivasagam NM, Kaye WH, Plotnicov KH, Greeno C, Weltzin TE, Rao R. Persistent perfectionism, symmetry, and exactness after long-term recovery from anorexia nervosa. Am J Psychiatry 1995;11:1630-4.

[19] Casper RC. Personality features of women with good outcome from restricting anorexia nervosa. Psychosom Med 1990;52:156-70.

[20] Garner DM, Olmsted MP, Bohr Y, Garfinkel PE. The Eating Attitudes Test: Psychometric features and clinical correlates. Psychol Med 1982;12:871-8.

[21] Kordy H, Kramer B, Palmer RL, Papezova H, Pellet J, Richard M, et al. Remission, recovery, relapse and recurrence in eating disorders: conceptualization and illustration of a validation strategy. J Clin Psychol 2002;58:833-46.

[22] Cooper Z, Cooper PJ, Fairburn CG. The validity of the eating disorder examination and its subscales. Br J Psychiatry 1989;154:807-12.

[23] Pike KM. Long term course of anorexia nervosa: response, relapse, remission and recovery. Clin Psychol Rev 1998;18:447-75.

[24] Pike KM, Walsh BT, Vitousek K, Wilson GT, Bauer J. Cognitive behavioral therapy in the post-hospitalization treatment of anorexia nervosa. Am J Psychiatry 2003;60:2046-9.

[25] Freeman RK, Walker MK, Ben-Tovim DI. Low levels of interrater reliability in a standard measure of outcome in eating disorders (the modified Morgan–Russell Assessment Schedule). Int J Eat Disord 1996;20:51-6.

[26] Shisslak CM, Crayo M, Estes LS. The spectrum of eating disturbances. Int J Eat Disord 1995;18:209-19.

[27] Herzog DB, Keller MB, Lavori PW. Outcome in anorexia nervosa and bulimia nervosa- a review of the literature. J Nerv Ment Dis 1988;176:131-43.

[28] American Psychiatric Association. Diagnostic and statistical manual of mental disorders, 4th ed text revised (DSM-IV-TR). Washington, DC:APA, 2000.

[29] Clausen L. Time course of symptom remission in eating disorders. Int J Eat Disord. 2004;36:296-306.

[30] O'Connor MA, Touyz SW, Dunn SM, Beumont PJ. Vegetarianism in anorexia nervosa? A review of 116 consecutive cases. Med J Aust 1987;147:540-2.

[31] Schebendach JE, Mayer LES, Delin MJ, Attia E, Contento IR, Wolf RL, et al. Dietary energy density and diet variety as predictors of outcome in anorexia nervosa. Am J Clin Nutr 2008;87:810-6.

[32] Kaye WH, Bulik CM, Thornton L, Barbarich N, Masters K. Comorbidity of anxiety disorders with anorexia and bulimia nervosa. Am J Psychiatry 2004;161:2215-21.

[33] Halmi KA, Sunday SR, Strober M, Kaplan A, Woodside DB, Fichter M, et al. Perfectionism in anorexia nervosa: Variation by clinical subtype, obsessionality, and pathological eating behavior. Am J Psychiatry 2000;157:1799-805.

[34] Lilenfeld LR, Kaye WH, Greeno CG, Merikangas KR, Plotnicov K, Pollice C, et al A controlled family study of anorexia nervosa and bulimia nervosa: Psychiatric disorders in first-degree relatives and effects of proband comorbidity. Arch Gen Psychiatry 1998;55,603–10.

[35] Milos G, Spindler A, Ruggiero G, Klaghofer R, Schnyder U. Comorbidity of obsessive-compulsive disorders and duration of eating disorders. Int J Eat Disord 2002;31:284-9.

[36] Strober M. Pathologic fear conditioning and anorexia nervosa: On the search for novel paradigms. Int J Eat Disord 2004;35:504-8.

[37] Toner BB, Garfinkel PE, Garner DM. Affective and anxiety disorders in the long term follow up of anorexia nervosa. Int J Psychiatry Med 1988;18:357-64.

[38] Crane AM, Roberts ME, Treasure J. Are obsessive-compulsive personality traits associated with a poor outcome in anorexia nervosa? A systematic review of randomized controlled trials and naturalistic outcome studies. Int J Eat Disord 2007;40:581–8.

[39] Saccomani L, Savoini M, Cirrincione M, Vercellino F, Ravera G. Long term outcome of children and adolescent with anorexia nervosa: study of comorbidity. J Psychosom Res 1998;44:565-71.

[40] Sullivan P, Bulik CM, Fear J, Pickering A. Outcome of anorexia nervosa: A case-control study. Am J Psychiatry 1998;152:1630-4.

[41] Bulik CM, Sullivan PF, Fear JL, Pickering A. Outcome of anorexia nervosa: Eating attitudes, personality, and parental bonding. Int J Eat Disord 2000;28:139-47.

[42] Strober M, Freeman R, Lampert C, Diamond J. The association of anorexia nervosa with anxiety disorders and obsessive-compulsive personality disorder: Evidence from a family study with discussion of neurodevelopmental and nosological implications. Int J Eat Disord 2007;40:S46-51.

[43] Fichter MM, Quadflieg N, Hedlund S. Twelve-year course and outcome predictors of anorexia nervosa. Int J Eat Disord 2006;39:87-100.

[44] Herzog DB, Dorer DJ, Keel PK, Selwyn SE, Ekeblad ER, Flores AT, et al. Recovery and relapse in anorexia and bulimia nervosa: a 7.5- year follow up study. Am Acad Child Adolesc Psychiatry 1999;38:829-37.

[45] Lowe B, Zipfel S, Buchholz C, Dupont Y, Reas DL, Herzog W. Long- term outcome of anorexia nervosa in prospective 21- year follow–up study. Psycol Med 2001;31:881-90.

[46] Zipfel S, Lowe B, Reas DL, Deter HC, Herzog W. Long–term prognosis in anorexia nervosa: Lessons from a 21- year follow- up study. Lancet 2000;355:721-2.

[47] Herzog W, Deter HC, Fiehn W, Petzold E. Medical findings and predictors of long- term physical outcome in anorexia nervosa: A prospective 12-year follow-up study. Psychol Med 1997; 27:269-79.

[48] Yackobovitch-Gavan M, Golan M, Valevski A, Kreitler S, Bachar E, Lieblich, A, et al. An integrative quantitative model of factors influencing remission and non-remission in anorexia nervosa. . Int J Eat Disord 2009;42:306-17.

[49] Metz CE. Basic principles of ROC analysis. Sem Nuc Med 1978; 8: 283-98.

[50] Garner DM. Eating Disorders Inventory-2 (EDI-2). Odessa, FL: Psychological Assessment Resources, 1991.

[51] Bachner-Melman R, Zohar AH, Ebstein RP. An examination of cognitive versus behavioral components of recovery from anorexia nervosa. J Nerv Ment Dis 2006;194:697-703.

[52] O'Dwyer AM, Lucey JV, Russell GF. Serotonin activity in anorexia nervosa after long-term weight restoration: Response to D-fenfluramine challenge. Psychol Med 1996;26,353-9.

[53] Hsu LG, Crisp AH, Callender JS. Recovery in anorexia nervosa: The patient's perspective. Int J Eat Disord 1992;11:341-50.

[54] Garrett C. Beyond Anorexia: Narrative, Spirituality and Recovery. Cambridge 1998: Cambridge University Press.

In: Treatment and Recovery of Eating Disorders
Editors: Daniel Stein and Yael Latzer

ISBN: 978-1-62808-248-7
© 2013 Nova Science Publishers, Inc.

Chapter 15

THE ROAD TO LIBERATION: METAPHORS AND NARRATIVES OF ILLNESS OF WOMEN RECOVERED FROM BULIMIA NERVOSA

Roni Elran-Barak[1,2§§§§], Yael Latzer[2,3], Eli Buchbinder[2] and Eynat Zubery[1]

[1] Eating Disorders Unit, Davidson (Hanotrim) Clinic, Shalvata, Raanana, Israel
[2] Faculty of Social Welfare and Health Sciences, University of Haifa, Israel
[3] Eating Disorders Clinic, Psychiatric Division, Rambam Medical Center, Haifa, Israel

ABSTRACT

This paper attempts to identify the unique way in which women who have recovered from bulimia nervosa (BN) describe their recovery process. This is a qualitative study, based on in-depth interviews with twelve women who have recovered from BN. Analysis of the interviews reveals that the women use metaphoric language to describe their recovery as a sharp transition transformation is described using three archetypal protagonists who embody three dimensions of change: the Self, the Bulimia, and the Environment. The recovery experience that emerges from the interviews is a complex and polarized one, encompassing a perception of achievement and victory over the disorder, coupled with a contradictory view of the Bulimia as chronic disorder. The findings of the research are discussed in reference to object relations theory and the use of the splitting mechanism.

Keywords: bulimia nervosa, recovery, eating disorders, narrative

---

§§§§ E-mail address: adironi@haifau.013.net.il

INTRODUCTION

Despite widespread agreement among clinicians and researchers that recovery from BN is not a static situation, but rather a long process that includes relapses and remissions (1), only few studies have described the complex recovery process in depth. Many researchers concentrate on the etiology of the disorder and the means of treating it. Others, who focus on recovery, deal primarily with physiological and behavioral parameters, while devoting little attention to emotional experiences: what women who recover from BN feel, or how they define and express themselves (2). Research has focused on treatment and prevention, while leaving limited space for the point of view of those who have actually recovered from the disorder: How do they describe their recovery, and what makes it possible for them to achieve and sustain this recovery?

BN was not defined as a syndrome separate from anorexia nervosa until the early 1980s. The definition of the disorder according to DSM4 (3) consists of five criteria, including recurrent episodes of binge eating and recurrent inappropriate compensatory behavior to prevent weight gain. The etiology of the disorder is unknown (4), and it is often regarded as multi-factorial. Research findings suggest that biological, social, and psychological factors operate jointly to form the basis for the disorder (5). The high prevalence and complex etiology of the disorder have led to the development of a variety of treatments, including cognitive-behavioral and psychodynamic approaches, in addition to nutritional consulting and pharmaceutical therapy (6). This wide range of therapies has done little to improve the poor prognosis for those who suffer from the disorder. Only 40% of patients who complete treatment achieve full recovery; 60% continue to live with at least some of the symptoms (7).

But what is recovery from BN? There is disagreement on how to define it. Some argue that recovery should be defined in physiological terms, based on disappearance of the symptoms. Others add psychological factors, such as change in perceptions regarding body shape and weight, while another approach suggests factoring in the duration of control over the symptoms (8). Recovery is usually defined as the complete disappearance of binge-purge behaviors for six consecutive months. This definition is based on longitudinal surveys which indicate that only total disappearance of the symptoms following treatment can predict non-recurrence in the long term (9). Therefore, it is common to distinguish between recovery and remission (10). Remission refers to a pause in exhibition of the symptoms, followed by a relapse. Recovery, on the other hand, refers to a longer period of cessation of the symptoms, a state in which the risk of relapse is significantly smaller.

Attempts to understand recovery from BN have not included the voices of women who have recovered from the disorder. Only a few studies have shed light on the experience of those patients. These few studies have mainly helped to describe the stages of the recovery process (11) and to differentiate between recovery from cognitive symptoms and recovery from the behavioral ones (12). These studies have also described psychological and social changes in the women's lives (2) and emphasized the importance of informal support systems (13). However, none of this research has looked at the unique language in which recovered women describe their own experiences.

This study aims to explore the distinctive voices of women who have recovered from BN by paying special attention to the language they use. The motivation to study their language stems from the perspective that human language enables people to endow their experiences with meaning (14). One way to study human language is through the use of metaphor. According to Lakoff and Johnson (15), the language of metaphor is the language of the spirit and reflects our inner lives. The purpose of this study is to identify and understand the metaphorical language by which women who have recovered from BN describe their recovery.

METHOD

This is a qualitative study based on in-depth interviews with women who have recovered from BN. The population of the study consisted of a purposive sample (18) of twelve women who had completed the treatment program at the eating-disorder outpatient unit, Davidson (Hanotrim) Clinic, Shalvata, Raanana, Israel. Participants' ages ranged from 20 to 53 years. The age of onset of BN ranged from 13 to 25, with treatment sought between the ages of 16 and 38. The participants' demographic characteristics varied: Some were married, with or without children, and some were single; some had completed a high school education, while others had higher degrees. In order to avoid language and cultural biases, only Jewish, Hebrew-speaking women were interviewed. All of the women met criteria for purging-type BN (based on DSM-IV) when they sought treatment, but had had no BN symptoms between the end of the treatment and the time of the survey. The interviews took place a year or more after the end of the treatment; the participants met the definition of recovery based on strict criteria of lack of symptoms for a year or more.

Data were collected through semi-structured interviews (19), which lasted between one and three hours. The interview guide covered several topics: factors that helped or hindered recovery, etiological factors, the treatment program, stages in the recovery process, and how recovery differed from illness. An eating-disorder diagnosis was performed three times using the EDE (20): when the women first sought treatment, at the end of the treatment, and at the interview.

Content analysis of both the surface (the text) and the deep structure (the subtext) of the interviews (21) was performed. Surface structure refers to the sum of the words as they were spoken, whereas deep structure refers to the interpretive constructs, meanings, and emotional and attitudinal implications of what was implied but not explicitly stated. In the analysis, we attempted to identify the different voices in the text and combine them (22). In other words, we analyzed both the clearly explicit and the underlying and unstated voices in the surface and the deep structure of the text.

FINDINGS

Analysis of the narratives shows that the women describe the recovery and illness experiences as two polar opposites. Therefore, in order to understand the recovery experience, it is necessary to grasp and define the illness experience. The latter is described in metaphors such as chaos, lack of control, loneliness, and suffering, while metaphors for recovery include regaining control of life, partnership with others, and victory in the fight against BN. These contradictory metaphors represent the perception of a drastic transformation from enslavement to liberation, from chaos to order, and from closedness to openness. The women's perception is that who they were then is completely different from who they are now, in the recovery stage.

The dramatic change is highlighted mostly by the transformation within the three protagonists of the recovery story: the Self, representing the image of the women interviewed; the Bulimia, which represents the illness; and the Environment, which represents the outer world, such as therapists, family, and friends. Those three protagonists are transformed during the move from illness to recovery, so that the metaphors used by the women to characterize the protagonists in the beginning of the story are exactly the opposite of those used to describe them at the end. This transformation is shown in Figure 1 and explained in detail in the following sections.

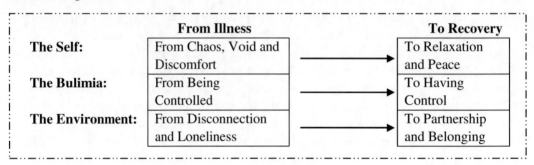

Figure 1. From Illness to Recovery

1. The Experience of Being Ill

The illness is narrated as deep physical dependency on food, which is perceived as an addictive substance. The interviewees tell of daily vomiting and of turning food into an object without which they cannot survive: It grants them positive sensations of enjoyment and relaxation and helps to turn away negative feelings of emotional pain and disappointment. The women say that being bulimic is like swinging between alternating moods and like living in an external and internal void. This existential feeling of a void creates a destructive urge to experience physical sensations of stuffing and emptying the body through overeating and vomiting. The women perceive themselves as useless, dependent, and passive, and they describe their lives as enslaved by the Bulimia, leaving little space for other facets of life.

The focus in the illness stage is on hiding the disorder, a secrecy which causes loneliness, alienation, and estrangement, as well as a rift between the inside and the outside. While in the outer world most of the women continue to function, to study, to work, and even to raise children, they feel chaos in their inner world. An experience of division among the three protagonists emerges: the Self, the Bulimia and the Environment.

1.1. The Self: Chaos and Void

The first protagonist, the Self, is described in the illness stage in terms of loss of control, consistency, and order, as well as a lack of capacity to foresee the future. The reigning chaos creates a sense of distance between the interviewees and themselves, even an estrangement: They do not recognize themselves and do not know who or what they are. The Self becomes a hollow entity that tends to disappear. It is an internal void, like an "inner suction pump" or a "black hole." This sensation manifests as an experience of imprisonment inside the illness with no way out. One of the women describes it as follows:

> "This was a crazy and messy period. To suggest that I had bulimia is to limit the scope, as I was bulimic and alcoholic; let's face it, I was compulsive with food, alcohol, and men[...] if I was not with a man then I would eat, and when I was eating with a man I would also drink. It was all around these three things[...] I lived in Tel-Aviv, in the craziest location, because I needed noise all the time, to overcome the inner noise." [Ronit]

Ronit's narrative reflects a sense of chaos and loss of control. Ronit is trapped in a cycle, with no way to move forward or to create a change. Her life rolls by of its own accord, at frightening speed, and her interests shrink to the fulfillment of only physical needs: food, sex, and alcohol. In this condition, even the noise coming from the street, perhaps representing the external reality, is too weak to "overcome the inner noise." Another interviewee describes:

> "All this scene of eating and vomiting was[...] I would wait for this detachment. I would become totally dazed, watching soap operas on TV. For two hours I was in another world and it was impossible to talk to me. No communication. Nothing. I would sit, eat, and throw up." [Yaarit]

Yaarit tells us that the eating and vomiting episodes helped her to "detach" herself from reality, to withdraw within her inner self, sealing off communication with the outer world. Food and TV became means of escape from the threatening external environment into "another world" in which she could construct a moment of peace. This running away to a virtual space is also Yaarit's escape from herself, from her unbearable emotional pain. The use of the term "dazed" suggests how intensely Yaarit needed to suffer in order to run away from her pain.

1.2. The Bulimia: Taking Over

The second protagonist, the Bulimia, is defined metaphorically, in the illness stage, as a ruler that totally controls the women's lives. They tell us that the Bulimia in this stage was so strong that they had to surrender to it. They describe it as a "whole," a total experience that controls their lives. Surrendering to Bulimia means that life is limited to obsessive preoccupation with food and weight, leaving no space for other interests or activities:

> "All the time with the Bulimia. To eat, not to eat. To throw up, not to throw up. Pills now, pills later[...] My entire life revolved around food and the bathroom. It was just throwing up constantly. I felt all of a sudden that I was living for the sake of hiding[...] That this was the essence of my life." [Sarit]
>
> "The Bulimia took over me. It was a lot of that and only that. It bothered me in every respect. I had no life. It was disgusting, awful, repulsive. I believe that cancer is a compliment and an easier term compared to Bulimia. It is eating and throwing up all day long, nothing else. I gave up lots of other things and practically stayed static, with no moving forward." [Nira]

These quotations capture the sense of enslavement and loss of identity during the illness stage. Bulimia is described as a separate entity, external to the women, having destructive capacity which swallows and conquers everything, even turning into the only "essence of life." This external entity makes Nira stand idle, motionless and essentially enslaved by the Bulimia, with no power to develop in other spheres of life as an independent human being. The enslavement experience is also compared with "cancer," a destructive, overpowering, dangerous disease that leaves the patient hopeless and scared.

The impression is that the Bulimia develops and expands in a way that makes the Self shrink. The second protagonist, the Bulimia, becomes the main actor on stage, leaving the first protagonist, the Self, on the margins. In reaction to the Bulimia taking over, the weak Self appears to attempt to push the monstrous Bulimia back and out by hiding it in the bathroom or in a secret, sealed chamber. But this attempt is destined to fail, as it is not based on real strength of the Self, but on an illusory capacity to conceal. The interviewees are ashamed of being bulimic, because it represents their dark side, the "disgusting" and "repulsive" one; hence their attempts to hide it, which in turn drive them into a circle of loneliness.

1.3. The Environment: Disconnection and Loneliness

The third protagonist, the Environment, represents the external world of the women. In the illness stage, its distance and alienation from the Self are emphasized. The women tell us how they ran their lives during their illness through secrecy and disconnection from the Environment.

> "I think that I lived in a kind of a bubble[…] I functioned well and felt nothing. I had no pain. I wasn't really anywhere, I was unattached." [Idit]

The "bubble" metaphor describes how Idit cut herself off from the Environment. This bubble wraps and protects her, but at the same time it also blocks the connection between her Self and the outside, to the extent of splitting her inner self from her external world. This disconnection is evident in the contrast between "I functioned well" and "I felt nothing," between what is visible from the outside and the chaotic inner experience.

The statements "I felt nothing," "I had no pain," and "I was unattached" articulate the heavy price Idit paid for the split between the inner and the outer world. Life continues outside, but Idit does not have the privilege to take part in it. It seems that the gap between the Self and the Environment – the first and third protagonists – is growing ever larger.

2. The Experience of Recovery

The experience of recovering, according to the women's perception, is the opposite of the experience of being ill. While the experience of being ill is narrated as chaos, void, lack of control, and loneliness, the experience of being recovered is narrated as being relaxed, as having control, meaning, and partnership with others. The interviewees explain that recovery entails a change on two levels: physical and emotional. In the physical sphere, the eating and vomiting episodes end, and the preoccupation with food, weight, and shape eases. In the emotional sphere, the change is described as stronger feelings of self-esteem, a sense of freedom and ease, as well as openness and association with other people. This new situation creates a change in the relationships among the protagonists: The second, the Bulimia, which overruled everything, diminishes, making room for the creation of a new life experience of liberation and peace.

Despite the dichotomizing of the recovery as a total opposite of the illness, some of the women say that the recovery experience is not a purely positive one. They suggest that recovery is a complex experience with ups and downs, and with continuous movement between two poles: peace and harmony on the one hand, and never-ending war on the other. The first pole represents a perception of full recovery, as the eating disorder is perceived as being over. The second pole represents a perception of the Bulimia as a chronic disease that entails relapses and remissions and that will never disappear. Some of the interviewees indicate that even though they have not had bulimic symptoms for a year or more, they continue to be afraid of falling back into the disorder. These women do not have a euphoric sensation of victory over the disorder; instead they continue to perceive their lives as a never-ending war with many crises and difficulties.

2.1. The Self: Relaxation and Peace
Most of the women characterize the first protagonist, the Self, in the recovery stage, in terms of relaxation and peace.

> "Over the last year I saw that I am apparently capable of doing other things beyond being ill or thinking about the illness or dealing with it, which is what I had been doing in the previous two years. I started to work on improving my math grades; I passed my qualifying exams and started taking courses at the University. Food became a secondary element in my life." [Sarit]
>
> "I have changed a lot. My present self is not the one I was before. I used to be a perfectionist, crazy. The change is internal. I became calm. I am not scared all the time. I know who I am and what I am and I know I have power and I know that I can have a happy life. I have gotten my life back." [Yaarit]

These two interviewees refer to the change the recovery made in their lives. Sarit describes the sense of capability and self-confidence that she now has. Her past obsession with food has become secondary, clearing the way for activities that are helping her grow and develop. This sense of power also emerges from the change in the relationship between the protagonists: The second one, the Bulimia, which overshadowed the first, the Self, in the illness stage, is now marginalized. It has become "a secondary element," enabling the recovered Self to thrive.

Yaarit compares the person she was before with the one she is today and defines two opposite images. This split describes the road to liberation as a total change, in which the one who sets out on the road and the one who reaches the end are not the same person. The first is "perfectionist and crazy" and the second is "calm." The road to liberation shapes the Self and enables its positive qualities to emerge.

While most of the interviewees express a degree of optimism for the future and describe their recovery as a positive experience of capability and security, some of them also define the Self – in the recovery stage – in a dual manner. They suggest that despite the feeling of recovery, they also have some doubts and disappointments.

"I managed to defeat the symptom, but the things that were underneath it are still unresolved." [Sarit]

"All that time I had been thinking that if I stopped vomiting my life would be beautiful and I would be able to do anything, and life would be so easy for me. But basically nothing, but nothing, has changed. I still find it difficult to face things. It is hard for me to face big challenges." [Idit]

The interviewees differentiate between two types of recovery: physical recovery, which involves overcoming the bulimic symptoms, and emotional recovery, which requires easing the emotional difficulties that underpin the symptoms. Furthermore, the relationship between the physical and emotional recovery is far from clear. Some interviewees feel that even though they have achieved physical recovery, they still face severe challenges on the emotional level. They understand that physical recovery does not make all their dreams come true. On the contrary, recovery can intensify a sense of hardship, because it exposes the need to struggle against the difficulties of life.

2.2. The Bulimia: Control and Never-Ending War

The Bulimia is the second protagonist that undergoes a significant change on the road to liberation, from having control over the Self in the illness stage to being controlled by the Self in the recovery stage. The powerful Bulimia that has been ruling the women's lives becomes feeble, which helps them understand that it is no longer a central component of their lives.

"I had to eat, so I ate. I wanted a sandwich, so I bought one. I craved chocolate, so I went for it. I got fat, so I got fat. Then I also lost the weight I had gained. It disturbed me a lot, but at a certain stage I managed to control it and get back to myself." [Naama].

Naama stresses that eating is no longer the center of her life. She controls her eating habits and her perception of her body. She is now able to make a choice regarding what, when, and how to eat, and how to perceive her eating. She is in control over the Bulimia. Food is no longer perceived as a threat.

"The temptation to run back to Bulimia is great, and the war is a 'never-ending war.' It is not easy to say: That's it. I do not return there. I do not starve, I do not throw up, and surely I do not return to where I have been." [Sara]

Sara describes how she succeeds, despite the hardship, in controlling the Bulimia. This sense of being in control is described as a "never-ending war." It is an ongoing struggle that may never end, a fight not to "run back to Bulimia" in difficult moments. The illness, according to this approach, continues to exist in the background throughout the interviewees' lives, even after their physical recovery.

"It is clear that something little will always remain there. It is slowly fading; it is no longer the center of my life. From the point of view of the symptom, it has been so long since I really exhibited it, but inside it still exists and it will always stay there." [Sarit]

Sarit emphasizes the concept of the "never-ending war" and describes how, despite her recovery, she is still threatened by the eating disorder: "I am still not certain that I really got out of it." The notion is that the present healthy Self continues to carry within itself particles of the ill Self. For that reason, it is not possible for her to be at ease; despite her recovery, Bulimia continues to be present.

2.3. The Environment: Partnership and Belonging

The third protagonist, the Environment, is narrated in the recovery stage through the metaphors of partnership and belonging. The partnership concept represents a change in the relationships of the interviewees with their surroundings, including their therapists, family, and friends. The recovered interviewees are able to share their secrets with their Environment, to rely on others and to establish new and trusting relationships:

> "She [the therapist] was all ears with me. She understood me and accepted me. I believe that she loved me. In the worst of times I always knew that there was someone there for me. The fact that she listened to me and understood me helped me face the challenges." [Sarit].

This quotation describes the therapeutic relationship as a crucial element in the recovery process. The connection is defined by the metaphor "all ears," which indicates that the therapist is perceived as absolutely attentive and supportive. These qualities enable Sarit to trust her, to confide her secrets and to give up her loneliness for the sake of cooperation. This relationship with the therapist also helped her create other constructive relationships with family members and friends.

> "It took me a while to understand that I needed to ask for my parents' help. You reach this point when you realize that you want to give someone a way in, even the smallest opening, so that he or she can look after you. To come to the bathroom with you, just to make sure you don't pass out after throwing up." [Hila]
>
> "When I told my friends that I throw up they accepted me. It was convenient that they accepted me, and all of a sudden it was all right. Suddenly I do not have to hide any more. It gave me confirmation that it is OK to be me." [Gila]

These words describe the transformation from disengagement and loneliness to a situation in which the women enable their family and friends to be part of the recovery process. This change is critical for recovery. It allows the first and the third protagonists, the Self and the Environment, to cease being enemies and connect in order to overcome the illness.

In sum, the findings of our research indicate a change in the relationship between the protagonists on the road from illness to recovery. Their relationship in the illness stage is characterized by disconnection and alienation: The Bulimia rules the Self, which is detached from the Environment. In the recovery stage, the three protagonists connect in order to support the process. The creation of a bond among the three protagonists symbolizes the powerful change that comes with recovery. It is not only a physical recovery, but rather a broad and real integration of three main elements: the Self, the Bulimia, and the Environment.

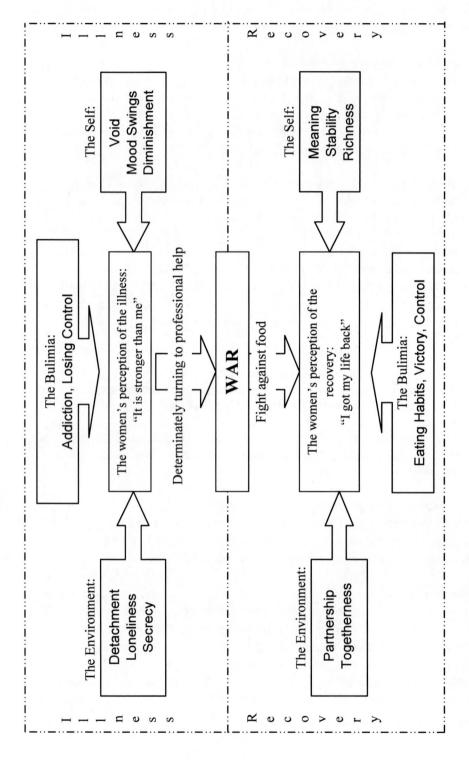

Figure 2. The Perception of Illness and Recovery.

DISCUSSION

This work uses qualitative methodology to examine how women who have recovered from BN perceive their recovery processes and how they describe their transformations in their own subjective voices. Two central findings emerge. The first is that the women's recovery stories feature three protagonists: the Self, the Bulimia, and the Environment. The second finding is that the women perceive illness and recovery as two opposite experiences. This perception becomes apparent through examination of the metaphorical language that the women use.

It is worthwhile to examine these findings in reference to object relations theory and the use of the splitting mechanism (23). According to object relations theory, the binging and purging mechanism is a symbolic manifestation of the splitting that bulimic women perform between positive and negative objects: between the good mother and the bad one (24), between the false self and the true self (25), and between the body self and the psychological self (26). In this sense, the bulimic episode can be seen as an escape from the good to the evil. When filling her body, the bulimic woman feels that she is not alone, but rather that she is one with the ultimate good, with her ideal mother. Then, the dread of fusion leads to emptying the body by vomiting, which helps the woman distance herself from the ultimate good and from her real mother (27,28). Splitting is a psychological defense mechanism which appears as a result of a failure to integrate inner objects, namely positive and negative self-representations. Consequently, the positive objects are constantly threatened by the negative ones, leading to instability in relationships, identity diffusion, and mood swings.

In this context, it is possible to understand the first finding – the splitting between the protagonists – as a split between good and bad internal objects. During the illness stage, bulimic women cannot integrate their internal good and bad objects and thus they split them. They fall into this pattern, for example, when they project negative characteristics onto the third protagonist, the Environment, and see it as an enemy that cannot understand, listen, or help.

With the transition from illness to recovery, there is a major change in the women's tendency to use the splitting mechanism. They start to perceive the protagonists in a more integrated manner. The perception of the Environment as an "enemy" changes, and they start perceiving it as a friend, someone that they can lean on. This shift is possible mainly due to the professional help that they receive. The very fact that they choose to seek help means giving up the secret of Bulimia. Telling the secret to their therapists paves the way to revealing it to family and friends. When the women experience the feedback of the Environment as helpful and accepting, there is a positive sensation of security. This feeling enables the split between the objects to heal: The Self and the Environment are allies now.

The second finding indicates that the interviewees see illness and recovery as two opposite experiences: "My present self is not the one I was before." This language might suggest that they continue, despite their recovery, to use a splitting mechanism between good and bad, or between wonderful recovery and unbearable illness. This perception might serve as grounds for seeing the recovered women as not fully recovered, in that they continue to use the splitting mechanism. A deeper understanding of the findings allows for another interpretation: The women make a clear distinction between illness and recovery, in order to make complex use of their definitions of these terms. This use entails the capacity to preserve the memory of the disorder within the recovery experience and to move freely between good and bad moods, between situations in which the fear of falling back into the Bulimia emerges and situations in which a sensation of security prevails.

Furthermore, splitting between illness and recovery may also be a positive driving force that helps the women to connect to their healthy selves. This splitting can help the women suppress and even forget the bad memories of the illness and focus on the present, on health, success, and strength. This perception of the splitting mechanism as a positive driving force is based on studies showing that positive growth after traumatic events indeed happens to those who have suppressed the trauma and have not been constantly preoccupied by it (29,30). The capacity not to remember may enable the women to push forward towards a complete recovery.

This study is based on qualitative methods. It is unique in its in-depth analysis of the distinct voices of women who have recovered from BN. This type of study has several methodological limitations, such as a small and perhaps non-representative sample, and an interview method which might entail personal and non-objective relations between the interviewer and the participants. Another drawback relates to the method of analysis, which inevitably involves the subjective view of the analysts. There may be a need for further research that examines the process of recovery from BN using quantitative and empirical tools.

Figure 2 shows how this study investigates the metaphorical language of women who have recovered from BN and describes their road to liberation. The study focuses on two points along this road: the beginning of the process and its end. Careful examination suggests that recovery from BN happens when the patient is willing to fight for her recovery and to turn to professional help with determination.

REFERENCES

[1] Olmsted, M.P., Kaplan, A.S., & Rockert, W. (2005). Defining Remission and Relapse in Bulimia Nervosa. International Journal of Eating Disorders, 38, 1-6.

[2] Peters, L., Fallon, P. (1994). The journey of recovery: dimensions of change. In Fallon, P., Katzman, M., & Wooley, S. (Eds.), Feminist Perspectives on Eating Disorders, (pp. 339-354). Guilford Press: New York London.

[3] American Psychiatric Association (1994). Diagnostic and statistical manual of mental disorders (4rd ed.). Washington, DC: APA.

[4] Fairburn, C.G. (2003). Eating disorders. The Lancet, 361, 407-416.

[5] Polivy, J., & Herman, C.P. (2002). Causes of eating disorders. Annual Review of Psychology, 53, 187-213.

[6] Andersen, A.E., & Corson, P.W. (2001). Characteristics of an ideal psychotherapist for eating disordered patients. The Psychiatric Clinics of North America, 24, 351-358.

[7] Thompson-Brenner, H., Glass, S., & Western, D. (2003). A multidimensional meta-analysis of psychotherapy for bulimia nervosa. Clinical Psychology-Science and Practice, 10, 269-287.

[8] Keel, P.K., Mitchell, N.E., Davis, T.L., Fieselman, S., & Crow, S.J. (2000). Impact of definitions on the description and prediction of bulimia nervosa outcome. International Journal of Eating Disorders, 28, 377-386.

[9] Maddocks, S.E., Kaplan, A.S., Woodside, D.B., Langdon, L., & Piran, N. (1992). Two year follow up of bulimia nervosa: the importance of abstinence as the criterion of outcome. International Journal of Eating Disorders, 12, 133-14.

[10] Field, A.E., Herzog, D.B., Keller, M.B., West, J., Nussbaum, K., & Colditz, G.A. (1997). Distinguishing recovery from remission in a cohort of bulimic women: How should asymptomatic periods be described? Journal of Clinical Epidemiology, 50, 1339-1345.

[11] Platt, C.M. (1992). Formerly chronic bulimic's perception of the process of recovery. Unpublished doctoral dissertation: California School of Professional Psychology, Berkeley.

[12] Rorty, M., Yager, J., & Rossotto, E. (1993). Why and how do women recover from Bulimia Nervosa? The subjective appraisals of forty women recovered for a year or more. International Journal of Eating Disorders, 14, 249-260.

[13] Wasson, D.H. (2003). A Qualitative Investigation of the relapse experience of women with bulimia nervosa. Eating Disorders: The Journal of Treatment and Prevention, 11, 73-88.

[14] Goolishian, H., & Anderson, H. (1987). Language systems and therapy: An evolving idea. Journal of Psychotherapy, 24, 529-538.

[15] Lakoff, G., & Johnson, M. (1980). Metaphors we live by. Chicago: University of Chicago.

[16] Lincoln, Y.S., & Guba, E.G. (1985). Naturalistic inquiry. Beverly Hills, CA: Sage.

[17] Weiss, R.S. (1994). Learning from Strangers: The art and methods of qualitative interview studies. The Free Press: New York.

[18] Patton, M.Q. (2002). Qualitative research & evaluation methods (third edition). Thousand Oaks, CA: Sage.

[19] Spradley, J.P. (1979). The ethnographic interview. New York : Holt, Rinehart and Winston.

[20] Cooper, Z. & Fairburn, C. (1987). The Eating Disorder Examination: A semi-structured interview for the assessment of specific psychopathology of eating disorders. International Journal of Eating Disorders, 6, 1-8.

[21] Bandler, R. & Grinder, J. (1975). The Structure of Magic: A Book about Language and Therapy. Science and Behavior Books, Palo Alto, CA.

[22] Gilligan, C., Lyons, N.P. & Hamner, T.J. (1990) Making Connections: The Relational Worlds of Adolescent Girls at Emma Willard School. Harvard University Press, Cambridge, MA.

[23] Kernberg, O.F. (1984). Severe Personality Disorders. Psychotherapeutic Strategies. New Haven, CT: Yale Univ. Press.

[24] Selvini-Palazzoli, M. (1978). Self Starvation. New York: Aronson.

[25] Johnson, C., & Connors, M.E. (1987). The etiology and treatment of bulimia nervosa. Basic Books: New York.

[26] Goodsitt, A. (1997). Eating disorders: A self-psychological perspective. In. D.M. Garner & P.E. Garfinkel (Eds.), Handbook of treatment for eating disorders. New York: The Guilford Press.

[27] Sours, J.A. (1980). Starving to death in a sea of objects. New York: Jason Aronson.

[28] Sugarman, A., & Kursh, C. (1982). The body as a transitional object in bulimia. International Journal of Eating Disorders, 1, 57-67.

[29] Solomon, Z. & Laufer, A. (2004). In the shadow of terror: Changes in world assumptions in Israeli youth. Journal of Aggression, Maltreatment and Trauma, 9, 353-364.

[30] Kaminer, H. (1989). Sleep patterns and dreaming as a function of adjustment to massive trauma. Unpublished doctoral dissertation: Technion, Israel.

In: Treatment and Recovery of Eating Disorders ISBN: 978-1-62808-248-7
Editors: Daniel Stein and Yael Latzer © 2013 Nova Science Publishers, Inc.

Chapter 16

RECOVERY IN BULIMIA NERVOSA

Phillipa Hay[*****]

Foundation Chair of Mental Health, School of Medicine, University of Western Sydney,
NSW, Australia, and Adjunct Professor of Psychiatry, School of Medicine,
James Cook University, Australia

ABSTRACT

This chapter addresses first issues in definition around the question of recovery in bulimia nervosa (BN), next the natural history, and third the outcome with treatment including predictors that may be modified to enhance remission and reduce relapse or later recurrence rates.

Remission in BN is most often defined as the absence of binge eating and purging behaviours. In addition some studies have used reduction in psychopathology as an alternate indicator of recovery. These studies were based on a quantitative measure of eating disorder weight/shape (or other) concerns e.g. being less than one standard deviation above the community mean of the global Eating Disorder Examination score. There is a consensus that remission is most likely sustained after one year and relapse after that time may be termed recurrence.

Naturalistic studies suggest that about half or more of those with BN may have a good outcome in the longer-term, but for the remainder the disorder is persistent. Treatment outcome studies indicate that for those who engage in specific interventions and evidence based treatments (particularly psychotherapies such as cognitive behaviour therapy for bulimia nervosa) developed since the 1980s the likelihood of recovery is significantly increased. Whilst there are mixed outcomes in studies of prognostic factors, consistent pre-treatment factors identified include a history of psychological advsersity, borderline personality structure, depression and obesity. Consistent post-treatment prognostic features are achieving abstinence and good psychosocial adjustment. Thus treatments should address improving psychological resiliency, coping and co-morbidities.

Keywords: bulimia nervosa, prognosis, recurrence, relapse, remission, natural history

---

[*****] E-mail address: p.hay@uws.edu.au

INTRODUCTION

Bulimia nervosa is a 'modern' eating disorder. It was first delineated in the late twentieth century and was the first eating disorder to be characterised by recurrent binge eating, namely episodes of eating unusually large amounts of food over which there is a sense of loss of control, in people of normal or above average body weight [1,2]. By definition, the sufferer of bulimia nervosa also engages in compensatory extreme weight-control behaviours. These behaviours may take the form of self-induced vomiting and/or laxative or diuretic use (purging), or fasting and/or intense exercise (the non-purging form of bulimia nervosa). Few changes to the impending revised American Psychiatric Association criteria are proposed, excepting to reduce the minimum frequency of binge eating and purging behaviours to once weekly [3]. In addition to disordered eating behaviours, people with bulimia nervosa also have specific eating disorder psychopathology whereby their self-view or self-evaluation is unduly influenced by concerns about their weight and/or shape [1].

Bulimia nervosa is common, and early cohort and clinical incidence studies [4,5] support an increase in the incidence of bulimia nervosa in the decade following its recognition in 1980, to be followed by a plateau or even a decrease in the 1990s and past decade [6]. A systematic review has put the estimated incidence of bulimia nervosa at 12 cases per 100,000 per year [7]. Findings from national surveys in North America [8] and Europe [9] indicate that the 12-month prevalence of bulimia nervosa is around 0.3-0.5% in the general population and in Australian samples current or point prevalence of bulimia nervosa is similar [10]. Bulimia nervosa is also a disorder with high morbidity. In community and clinic surveys bulimia nervosa and like eating disorders have been found to have significant impact on health related quality of life and adaptive function [11,12]. Fortunately, specific and efficacious psychotherapies and pharmacotherapies have been developed for bulimia nervosa [13]. This chapter will address first issues in definition around the question of recovery in bulimia nervosa, next the natural history, and third the outcome with treatment including predictors that may be modified to enhance remission and reduce relapse or later recurrence rates.

WHAT IS MEANT BY RECOVERY?

There are several ways to approach the question of what is meant by recovery in bulimia nervosa. Is this recovery with or without treatment? When is remission recovery? Inevitably, recovery is defined according to remission sustained over time (one year in the Kordy consensus definition [14]) such that the likelihood of relapse is remote, and after which time the term recurrence may be preferred.

Definitions of remission are problematic. In a large recent review of 79 patient series Steinhausen and colleagues found 22 synonyms for remission (including 'abstinent') [15]. Differing definitions may lead to different rates of remission being reported. For example, in a 3-year trial of 334 eating disorder patients [16] remission of the 126 participants with bulimia nervosa was 30.2% when defined as absence of extreme figure (shape) preoccupation and no vomiting/laxative use or binge-eating [14], but up to 44.4% when defined as absence of behaviours only using the criteria of Shapiro et al. (no binge-eating, vomiting or laxatives)

[17] or the Psychiatric Status Rating Scale Level 2 (i.e. does not meet DSM-IV bulimia nervosa criteria, has no binge eating, vomiting or laxative use, often has disturbing thoughts about shape and weight) [18]. Whilst it is desirable to include attenuation or elimination of core psychopathology of extreme weight and shape concern, this is delineated in diverse ways. In contrast, absence of behaviours may be more consistently applied, although how it is measured again can be problematic if self-report of binge eating is relied upon [19]. For this reason outcome meta-analyses are more often reported for binge eating/purging abstinence (e.g. those use in the National Institute for Clinical Excellence (NICE) guidelines [20] and Cochrane Library reviews [21]) than for a measure that reflects both psychological symptom reduction (e.g. that developed by Fairburn and colleagues where remission was defined according to being less than one standard deviation above the community mean of the global Eating Disorder Examination score [22]).

NATURALISTIC OUTCOME STUDIES OF BULIMIA NERVOSA

It is difficult to study the natural course of bulimia nervosa. There are many longitudinal general populations and similar studies, but few include large samples of people with eating disorders and even fewer samples of people meeting criteria for bulimia nervosa. For example, Patton and colleagues [23] followed 107 adolescents with an eating disorder over a 10-year period. Their findings suggested partial eating disorders were unlikely to progress to full eating disorders, but were associated with significantly increased psychiatric co-morbidity and persistent underweight. However, this study of a young cohort cannot be generalised to older samples with full syndromes of bulimia nervosa which has onset in later adolescence and young adulthood, albeit that the age of onset may be decreasing [24].

A naturalistic community based 5-year full syndrome study [25] of adult women with bulimia nervosa (n=102) and binge eating disorder (BED) found that 31% and 15% continued to have bulimia nervosa at 15 months and at 5 years respectively. At five years half of the bulimia nervosa sample (36 of 74) still met diagnostic criteria for an eating disorder (24 with eating disorders not otherwise specified [EDNOS]) while only 15% (5 of 34) of those with BED met diagnostic criteria. Although the McKnight longitudinal naturalistic 4-year outcome study of BED [26] indicated only a small proportion of BED recover spontaneously, a less favourable outcome for bulimia nervosa compared to EDNOS and BED has also been reported in a large (n=385) 4-year prospective study of a mixed sample where participants were recruited from both clinic and community settings (through media advertisement) [27]. In this study remission was defined as the first point after entry to the trial when the participant had no DSM-IV eating disorder diagnosis (during the preceding 6 months), and relapse was defined as the first time after a remission when symptoms for any eating disorder diagnosis including EDNOS were found. At the 4-year follow-up, 47% of those with bulimia nervosa were remitted compared to 78% of EDNOS, 82% of the BED group, and 57% of anorexia nervosa participants [27]. A more recent but smaller 5-year naturalistic study of 23 people with bulimia nervosa found a 74% remission at 5 years, with a 47% probability of relapse within the 5-year follow-up study of those in remission [28].

The inconsistencies in these studies, namely in the course and outcome of people with eating disorders from community samples, may occur when individuals affected do or do not receive evidence-based or other treatments. Most of those in the Agras et al. study did receive treatment [27] but this was not the case in the Fairburn et al. study [25] where 28% of those with bulimia nervosa and only 3% of BED participants had treatment. Ben-Tovim and colleagues [29] studied the effects of treatment in a sample of people with eating disorders followed for five years after presentation to treatment services (see also below). Neither this nor the 5-year naturalistic Oxford study [25] found a relationship between receiving treatment for an eating disorder and outcome. This does not of course mean treatment is ineffective, but rather that within the myriad of factors that influence outcome in the uncontrolled setting of naturalistic studies, it is difficult to find a significant effect for specific interventions. The large number of features that may influence course (in either clinical or community populations) include psychosocial stresses, inter-current psychiatric illness and co-morbidities, and personal vulnerability from innate characteristics, such as lower levels of psychological maturity reported in women with eating disorders [30,31]. Relationships can be complex, and those important at onset or early in the illness course may differ from those that maintain and perpetuate illness. For example, Ball and Lee [32] investigated the relationship between stress and coping in a general population sample of women with disordered eating over six-months. They reported strong cross-sectional, but weak longitudinal relationships between stressful life events and eating disorder symptoms [32]. Stice [33] also evaluated longitudinal studies of mixed samples in a meta-analytic review and found some support for eating disorder attitudes, such as body dissatisfaction, perfectionism, and negative affect as maintenance factors (the last a causal maintenance factor) for bulimic symptoms. Hay and colleagues investigated the 2-year course and putative predictors of outcome of 87 young community women with disordered eating (63% with recurrent binge eating), although only 13 had full syndrome bulimia nervosa [34]. In this study eating disorder psychopathology remained high and mental health quality of life (MHQoL) remained poor over the 2 years [34]. A higher baseline level of immature defence style significantly predicted higher levels of eating disorder symptoms, poorer MHQoL and more disability as measured by 'days out of role' [34]. In addition, higher educational attainment, baseline general psychological disturbance, lower body mass index (kg/m^2; BMI), and having main work outside the home, were associated with poorer MHQoL.

Retrospective nationwide community based twin studies of outcome have also been conducted by Wade and colleagues (in Australia) [35] and Keski-Rahkonen and colleagues [36] (in Finland) with consistent findings. The first paper identified 29 women with bulimia nervosa from a survey of 1002 twins, of whom 13 were asymptomatic based on abstinence and low eating disorder concerns on the EDE criteria (similar to Fairburn et al. above [22]). Onset of bulimia nervosa was a mean of 13.65 (SD6.3) years prior to assessment and this study suggested that over 50% were fully recovered at longer term outcome. The latter paper based definitions of recovery on Field et al 1997 [37] findings that suggested likelihood of relapse declined markedly after 12-months of binge eating and purging abstinence. Thus, their definition of clinical recovery was 12-month abstinence plus BMI of at least 19. In this study 59 of the 2281 women met the DSM-IV [1] and the proposed DSM-V [3] criteria for bulimia nervosa i.e. having weekly or more binge eating/purging behaviours. Of these 59, 61% met recovery during the study period and 55% met recovery criteria at 5-years. Whilst only 32% of cases were detected by health professionals, and this did not significantly change outcome, no significant predictors of outcome were identified [36].

Taken together, these 'naturalistic' studies suggest that about half or more of those with bulimia nervosa may have a good outcome in the longer-term but for the remainder the disorder is persistent. Genetic and socio-cultural features (especially body dissatisfaction) are relevant predispositions, and symptom severity. In addition, poor psychological resiliency, poor health literacy, and past sexual abuse are putative maintaining factors. Whilst it has proven difficult to show an effect on a population level for such prognostic features or treatment, interventions that have reduced symptoms and morbidity remain important for the individual and society they live in. This will be discussed in the next section which addresses outcomes with treatments and identified prognostic attributes.

OUTCOMES WITH TREATMENT

The majority of longitudinal studies of outcome in bulimia nervosa have in fact been from clinical case series and other treatment samples rather than naturalistic or community samples as described in the previous section. For example, in the NICE [20] systematic review only two of more than 20 outcome studies identified in bulimia samples were not from a treatment series. Findings have similarly been mixed or inconsistent and studies have been of widely varying duration.

Two longer-term 10-year studies of BN following treatment [38,39] report a generally positive outcome. The first study (n=50) people followed participants after a placebo-controlled trial of mianserin treatment. They reported 52% of participants receiving placebo or drug had fully recovered, 39% were in partial remission, and only 9% continued to experience full symptoms of bulimia nervosa. The second, and larger (n=222) study combined outcomes from a cohort of patients following clinic treatment and a cohort of patients following a controlled (antidepressant and structured intensive group psychotherapy) treatment trial. At mean follow-up of 11.5 years they also found 41.6% were in full remission (at least 6 months binge/purge abstinence and absence weight/shape concerns) and 28.3% were in partial remission. Those that still had an eating disorder were more likely to suffer from EDNOS than bulimia nervosa. Only 11% still met criteria for bulimia nervosa.

Franko et al. [40] followed 554 women (110 with bulimia nervosa) seeking treatment in a catchment area of New England between October 1987 and June 1990. The focus of the report was on suicide and its predictors rather than recovery. However, it is of note that they found co-morbidity (such as depression) and suicide risk in bulimia nervosa to be high (10.9% suicided) over nearly 9-year period. A large 5-year South Australian study of women who had presented for treatment included 88 with bulimia nervosa [28]. Whilst it failed to demonstrate effects of treatment (see above), the study found little crossover between diagnostic groups, and a generally better outcome for bulimia nervosa than in other series with 74% having no eating disorder at five years.

From a set of 220 published studies identified in a systematic search, a large and current review [15] has pooled data of 79 patient series (n=5653 patients) published between 1981 and 2007. Studies were included if they reported at least one of five outcome measures for bulimia nervosa and had a follow-up of 6-months post-treatment episodes. Fourteen additional studies were also included, that reported only on prognostic factors. The mean age of onset (n=2508 patients) was 17.2 years (SD=1.7), at follow-up was 28.4 years (SD=4.3), and duration of follow-up was 3.2 months (SD=3.3, 6 months to 12.5 years). The vast majority were women, there being only 75 or 3830 (1.9%) men reported. The five-outcome criteria were recovery (with 22 synonyms), improvement (mostly reported with recovery), chronicity (with 21 synonyms), mortality (all crude, none standardised), and crossover to another DSM-IV criteria eating disorder. In 27 studies (n=1235 patients) the mean percent recovery rate was 44.9% (SD 15.5, range 5-73), improvement was 27.0% (SD 12.9, range 4-67), and chronicity was 22.6% (SD 15.1, range 2-70). In 6 studies (n=383 patients) mean percent crossover was 5.1 (SD=8.6, range 0-28). The crude mortality rate was 0.32% (14 deaths in 4309 patients).

Variations in definition of outcomes, size of study and the inclusion of studies, from early periods when bulimia nervosa had just been described and specific interventions not yet developed, all likely contributed to the wide range of percent outcomes found in this review [15]. When examined, recovery was significantly higher where dropout rates were low (49.8% versus 36.8%), where follow-up was more than 4 years (66.6% if > 4years, or 44.0% if >1 years versus 39.2% if < 4 years), and where patients received psychotherapy (versus medical therapy or behaviour therapy, 62.89% compared to 49.21% or 31.89% respectively). Although the last figures were derived from only 10 patient series, the outcome for psychotherapy are strong and support the need to engage patients actively in evidence based therapies such as specific cognitive behaviour therapy developed for bulimia nervosa by Fairburn and colleagues (see also Chapter 8) [22] which is has the best evidence for early and sustained improvements [13].

There are four current systematic reviews of pre- and post-treatment prognostic factors, namely the reviews by Steinhausen and colleagues [15], NICE [20], Keel and Brown [41], and Berkman and colleagues [42]. The consistent findings from these are summarised in Table 1.

Table. Pre and post treatment (after treatment has commenced) unfavourable prognostic factors consistently found in four current systematic reviews [15, 20, 41, 42]

Pre-treatment	Post-treatment
Borderline personality structure	Poor social adjustment[1]
Depression	Early engagement[2]
Low motivation	Continued high level eating
History of obesity	disorder symptoms[1, 2]
Problematic familial environments	Non-abstinence at end treatment[1]
e.g. abusive	Psychiatric co-morbidity &
Poorer adaptive function	depression[1]
Cumulative psychiatric co-morbidity	

1. Distinguished in NICE review [20]
2. Distinguished in Steinhausen et al. review [15]

The list of inconsistent features or features that have not been found to predict treatment outcome is very long and includes duration of illness, pre-treatment levels, binge eating &/or

purging, pre-treatment weight and/or shape concerns, BMI, history of weight fluctuations, age of onset, history of anorexia nervosa, low self-esteem, co-morbid substance misuse, neuroticism, obsessionality and a history of self-harm or suicidality (excepting where there is borderline personality structure – see Table 1).

However, prognostic factors that have been consistently found are potentially remedial. In particular, the role of problematic interpersonal function, often with a history of poor early life attachment and/or abuse, and features of borderline personality structure are receiving attention in treatment developments such as the 'transdiagnostic' broad cognitive behaviour therapy [22]. This therapy has additional modules addressing clinical perfectionism, mood intolerance, interpersonal function, and low self-esteem. It has been found to offer advantage for subgroups of normal weight eating disorder patients with bulimia nervosa and other eating disorders concurrent with these vulnerable personality traits [22].

Obesity is an increasing public health problem and also likely associated with the rise in particularly binge eating problems in Western societies [10,43] and is also a consistent prognostic factor in bulimia nervosa outcome. Preventative programs that address both disordered eating and obesity cannot be un-helpful in thus improving outcomes for bulimia nervosa. Attention to putative strategies that enhance engagement and minimise treatment drop-out (e.g. more frequent appointments in the first weeks of treatment, actively treating and not neglecting co-morbidities) will also likely lead to an improved result.

POST-TREATMENT RECOVERY RATES

Keel and colleagues [44] for nine or more years have followed 136 women with anorexia nervosa and 110 with bulimia nervosa who sought treatment, to specifically examine factors that might reduce likelihood of relapse. Over the time of follow-up 96% received treatment, 83 (75%) of those with bulimia nervosa achieved remission, and of these 29 (26% of total) relapsed. Whilst remission rates were higher in bulimia nervosa, relapse rates were similar for both eating disorders i.e. just over a third of those who remitted relapsed. The two variables that emerged as significant in predicting relapse in the multivariate model were psychosocial function and level of weight and/or shape concerns. The authors concluded that (as in treatment) relapse prevention interventions should test approaches that may reduce body image concerns but also improve adaptive function and resiliency to stress.

CONCLUSION

Naturalistic and treatment outcome studies indicate that between a third and a half of people with bulimia nervosa will recover and a quarter or more will significantly improve in the medium to longer-term. It is likely that specific interventions and evidence based treatments (particularly psychotherapies such as congitive behaviour therapy for bulimia nervosa combined with SSRI treatment) developed since the 1980s increase the likelihood of recovery. In addition, to optimise treatment specific to the the eating disorder addressing concurrant problems, improving psychological resiliency and coping are promising areas for increasing recovery and reducing relapse.

REFERENCES

[1] American Psychiatric Association. Diagnostic and Statistical Manual of Mental Disorders 4th edition (DSM-IV). Washington, DC: American Psychiatric Association, 1994.

[2] World Health Organisation. The ICD-10 Clssification of Mental and Behavioural Disorders. Clinical Descriptions and Diagnostic Guidelines. Geneva: World Health Organisation, 1992

[3] American Psychiatric Association. DSM-5 Development, 2010 http://www.dsm5.org/ProposedRevisions/Pages/proposedrevision.aspx?rid=25.

[4] Bushnell JA, Wells JE, Hornblow AR, Oakley-Brown MA, Joyce P. Prevalence of three bulimic syndromes in the general population Psychol Med 1990; 20: 671-680.

[5] Hall A, Hay PJ. Eating disorder patient referrals from a population region 1977–1986. Psychol Med 1991; 21: 697–701.

[6] Keel PK, Heatherton TF, Dorer DJ, Joiner TE, Zalta A. Point prevalence of bulimia nervosa in 1982, 1992, and 2002. Psychol Med 2006; 36: 119-127.

[7] Hoek HW, van Hoeken D. Review of the prevalence and incidence of eating disorders. Int J Eat Disord 2003; 34: 383–396.

[8] Hudson JI, Hiripi E, Pope HG, Kessler RC (2007) The prevalence and correlates of eating disorders in the National Comorbidity Survey Replication. Biol Psychiatry 2007; 61: 348-358.

[9] Preti A, Girolamo G, Vilagut G, Alonso J, Graaf R, Bruffaerts R, Demyttenaere K, Pinto-Meza A, Haro JM, Morosini P. The epidemiology of eating disorders in six European countries: results of the ESEMeD-WMH project. J Psychiatr Res 2009; 43: 1125-32.

[10] Hay P, Mond J, Buttner P, Darby A. Eating disorder behaviors are increasing: Findings from two sequential community surveys in South Australia. PLOSOne, 3(2) e1541, 2008, 6 February.

[11] Hay PJ, Mond J. How to 'count the cost' and measure burden?: a review of health related quality of life in people with eating disorders. J Ment Health 2005; 14(6): 539-552.

[12] Mond JM, Hay PJ, Rodgers B, Owen C, Beumont PJV. Assessing quality of life in eating disorder patients. Qual Life Res 2005; 14: 171-178.

[13] Hay P, Claudino A. Bulimia Nervosa. BMJ Clinical Evidence. 2008; 06: 1009.

[14] Kordy H, Krämer B, Palmer RL, Papezova H, Pellet J, Richard M, Treasure J. Recovery, Relapse, and Recurrence in Eating Disorders: Conceptualization and Illustration of a Validation Strategy. J Clin Psychol 2002; 58: 833–846

[15] Steinhausen H-C, Weber S. The Outcome of Bulimia Nervosa: Findings From One- Quarter Century of Research. Am J Psychiatry 2009; 166: 1331–1341.

[16] Bjork T, Clinton D, Norring C. The Impact of using difference outcome measures on remission reates in 3-year follow-up of eating disorders. Eur Eat Disorders Rev Online July 2010.

[17] Shapiro JR, Berkman ND, Brownley KA, Sedway JA, Lohr KN, Bulik CM Bulimia nervosa treatment: A systematic review of randomised controlled trials. Int J Eat Disord 2007; 40: 321-336.

[18] Herzog DB, Sacks NR, Keller MB, Lavori PW, von Ranson KB, Gray HM: Patterns and predictors of recovery in anorexia nervosa and bulimia nervosa. J Am Acad Child Adolesc Psychiatry 1993; 32: 835–842.

[19] Mond JM, Rodgers B, Hay PJ, Owen C, Beumont PJV. Validity of the Eating Disorders Examination Questionnaire (EDE-Q) in screening for eating disorders in community samples. Behav Res Ther 2004; 42: 551-567.

[20] National Institute for Clinical Excellence (NICE).(2004).'Eating Disorders- Core Interventions in the Treatment Management of Anorexia Nervosa, Bulimia Nervosa and Related Eating Disorders.' www.nice.org.uk (accessed 4 December 2005).

[21] Hay PJ, Bacaltchuk J, Byrnes RT, Claudino AM, Ekmejian AA, Yong PY. Individual psychotherapy in the outpatient treatment of adults with anorexia nervosa. Cochrane Database of Syst Rev 2003, Issue 4. CD003909. DOI: 10.1002/14651858.CD003909. Updated 2008.

[22] Fairburn CG, Cooper Z, Doll HA, O'Connor ME, Bohn KB, Hawker DM, Wales JA, Palmer RL. Transdiagnostic Cognitive-Behavioral Therapy for patients with Eating Disorders: A two-site trial with 60-week follow-up. Am J Psychiatry 2009; 166: 311-319.

[23] Patton GC, Coffey C, Carlin JB, Sanci L, Sawyer S. Prognosis of adolescent partial syndromes of eating disorder. Br J Psychiatry 2008; 192: 294-299.

[24] Favaro A, Caregaro L, Tenconi E, Bosello R, Santonastaso P. Time trends in age at onset of anorexia nervosa and bulimia nervosa. J Clin Psychiatry 2009; 70: 1715-1721.

[25] Fairburn CG, Cooper Z, Doll HA, Norman P, O'Connor M, The natural course of bulimia nervosa and BED in young women. Arch Gen Psychiatry 2000; 57: 659-665.

[26] Wifley DE, Wilson GT, Agras WS The clinical significance of binge eating disorder Int J Eat Disord 2003; 34: S96-S106.

[27] Agras WS, Crow S, Mitchell JE, Halmi KA, Bryson S. A 4-year prospective study of eating disorder NOS compared with full eating disorder syndromes. Int J Eat Disord 2009; 42: 565-570.

[28] Grilo CM, Pagano ME, Skodol AE, et al. Natural course of bulimia nervosa and of eating disorder not otherwise specified: 5-year prospective study of remissions, relapses, and the effects of personality disorder psychopathology. J Clin Psychiatry 2007; 68: 738–746.

[29] Ben-Tovim DI, Walker K, Gilchrist P, Freeman R, Kalucy R, Esterman A. Outcome in patients with eating disorders: A 5-year study Lancet 357; 9264: 1254-1257.

[30] Stiener H. Defence styles in eating disorders. Int J Eat Disord 1990; 9: 141-151.

[31] Schmidt, U., Slone, G., Tiller, J., & Treasure, J. Childhood adversity and adult defense style in eating disorder patients- A controlled study. Br J of Med Psych 1993; 66: 353-362.

[32] Ball, K., & Lee, C. (2001). Psychological stress, coping, and symptoms of disordered eating in a community sample of young Australian women. Int J Eat Disord 2001; 31: 71-81.

[33] Stice, E. (2002). Risk and maintenance factors for eating pathology: a meta-analytic review. Psychological Bulletin 2002; 128: 825-848.

[34] Hay PJ, Buttner P, Mond J, Paxton SJ, Rodgers B, Quirk F, Darby A . Quality of Life, Course and Predictors of Outcomes in Community Women with EDNOS and Common Eating Disorders. Eur Eat Disorders Rev 2010; 18: 281–295.

[35] Wade TD, Bergin JL, Tiggemann M, Bulik CM, Fairburn GC. Prevalence and long-term course of lifetime eating disorders in an adult Australian twin cohort. Aust NZ J Psychiatry 2006; 40: 121–128.

[36] Keski-Rahkonen A, H. W. Hoek HW, Linna MS, Raevuori A, Sihvola E, Bulik CM, Rissanen A, Kaprio J. Incidence and outcomes of bulimia nervosa: a nationwide population-based study. Psychol Med 2009; 39: 823-821.

[37] Field AE, Herzog DB, Keller MB, West J, Nussbaum K, Colditz GA. Distinguishing recovery from remission in a cohort of bulimic women: how should asymptomatic periods be described? J Clin Epidemiology 1997; 50: 1339–1345.

[38] Collings S, King M. Ten year follow-up of 50 patients with bulimia nervosa. Br J Psychiatry 1994; 64: 80–87.

[39] Keel PK, Mitchell JE, Miller KB, Davis TL, Crow SJ. Long-term outcome of bulimia nervosa. Arch Gen Psychiatry 1999; 56: 63–69.

[40] Franko DL, Keel PK, Dorer DJ, Blais MA, Delinsky SS, Eddy KT, Charat V, Renn R, Herzog DB. What predicts suicide attempts in women with eating disorders? Psychol Med 2004; 34: 843-853.

[41] Keel PK, Brown TA. Update on course and outcome in eating disorders. Int J Eat Disord 2010; 43: 195-204.

[42] Berkman ND, Lohr KN, Bulik CM. Outcomes of eating disorders: A systematic review of the literature. Int J Eat Disord 2007; 40: 293-309.

[43] Darby A, Hay P, Mond J, Quirk F, Buettner P, Kennedy L. The rising prevalence of co-morbid obesity and eating disorder behaviours from 1995 to 2005 Int J Eat Disord 2009; 42: 104-108

[44] Keel PK, Dorer DJ, Franko DL, Jackson SC, Herzog DB. Post-remission Predictors of Relapse in Women With Eating Disorders Am J Psychiatry 2005; 162: 2263–2268.

In: Treatment and Recovery of Eating Disorders
Editors: Daniel Stein and Yael Latzer

ISBN: 978-1-62808-248-7
© 2013 Nova Science Publishers, Inc.

Chapter 17

ABOUT THE EDITORS

Daniel Stein, MD, is a certified psychiatrist and child and adolescent psychiatrist. Since 1998, the director of the Pediatric Psychosomatic Department, Edmond and Lily Safra Children's Hospital, Chaim Sheba Medical Center, Tel Hashomer, Israel. He is an associate professor at the Department of Psychiatry, Head of the Section of Child and Adolescent Psychiatry and instructor at the School of Psychotherapy, all at the Sackler Faculty of Medicine, University of Tel Aviv, Tel Aviv, Israel. His main topics of interest include child and adolescent psychiatry, eating disorders and suicidology. He specializes in psychodynamic psychotherapy and cognitive behavioral therapy. Professor Stein is a member of numerous Israeli and international organizations, including the International Society of Child and Adolescent Psychiatry, the Academy of Eating Disorders, the Eating Disorders Research Society and the European College of Neuropsychiatry. He has participated in numerous international conferences and won several scientific awards. He is the co-founder and past deputy chairman of the Israeli Academy of Eating Disorders and a reviewer in several important Israeli and international peer-reviewed journals. He has written more than 120 articles and book chapters published in prominent international journals and books. Dr. Stein has recently edited, along with other prominent Israeli experts, a book on the integration of culture, psychology and biology in the study of eatong disorders. Dr. Stein is locally and internationally recognized as an expert in the field of eating disorder treatment and research.

E-mail: danil49@netvision.net.il; daniel.stein@sheba.health.gov.il; danstein@post.tau.ac.il
Website: www.safra.sheba.co.il/pediatric psychosomatic department

Yael Latzer, DSc, graduated from the University of Haifa with both her BA and MA Degree in Clinical Social Work. This was followed by obtaining her D.Sc at the Technion Medical School in Haifa, Israel. She received additional certification in psychotherapy, family and couple therapy. She held a two-year (1989-1991) fellowship position, training in the treatment of eating disorders at the Psychoanalytic Institute, Menninger Foundation, in Topeka, Kansas, USA.

Professor Lazter founded the Institute for the Treatment and Study of Eating Disorders in the Division of Psychiatry at Rambam Health Care Campus, Haifa, Israel in 1992 and has since served as its director. She is currently an associate professor in the Faculty of Social

Welfare and Health Sciences at the University of Haifa. She has served as the head of various academic programs, including a family therapy MA program, a clinical program, and most recently, a trauma program. In addition, in 2008, Professor Latzer has developed an MA for registered dietitians, a programe with an emphasis on behavioral and psychological related factors to eating and nutrition . She remains the head of this program since its establishment.

Prof. Latzer has published more than a hundred articles in scientific and clinical journals, as well as more than 30 chapters in various books. She edited a book entitled "Eating Disorders: Diagnosis, Epidemiology, Etiology and Prevention", which was published in 2011 and "The Dance of Eating and Sleeping among Adolescents: Normal and Pathological Perspectives" that will be published soon.

She has actively participated in many international and national scientific conferences and serves as a reviewer for a variety of international and local scientific journals. She was also nominated as the president of the Israeli Academy of Eating Disorders. During 2006-2008, she spent her sabbatical in New York, teaching at Yeshiva University, Ferkauf Graduate School of Psychology, and at the Nutrition and Behavior Faculty of Columbia University. Recently, she developed a rehabilitation program for young women with eating disorders in a residential hostel setting.

Prof. Latzer is both nationally and internationally recognized as an expert in the field of eating disorder treatment and research.

E-mail: latzer@zahav.net.il;
Website: http://hw.haifa.ac.il/social/cv/Yael_Latzer.html

In: Treatment and Recovery of Eating Disorders   ISBN: 978-1-62808-248-7
Editors: Daniel Stein and Yael Latzer   © 2013 Nova Science Publishers, Inc.

Chapter 18

ABOUT THE PEDIATRIC PSYCHOSOMATIC DEPARTMENT, EDMOND AND LILY SAFRA CHILDREN'S HOSPITAL, CHAIM SHEBA MEDICAL CENTER, TEL HASHOMER, ISRAEL

The Pediatric Psychosomatic Department of the Safra Children's' Hospital, Chaim Sheba Medical Center at Tel Hashomer, Israel, was founded in 1987 by Edith Mitrani MD. Serving as a nationwide referral center, this department specializes in the treatment of eating disorders in children and adolescents. Twenty patients are hospitalized at each period of time and around 80 patients are hospitalized yearly. The department runs a halfway out day center and an ambulatory follow-up service. The halfway out day center serves between 15-20 patients at each period of time and between 40- 50 patients are treated there every year. The ambulatory clinic currently treats around 100 patients yearly. The department has treated over 1,200 patients since its foundation.

Treatment is based on behavioral rehabilitation of disordered eating performed by a multi-professional team. Patients receive specialized individual, family and group therapies. Treatment is geared toward the amelioration of disordered eating preoccupations and behaviors, alongside promoting the ongoing developmental needs of the adolescents, and encouraging appropriate change in the family to reduce the risk for relapse following discharge.

As a university-affiliated teaching department, the Pediatric Psychosomatic Department trains students from different professions. The department runs several research projects in diverse topics related to eating disorders, suicidality, and psychosocial aspects of pediatric medical disorders.

About Sheba

CONTACT

Associate professor Daniel Stein, MD
Director, Pediatric Psychosomatic Department
Edmond and Lily Safra Children's Hospital
Chaim Sheba Medical Center
IL-52621 Tel Hashomer
Israel
E-mail: danil49@netvision.net.il; daniel.stein@sheba.health.gov.il; danstein@post.tau.ac.il
Website: www.safra.sheba.co.il/pediatric psychosomatic department

In: Treatment and Recovery of Eating Disorders   ISBN: 978-1-62808-248-7
Editors: Daniel Stein and Yael Latzer   © 2013 Nova Science Publishers, Inc.

Chapter 19

ABOUT THE FACULTY OF SOCIAL WELFARE AND HEALTH SCIENCES, UNIVERSITY OF HAIFA, ISRAEL AND ABOUT THE INSTITUTE OF THE TREATMENT AND STUDY OF EATING DISORDERS, DIVISION OF PSYCHIATRY, RAMBAM HEALTH CARE CAMPUS, HAIFA, ISRAEL

THE FACULTY OF SOCIAL WELFARE AND HEALTH SCIENCES

The Faculty of Social Welfare and Health Sciences was established in 1996 by the University of Haifa and the Council for Higher Education. The impetus for its founding was the intense and rapid professionalization in Israel and throughout the world of the various disciplines encompassed by the Faculty. In addition, the new Faculty reflects the need for an academic institution of higher learning in the north of Israel to train professionals in the areas of social welfare and health sciences.

Following its establishment, the Faculty of Social Welfare and Health Sciences has strengthened cooperation and collaboration between the University of Haifa and the Technion and the Rappaport Faculty of Medicine by offering specialization in the areas of behavioral sciences and administration, on the one hand, and medical sciences on the other. Each institution contributes and gains from the programs.

At present, the Faculty of Social Welfare and Health Sciences includes the School of Social Work, the School of Public Health, the Department of Human Services, the Department of Occupational Therapy, the Department of Nursing, the Department of Physical Therapy, and the Department of Gerontology.

THE INSTITUTE FOR THE TREATMENT AND STUDY
OF EATING DISORDERS

The Institute for the Treatment and Study of Eating Disorders was founded in 1992 as part of the Division of Psychiatry at Rambam Health Care Campus in Haifa, Israel. Prof. Yael Latzer, who founded the eating disorders clinic, has been the director since its establishment. The clinic serves as a nationwide referral center (though its clients are primarily from the North of Israel), specializing in the assessment, diagnosis, and treatment of eating disorders in adolescents and adults. An average of 12 new patients is referred every week, and approximately 150 new patients are treated yearly. The clinic treatment model is based on a multidisciplinary framework with a focus on family therapy. Based on this model, the clinic provides a two-year continuing education program for experienced clinicians from all disciplines. The clinic has undergone an enormous amount of professional and clinical development over the years and has become a recognized leader in the field of eating disorders, both within Israel and in the international professional community.

The eating disorders clinic is affiliated with the Faculty of Social Welfare and Health Sciences at the University of Haifa, providing a training, practicum and research setting for BA, MA, and PhD students. As a university-affiliated teaching department, the clinic trains students from different professions and conducts research projects on many diverse topics related to eating disorders.

Recently, the clinic launched a rehabilitation program for young women with eating disorders who have entered their recovery phase of treatment. This pioneering and unique program, supported by the National Insurance Institute of Israel and approved by the Ministry of Health and Ministry of Social Affairs and Social Services, aims to provide residence in a hostel setting for eating disorder patients during their recovery period. The house, "Zeyda Laderech," was opened in July 2009.

Contact
Yael Latzer, DSc,
Eating Disorders Clinic Rambam Medical Center,
University of Haifa, Faculty of Social Welfare and Health Sciences
Mount Carmel, Haifa, 31905 Israel.
E-mail: latzer@zahav.net.il

In: Treatment and Recovery of Eating Disorders   ISBN: 978-1-62808-248-7
Editors: Daniel Stein and Yael Latzer   © 2013 Nova Science Publishers, Inc.

Chapter 20

ABOUT THE BOOK SERIES "HEALTH AND HUMAN DEVELOPMENT"

Health and human development is a book series with publications from a multidisciplinary group of researchers, practitioners and clinicians for an international professional forum interested in the broad spectrum of health and human development.

- Merrick J, Omar HA, eds. Adolescent behavior research. International perspectives. New York: Nova Science, 2007.
- Kratky KW. Complementary medicine systems: Comparison and integration. New York: Nova Science, 2008.
- Schofield P, Merrick J, eds. Pain in children and youth. New York: Nova Science, 2009.
- Greydanus DE, Patel DR, Pratt HD, Calles Jr JL, eds. Behavioral pediatrics, 3 ed. New York: Nova Science, 2009.
- Ventegodt S, Merrick J, eds. Meaningful work: Research in quality of working life. New York: Nova Science, 2009.
- Omar HA, Greydanus DE, Patel DR, Merrick J, eds. Obesity and adolescence. A public health concern. New York: Nova Science, 2009.
- Lieberman A, Merrick J, eds. Poverty and children. A public health concern. New York: Nova Science, 2009.
- Goodbread J. Living on the edge. The mythical, spiritual and philosophical roots of social marginality. New York: Nova Science, 2009.
- Bennett DL, Towns S, Elliot E, Merrick J, eds. Challenges in adolescent health: An Australian perspective. New York: Nova Science, 2009.
- Schofield P, Merrick J, eds. Children and pain. New York: Nova Science, 2009.
- Sher L, Kandel I, Merrick J. Alcohol-related cognitive disorders: Research and clinical perspectives. New York: Nova Science, 2009.
- Anyanwu EC. Advances in environmental health effects of toxigenic mold and mycotoxins. New York: Nova Science, 2009.
- Bell E, Merrick J, eds. Rural child health. International aspects. New York: Nova Science, 2009.

- Dubowitz H, Merrick J, eds. International aspects of child abuse and neglect. New York: Nova Science, 2010.
- Shahtahmasebi S, Berridge D. Conceptualizing behavior: A practical guide to data analysis. New York: Nova Science, 2010.
- Wernik U. Chance action and therapy. The playful way of changing. New York: Nova Science, 2010.
- Omar HA, Greydanus DE, Patel DR, Merrick J, eds. Adolescence and chronic illness. A public health concern. New York: Nova Science, 2010.
- Patel DR, Greydanus DE, Omar HA, Merrick J, eds. Adolescence and sports. New York: Nova Science, 2010.
- Shek DTL, Ma HK, Merrick J, eds. Positive youth development: Evaluation and future directions in a Chinese context. New York: Nova Science, 2010.
- Shek DTL, Ma HK, Merrick J, eds. Positive youth development: Implementation of a youth program in a Chinese context. New York: Nova Science, 2010.
- Omar HA, Greydanus DE, Tsitsika AK, Patel DR, Merrick J, eds.   Pediatric and adolescent sexuality and gynecology: Principles for the primary care clinician. New York: Nova Science, 2010.
- Chow E, Merrick J, eds. Advanced cancer. Pain and quality of life. New York: Nova Science, 2010.
- Latzer Y, Merrick, J, Stein D, eds. Understanding eating disorders. Integrating culture, psychology and biology. New York: Nova Science, 2010.
- Sahgal A, Chow E, Merrick J, eds. Bone and brain metastases: Advances in research and treatment. New York: Nova Science, 2010.
- Postolache TT, Merrick J, eds. Environment, mood disorders and suicide. New York: Nova Science, 2010.
- Maharajh HD, Merrick J, eds. Social and cultural psychiatry experience from the Caribbean Region. New York: Nova Science, 2010.
- Mirsky J. Narratives and meanings of migration. New York: Nova Science, 2010.
- Harvey PW. Self-management and the health care consumer. New York: Nova Science, 2011.
- Ventegodt S, Merrick J. Sexology from a holistic point of view. New York: Nova Science, 2011.
- Ventegodt S, Merrick J. Principles of holistic psychiatry: A textbook on holistic medicine for mental disorders. New York: Nova Science, 2011.
- Greydanus DE, Calles Jr JL, Patel DR, Nazeer A, Merrick J, eds. Clinical aspects of psychopharmacology in childhood and adolescence. New York: Nova Science, 2011.
- Bell E, Seidel BM, Merrick J, eds. Climate change and rural child health. New York: Nova Science, 2011.
- Bell E, Zimitat C, Merrick J, eds. Rural medical education: Practical strategies. New York: Nova Science, 2011.
- Latzer Y, Tzischinsky. The dance of sleeping and eating among adolescents: Normal and pathological perspectives. New York: Nova Science, 2011.
- Deshmukh VD. The astonishing brain and holistic consciousness: Neuroscience and Vedanta perspectives. New York: Nova Science, 2011.

- Bell E, Westert GP, Merrick J, eds. Translational research for primary healthcare. New York: Nova Science, 2011.
- Shek DTL, Sun RCF, Merrick J, eds. Drug abuse in Hong Kong: Development and evaluation of a prevention program. New York: Nova Science, 2011.
- Ventegodt S, Hermansen TD, Merrick J. Human Development: Biology from a holistic point of view. New York: Nova Science, 2011.
- Ventegodt S, Merrick J. Our search for meaning in life. New York: Nova Science, 2011.

Contact

Professor Joav Merrick, MD, MMedSci, DMSc
Medical Director, Health Services, Division for Mental Retardation
Ministry of Social Affairs, POBox 1260
IL-91012 Jerusalem, Israel
E-mail: jmerrick@internet-zahav.net

INDEX

C

D

Q

R

T

U